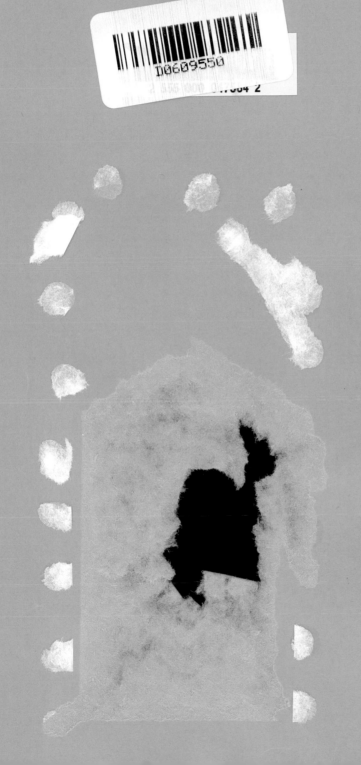

UNITED STATES MARSHALS

The United States Marshals of New Mexico and Arizona Territories, 1846-1912

Larry D. Ball

UNIVERSITY OF NEW MEXICO PRESS

Albuquerque

Library of Congress Cataloging in Publication Data

Ball, Larry D.   1940-
    The United States Marshals of New Mexico and Arizona
Territories, 1846-1912.

    Bibliography: p. 281
    Includes index.
    1. Law enforcement—New Mexico—History.   2. Law
enforcement—Arizona—History.   3. United States.
Marshals Service.   I. Title.
HV8145.N6B34   363.2   76-57543
ISBN 0-8263-0453-2

© 1978 by the University of New Mexico Press. All rights reserved
Manufactured in the United States of America
Library of Congress Catalog Card Number 76-57543
International Standard Book Number 0-8263-0453-2
First Edition

*This book is dedicated to
all the frontier United States marshals—
they enforced the laws of the land.*

Contents

Acknowledgments

This book is a product of the labors of many persons. Credit should go to Professor Clifford P. Westermeier who, in 1969–70, nursed an unsteady graduate student through the trials of his dissertation. That composition was the birth pang of the present book. My thanks also go to Mrs. Westermeier who kindly read the dissertation and to Professor Robert G. Athearn who, as second reader, made useful comments. Among others, special mention should be made of the following: Henry P. ("Pick") Walker, C. L. Sonnichsen, and Harwood P. Hinton, all of Tucson; Mrs. Burton Devere of Tombstone; J. Benson Newell of Las Cruces; Miss Mary Foraker of Albuquerque; Mrs. Laura M. Mullins, Jane Foraker-Thompson, and Romulo Martinez, all of Santa Fe; and Laurence P. James of Denver.

My thanks also go to the following institutions: the Norlin Library of the University of Colorado (Boulder); the Public Library, and the Library of the Colorado State Historical Society, both in Denver; the State Records Center and Archives, and the Museum of New Mexico, both in Santa Fe; and the Special Collections Department of Zimmerman Library at the University of New Mexico, in Albuquerque; the Arizona Historical Society, and the Special Collections Department of the University of Arizona, both in Tucson; the Department of Library and Archives, the Special Collections, and the Arizona Historical Foundation of Arizona State University, in Tempe; the National Archives in Washington, D.C., and branches at Bell, California, and Fort Worth, Texas; and the United States Marshals Service, in Washington, D. C.; the Marshal's Office in Phoenix; the United States Marshals Historical Society, of Miami, Florida; and Arkansas State University for a research grant to carry on this work. The author wishes to single out Marshal Dorotero Baca of Albuquerque, who so generously made a donation of the territorial papers of his office to the University of New Mexico

And finally, my heart goes out to Ruth, my wife, and Dur, my son, both of whom have patiently endured the fret and worry of such an undertaking and have worked alongside me throughout the entire endeavor. And to all those persons who have in some way contributed to this book—but whom I have neglected to mention—many thanks.

Jonesboro, Arkansas
March 1977

1

Introduction

In a report dated December 1, 1865, the United States Marshal of Arizona Territory, Milton B. Duffield, informed a superior in Washington that he had recently encountered a troublemaker in Tucson. One Lieutenant Colonel Kennedy, a former Confederate officer, had called Duffield into the street and threatened to "chastise" him for investigating the activities of the former rebel and his friends. The marshal wrote that in self-defense he had knocked Kennedy down and administered "some sound kicks . . . about his head," after which the soldier "ran like a dog leaving his chivalry behind." In order to drive the lesson home, Duffield added that he had "sent a Derringer Pill after" Colonel Kennedy, "making an issue through his right ham." The marshal concluded, gloating, that the shot "had a tendency to terrify the rest of Kennedy's associates."[1]

This exhibition of bravado, while out of character among frontier United States marshals, may have conformed closely to the ancient tradition of Milton B. Duffield's office. The word "marshal" derives from the Old High German, *marah*, meaning horse, and *calc*, meaning servant. Together the words meant "horsekeeper." From humble beginnings in the service of the Germanic war chieftains, the marshal rose to the position of Marshal of Cavalry in the armies of the Frankish kings and acquired the rank of knight in the nobility.[2]

As the status of the marshals improved in European society, the kings added to their duties the maintenance of law and order at the court. The crown permitted the marshals to appoint deputies;

eventually the chief lawman became the executive officer to the royal judiciary. In England the *Mareschal du Banc du Roy*, or Marshal of the King's Bench, survived into the nineteenth century. The military aspect of the medieval marshal survived as well, in the offices of provost marshal and field marshal.[3]

These traditions of the marshalcy were transplanted to the English colonies. A provost marshal, or high marshal, exercised some sway over the Roanoke settlement in 1584. He may have performed civil as well as military duties since, in their earliest stages of growth, many plantations were semimilitary in nature. Marshals also served Jamestown, Plymouth, and Massachusetts Bay. They supported the courts and cared for prisoners until, near the end of the seventeenth century, some colonies, most notably Massachusetts Bay, substituted the office of sheriff for the marshalcy. Other colonies, such as Georgia, retained the latter position until the American Revolution. An emasculated form of the colonial marshalcy survived, also, in the village or city marshalcy.[4]

As the marshalcy of the American colonies lost power, another office with the same title appeared in the British Empire. In 1697, the crown established the vice-admiralty courts to enforce revenue laws and to suppress smuggling and piracy. The courts' new officials served the process of the admiralty courts and cared for confiscated property, assignments not unlike those of the colonial sheriffs. The similarities ended here, since the new marshals performed their tasks on a higher, or federal, plane. As the parvenu courts extended their jurisdiction (even into inland waters of the colonies), the marshals began to collide with the sheriffs in matters of jurisdiction.[5]

These energetic officers expanded their jurisdiction until the American Revolution, when the rebels abruptly extinguished the British Imperial Judiciary. The notion of a strong federal court system, with its supporting marshalcy, fell out of favor. The founders of the first American government refused to entertain any serious thoughts about a centralized national judiciary. Justice remained in the hands of individual states into the 1780s. Sheriffs and other local law officers regained prestige and authority.

American distaste for a centralized judiciary was unrealistic. The Articles of Confederation failed to resolve dangerous conflicts either within or between the states. Some of the new governmental leaders desired a stronger federal government, one that could adjudicate legal problems between the states. In June 1783, Alexander Hamilton introduced a resolution into the Confederation Congress, calling for a stronger central government, one that would have a strong judiciary. Three years later a demonstration by rebellious Massachusetts citizens revealed the inadequacies of the small states and their judiciaries. In the absence of a federal judiciary to provide aid to the weakened state, Massachusetts had to quell the uprising—Shays's Rebellion—alone.[6]

This incident caused the advocates of a powerful central government to agitate for reform of the Articles of Confederation. To this faction, later called the Federalists, the British vice-admiralty courts and their marshals provided a ready example of a powerful law-enforcement instrument. This English precedent "laid the jurisdictional foundation . . . of the federal courts of the United States."[7]

In 1789, the first American Congress paid special attention to courts and law officers. Two conflicting opinions existed about the new judiciary. One faction followed the lead of James Madison's *Federalist Paper* (number forty-five) in which he concluded that the American people would demand that the state courts retain the judicial authority of the Union and would hear federal as well as local cases. Congressman Samuel Livermore of New Hampshire spoke for this group. Duplication of court systems was wasteful, he declared, especially since the state courts were "fully competent" to conduct the business of the federal government. He argued that Americans would be "irritated to see their neighbors dragged before two tribunals [state and federal] for the same offense." Furthermore, the new United States courts would be expensive, since they would require paying many new officers, such as marshals.[8]

The proponents of a separate judiciary—including James Madison, who now sided with the Federalists on this issue—prevailed. In September 1789, Congress passed the Judiciary Act, which provided for the federal court system, made up of district, circuit, and supreme courts. The act divided the states into fifteen judicial districts, including one for Maine (attached to Massachusetts for government), and one for Kentucky, the counties of Virginia beyond the Appalachian Mountains.[9]

Several supporting personnel served these courts. In addition to judges, clerks, and district attorneys, a marshal was attached to each United States District Court. When the circuit or supreme court convened in a particular district, the lawman supported that session. This officer, who has become (under the guise of a frontier peace officer) the symbol of law and order to many Americans, closely resembled the marshal of the British vice-admiralty courts. By the Judiciary Act, the marshal was authorized to execute "all lawful precepts" directed to him by the federal benches. He was empowered to employ deputies, and when necessary, to "command all necessary assistance" in the form of the *posse comitatus* (all able-bodied citizens aged sixteen to sixty-five). Subsequently, he acquired additional duties: the custody of federal prisoners; the rental and provision of the physical needs of the court; the disbursement of court funds (for which he was required to post a bond); and the custodianship of condemned property. He would also have the duty of executing prisoners.[10]

These duties required very little time, since the business of the federal courts was light. Congress filled the void with many odd tasks, so that the marshals became the "handymen" of many government agencies in the early years of the Republic. They conducted the census. They supported the courts-martial of the state militias, by serving process against delinquent militiamen. In the 1790s, these lawmen deported unwanted aliens on the order of the president. The United States marshals acquired custody of ships and goods seized by the United States revenue officers. Additional tasks included the protection of public lands and the enforcement of the neutrality laws.[11]

The men who drafted the Judiciary Act of 1789 were very conscious of the powers of this federal lawman and made special efforts to prevent abuse of the office. They restricted the marshalcy to a term of four years, a qualification placed upon no other appointive office in 1789. Oliver Ellsworth may have proposed this unique provision. An experienced lawman from Connecticut, Ellsworth had observed the colonial practice of restricting sheriffs to fixed terms. He probably suspected that the marshal of the United States, like his counterpart in the county, the sheriff, would help to select juries. This power could make the federal marshal "dangerous."[12]

Marshals were appointed by the president, with the consent of the Senate. The first chief executive, George Washington, inquired personally about the candidates. The first battery of lawmen were "an able group," and included physicians, lawyers, and statesmen. Several of them were formerly members of the Continental Congress; almost all were veterans of the Continental Army. Two had been generals; six had reached the ranks of colonel or lieutenant colonel. Clement Biddle, the first Marshal of Pennsylvania, had been Washington's financial agent in Philadelphia.[13] The president dispatched a letter to the first marshals on September 30, 1789, in which he urged them to "discharge their respective trusts with honor to themselves and advantage to their country."[14]

The majority of the new public servants, including the marshals, were remunerated by the fee system rather than by salary. There were several reasons for this practice: the fledgling government was "impoverished" and lacked not only an adequate supply of currency, but also the "means of moving funds readily from place to place." These conditions made the fee system a godsend to the new administration:

> Officials were compensated if there was a demand for their services; otherwise the government expended nothing. They were paid on the spot, by . . . [persons whom] the law required to deal with them. There was no problem of collection—the self-interest of the official was sufficient.[15]

In the early years, pay under the fee system proved very low. The Marshal of North Carolina reported an income of only $606.47 in 1792, while his colleagues in Massachusetts and Maryland earned $289 and $253.72, respectively. Most surprising was the income of the Marshal of New York, a mere $48.63. Evidently, New York City was outside his district.[16]

This meager income discouraged energetic young men from seeking the post. Edmund Randolph of Virginia, the first (and very conservative) attorney general, characterized the return from fees of the marshalcy as mere "trifles." In 1791, Randolph urged Congress to provide the federal lawmen with an income at least "equal to a livelihood." He argued that, since these officers were always on call, "they are precluded from any [other] gainful employment." Alexander Hamilton wrote off the marshalcy as "troublesome and unprofitable." Meanwhile, President Washington publicized the more rewarding side of the office, "a step" upward in an official career.[17]

The fee system might appear beneficial to a poverty-stricken government, but many persons objected strongly to it. In February 1793, in a congressional debate over the use of fees, Thomas Fitzsimons of Pennsylvania argued that not even the watchful eye of the government could guard against "abuses and frauds" by officers on the fee system. He was undoubtedly referring to the inclination of government agents to "make" fees by trumping up charges and making arrests on insufficient cause.[18]

These arguments failed to impress most congressmen, although some measures were taken to guard against abuses of the fee system. Stringent penalties were imposed on those who charged excessive fees. Another measure required the publication of lists of official fees. In 1789, the national lawmakers permitted the marshals to charge fees equal to those of state officers. Ten years later, Congress assigned the lawmen a limited, but uniform, fee list: $2 for the service of a writ or subpoena; $.05 per mile for travel on official business; $.50 for the commitment or discharge of a prisoner; and $4 per day for attendance upon the court when in session. Unfortunately, this list was limited and federal lawmen continued to use the fee bills of the various states, bills that varied greatly.[19]

In the performance of his duties, the marshal relied heavily upon deputies. The power to employ "one or more" subordinates had been granted by the Judiciary Act. The arrangement between the marshal and underling was unique. The deputy was an employee of the marshal, and not an officer of the court. The marshal and subordinate made a private arrangement about income, and the marshal retained a percentage of the deputy's fee income. This procedure often encouraged the deputies to "make" fees. The deputyship was a part-time position, one that required the occupant to retain full-time employment elsewhere. Often the deputies were concurrent sheriffs, deputy sheriffs, or constables.[20]

The deputy marshals were empowered to perform most of the duties of the marshal—to serve the process of court, to deputize temporary deputies, and to summon the *posse comitatus*. If a marshal died, the deputy filled the post temporarily. In the early 1800s, as court business increased, the ranks of the deputies divided into two categories—office deputies and field deputies. The former worked in the headquarters and performed bookkeeping tasks; the latter resided in remote corners of the judicial district and served the marshal during sessions of court.[21]

Some doubt about the legal status of the deputies arose among early federal judges. They were merely employees of the marshals and not officers of the court. The judges doubted that the deputies could legally serve the process of court. However, in 1844 Attorney General John Nelson laid these objections to rest by ruling that their oaths of office qualified deputies to serve the process of court. It had long since been established that they might be fired, by the marshal or by the district judge. In the quaint words of Attorney General Edmund Randolph, "the judge is armed with authority to stop his [the deputy's] improper career."[22]

After only a few years of service it became apparent that the marshalcy lacked the confidence of many Americans. Many citizens, like their English ancestors, distrusted official positions created by sudden acts of Congress, preferring that government posts arise through custom and tradition, that is, through common law. The county sheriff's office was such a product, having appeared in England in the seventh century before the earliest written records about the shrievalty.[23]

To resolve this dilemma, Congress attempted to surround the marshalcy with the majesty of the common law and at the same time, to increase the power of the office. In May 1792, the national legislators provided that "the marshals shall have, in each state, the same powers as sheriffs in executing the laws of the United States." By statute the federal lawmen acquired a position in the sphere of the federal laws akin to the place of the sheriffs. Deputy marshals were granted powers equivalent to deputy sheriffs. In 1827, to eliminate duplication, the attorney general ruled that, while the federal lawman must conform to common law rules, he was not required to conform exactly to the "duties of a sheriff."[24]

Although the marshals acquired some guidance from an acquaintance with the duties of the sheriffs, the federal lawmen fell under the immediate control of judges and United States district attorneys. The federal judges not only determined the process to be served by the lawman, but also influenced the appointment of the marshals. Judges could not remove a marshal from office or refuse to administer the oath to the president's choice, but could obstruct the appointment by raising questions about the marshal's bond and sureties. It was many years later, in 1863, before the federal judges were empowered to appoint interim marshals.[25]

In spite of the power of the judges, much of the prestige of federal justice depended upon the marshals and attorneys, whom Thomas Jefferson characterized as the "doors" to the United States courts. The marshals worked closely with—and sometimes against—the district attorneys, the officers who prosecuted and defended federal cases. The attorneys were men of the bar and usually men "of ability and standing" in their communities. The marshals, not normally lawyers and often held in less esteem, frequently regarded the attorneys as impractical. The lawyers caused the lawmen to deliver warrants in remote areas, to hostile persons, and then dropped the case. These government lawyers possessed a wide range of discretionary powers, to include the power to judge whether Washington could win such cases or not. It might be in the best interest of the government to drop, rather than lose, the case.[26]

The marshals and their colleagues in the court system were part of a rapidly growing administrative network of lawmen that stretched all the way from the national capital to the ever expanding frontier line in the West. From a mere fifteen judicial districts, each with a marshalcy, in 1789, the number grew to twenty-two only twelve years later. Each new state and, after 1813, each new territory, acquired a marshal. By 1850, there were twenty-one states and four vast territories. Some heavily populated states were subdivided into two (or even three) judicial districts, with a marshal for each district.[27]

Within the administrative organization of the federal government, the marshals were a part of "field services" (as opposed to central administration). The Founding Fathers considered field officers to be absolutely necessary for the efficient application of governmental policy and for the convenience of the citizenry. The judiciary was no exception, and the marshals and district attorneys were two of the first field officers that Congress created. As a concession to the inhabitants of each judicial district, marshals were often appointed from among residents of the area. Appointees to higher office were normally "persons of national consequence."[28]

The fact that the federal lawmen were stationed far from the center of government caused many administrative problems, problems aggravated by slow and uncertain postal and transportation systems. The national authorities attempted to maintain a mutually beneficial relationship between the "center and circumference" as well as "to maintain energy and consistency" in the routine affairs of subordinate departments. This was exceptionally difficult, since lower-echelon field offices had to "possess some discretion."[29]

The marshalcy presented national administrators with peculiar problems in this regard, since the lawmen were only ministerial officers. In this capacity they merely executed "all lawful precepts" of the court. Unlike their colleagues, the district attorneys, the marshals possessed little discretionary power. Nevertheless, a tug-of-war occurred between the marshals, who were keenly aware of the peculiarities of their districts, and their superiors in Washington, who demanded that the policy of the government be carried out to the letter.[30]

Various administrators were empowered to superintend some activities of the lawmen and to discipline or remove an officer. The procedures for superintending them included sending out instructions, circulars, rulings, and reviewing particular cases upon appeal. If routine discipline failed, a lawman's superiors might bring suit to compel him to perform his duty, or to cause him to account for his negligence. If all these procedures failed, the errant lawman might be removed from office by the president. In his eight years as chief executive, from 1801 to 1809, Thomas Jefferson removed eighteen marshals for various abuses, including the use of their offices for political purposes.[31]

While Congress assigned the field services of the early republic to one of the branches of government, it neglected to consolidate the judiciary. As a result, the marshals acquired many superiors. The secretary of state issued instructions of "a general nature" to lawmen. The secretary of the treasury supervised the marshals' spending of public moneys. In 1849, when the Department of the Interior was created, its secretary assumed some responsibilities formerly held by the secretary of state. The attorney general, the most likely candidate for supervisory powers over the judiciary, remained a part-time legal consultant to the government for many years,[32] and had little to do with the problems of the marshalcies.

The absence of an immediate supervisor inhibited the routine administration of justice, though a vague and general supervisory power always lurked in the background in the form of the chief executive. His interests in the marshals were both political and constitutional. Since he normally appointed the federal lawmen from his political party, the president possessed a vested interest in their performance; and the Constitution charged the executive to "take care that the laws be executed." The chain of command remained unclear for many years until ultimately the president became the "supervisor of law enforcement."[33]

Of all the officials who exercised authority over the early marshals, the secretary of the treasury was the most important. Always suspicious of human weakness, the Founding Fathers had established a tight system of financial accountability. The treasurer required them to post a bond ($20,000 and often more) with sureties. The lawmen were required to make periodic reports of their collections and to deposit them in the Bank of the United States or some other designated depository. Before a session of federal court, the treasurer advanced a sum of money to the lawmen, who used it for jurors and other expenses. The marshals submitted accounts of their expenditures, with accompanying receipts. The treasurer examined these accounts carefully for unauthorized expenditures, or other irregularities, and then made a "settlement" with the marshals. By 1823, the lawmen were required to make quarterly financial reports.[34]

In the early 1800s, with the increase in the amount of judicial work, the marshals pleaded for better compensation. After 1820, they complained bitterly about poor remuneration, but with little success. When they performed a unique service, one not covered by the fee list, the marshals were permitted to apply for "extra compensation." In an effort to earn livelihoods, they became "most persistent claimants for extra compensation."[35]

Some marshalcies, especially those in districts with large cities, became very profitable. In 1841, General Solomon Van Rensselaer, a member of a very distinguished Dutch family of New York, aspired to the marshalcy of the Southern District of New York. An acquaintance informed him that the office earned as much as $18,000 per year. Not only was the post profitable, but also it was "genteel," since deputy marshals performed most of the tasks of the office. Senator Daniel Webster of Massachusetts sought the marshalcy of his state for his ambitious son, Fletcher. The senator considered the office to be appropriate, since Fletcher would receive an income without having to work and thus be able to continue his law practice. Fletcher eventually became surveyor of the Port of Boston rather than marshal.[36]

This discrepancy between the incomes of urban and rural marshals caused Congress to legislate uniform fee incomes for marshals. In 1842, only a year after General Rensselaer had sought the profits of the office, the lawmakers placed a ceiling of $6,000 on the annual income of the lawmen. Any fees collected above that figure were to be turned over to the Treasury.[37]

In addition, Congress belatedly established a uniform fee list for the marshals. An act of 1853 discarded the antiquated procedure of requiring the marshals to employ the fee list of county sheriffs. Among the most important provisions of the new fee bill were: $2 for service of a warrant; $.50 for service of subpoena; $.06 per mile for travel; $.50 for each bail bond; $5 per day for serving court in session; $5 for drawing and executing a deed; $.10 per mile for escorting a prisoner to jail; actual expenses when endeavoring to arrest a criminal, not to exceed $2 per day; and two percent of money disbursed to jurors and witnesses.[38]

The federal lawmen continued to depend on the sheriffs and other lesser officers for many services. Since the marshals possessed no facilities for housing federal prisoners, the lawmen requested the use of county jails or state penitentairies. In 1789, Congress persuaded most states to care for federal charges for $.50 per month. After many complaints about the inconvenient locations of federal courts, the United States permitted state courts to hear certain federal cases. The marshals adopted the methods of the states in the selection of juries and instituted similar paperwork. The two arms of law enforcement also exchanged information about criminals.[39]

The marshals appreciated the assistance of local authorities, since Washington gave the marshals few funds for the pursuit of criminals. Congress evidently feared a strong detective arm in the marshalcy and, at the same time, regarded it the duty of every loyal citizen—as informant or juryman—to report the whereabouts of criminals. Congress authorized rewards to these informants, although some objections were raised to bounties. Vindictive persons, said the critics, might make malicious accusations in order to earn bounty money. However, the object of the lawmakers was "to induce *private citizens* to observe the law" and to report violations of federal statutes. District attorneys were also expected to be alert and to assist the marshals. These institutions were supplemented by small detective agencies within several branches of government, especially in the Treasury and Post Office departments.[40]

Nevertheless, among the agencies of detection, the marshals occupied a central place. Although they were simultaneously the ministerial officers of the courts, they were "expected to spare no effort to detect and apprehend violators of the law." The federal lawman was "the original law enforcement officer in the federal system and constituted the first line of defense on occasions of domestic disturbance."[41]

In spite of his considerable powers, the marshal was weakened by severe handicaps. The government paid the same small fee for the arrest of a hardened criminal as for the service of a warrant upon a harmless citizen. Congress neglected to provide stiff penalties for the protection of the federal lawmen from violent resistance. In 1790, the national lawmakers timidly provided for a fine of $300 and imprisonment of twelve months for assault upon a federal officer. Congress concluded that the criminal laws of the states were sufficient to protect all citizens (including the marshals) against violence. Yet, as the sectional crisis (the hostility between North and South over slavery) arose in the early 1800s, the states often used their courts against the marshals.[42]

The Judiciary Act anticipated this circumstance and permitted the lawmen to command "all necessary assistance" in the form of the *posse comitatus* ("power of the county"), another feature of English common law that the United States judiciary adopted. The sheriff in England was authorized to summon every person aged fifteen or older and able to travel. Persons who refused to serve as possemen were liable to a fine and imprisonment. The United States marshals seldom called all able-bodied men. Instead they assessed the degree of the emergency and appointed possemen "by tens, hundreds, or thousands where need required."[43]

The *posse comitatus* often presented officers with administrative problems. The possemen expected pay for their services but funds for such services fell under the classification of emergency or "extraordinary expenses" in Washington. The approval of the president was required before payment was made. Only in 1854 did the attorney general rule that these emergency expenses were binding upon the government. Even so, the Treasury Department continued to scrutinize the marshals' accounts for posses and disallowed many.[44]

Occasionally, a marshal was embarrassed to learn that the citizens of his district were in rebellion and unwilling to serve as possemen. The lawman could turn only to the military for assistance. Thus, in 1792, when rebellious whiskey distillers of western Pennsylvania resisted the marshal, Congress authorized the president to dispatch the militia to aid the federal lawman. The chief executive could issue orders to the militia only if there were a clear demonstration that the marshal was overpowered by the dissidents and only after he (the president) had issued a proclamation urging the dissidents to return peacefully to their homes. The militia did not become a part of the *posse comitatus*, it merely supported the marshal until he could serve the process of court without interference. In 1807, when President Thomas Jefferson encountered obstructions to the Embargo Act, Congress empowered him to dispatch regular army units to aid marshals under the same proclamation procedure.[45]

The chief executives complained many times about this time-consuming process, and in 1854, Attorney General Caleb Cushing concocted a means to circumvent the proclamation. When violent obstructionists confronted the marshals, the lawmen could deputize any individual, or *body of organized persons*, within their districts. This ruling not only permitted the federal lawmen to summon the army as a posse, but also it circumvented the requirement that the president issue a proclamation before he placed troops under the marshals. President Franklin Pierce went one step further when he deliberately assigned troops to a judicial district (Kansas Territory) in which widespread resistance to the marshal was occurring, thus assuring the lawman a reliable posse.[46]

The outbreak of serious sectional violence in frontier Kansas in the 1850s presented a dangerous challenge to the marshalcy and federal courts. In December 1858, the belligerents—pro- and antislavery parties—alarmed Marshal William Fain to such an extent that he summoned several hundred civilians as possemen. He kept the posse under arms for several weeks as a kind of "standing army" and presented a bill to the Treasury. The authorities in Washington were shocked by Fain's behavior and ordered him to disband his "army."[47]

This incident forced the attorney general to define the limitations of the marshal's posse. In theory "there is no defined limit" to the powers of the marshal to increase the size of his posse. Practically, however, the marshal's resources "are decidedly limited" by financial means and by the nature of the marshal's district. The lawman, says historian James G. Randall

> is a ministerial officer intrusted with the execution of specific judicial orders or writs, and . . . he is by no means authorized to maintain a quasi-military force or to keep a large body of men in the field for an indefinite period in order to break up an insurrection. . . . [The] suppression of insurrection is the executive, not a judicial, function.[48]

The attorney general instructed Marshal Fain to employ a posse for short periods only and for a specific purpose. A posse could not take on the coloration of a military expedition. This incident in the turbulent Kansas Territory emphasized the limitations of the office and pointed out the first purpose of the marshalcy—to serve the process of the federal court, and not to suppress large-scale uprisings.[49]

In 1789, the Founding Fathers had given little thought to justice in the western territories. The lands west of the Appalachians were too immature for a costly legal system. Only Kentucky, then a part of Virginia, received a marshal and a United States District Court. The Northwest Territory received a judiciary of only three judges, any two of whom sitting together (later only one was necessary) constituted a superior court with common-law jurisdiction. Since these tribunals lacked federal jurisdiction, the territories required no United States marshals.[50]

The subject of territorial court jurisdiction over United States cases became a thorny one, especially when the Supreme Court refused to entertain judicial appeals from the western courts. As early as August 1789, Governor Arthur St. Clair of the Northwest Territory deplored the failure of Congress to provide a United States attorney for his district, an officer "to sue for, or defend, the property of the United States in civil cases." The pleas of St. Clair and others fell upon deaf ears in Congress until 1801, when the lame duck Federalist Congress provided for an elaborate system of United States circuit courts. The Northwest Territory (by now confined to Ohio) and Indiana Territory fell under this new judiciary. The incoming Jeffersonian Congress quickly repealed the act. The superior courts of the territories, however, were given jurisdiction over the United States cases that had arisen during the brief existence of the circuit courts. Only in 1805 did Congress formally bestow upon the territorial courts the concurrent powers of a United States district court.[51]

While the Act of 1805 granted federal jurisdiction to the superior courts of the territories, it did not provide for a permanent staff of federal officers, most notably a marshal and attorney. Congress resorted to expediencies. A governor or judge appointed a person, usually a sheriff, temporarily to "act as marshal." A special United States Land Commission appointed a marshal in 1805 for the purpose of serving the process of the commission. This body, which adjudicated land disputes in the remote Illinois (Kaskaskia) Country, was empowered to subpoena witnesses. Since the congressional charge to the commission did not authorize a marshal, the officers assumed "a constructive power" to appoint a lawman to serve the process of the land court.[52]

In the first decade of the nineteenth century the amount of federal business increased appreciably in the territories. The government became concerned about intruders on the public lands, something that persons "acting as marshals" failed to prevent. In Michigan and Mississippi the problem of maritime law on the Great Lakes and Gulf Coast became serious. In 1806, Mississippi also experienced a spectacular dispute between territorial and federal authorities over the custody of the suspected revolutionary, Aaron Burr.[53] Several years later, in 1813, when Delegate George Poindexter of Mississippi (a temporary federal attorney in 1806) entered Congress, he agitated for permanent marshals and attorneys for all territories. On February 27, 1813, Poindexter won his case. The national lawmakers belatedly provided that each territory should have a battery of federal officers. The marshal

> shall execute all process issuing from the territorial courts when exercising their jurisdiction as circuit and district courts of the United States. He shall have the power to perform the duties, and be subject to the regulations and penalties, imposed by law on the marshals for the several judicial districts of the United States.

Thereafter, when Congress created a new territory, the act of organization included a federal lawman. Congress also declared that each territory should have a district attorney. These two officers, the "doors" to the United States courts, became a permanent and important part of federal justice in the territories for the next century.[54]

Even though Congress had legislated piecemeal for the territorial judiciaries during the early years of the Republic, its members had been aware of the peculiar conditions of frontier law enforcement, and occasionally, had acted on same. In 1804, when the organization of the Louisiana Purchase began, Congress designated the southern Mississippi Valley the Territory of Orleans and took the unprecedented step of giving it a United States district court (not a concurrent territorial court) with a marshal and assorted officers. Francis J. L. D'Orgenay, a highly respected creole, was appointed marshal by President Thomas Jefferson on December 12, 1804,[55] and became the first "western" marshal.

Congress also imposed upon several territorial marshals the duty of policing vast tracts of Indian lands in the Louisiana Purchase. By the 1830s some one hundred thousand Indians had been deported from their homes in the East to the Indian Country adjacent to Arkansas and Missouri. The tribes established local courts for the trial of cases involving only Indians, but the Indian Intercourse Act of 1834 extended "the general laws of the United States" into the Indian Country and provided that the United States courts of Missouri and the Territory of Arkansas should hear cases that arose between Indians and whites.[56]

The task of policing the western territories placed an incredible strain upon the frontier marshals, who were fortunate to have the western army to assist them. As early as June 1791, Governor Arthur St. Clair of the Northwest Territory outlined the civil responsibilities of the frontier army. "Every necessary aid," said the executive, "either in suppressing tumults, apprehending offenders or safely keeping them after they are apprehended, to which the Power of the County [*posse comitatus*] may be inadequate, will be cheerfully rendered by the military." This relationship between the military and the marshals became more firmly bonded in 1854, when Attorney General Caleb Cushing circumvented the presidential proclamation provision and authorized the marshals to summon the Army as a *posse comitatus.*[57]

Territorial marshals both resembled and differed from their eastern colleagues. They were appointed by the president, and confirmed by the Senate, for four-year terms. In 1806, Congress extended the fee system to the territories, but the cost of living was so high that the national lawmakers eventually granted the territorial marshals an annual salary of $200, plus fees, not to exceed $4000 per year.[58]

It is difficult to assess the effectiveness of the United States marshals in the early territories. By 1850, federal lawmen served the courts across a vast frontier to the Pacific Ocean. A battery of lesser lawmen—county sheriffs, city marshals, and precinct constables—cooperated in the same endeavor. However, the counties were often too large for one sheriff to police and the territories were much too vast for the United States marshals to cover adequately. Within their districts, these latter officers attempted to protect public lands and assist the Indians against encroachments by whites, as well as to quell domestic insurrections. These activities, and others, have prompted one historian to conclude that, by 1850, the United States marshals had "acquired the primary duty of [law] enforcement within the territories" and were often "the sole police power in pioneer communities."[59]

2

The Marshalcy in Antebellum New Mexico Territory

Among the new mid nineteenth-century marshalcies west of the Mississippi River, the New Mexico office stood out. In 1851, when John G. Jones assumed the mantle of federal law enforcer under the territory's first permanent civilian government, his district included not only New Mexico but also Arizona. Jones's precinct contrasted sharply with many western districts, not only in size, but in other ways. It had a unique geography of barren deserts and mountains, dotted by sparsely settled villages, and a complex mixture of peoples, many of whom were accustomed to Mexican justice (based on Roman, not English, legal structures). The Indians were receptive only to their own laws. Jones and his successors wrestled with these problems, and by 1861 they had laid the foundation of federal law enforcement in the Southwest. The victory was not clear-cut. The Hispanos were occasionally rebellious. The Indians were warlike and thus out of the lawman's purview. In serious crises the marshals had to rely on support from the army and energetic governors.

Marshal Jones and his successors prudently confined their official activities to the few settlements of the territory, chief among them Santa Fe. Settled by Spaniards about 1608, Santa Fe was one of the northernmost outposts of Spanish civilization for centuries. It rested atop a rough triangle of waterways formed by the two most important rivers of New Mexico—the Rio Grande and the Pecos. Including its environs, Santa Fe counted possibly 6,000 citizens in 1851. The city impressed visitors differently. Trader Thomas James, who saw Santa Fe in 1822, declared that it

18

"presented a fine appearance." In 1832, merchant Josiah Gregg was disheartened at his first sight of the village. It appeared life-less. Gregg mistook the adobe residences of the New Mexicans for brick-kilns. However, as Harvey Fergusson has observed, Hispano towns are like desert plants; they "tend to reach a certain modest size and then grow very slowly if at all."[1]

In addition to Santa Fe, the marshals visited other villages on or near the Rio Grande. Sixty miles above Santa Fe was Taos, complemented by an ancient Pueblo Indian community. It had long served as a haven for American fur traders and as a port of entry for foreign merchants. South of Santa Fe, along the old Royal Road (el Camino Real) to Mexico, the most important stopover was Albuquerque, which probably numbered no more than the 2,547 persons recorded in 1828. Farther south was Socorro. The mar-shals dreaded this spot. It was a haven for outlaws from Texas and elsewhere, men who made Socorro feel "the shock of gun-rule."[2]

With the addition of the Gadsden Strip—the Mesilla and Gila valleys—to New Mexico in the 1850s, the marshals acquired jurisdiction over several villages on the lower Rio Grande and to the west in "Arizona." The marshals were anxious to impress upon the inhabitants of Dona Ana, Las Cruces, and Mesilla, that the Santa Fe government could enforce the laws. Texans had claimed New Mexico east of the Rio Grande and in 1841, had invaded that region unsuccessfully. Franklin (El Paso), Texas, still intimidated the New Mexican communities in the Strip economically.

Much to the dismay of the federal enforcers, they were unable to take the federal laws into the westernmost portion of the Purchase, "Arizona." The only route from Santa Fe to this remote spot was roundabout—to Mesilla and west along an old Spanish route. In 1858, this road became the Butterfield Overland Mail. Tucson, the largest community in Arizona, contained 760 persons in 1851. (A visitor described the village of adobes as "a city of mud-boxes, dingy and dilapidated.") Most of the inhabitants were Hispanos but, unlike the case in New Mexico, the few Anglo-Americans of southern Arizona threatened to dominate the Hispanos. This fact would play a significant part in the operations of the marshalcy many years later.[3]

Elsewhere in Arizona, civilization was restricted to the village of Tubac (250 residents) and Yuma. Many of Tubac's residents were American prospectors or representatives of eastern mining firms,

attracted by reports of gold in the area. Yuma, situated where the
Gila River emptied into the Colorado, consisted of a few shanties
clustered about a ferry site. In 1860, the first census of Arizona
counted about 2,000 settled persons, Anglo-American and Hispano. The Indians, many of whom were hostile, numbered about
25,000. It is no wonder that the marshals in Santa Fe placed this
area in the hands of the army and vigilante justice.[4]

In the Rio Grande Valley, persons of Spanish descent constituted an overwhelming majority of the peaceful population. The
majority of the Hispanos in New Mexico (about 58,000 in 1851)
were peaceful and industrious farmers and herders. Many American visitors refused to recognize this and alleged that the Hispanos
were "depraved" and "lawless" desperadoes, or "demented and
besotted brutes." These observations were colored by the fears of
Anglo Protestants who anticipated a resurgence or rebellion by the
Catholic Hispanos.[5]

In addition to the Hispanos, New Mexico district contained an
estimated 25,000 Indians. Only a few tribes were peaceful. The
Pueblos, Zuni, and Moquis, about 7,000 in number, were sedentary and resided in tight-knit communities. They were a deeply
religious people who had mixed Catholicism and their own ritual.
"In every [Pueblo] village," wrote Harvey Ferguson, "one building
stands apart . . . ." Often "oblong or circular," this is the kiva
"where many gods . . . are worshipped." In theory the Pueblos
possessed American civil rights, and in 1855, the territorial legislature declared the tribes corporate bodies. Of all the Indians in New
Mexico in 1851, only these fell under the immediate purview of the
marshals.[6]

The balance of the Indians in the district were hostile and
outside the officers' concern. Inasmuch as the Apaches and Navajos
occupied four-fifths of the lawmen's district, however, and
equalled in number the peaceable citizens, they effectively
obstructed the marshalcy in outlying areas. In 1864, an angry
judge, upset at the power the military wielded over the Indians,
averred that he would issue process against any Indian lawbreaker
and present the warrant to the marshal who "was duty bound to
serve any warrant that the court might issue." Needless to say, the
thought that he and his posse might be constrained to face the
Apaches must have less than pleased the marshal.[7]

The most influential residents of the territory in 1851 were the

Americans, some 5,000 in number. Some of them were soldiers; others were merchants who represented eastern firms. The latter contracted supplies to the army and thus provided much of the currency for the territorial economy. Some of the Anglo-Americans had entered the Southwest in the 1820s when ambitious Missouri traders opened a lucrative commerce, the famous Santa Fe Trade, with Mexican New Mexico. A few married into the Hispano families. The resultant merchant clique, supplemented by a few European immigrants, was to furnish political leaders for New Mexico Territory during the next generation. They maintained a keen interest in the marshalcy, since commerce could flourish only where law and order existed. Several of the early federal lawmen were a part of this narrow but energetic community.[8]

Marshal John G. Jones and his successors were dismayed by the machinery of Mexican justice that they confronted. The more important institutions—church, army, trades, and professions—were permitted to administer justice in their own courts. Civil cases went before the official tribunals, the courts of the alcaldes, where the burden of proof was not upon the judges, but upon the plaintiffs.[9]

The inhabitants of New Mexico Territory were vaguely familiar with the office of United States marshal in 1851. In September 1846, a month after the surrender of the Mexican governor to American forces, General Stephen Watts Kearny proclaimed a temporary government and appointed civilian officials. For marshal, Kearny chose Richard Dallam, a member of an enterprising St. Louis family, who was engaged in mining and merchandizing around Santa Fe.[10]

Chief Justice Joab Houghton, whom Dallam would be required to support, quickly divided the territory into three judicial districts: The First, at Santa Fe; the Second, with Albuquerque as headquarters; and the Third, centered around Taos. Although the marshal was permitted to locate his office wherever he desired (federal law enforcement was still rather informal), Dallam chose the capital city. The first session of the Territorial Court, which heard United States cases, met on December 1, 1846, in Santa Fe. No doubt Marshal Dallam attended.[11]

The peremptory fashion in which the conquerors launched the government in Santa Fe offended the ruling class of Hispanos, since the vast majority of Kearny's appointees, including the chief federal lawman, were Anglos. Resentment smoldered until January 1847, when the counties north of Santa Fe launched the bloody Taos Rebellion. They murdered Governor Charles Bent, the sheriff of Taos, and other officers. Marshal Dallam was not equipped to suppress an insurrection, but he promptly joined a militia unit as sergeant and marched against the rebels.[12]

After the rebellion was put down, few civil lawmen were left in the area. The Americans massacred some of the insurgents, but, in order to maintain a semblance of legality, the victors actually tried—and executed—others. Many years after the affair in Taos, an old pioneer of New Mexico, "Uncle Dick" Wootton, recalled that his comrades had designated him "marshal" of the summary tribunal.[13]

As peace returned to northern New Mexico in the spring of 1847, the legitimate marshal, Richard Dallam, and the courts resumed operation. In March, Dallam opened an official session of the Third District Court in Taos to try one of the surviving rebel leaders, Antonio Maria Trujillo. Other insurrectionists were jailed in Santa Fe and tried at the spring session of the United States court in that city. Many of them were eventually released.[14]

The bitter resistance of the natives to American domination convinced Congress that New Mexico was not prepared for civilian rule. As early as January 11, 1847, the War Department ordered the abolition of the marshalcy and district attorney's office. These offices were inconsistent with the de facto military rule in the district. Dallam and the attorney continued to serve, however, until June 22, possibly to assist in the trial of the rebels. In February 1848, General Sterling Price officially eliminated the office of marshal. And in October, the governor was replaced by a military officer. Congress applauded these steps, since the presence of a military governor degraded the marshalcy and other civilian posts.[15]

Some citizens resented this irregular regime in Santa Fe, especially since it delayed statehood, the ultimate goal of the Anglo-Americans of New Mexico. The advocates of a regularized government petitioned Congress and protested the removal of the marshalcy and other offices. The prospects of a receptive Congress were better after the Treaty of Guadalupe Hidalgo was ratified (1848) and the United States had formally annexed New Mexico. Only the question of chattel slavery in the Southwest hindered the formation of the new territorial government. Thus, any mention of slavery was avoided in the Organic Act of September 1850, which created the Territory of New Mexico. On March 3, 1851, the new regime went into operation.[16]

John G. Jones became New Mexico Territory's first marshal under civilian rule. A longtime resident of the Southwest, he had served as advisor to the government on Indian policy. When he assumed the marshalcy on March 12, 1851, he was also sheriff of Santa Fe County.[17]

Charles S. Rumley, who succeeded Jones as marshal on April 5, 1853, served only a short time—about five months. He was very close to the merchant clique of former territorial delegate Hugh N. Smith and became the first initiate into the Masonic Lodge of Santa Fe. Such a distinction would not have been accorded had this narrow order not respected Rumley.[18]

Rumley was followed by Charles Blumner, who took the oath of office on December 10, 1853. As early as 1837, Blumner had been a participant in the Santa Fe trade, often signing his name "Carlos" to indicate his affinity with the local population. He was territorial treasurer before and after his marshalcy. When he resigned the latter position in 1857, his colleagues gratefully presented him with a party and a silver pipe for his contribution to federal law enforcement. Like Charles Rumley, Blumner was a Mason.[19]

Prussian-born Charles P. Clever was the last marshal of New Mexico during the pre–Civil War period. Upon his arrival in the territory in 1850, Clever obtained U.S. citizenship and formed a partnership with Sigmund Seligman, a member of an influential commercial community of German Jews. He became a director of the *Santa Fe Weekly Gazette* and was soon admitted to the bar. He served as constable in Santa Fe and as a deputy United States marshal. His appointment to the marshalcy on March 30, 1858, was the result of the influence of territorial delegate Miguel A. Otero. Although his term expired in 1861, Clever remained in office until August 16, 1862. His successor, Albert W. Archibald, failed to post an adequate bond and was disqualified.[20]

The federal court system remained substantially unchanged under the new territorial government. The Gadsden Purchase (or Dona Ana County) was arbitrarily added to the southern (the Second) judicial district in 1853. The president appointed three territorial judges who sat concurrently in the federal and territorial courts. Each judge held two terms annually, in the spring and fall, with sessions in several counties. Upon the completion of a session of the United States court, the same judge opened a territorial session. Two grand juries were summoned, one for each side of the judiciary: the United States district attorney prosecuted in the federal side of court; the territorial attorney general or county prosecutor served the territory.[21]

The judicial system of the territories was "one of the weakest" links of frontier government. The president appointed territorial justices without regard for the desires of the residents of the territories. Many appointees were incompetent or refused to serve their districts faithfully. Because of this, the New Mexico legislature conferred upon probate judges some jurisdiction normally reserved for federal courts. Local justices of the peace, who held court often instead of twice a year, could convene a hearing at a moment's notice and determine to which court, United States or territorial, a case belonged.[22]

Federal statute required that prisoners of the United States be guarded by a deputy marshal. Because New Mexico Territory had no federal prison, the marshal contracted with the county sheriffs (who were often made deputy marshals) for penitentiary space. These county officers were probably the most qualified men to serve as deputies to the federal lawman, but not necessarily the most trustworthy. The sheriffs worked in the interest of the local courts first and the United States courts second.[23]

Not the least of the marshals' problems was finding deputies who spoke Spanish. In the instance of Simeon H. Smith, Marshal Charles Blumner evidently found an Anglo fluent in Spanish, although this interesting man earned most of his livelihood as a quack healer and horse doctor. Most deputies with language capabilities were found in the Hispano population, since the ruling Anglos had wisely realigned with the dons since the Taos Rebellion. In May 1858, the *Santa Fe Weekly Gazette* noted that Marshal Charles P. Clever had recently appointed Sheriff Jesus Maria Sena y Baca as a deputy. After congratulating Clever on the wise selection (Clever was a director of the paper), the editor characterized Baca as "a young man with business habits, [who] understands both languages."[24]

While the marshals were concerned with ensuring federal law enforcement among the Hispanos, they were also anxious to place deputies among the Indian population. Marshal John G. Jones selected as his subordinate for the northern (Third), heavily Indian judicial district, Lafayette Head, a veteran of the Mexican War and an energetic merchant in Abiquiu, Rio Arriba County. Head was a special agent for the Jicarilla Apaches and the Utes. He was also married to Martina Martinez, a member of a very influential family. Eventually he became a highly respected member of the Territorial Assembly.[25]

The marshals personally opened each session of federal court, although the attorney general subsequently permitted deputies to carry out this task. William Watts Hart Davis, who became United States district attorney in 1854, outlined the itinerary of Marshal Charles Blumner and members of the bar for one spring circuit of federal court. The judicial party traveled from Santa Fe to Taos in order to open court on the first Monday of March. From that village, Blumner rode to Chamita, and then to Santa Fe on March 20. In mid April, he went to Albuquerque; from there, the marshal rode to Socorro, and on to Las Cruces, the southernmost point on the lawman's route. Davis estimated that the marshal and the legal community traveled a thousand miles by horseback in eight weeks. This itinerary was repeated in the fall. The early marshals attended the courts faithfully. The *Santa Fe Weekly Gazette* noted regularly the departure of these officers for sessions of court.[26]

The problem of supporting the federal side of the courts was aggravated for the marshal in August 1856, when Congress consolidated the county sessions of federal court into one session in each judicial district. Constituents complained that they could not leave their crops or herds and travel unescorted through Indian country to the new, and more remote, locations of the single sessions. At the Socorro court in 1858, Marshal Charles P. Clever delayed the opening of the court because many persons refused to attend. The *Weekly Gazette* noted the unfortunate delay but added that a prospective juror could not be expected to ride two hundred miles to court. Clever's problem was complemented by the failure of the territorial assembly to appropriate funds to pay the jurors for their services to the territorial side of the court. The marshal paid the balance due the jurors, since the same panel sat for the United States side of the court. The harassed federal policeman merely endured this law. In 1858, the "Consolidation Act" was wisely abolished.[27]

In addition to these complications, the marshals found court-house and jail facilities almost nonexistent in the 1850s. Most of the federal offices, and presumably the marshal's headquarters, were located in the Palace of the Governors in Santa Fe. Federal author-ities, who had leased the building from the territorial assembly, were required to keep the building in good repair, although Gov-ernor Abraham Rencher recalled that when he arrived at his post, in 1857, the structure was "in ruinous condition." This ancient building became the site for many notable sessions of federal court.[28]

The marshals rented courtrooms wherever available. In August 1851, Marshal John G. Jones nearly precipitated a Hispano riot when he revealed plans to lease a vacant church building in Santa Fe. The edifice was used by the army for storage purposes. The courtroom for an 1854 session at Chamita was an unfurnished building which the marshal rented for $1 per day.[29]

The jails were little better. The most secure jails were the military guardhouses, which the army often made available to the federal lawman. District Attorney William W. H. Davis described the "jail" at Taos as a small room that adjoined the courtroom. The "cell" had no lock but was secured by a piece of "twine string." Marshal Jones was deeply humiliated in March 1852, when the county officials revealed that there were no more funds for the subsistence of prisoners. With no other recourse, Jones, Sheriff R. M. Stevens (Stephens), and Probate Judge Tomas Ortiz certified to the governor that the county was "without means to feed pris-oners" and that "the poor 'wretches' must inevitably die or rot in jail" unless the executive intervened. The governor reluctantly pardoned the fourteen inmates on the condition that they leave the territory within twenty-five days.[30]

Near the end of the 1850s, Governor Rencher asked the territor-ial legislature for an appropriation to complete a prison. Congress had authorized the structure many years earlier. Nevertheless, prisoners were housed in the partially completed structure. Only in 1882 did the territory belatedly complete the penitentiary.[31]

The marshal encountered even more problems in the remote Third Judicial District. For example, before the Gadsden Purchase in 1853, the community of Mesilla lay in a disputed zone with Mexico. Consequently, when several Mexicans murdered an Apache chief in the American village of Dona Ana and fled to

Mesilla, Marshal Charles S. Rumley asked Mexican officers to arrest the suspects. The Mexicans refused. Rumley and the sheriff organized a posse to recover the murderers and requested forces from nearby Fort Fillmore. When the post commander refused, Rumley discreetly disbanded his posse.[32]

Not the least of the marshals' frustrations in Dona Ana County arose from violations of the customs laws. In 1854, Congress created the Customs District of Paso del Norte (El Paso) which included not only New Mexico Territory but Texas west of the Pecos River. The federal court for the Third Judicial District, at Dona Ana, New Mexico, was empowered to try all customs cases in western Texas and New Mexico. The Texas legislature, outraged at this encroachment, resolved not to obey Marshal Charles Blumner, the first marshal to enforce this law, and urged its citizens to ignore him and his deputies. By November 1856, the United States court had more than one hundred indictments against Texans. Many Texans, who had to travel many miles out of their way to pay the customs duties, deliberately violated the laws. The editor of the *Weekly Gazette* discreetly urged the federal judge to fine only the most flagrant violators. At the same time, the writer denied the right of the Texas legislature to direct its citizens to refuse to obey the New Mexico marshal.[33]

The marshals were sometimes embarrassed by their customs duties. The frontier army posts of western Texas and southeastern New Mexico purchased many supplies from Mexico and, like civilian traders, refused to take the roundabout trails to distant customs offices. In 1856, Deputy Marshal Samuel G. Bean of Mesilla traveled to Texas to arrest Major James Longstreet for "resisting" a customs officer. Longstreet was fined $300 and released. An anonymous observer of these proceedings grumbled to a Santa Fe journalist that the army officers should not be subject to the "nuisance" of the federal courts. Evidently the judges agreed, and they dismissed many of the customs cases.[34]

In "Arizona," in contrast to the situation in Texas, the federal lawmen did as little as possible. As late as July 1856, United States District Attorney W. Claude Jones, who resided at Las Cruces, informed the governor that "there is a great necessity for civil officers at Tuson [*sic*] . . . ." He added that "people are continually passing into our new territory . . . and they require protection."

The attorney added that "a gentleman of standing" had recently arrived in Las Cruces from Kentucky and requested an appointment to some civil office in Arizona. This Kentuckian was Charles D. Poston, who would later acquire the title "Father of Arizona." Poston received an appointment as deputy county recorder for Dona Ana County, with headquarters in Tucson, and had a friend appointed deputy sheriff. However, Poston was disappointed when the outcasts of Tucson refused to obey him or the deputy sheriff. "The 'rawhiders' refused to pay taxes, [to buy] licenses, or to recognize New Mexican authority," he recalled many years later. "The new purchase of Gadsden began its career in chaos & lawlessness." Aside from an occasional visit by the sheriff and deputy marshal of Mesilla, Samuel G. Bean, a decade passed before this remote area acquired law enforcement.[35]

An example of the impotency of the marshalcy occurred early in 1857, when "Colonel" Henry A. Crabb led a band of filibusters through New Mexican territory and into Mexico. Crabb had vague notions about creating an independent state in Sonora. Some two dozen residents of Tucson, led by Granville Oury, attempted unsuccessfully to join the Crabb party. Mexican authorities executed the "colonel" and his immediate force. From his office in Santa Fe, Marshal Charles P. Clever could do nothing about such violations of the neutrality laws.[36]

The failure of the federal lawman to enforce the laws in remote Dona Ana County provoked an independence movement in the Gadsden Purchase. Beginning in 1856, citizens of Tucson and Mesilla memorialized Congress regularly for separation from New Mexico. Among other grievances, the residents of Arizona cited the absence of federal law officers. No redress was forthcoming. In 1860 the petitioners created the extralegal "Territory of Arizona." Lewis Owings became governor and, surprisingly, Samuel G. Bean accepted the marshalcy. The fact that Bean had served as a sheriff and deputy marshal for years made him a logical candidate for this illegal post.[37]

This separatist movement alarmed Governor Abraham Rencher, who recommended that the Tucsonians be provided with a separate judicial district. The territorial assembly refused his request. In 1861, when the New Mexico Assembly belatedly established the county of Arizona, the Civil War precluded any practical effects of the new creation. It appears that no deputy marshal was ever appointed for Arizona, although one angry Arizonian noted with disgust that the taxes were always collected (by the customs officers) to support the government.[38]

In the face of so many obstacles, the marshals had to depend on the army for support. Many observers have commented unfavorably about the performance of the military as a civil law enforcement agency, but the regulars were the "only disciplinary arm of government" in the remote territories. Hubert Howe Bancroft, who observed the bluecoats in action against desperadoes, characterized the frontier garrisons as "lazy, careless, indifferent, and stupid." They "were no match for" desperate men on the frontier. Scholar Frank Richard Prassel concluded that, while the army was the only institution that could "maintain order" in the territories, it nevertheless "failed."[39]

Still, the marshals of New Mexico were happy to have the assistance of the troops. In 1858, when a militia unit, the Mesilla Guard, massacred eight Apache Indians, Marshal Charles P. Clever requested the assistance of the local army post. The populace sympathized with the killers and refused to serve in his *posse comitatus*. The army cooperated, however, by swearing out a complaint and providing an escort. Clever arrested the leader, Juan Ortega, and thirty-five members of the Mesilla Guard. The prisoners were lodged in the post guardhouse at Fort Thorn. On the day of the trial in Socorro, a detachment accompanied the marshal and his charges to court.[40]

The cooperation between the marshalcy and the military benefited the army as well. In 1852, Major James H. Carleton, commander of Fort Union, complained about illegal saloons on the military reservation. Governor James Calhoun directed Marshal John G. Jones to remove the illegal occupants. The task fell to Deputy Marshal R. M. Stephens who zealously destroyed the "grog shops" and confiscated the alcoholic beverages under the Intercourse Act of March 3, 1847. The disgruntled owners attempted to prosecute the deputy and Major Carleton, but the court dismissed their cases in September 1853.[41]

The fact that the marshals and other territorial lawmen depended upon the military for support caused some persons to scoff at the civilian government. Among the most caustic critics Colonel Edwin V. Sumner, commander of military forces in New Mexico, occupied a prominent place. In a much publicized letter to the secretary of war—published in the *New York Times* on January 11, 1853—the colonel declared that the territory was not ready for self-government and that "no civil government can be maintained here without the aid of a military force." Every branch of government had failed, including the local judiciary. The federal courts suffered from the "total incapacity" of the judges, jurors lacked "principle," and the prison system failed because the citizenry refused to be taxed for its upkeep. Sumner recommended that the United States withdraw and leave the New Mexicans to their own political devices—the *pronunciamiento* system of monthly revolutions.[42]

At the heart of this bitter critique lay Sumner's doubts about the ability of the Hispanos to serve on local and federal juries. It was true that the federal lawmen did encounter problems with the native population. The marshals were constrained to post official notices in Spanish, as well as English, and to hire interpreters. New Mexican jurors did tend to be lenient, as Colonel Sumner charged, but hardly unprincipled. When a native jury acquitted an alleged murderer in 1857, the angry judge promptly dismissed the jurors. Marshal Charles Blumner reluctantly went to the expense of summoning another jury.[43]

Much of Colonel Sumner's hostility arose because of his resentment of irresponsible civil officials. Many territorial officers were chronically absent from their posts. In May 1852, the majority of the territorial officers—governor, secretary, attorney general, two judges, and two Indian agents—were all absent. Some years later the *Weekly Gazette* announced that "New Mexico is without a government," since Governor David Meriwether, the secretary, and chief justice, were absent from their posts. In October 1858, the editor again noted absences and wrote, "Is our judiciary ever to operate fully?"[44]

Fortunately, the marshals of the 1850s were not absentee officials. The federal lawmen were permanent residents of the territory. Marshal Charles P. Clever became a strong advocate of the appointment of residents to all important territorial posts. Clever defended his position before an informal group, the Santa Fe Literary Club, but the society (heavily attended by nonresident appointees) voted for appointments from outside the territory.[45]

The rivalry between these home rule and anti-home rule factions greatly influenced the fortunes of the marshalcy in the decade before the Civil War. The anti-home rule group, or American party, led by Hugh N. Smith, obtained the support of the administration of President Franklin Pierce. In 1853, Smith persuaded Pierce to appoint Charles Rumley to the marshalcy. In 1858, when the office was again vacant, the home rule clique, led by Delegate Miguel A. Otero, exerted much political power in New Mexico. Otero, a man with Southern leanings and an advocate of a slave code for his district, nominated Charles P. Clever, a man with similar political leanings. President James Buchanan obligingly appointed Clever to the marshalcy over the objections of former Governor William Carr Lane. Lane, who represented an influential group of merchants in St. Louis, recommended young Samuel Ellison for the marshalcy. Ellison became a life-long public servant in New Mexico (although he lost this first bid for public office.)[46]

Appointment to public office in New Mexico made the incumbent fair game for all political enemies. The marshalcy was no exception. Soon after Charles P. Clever became federal lawman, a disgruntled Socorran informed the secretary of interior that Clever was a poor choice for this important office. As a deputy marshal under Charles Blumner, Clever had "speculated in jurors' certificates"—that is, purchased them from jurors at a discount—and had consequently been dismissed from his post. Furthermore, Clever was a political liability, a "German freesoiler" who kept a Mexican mistress openly. In 1859, when the sheriff of Santa Fe attempted to attach mercantile goods belonging to Marshal Clever and others, the lawman stood his ground in court. The United States district attorney who defended Clever concluded, correctly, that the Prussian immigrant exerted "great influence" in the community.[47]

The federal lawmen were fortunate that New Mexico was not directly involved in the violent controversy over the Fugitive Slave Act of 1850. The marshals in the East encountered much hostility as they attempted to return runaways to their southern masters. Some sentiment existed in the Southwest in favor of slavery, and peonage and Indian slavery did flourish. In 1859, the territorial legislature adopted a slave code, but this accommodation with Negro slavery ended with the outbreak of the Civil War. The speaker of the house in the territorial legislature, Levi J. Keithley, raised strong objections to this code, but his colleagues ejected him. Such strong antislavery feelings impressed President Abraham Lincoln, who later regarded Keithley as a potential candidate for the marshalcy.[48]

With so many hindrances in their paths, it is remarkable that the marshals supported the federal judiciary so successfully in New Mexico Territory. The 1850s were critical years for the courts, since the Hispano citizenry began to reconcile themselves to the United States judicial process during those years. The marshals played an important part in that assimilative process. Among the servants of the courts, they and their deputies were most visible to the Hispanos and the sedentary Indians. The biannual trek of the lawmen from Taos to Mesilla and the service of hundreds of pieces of process did much to indoctrinate the people in the American judicial process. The fact that the marshals were the paymasters of the juries reinforced the growing allegiance of the natives. The marshals did much to accommodate the courts to native customs. When the devout and hardworking farmers of New Mexico refused to answer summonses to court during holy days or critical planting and harvesting season, the marshals and the judges merely adjusted the calendar of the tribunals.

By 1861 the broad lines of federal law enforcement existed in New Mexico, although the marshals still confronted serious problems. They routinely served the process of the federal courts and maintained deputies in strategic communities, though the office continued to suffer maladies common to all frontier marshalcies. The marshals served part-time, and the deputies were normally concurrent sheriffs. The county officers subordinated the interests of federal justice to local matters and often bowed to the pressures of their constituents. When the people objected to a decision of the federal court, the marshals could write off the prospects of summoning a *posse comitatus*. Congress contributed to the problems of the federal lawmen by haphazardly adding newly acquired land to the territory. The marshals fretted helplessly about the administration of justice in the Gadsden Purchase. With such insuperable problems before them, the harried lawmen resorted to the only forces available—the governors and the army. These institutions, with the marshals, formed a law enforcement triad that endured during the entire territorial period.

3

The Wartime Marshalcy

In spite of the remoteness of New Mexico from most Civil War action, the marshals were forced to subordinate routine affairs to the demands of war. They were required to confiscate rebel property and to suppress treason. The aggravation of martial law, and the arrogance of military governors, further complicated their lives.

Civil War violence erupted in New Mexico in July 1861, when Confederate forces occupied Mesilla and prepared to send columns into the upper Rio Grande Valley and into southern "Arizona." After secessionist conventions in Mesilla and Tucson appealed to the Confederacy for recognition, Colonel John R. Baylor created the Confederate Territory of Arizona from the lower half of New Mexico. Baylor made himself governor and appointed subordinates to lesser posts, including George Frazier as marshal.[1]

In February 1862, Brigadier General Henry Hopkins Sibley, commander of the Confederate "Army of New Mexico," began to march north toward Santa Fe. Sibley's troops pushed back the Union forces from the important ford across the Rio Grande at Valverde, occupied Socorro and Albuquerque, and entered Santa Fe on March 10. Governor Henry Connelly evacuated the capital and set up temporary headquarters at Las Vegas. Meanwhile, a small Confederate force under Captain Sherod Hunter occupied Tucson (where there was no resistance) and reconnoitered as far west as Yuma, on the Colorado River.

In spite of these early successes, the Confederate occupation of the Southwest was short-lived. The Sibley and Hunter columns had overextended their supply lines and alarmed the loyal union populations of Colorado and California. Colonel John P. Slough led the First Colorado Regiment southward where, in cooperation with the Union Forces of Colonel Edward R. S. Canby, he stopped the rebel advance at Glorieta Pass, east of Santa Fe. Likewise, Captain Hunter's small party in Arizona could not withstand the advance of General James H. Carleton's California Column which appeared in southern Arizona in the spring. In June 1862, Carleton occupied Tucson, where he established a "Territory of Arizona" under a military governor. In September, as the commander of Union forces of the Far Southwest, he entered Santa Fe.

Since many officials of the territories had shifted their loyalties to the South, President Lincoln and Attorney General Edward Bates took pains to place loyal Republicans in the marshalcies of New Mexico (and soon after, in Arizona). Marshal Charles P. Clever, who had many separatist friends, was removed from office in 1862. However, when threatened with disbarment, he discreetly swore loyalty to the Union.[2]

Persuading a dependable citizen to accept the marshalcy was not easy. The search had begun in the spring of 1861, when the attorney general offered the post to a prominent Las Vegas merchant, Levi J. Keithley. Keithley had acquired a reputation of loyalty when he fought the territorial slave code. But he could enumerate many reasons for refusing the marshalcy: the cost of living in Santa Fe was outrageous; the small amount of business in the federal courts earned few fees; if he took the position, he would not be able to support a family. As a correspondent to the *New York Times* observed, the New Mexico marshalcy "is a position of much labor without sufficient emoluments to keep soul and body together."[3]

On September 13, 1861, the president appointed Albert W. Archibald, a young Nova Scotian gold seeker, to the office. Archibald arrived in New Mexico in 1858 or 1859, and worked for the great land baron, Lucien B. Maxwell. Maxwell may have recommended Archibald—who was only twenty-one years old—for the post of marshal. By the time his appointment was confirmed, however, he had decided to move to Trinidad, Colorado. Judge Kirby Benedict, who was desperately searching for a marshal, persuaded Charles P. Clever to remain in office until a new selection could be made.[4]

The president, meanwhile, began looking outside the territory for a prospect. At the recommendation of Senator James H. Lane of Kansas, Lincoln appointed Abraham Cutler of Kansas to succeed Charles P. Clever. Born in New York, and Free State partisan in the Kansas Border Wars, Cutler earned a reputation as a strong antislavery advocate. A Leavenworth editor observed, as Cutler prepared to leave for New Mexico in May 1862, that "He will probably get a rush of business when he gets there." Chief Justice Benedict noted with relief that Cutler took the oath of office on August 16, 1862. The judge added that the new marshal "appears very well indeed" and hoped that "he will make a good marshall [*sic*] which the conditions here will greatly need."[5]

Abraham Cutler had hardly occupied his new office when Congress separated Arizona from his district. On March 10, 1863, President Abraham Lincoln appointed Milton B. Duffield to the Arizona marshalcy. Duffield, a fanatical unionist, was born in present-day West Virginia about 1810. Subsequently, he became associated with Senator Samuel Pomeroy of Kansas in President Lincoln's scheme to colonize former slaves in Central America; when the plan did not materialize, Pomeroy recommended Duffield for the Arizona marshalcy. Charles Poston, a pioneer of Arizona, declared that the appointment of Duffield had been for the benefit of the "African element" of the territory. Duffield was strong enough to practice his beliefs; he kept an octoroon wife openly in Tucson (in addition to an Anglo wife elsewhere).[6]

The new marshals had very little time to establish themselves before Congress passed two acts to provide for the seizure of rebel property—the First and Second Confiscation Acts, on August 6, 1861, and July 17, 1862, respectively. The first provided only for the seizure of property devoted to "hostile use," but the latter was much broader. Congress intended to punish the rebels, and the confiscation of property was the penalty for treason to the Union. Attorney General Bates, the chief legal advisor to President Lincoln, expressed many doubts about such a policy and delayed the application of the acts. As a loyal unionist from the border state of Missouri, he was torn between duty and discretion. At first, he refrained from interference in the confiscation and permitted the federal courts to carry out the seizures. When reports reached him about excesses in the seizures and of military interference with the marshals, the attorney general determined to take a closer look. On

November 13, 1862, President Lincoln directed Bates to assume full responsibility for the application of the Confiscation Acts.[7]

The procedures for the confiscation of the property of Confederates and their sympathizers varied. The goods of Confederate officers were seized "without qualification," but persons who merely supported the rebellion were given sixty days to return allegiance to the Union. All confiscation proceedings began in the federal courts (or in the territorial courts). All court actions followed the procedure in admiralty or revenue cases.

> In the beginning suit, a libel of information, analogous to that directed against smuggled goods, would be filed by the district attorney. A monition or public advertisement would then be issued by the marshal, summoning the owner to appear in court and establish his loyalty. If the owner appeared to answer the libel, a hearing of both sides would usually follow, though there were cases where the owner was not permitted any hearing. Where the owner did not appear, an *exparte* hearing was conducted. In the case of condemnation, the marshal would be directed to sell the property at public auction, turning the proceeds, after payment of costs, into the public treasury.

On January 8, 1863, Attorney General Bates issued belated "Instructions in the Confiscation of Property" to the district attorneys and marshals. Bates cautioned the lawmen to seize property only upon the written directions of the attorneys, to avoid hasty action, and to keep careful records of their seizures.[8]

The loyal New Mexicans were especially anxious to enforce the Confiscation Act, since the eastern press had accused the territory of disloyalty in 1861. By coincidence, in September 1862, Governor Henry W. Connelly had fallen ill, and Secretary William F. M. Arny, a fervent unionist, had become acting governor. Arny was acquainted with Marshal Abraham Cutler, both men having been active Free-Soilers in Kansas. In late September, the acting governor directed Cutler and United States District Attorney Theodore D. Wheaton to begin legal action against the rebels. Although the combination of the two former Free-Soilers, Arny and Cutler, seemed fortuitous for the Union cause in New Mexico, the two men soon fell into opposing political camps.[9]

Although Congress preferred that the civil authorities conduct the confiscations, the army conducted some seizures in New Mexico in the first months of the war. In Arizona County, where the marshal's authority hardly existed, General James H. Carleton began the confiscations in June 1862. In Tucson he occupied the property of Palatine Robinson, the former receiver of property for the Confederacy. Southeast of Tucson, at Patagonia, the general seized the mine of Sylvester Mowry (a graduate of West Point), who had allegedly aided the rebels.[10]

In the lower Rio Grande Valley, many persons assisted the rebels. Governor Arny urged Marshal Cutler and Attorney Wheaton to prosecute these sympathizers with firmness. Many native families—the Armijos of Albuquerque and the Barelas of Dona Ana—were victims of the Confiscation Act. Former territorial officials, such as Spruce Baird and Samuel G. Bean, once a deputy marshal, also fell prey to the federal lawmen.[11]

As Cutler carried out these confiscations, he became aware of unlibeled rebel property in nearby El Paso, Texas. The courts had "ceased to function" in El Paso County, and a Union occupation force constituted the sole authority. With the support of Judge Joab Houghton of the Third Judicial District (which in a reshuffle in 1860, became the southernmost district), the marshal entered El Paso. Cutler declared that his jurisdiction in the Customs District of Paso del Norte—which comprised New Mexico and El Paso County, Texas—provided him with this power. Furthermore the procedure for seizures under the Confiscation Act practically duplicated those of the admiralty (customs) laws.[12]

Whatever the legality of the seizures in Texas, Marshal Cutler began proceedings in 1864. He occupied Fort Bliss, at that time the property of merchant James Magoffin, who had headed the Confederate Commission in El Paso. An unfortunate emigrant, Jesse Slade Franklin, lost his wagon train to the possessive lawman. On December 8, 1865, a sarcastic dispatch from Mesilla to the *Santa Fe New Mexican* reported that "Indians" (obviously the marshal) had libeled cattle in Texas. The flour mill and ranch of Simeon Hart, an active rebel agent, fell to the marshal. The *New Mexican*, which opposed the lawman's activities in Texas, estimated that Cutler had seized about $500,000 worth of property in Texas.[13]

Many knowledgeable people objected strongly to the marshal's confiscations outside his district. In October 1864, Judge John S. Watts of New Mexico informed General Carleton that Cutler's seizures in Texas "were illegal and void." Carleton agreed. He replied that when Cutler began the confiscations in El Paso, he (Carleton) had asked the attorney general to persuade Congress to create a temporary judicial district for West Texas. Such a district would require a new marshal. Many years later, W. W. Mills, the United States Collector of Customs at El Paso during the Civil War, admitted that he supported the subordination of his district to Marshal Cutler and the New Mexico courts. But he "did not then even dream of the confiscation of anyone's real estate." Mills thought the New Mexican courts would "enable me to condemn and sell goods smuggled into El Paso County." Not until 1866 was this nettlesome problem resolved, when the Supreme Court ruled that the New Mexican court, and thus Marshal Cutler, had no authority to seize property in El Paso County, Texas.[14]

Marshal Abraham Cutler's confiscations in Texas and New Mexico exposed him to charges of peculation. Such abuses were possible. The First Confiscation Act (it was not superceded by the Second) provided that a share of the spoils of the confiscations go to the informant. Cutler allegedly began the seizures in New Mexico by fabricating a letter from an "informant." The marshal could charge exorbitant fees to libel property and purchase condemned property under fictitious names. Some victims of Cutler's confiscations confronted him and Judge Joab Houghton in court at Mesilla, in December 1865, and accused them of being "unmitigated scoundrels."[15]

The federal lawman acknowledged considerable profits from his confiscations, when he filed an account with the Third District Court in Mesilla. In the case of Jesse Slade Franklin, Cutler charged:

For the hire of herders, houst [sic] rent, etc.	$325.00
For charges and responsibility of property, 40 days at $10 per day	400.00
For serving monition on same	10.00
For mileage, for going and returning from the Cottonwoods [the location of the seizure], 40 miles at $.50 per mile	20.00
For publication in Santa Fe Gazette	30.00
Total	$785.00

The lawman's expenses hardly justified the charges—the herd consisted of "eight yoke of oxen and five mules."[16]

In addition, the marshal purchased several pieces of libeled property, an indiscretion of considerable magnitude. In July 1864, he reportedly purchased an interest in Sylvester Mowry's confiscated mine in southern Arizona. He also bought the libeled goods of former Deputy Marshal Samuel Bean. In El Paso the greedy marshal paid $30 for an estate of 320 acres, and blandly signed the deed Carrie F. Cutler, the name of his wife.[17]

Among the most outspoken enemies of the federal officer was Sylvester Mowry. Mowry filed a suit in San Francisco, California, against Cutler, his deputy, Frederick Beckner (Burckner), and General James Carleton, for damages totaling $1,129,000. To publicize this suit, Mowry planted highly exaggerated letters in eastern newspapers. Cutler responded with a staged demonstration in Albuquerque, Mowry's case eventually died on a demurrer.[18]

But the marshal did not escape so easily. When he left office in early 1866, an Albuquerque grand jury charged him with embezzlement. The judge directed Cutler to make a return of collections from the sale of all libeled property. The former lawman presented a vague and unitemized report in which he claimed that the government owed him $571.29. The astonished judge noted that Cutler's report admitted collections worth $52,000 in the Third Judicial District alone.[19]

The court was chagrined. The judge recalled that a previous court had allowed Cutler $30,000 in expenses. The bench ordered him to post a $10,000 bond and to be held accountable to the new marshal, John Pratt, until he, Cutler, presented an accurate and itemized account of his collections. In May 1867, the former marshal produced a belated but detailed statement and pleaded not guilty. The following October, a sympathetic jury found Cutler not guilty of embezzlement. A private citizen promptly presented a claim against Abraham Cutler for damages and levied an attachment for $4700 against his property. But the former lawman had departed the territory, and the outcome of the claim is unknown.[20]

By late 1865, the United States government had tired of the costs of prosecuting the confiscation cases. At the October sessions of court in New Mexico, the government quietly dropped many of the cases. Sylvester Mowry repossessed his mine, only to die shortly thereafter. William S. Oury of Tucson, among many others, recovered his property under the presidential amnesty of July 1868. Some cases were appealed to the United States Supreme Court, which dismissed them in 1869.[21]

Marshal Abraham Cutler did not spend all of his term enriching himself. He spent a goodly amount of time dealing with the complexities of martial law. In 1861, when Colonel Edward R. S. Canby learned that southern spies were subverting his already shaky territorial volunteers, he suspended the writ of habeas corpus. Canby cautioned his subordinates against irritating civilian officers and urged the army to "unite with and assist the civil authorities in maintaining order." In September 1862, General James H. Carleton abandoned this discreet policy and established martial law. The army's provost marshals (the military counterparts to the civilian marshals) reduced the federal lawman's jurisdiction considerably. A. F. Banta, a newspaperman in Albuquerque in 1863, recalled that a provost marshal and two companies of infantry commanded the town. "The little law left over after the military got through," reflected Banta, was represented by three lawyers, an alcalde's court, and John Hill, the deputy United States marshal. "But suffice it to say," concluded the old-timer facetiously, "[Hill] had no writs of habeas corpus to serve as such trivial writs were attended to or ignored by the provost marshal."[22]

In 1864, New Mexicans hostile toward martial law formed a political faction that championed the rights of the marshal. Judge Joseph Knapp, who resented the travel restrictions imposed under martial law by Carleton, accused the general of preventing Marshal Cutler's deputies from serving the process of Knapp's court. A federal grand jury in Dona Ana County leveled similar charges. In the last months of the Civil War, the influential Judge Kirby Benedict joined the Knapp forces. As part owner of the *Santa Fe New Mexican*, Benedict was able to gain sympathy for the marshal and the courts.[23]

Still, Marshal Cutler had to rely heavily on the military to maintain control in the southern part of the district. In 1861, rebels established their counterpart to the Union marshal in Mesilla and warned the United States judge to stay away. "The comings were easy enough," said a hostile Mesilla editor, "but the going away is beset with difficulties." On October 3, 1862, Cutler formally requested the support of troops to enter Dona Ana County. "I am informed," he told General Carleton, "That in the discharge of my duties in the Messilla [*sic*] Valley and elsewhere South of here I will require the assistance of United States troops."[24]

When Carleton's California Column arrived in Dona Ana County in August 1862, he learned that the troubled area had been without civil law for three months. The rebel judiciary held only one term of court. Carleton quickly proclaimed martial law, established a military court, and permitted the civilian court to try only minor cases. As a concession to the Hispano population, he permitted the appointment of an alcalde.[25]

The Union general realized that military rule in Dona Ana County disturbed the civilian government in Santa Fe, and he urged Acting Governor William F. M. Arny to appoint civil officers for the county as soon as possible. Arny complied by proclamation on March 28, 1863. For sheriff, he selected Frederick Beckner, whom Marshal Cutler promptly deputized. Arny discreetly praised Carleton for maintaining order in Dona Ana, since the area had been without "any organization" for many months. By letter, Arny also urged the new appointees "to try to get along harmoniously with the military authorities."[26]

A gloomier situation prevailed in Arizona. The marshals seldom, if ever, visited Tucson personally in the 1850s, and Abraham Cutler failed to improve upon their performance. In October 1862, the military authorities at Yuma asked Judge Kirby Benedict to transfer rebel Sylvester Mowry to Albuquerque for trial. Benedict refused, explaining that Marshal Cutler did not possess the resources to travel to Yuma for one prisoner. The army, Arizona's only authority, eventually released Mowry.[27]

Some hope appeared for the neglected inhabitants of the Gila Valley, in February 1863, when Congress awarded territorial status to the Arizonans. That November, Santa Feans feted the official train of Governor John N. Goodwin as it passed through New Mexico. The officials in Santa Fe were happy to have the burden of Arizona removed from their shoulders. The destination of Goodwin's party was a small army post in central Arizona, Fort Whipple, in the Chino Valley. General James Carleton urged the new territorial executive to locate his capital there, since several gold mines had been discovered in that area. Goodwin accepted this advice, since Tucson, the only likely spot elsewhere in the territory, was a haven for former secessionists.[28]

The task of establishing a judiciary for the vast and unpopulated territory was not easy. On April 9, 1864, Governor Goodwin began the process by establishing three judicial districts. Each district incorporated scattered clusters of settlements. The area south of the Gila River and east of the 114th meridian constituted the First Judicial District. Judge William T. Howell presided over this district, and maintained headquarters in Tucson. To Judge Joseph P. Allyn fell the Second Judicial District, which lay west of the 114th meridian. La Paz, on the Colorado River, became his residence. The Third Judicial District of Judge William F. Turner included the northeast portion of the territory and centered around Prescott (Fort Whipple).[29]

When Marshal Milton B. Duffield arrived in his new district early in 1864, the military still commanded the region. On November 25, 1863, General Carleton had ordered Major Edward B. Willis at Fort Whipple to suspend martial law as soon as Governor Goodwin established a civil government. Carleton, however, assumed that the military would still be required to support the marshal and other officials. "While your troops are not, as a matter of course, to be used as a constabulary," said the general, "still, in that new and distant country where society has got to be regulated out of the most discordant materials, you will not cavil or split hairs." Carleton charged Willis to "always be ready with force—when called upon by the Governor or by the Marshal of the Territory."[30]

The primitive resources of the new Arizona marshalcy imposed many hardships upon Duffield. He had to set up an office in his private residence and order official stationery from San Francisco. Since the newly created territory had no jails, Duffield used military guardhouses and on at least one occasion, he chained a prisoner to the wall of a house. He conducted his first official duty, the supervision of the census, during an Indian uprising. And in Prescott someone stole his horse. The outraged lawman posted a small reward and then demanded $300 in damages from the federal government.[31]

Marshal Duffield considered the presence of unreconstructed rebels in southern Arizona to be his most important problem. He chose Tucson for his headquarters in order to watch them. In the first months of his term, he sternly enforced the Confiscation Acts. However, Governor Goodwin and District Attorney Almon Gage refused to prosecute the rebels. The Goodwin Administration desired to "mollify" the former Confederates and to unify the territory. The government suspended all confiscation proceedings when District Attorney Gage lost papers pertinent to them while crossing a river.[32]

The angry marshal continued to observe the movements of the ex-rebels and provoked a former Confederate officer, one Kennedy, to confront him on the streets of Tucson:

> He [Kennedy] called me out a few days ago with all the chivalric airs imaginable to chastise me for inqui[r]ing into his character, when I was compelled to knock him down and administered some sound kicks, about his head, when I allowed him to get up, he then ran like a dog leaving his chivalry behind, and for the purpose of extracting any remainder that might be left, I sent a Derringer Pill after him making an issue through his right ham.

Duffield wrote Secretary of State William Seward, "If I am molested again I will go to work in earnest and place the balls a little higher up."[33]

Duffield's hatred of rebels was extreme. Soon after the feud with Colonel Kennedy, the marshal arrested another rebel officer, Cristopher C. Dodson, on a murder warrant issued by Judge Joab Houghton of New Mexico. Dodson's friends obtained a writ of habeas corpus for his release, but the lawman stubbornly refused to unchain his prisoner. According to Duffield, the right of habeas corpus had not been restored to the territory. When Duffield belatedly released Dodson, it was only because he had received no further instructions from New Mexico.[34]

Marshal Duffield did not spend all his time harassing rebels. He also appointed deputy marshals to help him. In spite of extremely low incomes, Gilbert W. Hopkins, an engineer for the Maricopa Mining Company, and Amasa G. Dunn, a carpenter from Prescott, became deputy marshals for the First and Third Judicial Districts, respectively. Duffield's census deputy, Charles A. Phillips, probably continued as a permanent subordinate in the Second Judicial District. When, in 1868, Dunn accepted reappointment, the Prescott *Arizona Miner* expressed surprise since the deputy marshalship did not "amount to much."[35]

The poor income of the marshalcy did not go unnoticed. Most lawmen maintained full-time businesses and assumed that the marshalcy was a part-time job. When Marshal Abraham Cutler entered a sutler's business in Albuquerque, the *New Mexican* commented, "We are glad Mr. Cutler has some other business, besides that of Marshal. That scarcely pays." In June 1867, the *Arizona Miner* observed that the small salary and fees were inadequate. After Milton Duffield resigned because of the poor income, the *Arizona Miner* commented sympathetically: "Duffield, with all his self denial, could not have survived, but for the little operation in his mines." The editor recommended a salary of $2,500 per year and urged the territorial delegate to take up the problem in Washington. Governor Richard McCormick also went on record for higher salaries for the marshals, although many years elapsed before Congress rectified this problem.[36]

Although many territorial officers recommended a higher salary for Marshal Duffield, this did not mean they liked him. During his term of office, Duffield alienated nearly every territorial politician. His neurotic sense of persecution at the hands of "unreformed" rebels and their allies in the territorial capital, caused him to keep up a constant flow of letters of protest to Washington. Although written in the year after his resignation, this letter to the New York *Tribune* is by no means out of character:

> On the 24th of June [1867] a friend writes me from Tucson that seventeen men were killed [by Indians] in my county, (Pima), and herds driven off . . . . The Indians have come down in the daytime and taken animals from the Government Corrals in sight of soldiers. Whiskey, cards, fandangos, and prostitutes have been occupying the military in Arizona since the first organization of the Territory.

A demoralized army was not the only enemy of the territory:

> Arizona seems a kind of "Rogues' Paradise" for a class of government contractors, and quiet, pleasure seeking officers; and to give the appearance of action, occasionally are read accounts of successes obtained by the troops . . . I do not hesitate, over my own signature, to declare them false.[37]

The officers of the territory did not take the ravings of Marshal Duffield passively. Territorial Delegate Charles Poston considered Duffield "unworthy," and in 1865 recommended to President Lincoln that he be removed and that former Confederate King S. Woolsey be appointed marshal. Duffield resigned that same year (effective April 1, 1866). When the *Arizona Miner* learned the "pleasing intelligence" that Duffield had left office, the editor commented, "Having long since put Duffield down as insane . . . we seldom have mentioned his name in these columns." When the journalist heard that the former lawman was making a third trip to Washington to settle his accounts, the commentator hoped that the fractious former marshal would "stay there."[38]

The authorities in Washington were well aware of weaknesses in the territorial marshalcies and devoted special attention to them during the war years. Whereas the presidents chose marshals from residents of New Mexico in the 1850s, Lincoln also appointed loyal outsiders to the posts in Santa Fe and Tucson. He set a precedent subsequent chief executives followed for many years. Lincoln encouraged the centralization of the loose federal court system, and in 1861, the attorney general assumed direction of the marshals and district attorneys. This decision presaged the growth of the marshalcies, but did not affect the southwestern officers for several years.

The decision of Congress to confiscate rebel property made the marshals of New Mexico and Arizona divisive forces in their districts. The absence of precise instructions and the opportunity for easy money opened the offices to corruption. The confiscations also distracted the marshals from the promotion of the jury system among the Hispanos and peaceful Indians. As late as 1870, the judges in New Mexico "were still struggling to introduce the jury system and American [legal] procedures into their courtrooms."[39]

In spite of these distractions, the Civil War contributed indirectly to the efficiency of federal law enforcement. By creating Arizona Territory, Congress relieved the marshalcy in Santa Fe of a responsibility that it had seldom fulfilled during the 1850s. Future marshals could confine their energies to a compact district in the Rio Grande Valley. While the assignment of a marshal to Tucson improved federal justice measurably in Arizona, the new lawmen lacked the advantages of their colleagues in New Mexico. Unlike the larger and more stable society in New Mexico, Arizona's population was scattered and fragmented, consisting of a small Hispanic group, warlike Indians, and politically divided Unionists and Confederates. The Arizona marshals had to exercise tact and diplomacy to enforce the federal laws, qualities that the first lawman, Milton B. Duffield, lacked. In 1866, the incoming marshals possessed many advantages over their predecessors, but the hatreds of the Civil War died slowly. The future of federal law enforcement would depend upon the tact and diplomacy of the presidents' appointees.

4

Marshal John Pratt, 1866–76

In 1866, New Mexico Territory was on the verge of economic expansion. Hundreds of settlers moved to the Southwest, most of them anxious to find a peaceful place where they could forget wartime hatreds. Since legal problems always accompanied migration, the federal courts anticipated many new responsibilities. The new United States Marshal, John Pratt, expected an increase in the service of process. The enlargement of the reservation Indian population resulted in closer relations between Indians and United States courts. Several problems were left over from the Civil War: white enslavement of Indians persisted; debt peonage was prevalent; a residue of confiscation cases also remained. These conflicts descended upon the marshalcy in the late 1860s and threatened to involve the office in heated political factionalism.

Postwar New Mexico had a very different social complexion from that of the 1850s, when the first federal lawmen arrived in the Southwest. Hostile Indians no longer confined settlement to the Rio Grande Valley. The vigorous campaign of General James H. Carleton in 1863 reduced the great Navajo and Apache warriors, so that Indian warfare became the exception rather than the rule in New Mexico. The government began to impose the laws of the United States upon the tribes. This procedure was slow and tedious, and the extent of the authority of the federal courts upon the reservations remained very limited. Indian agents guarded their wards jealously and restricted the marshals to preventing white encroachment on the reservations.[1]

The reduction of the Indians opened new land to the whites and increased the responsibility of the marshals. In the northeast,

47

farmers and miners filtered into the upper Cimarron River Valley. In 1869, the legislature created Colfax County to accommodate these new arrivals and Cimarron became the seat of local government. In the southeast, the grasslands along the Pecos River invited Texas cattle barons, such as John Chisum. Other ranchers included men like Lawrence G. Murphy, a veteran of the Union Army. The village of Lincoln (formerly Placitas) became the county seat for Lincoln County, created in 1869. In the southwestern corner of New Mexico interest grew in mining on the Gila River around Pinos Altos. In 1868, Dona Ana County was divided, the western half becoming Grant County. Silver City eventually became the county seat and a center for mining and cattle.[2]

Among the migrants to New Mexico in the postwar years, young ambitious lawyers were most conspicuous. Two members of the bar stood out—Stephen B. Elkins, a Union veteran, and Thomas B. Catron, a former Confederate. They were friends despite their war records, having been classmates at the University of Missouri. In New Mexico they formed a law partnership, supported the new Republican Party, and proceeded to build a political and economic machine, called the Santa Fe Ring. The nature of this combine is uncertain. Some people insist that it did not exist. Probably, the Ring possessed "no fixed membership or formal organization," but consisted of "a group of persons, [mostly Republicans], with common political and economic interests."[3]

With the support of the growing Republican party (an outgrowth of the Unionist party of Judge Kirby Benedict), Elkins and Catron controlled the political patronage and economic resources of the territory. They invested in mining and cattle, and became deeply involved in the Spanish land-grant problem. In 1848, the United States had guaranteed these grants, but many boundaries were unclear. Lawyers, including Elkins and Catron, earned sizeable fees from litigations over the grants. They often won their cases because fellow members of the Santa Fe Ring occupied important judicial offices. By 1867, Stephen Elkins had been made United States district attorney. Two years after that Thomas Catron became attorney general of the territory.[4]

Any ambitious new arrival in the territory had to come to terms with the Republican machine of Elkins and Catron, and Marshal John Pratt was no exception. Pratt's background is obscure. He was born in Massachusetts and often returned to Boston on leaves of absence. Like his predecessor, Abraham Cutler, Pratt had been a resident of Kansas and had served as a company adjutant in the Second Kansas Cavalry in 1862. He accepted the marshalcy on March 3, 1866. Pratt retained many Kansas commercial and speculative connections after he settled in New Mexico. He was a staunch Republican and a devout Episcopalian.[5]

The new officer faced many problems, among them a loss of public faith in the responsiveness of the marshal's office. Most of Marshal Pratt's federal court business lay in the southern districts rather than in Santa Fe, and like his predecessor he fixed his headquarters at Albuquerque. The inhabitants of the Third Judicial District were agitated by the failure of the federal courts and territorial officials to provide them with timely justice, and as late as 1863, they attempted to form the territory of "Montezuma." Perhaps Marshal Pratt could overcome this disaffection with speedy responses from Albuquerque.[6]

The marshal also selected energetic deputies in another attempt to restore the faith of the people of his district. He retained John Hill, a Cutler appointee, in Albuquerque and chose the Hispano sheriff, Jose D. Sena, as deputy for Santa Fe. Only thirty-two years of age, Sena possessed many attributes that fitted the needs of the office: a command of Spanish and English; an education in an eastern school; and service in the Union army. In cases where an additional deputy was needed, the marshal could authorize temporary appointments. In July 1867, Pratt dispatched a blank deputation to District Attorney Stephen B. Elkins in Santa Fe with the request that he deputize a person to serve only "necessary preliminary process." Pratt added that he would not make a permanent appointment "until I can see you [Elkins]" about the appointee.[7]

Among his first duties, Marshal Pratt assisted District Attorney Elkins with the prosecution of Abraham Cutler. After taking Cutler into custody, Pratt released him on bond with the stipulation that Cutler remain in the territory. Much to the surprise of the marshal, Cutler abruptly departed for the East (possibly to settle his accounts personally in Washington). This incident appeared suspicious to the editor of the *New Mexican* who demanded an explanation for Pratt's "excessive simplicity." Cutler returned voluntarily for trial and Pratt was exonerated.[8]

In July 1867, Pratt informed Attorney Elkins that many official documents, including those related to the Cutler case, were missing from the office of the court clerk in Albuquerque. An investigation revealed that thieves had stolen the documents and were holding them for ransom. As the trial date approached, Clerk Benjamin Stevens informed the anxious marshal that he had recovered the Cutler papers. The clerk added that the thieves (who were former soldiers) had forced him "to come down with the *cash.*"[9]

While the marshal massed the evidence, District Attorney Elkins attempted to make a case against Abraham Cutler. It was not easy since Cutler was strengthening his position. In July 1867, the former marshal settled his accounts in Washington. This did not, however, clear up the embezzlement charge. The government said that the former marshal had received fees from the proceeds of illegal confiscations in Texas and was guilty of embezzlement. Elkins advised the solicitor of the Treasury that the jury would almost certainly acquit Cutler, since the United States court at Albuquerque had, in the first place, erroneously awarded this money to Cutler. The court had erred, not the former lawman. The lawyer predicted correctly. At the fall term of court in Albuquerque, the jury exonerated Cutler. This decision did not erase private suits, which continued to follow Cutler.[10]

The most pressing consequence of the confiscations remained— the proper disposal of libeled property. In 1866, the outraged Texas victims of Marshal Cutler's seizures argued before the territorial Supreme Court in Santa Fe that the federal courts of New Mexico did not possess the authority to confiscate in El Paso. The tribunal agreed. When the United States Supreme Court upheld this ruling, the libelees demanded the return of their property. Matters were further complicated when the government was constrained to expel (and also compensate) persons who had purchased the libeled property at auction and who were appealing for a refund of money. Marshal Pratt was no doubt happy that the decision in this matter was outside his purview.[11]

As the government laid the confiscation cases to rest, Congress resolved to ensure the victims of slavery their civil rights. The Plan of Reconstruction included the inhabitants of the territories. Accordingly, the national legislators passed several acts for the benefit of the territories: Negro slavery was abolished (1862); bigamy was forbidden (1862); no denial of the elective franchise on account of race, color, or previous condition of servitude was permitted (1866); Indian slavery and peonage were abolished (1867); and revenue laws were rigorously enforced in order to prevent the illegal manufacture of alcoholic beverages (1867). These acts provided the marshal with a good deal of work.[12]

Several southwestern territories, including New Mexico, continued to practice chattel slavery in violation of the act of 1862. The New Mexican grandees considered this act to apply to Negroes, not Indians, and to have absolutely no effect upon peonage (personal bondage as a consequence of indebtedness). On March 2, 1867, President Andrew Johnson signed a bill "To Abolish and Forever Prohibit the System of Peonage in the Territory of New Mexico and Other Parts of the United States." By this law (and the Civil Rights Act of the previous year), the Republicans hoped to end these injurious practices. Violators were subject to a fine and imprisonment.[13]

Although Congress authorized the army to support John Pratt, the burden of the new law fell largely upon the marshal. Pratt and a force of extra deputies massed evidence against practitioners of peonage and slavery. On September 26, 1868, he reported to District Attorney Stephen B. Elkins that his subordinates had delivered 150 violators of peonage to Special Commissioner William Griffith, who administered the new laws in New Mexico. After an examination, Griffith bound them over for trial in Taos since the majority of the violations had occurred in that area. Pratt added that his office had also freed about 500 Indian slaves and that they outnumbered the manumitted peons. The marshal learned about many cases in remote parts of his district, but lacked funds to investigate.[14]

Several obstacles stifled the efforts of the marshal. The impatient Radical Republicans concluded that Pratt moved too slowly. By joint resolution in July 1868, the lawmakers directed the army to liberate slaves among the Indians, especially the Navajos.[15] Pratt hesitated with his work and asked Elkins if, in view of the participation of the army, he should "make any change in the manner of performing my duty." The successes of John Pratt among the peons and slaves convinced the district attorney that the army should not interfere. He advised General George Getty, the commander of the New Mexico Military District, that Pratt's office had completed most of the task. "It is possible," Elkins advised the general, that the success of the marshal "might preclude the military [from] taking any measures" under the congressional resolution.[16]

In addition to the threat of military interference, Congress balked when the expense of releasing the slaves and peons exceeded expectations. When the Treasury refused to honor the requisitions of Commissioner Griffith, he simply discontinued the manumissions. The attorney general also refused Marshal Pratt's requests for funds to transport freed Indians to their homes. These stumbling blocks prolonged peonage and slavery, although Marshal Pratt's deputies contributed significantly to the demise of these forms of bondage.[17]

Congress also desired to ensure the new citizens their right to exercise the franchise and authorized the marshals to appoint special deputies to protect these rights at the polls. Marshal Pratt assigned numerous deputies to the voting places during the delegate election in September 1867. The defeated candidate, J. Francisco Chavez, promptly charged the federal lawman with improper interference with the voters. Ironically, the victorious candidate was former Marshal Charles P. Clever. The *Santa Fe New Mexican* concurred with Chavez and accused Pratt of aligning with Clever and the "European merchants" (the German Jewish group who immigrated to New Mexico in the 1850s).[18]

This scandal provoked the assembly to conduct a full-scale inquiry. R. M. Stephens, a former deputy marshal, testified that Pratt had refused to deputize any Chavez followers and that his subordinates had intimidated Chavez voters at the Santa Fe polls. William Breeden, assessor of internal revenue, said that some deputies ordered Chavez voters from the polls.[19]

Many irregularities had occurred in the southern districts, but one deputy marshal from Albuquerque reported that, contrary to reports, Chavez partisans had prevented Clever supporters from voting in that town. This deputy had also seen a judge throw out some ballots for Clever. Brigadier General of Militia Jesus M. Baca y Salazar testified that he saw many noncitizens vote. (These persons were residents, but they had refused citizenship under the terms of the Treaty of Guadalupe Hidalgo, in 1848). Salazar implied that these noncitizens had voted for Clever. Deputy Court Clerk William T. Jones in Dona Ana swore that noncitizens had voted for Chavez. The awarding of the contested delegate's chair to

J. Francisco Chavez indirectly comdemned the marshal for improper interference.[20]

In addition to guarding the polls, Congress directed the marshals to enforce the revenue laws. The purpose of these laws was to stamp out illegal liquor distillers, who refused to purchase a liquor license from the government. The national legislators were alarmed most by the moonshiners in the former slave states, but the frontier territories experienced similar violations. In New Mexico, the manufacture and sale of illegal spirits, especially to the warlike Indians, reached alarming proportions in the 1860s and 1870s. One newspaper editor "reasoned" that a drunken Indian was a murdering Indian and characterized the illicit traffic in alcoholic beverages as "a terrible incentive to savage rapine and murder." He urged the authorities to prosecute violators "severely."[21]

Marshal Pratt's office attempted to enforce the revenue laws, but the task soon exceeded his resources. Cases fell into two categories: the routine service of process upon illicit distillers in established communities; and the arrest of illegal manufacturers and peddlers in the remote plains of eastern New Mexico.

The marshalcy devoted considerable time and effort to serving warrants and subpoenas in local cases. The promise of a $300 reward for information about moonshiners greatly helped the marshal. In August 1867, the Santa Fe court heard more than 125 cases. The *New Mexican* congratulated U.S. District Attorney Stephen B. Elkins for winning the first revenue convictions in the territory and praised "the present efficient and energetic marshal, Captain John S. Pratt, and his deputies" for their work. Such devotion to duty, said the newspaper, made Pratt "an officer and a gentleman."[22]

The arrest of moonshiners in remote districts was more difficult. Pratt had to rely upon the army since he could not afford a force of deputies. Only the army possessed the resources to run down the illegal liquor traders in eastern New Mexico and western Texas. In March 1867, General William T. Sherman, commander of the Division of the Missouri, ordered his subordinates in New Mexico to cooperate with the civil authorities in the suppression of the trade. Sherman directed the commander at Fort Bascom, on the Canadian River in eastern New Mexico, to search the goods of all traders entering and leaving the plains. If any returning parties had "new horses," the commander was to presume the animals stolen and to confiscate them. The Indians stole Texas stock to pay for whiskey, guns, and ammunition.[23]

The federal lawman and his military assistants often arrested the traders, rather than the distillers, under another federal law—the Indian Intercourse Act of 1834. As the crusade against the traders mounted, the army made numerous arrests in the late 1860s and early 1870s. The *New Mexican* announced in July 1871, that a patrol from Fort Bascom had arrested several Hispanos and an Indian woman and placed them in the hands of the marshal. They were charged with violation of the Indian Intercourse Act.[24]

The bluecoats often complained that the civil authorities failed to fulfill their responsibilities against the unlawful merchants. After a patrol turned over several traders to Marshal Pratt, in April 1867, the judge refused to hold them. The evidence was insufficient, and the judge ordered the whiskey returned to the prisoners. This sort of failure in cooperative effort imposed a handicap that "the military would never completely overcome in its efforts to stop cattle smuggling" on the plains.[25]

It was the marshal's job to dispose of any stock seized by the army, although the procedure was protracted. First, the court had to rule that the livestock were "perishable property" and thus could not be protected indefinitely. The marshal then published a public notice of a hearing to inform interested parties that he planned to auction them in the near future:

> I hereby admonish and summon all persons claiming any interest in said property or knowing or having anything to say why the same [stock] should not be decreed to be forfeited to the United States and comdemned and sold to answer the prayer of said information, that they appear [at the hearing].

If the rightful owner failed to claim the livestock, the marshal sold the cattle to the highest bidder.[26]

As the marshal extended his activities onto the eastern plains, he also strengthened the office in the Third Judicial District. In 1860, the assembly changed the designation of this southern district to the "Third," and some years later, divided Dona Ana County (which coincided with the Third District) into Grant, Dona Ana, and Lincoln counties. The dangerous trip across the desert from

Albuquerque to Mesilla occasionally prevented judicial officers from holding regular sessions of court in the south, although the promptness of Marshal Pratt and the federal judges helped to prevent any renewal of secession movements in Dona Ana County.

In November 1871, the *New Mexican* noted with relief that Judge Daniel B. Johnson had arrived safely in Mesilla and was destined for Grant County, where only two terms of court had been held in four years. Aside from empannelment of a grand jury in Lincoln County in 1870, that southeastern region had not had court at all. Such judicial delinquency, according to the *New Mexican*, was just "cause for grief" in the south. "The interest of law and order as well as the business and financial interests of that region" demanded punctual authorities. Marshal Pratt encountered only routine problems, such as smuggling, in those southern counties.[27]

Pratt depended upon the usual judicial expediencies to staff his offices in these new counties. He made local officers concurrent deputy marshals. In this way, one lawman, at once a county and federal officer, served one session of the territorial court (also possessing concurrent powers to try federal cases). This stopgap measure cut the costs to the federal government in the short run, but maimed the marshalcy in the long run. The sheriffs often failed to uphold territorial laws, not to mention the laws of the United States. In December 1866, Acting Governor William F. M. Arny advised the Assembly that he had received several "well founded" complaints about negligent sheriffs. He exhorted the county officers to execute the laws faithfully, since "crime throughout the territory is on the increase." Such ineptitude among the sheriffs, who were also deputy marshals, must have disconcerted Marshal Pratt.[28]

As federal court business increased, the marshal was forced to provide housing for a larger number of prisoners. Neither the federal government nor the territory possessed a penitentiary in New Mexico. United States prisoners resided in the county jails or in military guardhouses. The legislature petitioned regularly for funds to complete the prison (begun in 1854), but Congress refused. The secretary of interior authorized temporary arrangements with neighboring state or territorial prisons. John Pratt contracted with the Missouri State Penitentiary at Jefferson City. Normally, he combined his official leave with the delivery of prisoners, usually after the fall and spring sessions of federal court.[29]

Such absences caused the deputy marshals to become more important in the marshalcy. Deputy James T. Newhall filled in for his superior in April 1873. Subordinates also opened sessions of court. Deputy William Rosenthal officiated with "efficiency and courtesy" at one session in the absence of the marshal. Sheriff Mariano Barela of Mesilla, a concurrent deputy marshal, represented Pratt at another session.[30]

Just as the affairs of the marshalcies of New Mexico and neighboring territories became more demanding after the Civil War, the load of the judiciary increased in the national capital. A mass of legal business accrued during the Reconstruction Era. Each department of government attempted to resolve the dilemma by appointing numerous attorneys, but merely proliferated the bureaucracy. In 1867, Congress complained about the unnecessary waste of expense of these men of the bar. Yet, the legislators feared the solution to this problem—a centralized "department of law." The powerful Committee on Retrenchment, which exalted savings above all other virtues, broke down the resistance in Congress. The committee recommended the centralization of federal legal business. On June 22, 1870, President Ulysses S. Grant signed the Department of Justice Act.[31]

The Department of Justice altered the procedures of federal justice immediately. The attorney general, who presided over the new creation, provided expert assistance to the president and all departments in Washington. He consolidated his authority over the district attorneys and marshals (he had begun to supervise them in 1861) by acquiring control of their financial accounts from the Department of the Interior. The new *Annual Reports* of the attorney general apprised Congress of the present state of federal justice and included recommendations for improving it.[32]

Congress instructed the head of the Department of Justice, George A. Williams, to impose strict monetary controls on the marshals. In 1873, Williams informed Congress that he had directed the marshals to economize, "but not altogether with satisfactory effect." He instructed his subordinates to submit estimates of expenses for the coming fiscal year, and he "pruned" the marshals' projections. The following year Williams supported a bill of the House Committee on Expenditures that would tighten the regulation of fees and costs allowed the marshals and other officers.[33]

The efforts of Marshal John Pratt to economize failed to satisfy Attorney General Williams. On November 30, 1874, the attorney general asked Pratt to explain the "goodly" increase of federal court expenses in New Mexico. The marshal replied that the fees of jurors and witnesses, over which he had no control, made up most of his accounts. He estimated his expenses for the fiscal year 1875 at $24,856. Although the attorney general's reply to this estimate is lost, the Department of Justice allowed Pratt's successor, in 1877, only $23,000. In 1877, the attorney general also demanded that the marshals file weekly financial returns.[34]

In addition to economization, the Department of Justice desired to improve the detection and pursuit of criminals. The government had no central detective agency, but permitted numerous special agents (Treasury or Secret Service) to serve various departments in Washington. Each agent investigated "special subjects" and enforced "particular laws," but Congress refused these detectives permission to enforce the "fundamental statutes" of the nation. Many Americans feared that a central detective agency would abuse its powers. When judges or marshals requested permission to employ a detective for some task, the Treasury refused them federal moneys. Congress made a timid beginning to erase this shortcoming in 1871, when it gave the attorney general $50,000 for the purposes of detection and prosecution of crimes against the United States. While this small sum had little immediate importance, "this appropriation . . . was to become the basis of the centralized investigative function of the Department of Justice." The attorney general continued to receive funds annually for investigative purposes. In 1873, the Department received funds to detect and punish violators of all the Indian laws. The attorney general also acquired money for the examination and prosecution of crimes within the Department of Justice, such as peculation or falsification of accounts. These various appropriations opened the way for the attorney general, through his marshals and other subordinates, to enter a relatively new field of work—the detection of violators of the federal laws.[35]

While the attorney general was trying to increase the efficiency of the marshals, Congress hindered his efforts. A proviso to the Army Appropriation Bill of June 16, 1874, provided that "only actual traveling expenses shall be allowed to any person holding employment under the United States." Attorney General George

A. Williams complained that the new law would "work a great hardship to the marshals." The marshals earned only $200 per annum, plus fees, including mileage. This proviso removed the larger mileage allowance.[36]

The marshals responded angrily. A somewhat alarmed Williams advised Congress that the "marshals are often obliged to travel hundreds of miles to serve process" and that the overworked officers must receive the mileage fee. Several of his best marshals, and deputy marshals, who received such small incomes and depended heavily upon the mileage allowance, threatened to resign unless Congress rescinded the act.[37]

Not only did the Department of Justice take a keener interest in the marshalcies, but the decisions of the bureaucrats in the department reached the lawmen more quickly than ever before. Communications improved significantly in the Southwest in the late 1860s. The military telegraph reached Santa Fe in 1868. It spanned the Rio Grande Valley to Las Cruces, thence westward to Silver City, and eventually to San Diego, California. A Western Union Telegraph Company line stretched from Santa Fe eastward to Las Vegas, Fort Union, Cimarron, and Trinidad, Colorado. These lines tied Marshal Pratt to Washington and, at the same time, placed him much nearer his deputies. Federal justice became much swifter in New Mexico.[38]

In spite of these innovations Marshal Pratt was more preoccupied with territorial party politics than with the Justice Department. The political parties feared the marshal and attempted to control him. Through his power to appoint deputies to guard election polls or to supervise the census, Marshal Pratt exerted great influence. The Republican editor of the *New Mexican*, who desired to increase the chances of statehood through an inflated census return in 1870, brazenly announced that "as a matter of course Marshal Pratt will select his [census] assistants from the ranks of the Republican Party." Even more, said the editor, "We desire and expect that all patronage of the marshal's office shall be given to Republicans." The federal lawman evidently satisfied his political friends: "We congratulate Marshal Pratt," said the *New Mexican* after the census and patronage appointments had been announced, "our marshal has . . . acquired a new title to public confidence."[39]

John Pratt's place in party politics appeared insecure in 1866, when he assumed office. As an appointee of the unfortunate Border Democrat, President Andrew Johnson, Pratt remained loyal to his patron. He married the daughter of the influential Hispano, Ambrosio Armijo, who leaned toward states rights and the Democratic party. Soon after his arrival, Pratt accompanied former Marshal Charles P. Clever and General James H. Carleton, both Democrats, on a prospecting trip to the ore-bearing region soon to become Grant County. With such political leanings, it is no wonder that the territorial legislature condemned him for interfering on the side of Clever in the 1867 delegate election.[40]

The high hopes of the Clever faction, however, were soon dashed. The canny marshal joined Thomas B. Catron and the Santa Fe Ring. The economic resources of this clique enabled the Ring to dictate the political direction of the territory. Pratt engaged in a remarkable range of enterprises—contracting wheat to the army, and investing in the Rio Grande and the Kansas Pacific railroads. When, in 1870, he was elected to the board of the newly created Maxwell Land Grant and Railroad Company, Pratt's place in the Santa Fe Ring was beyond doubt. This massive Spanish grant, which sprawled across northeastern New Mexico and southern Colorado, fell into the hands of the Ring—Thomas B. Catron, Stephen B. Elkins, Pratt, and others—for $1,350,000. From 1871 to 1876, Pratt also served on the board of directors of Stephen B. Elkins's First National Bank of Santa Fe.[41]

As a participant in the Santa Fe Ring, John Pratt courted accusations of a conflict of interest between his official duties and his private enterprises. The difficulties between the Maxwell Land Grant Company and squatters on company land exposed the marshal's sensitive position. This conflict, called the Colfax County War, arose after prospectors discovered gold on grant land in 1867. Many settlers moved onto property claimed by the company and prepared to stay indefinitely. The "war" erupted in the fall of 1875 when assassins murdered Parson T. J. Tolby near Cimarron. Tolby considered himself a spokesman for the settlers on grant land. A few days before his death, Tolby threatened to expose some shady dealings of Judge Joseph Palen, an associate of the company. Partisans of Tolby suspected the company's henchmen in Colfax County of carrying out the murder.[42]

When the local authorities failed to find the killers, Tolby's friends collected "evidence" that allegedly implicated several Hispanos and county officials in Cimarron. While extracting "confessions" from two alleged killers, the vigilantes lynched the unfortunate men. When the confessions implicated County Probate Judge Robert Longwill, the frightened official fled to Santa Fe. For some unexplained reason, he placed himself in the protective custody of Marshal John Pratt. Longwill may have concluded that since the Maxwell Company was involved in federal bankruptcy proceedings, the marshal could legally care for him. (The uniform bankruptcy law of 1867 made the marshal the executive in the disposal of these cases.)[43]

When the sheriff of Colfax County failed to contain the feud, Governor Samuel B. Axtell declared the county to be in a state of "riot and anarchy." In January 1876, the territorial assembly abolished the Colfax County courts and attached the county to Taos County for judicial purposes. Axtell dispatched special agent Ben Stevens to Cimarron and provided him with a detachment of regular troops. Stevens's assignment was an unenviable one—to arrest the violent ringleader of the vigilantes, Clay Allison. He failed, but Allison surrendered voluntarily.[44]

The Colfax County War was largely a matter for the territorial courts, and John Pratt avoided the controversy until July 1875. In that month the federal courts charged Mrs. William R. Morley, wife of the president of the Maxwell Land Grant Company, with robbery of the mails at Cimarron. She allegedly removed an envelope from the post office illegally. United Stated District Attorney Thomas B. Catron, an enemy of William R. Morley, presented Marshal John Pratt with a warrant for her arrest in August 1875.

Catron probably intended the warrant to harass his political enemy and may have instructed Pratt not to serve it. Later that month, Pratt went east on business, but informed Mrs. Morley's husband, William, that he intended to serve the process upon his return. Morley reportedly replied, "Tell Mr. Catron to crack ahead with it [the case]. What he has already done will cost [Stephen] Elkins 500 votes" in the coming election.[45]

Although the federal lawman returned from the East in September, he neglected to serve the warrant against Mrs. Morley. Several stories appeared to explain the marshal's failure: one tradition declares that gunfighter Clay Allison, who respected Mrs. Morley's pluckiness (but was on the opposite political side), warned Pratt and Attorney Catron, "Bring that woman to trial and not a man will come out of the courtroom alive"; a second account states simply that Mrs. Morley was pregnant and Catron refused to bring her to trial. William Morley informed the attorney general that Catron refused the marshal permission to arrest his wife, because a trial would have exposed the indictment as a malicious attempt to injure the reputation of Morley. In any event, Marshal Pratt avoided an embarrassing incident for federal justice in New Mexico.[46]

The angry settlers on the Maxwell Grant perceived a conspiracy among the federal officials in Santa Fe, and they lodged numerous complaints in Washington. Mary E. McPherson, mother-in-law of William Morley, charged that Thomas B. Catron and a group of "U.S. officials" masterminded the murder of Parson Tolby and falsified charges against Mrs. Morley (the writer's daughter). Catron also manipulated the disestablishment of the Colfax County court. William Morley informed the attorney general that Catron attempted to undermine Morley's place in Cimarron society, when Catron charged that Morley's newspaper, the *Cimarron News and Press*, deliberately whipped up the vigilantes. While Catron replied persuasively to these charges, the accusations disturbed the attorney general and publicized the existence of political partisanship within the federal judiciary of New Mexico. The close relationship of Marshal Pratt with the controversial district attorney inevitably colored the reputation of the marshalcy.[47]

The Colfax County War accentuated Pratt's importance in territorial politics. His political enemies had already made several efforts to replace him, after his participation in the disputed delegate election of 1867. Two years later, the *New Mexican* reported a rumor that the marshal, who was the last appointee of President Andrew Johnson in New Mexico, had been removed. This rumor probably resulted from the machinations of Delegate J. Francisco Chavez, who nominated as Pratt's replacement James M. Wilson of Santa Fe. Governor William A. Pile, who opposed Pratt, endorsed Wilson and "earnestly" hoped that "the appt. [appointment would] be made."[48]

Political fighting continued between the resourceful lawman and his enemies. In August 1869, an anonymous correspondent from Santa Fe informed the St. Louis *Missouri Democrat* that several "conservative republican federal office holders," including Pratt, were assisting the "demoralized democracy," the Democratic party, in "a ghastly effort" to defeat Delegate Chavez at the next election. Pratt replied immediately through the *New Mexican*, a staunch Republican journal, that his purpose was "to support the nominee of the republican convention." In May 1871, Chavez admitted that he supported Herman H. Heath, the former territorial secretary, for the marshalcy. By this time the canny Pratt had become firmly intwined in the Santa Fe Ring.[49]

Marshal John Pratt led an active social life in spite of these distractions. He progressed through the ranks of the Montezuma Lodge of the Masonic Temple, also a bastion of the Santa Fe Ring. He was elected vestryman in the local Episcopal Church. When death claimed the eminent chief justice, Joseph G. Palen, Marshal Pratt led the funeral cortege. He was an organizer of the annual Fourth of July celebration—Marshal of the Day, in 1873. At the all-important Centennial Celebration in 1876, Pratt's speech "held captive his hearers by his fine flow of language."[50]

Even as upright a citizen as John Pratt was constrained to come to terms with the hardships of the harsh desertlands. He grasped fervently the few pleasures that New Mexico offered. Major John G. Bourke, a veteran army officer on the frontier, encountered the marshal in one of his more passionate moments. A delightful storyteller, Bourke preserved this gem about the federal lawman:

In October 1869, First Lieutenant L. L. O'Connor, deep in his cups, had allowed his wife to drive his four-mule team down a steep grade called La Bajada near Santa Fe. Unaware that Marshal Pratt and his party were walking ahead and out of sight of the O'Connor family, the team suddenly caught up with the lawman. "Why! My God Almighty! Man!" exclaimed the surprised marshal, "I wouldn't drive down La Bajada myself!" "No," replied the inebriated soldier, "Nur Oil [nor I]." Mrs. O'Connor had driven down. The lieutenant offered Pratt and his party a drink of sherry To'Kay or Hock [a modification of Hochheimer, a Rhine wine], when Mrs. O'Connor interjected that they had only whiskey. "Well," said the tipsy lieutenant, "Damn their furrin ingray-jints [foreign ungratefulness] any how—shure fish-key's [whiskey] the dhruink fur a gintil min [gentleman] all-ways"; so the whole party turned themselves loose on the black bottle.[51]

After more than ten years as marshal of New Mexico Territory,

John Pratt stepped down in May 1876, to make room for John E. Sherman, Jr., a member of the prestigious Ohio family. The procedure by which Pratt lost his post provides a good example of the manipulation of territorial officials. In 1881, former Delegate Stephen B. Elkins explained the removal of Pratt to Senator John P. Jones of Nevada. In order to make a place for Sherman in the marshalcy, President Ulysses S. Grant appointed Pratt secretary of New Mexico Territory and relieved the incumbent, William G. Ritch. Ritch importuned Elkins to have him reappointed to the secretaryship but, recalled Elkins, President Grant "would not do it unless by my consent." Elkins approved the reappointment of Ritch, but also acquired a consulship for Pratt. This political maneuvering placed John E. Sherman, Jr., in the marshalcy.[52]

John Pratt's ten-year term witnessed important developments in federal law enforcement. As a participant in the Republican Congress's efforts to remove the last vestiges of human bondage from the nation, the marshal briefly became a reformer. As a subordinate in the newly created Department of Justice, Pratt acquired broadened powers of office—to include potential detective powers. As custodian of federal prisoners, Pratt provided better care for his charges in eastern penitentiaries. Within his district, Pratt cultivated the good will of the county sheriffs, whom he depended upon to serve as deputies. The deputies also increased their range of duties, and improved the administration of the marshalcy.

These improvements occurred in spite of instances of flagrant abuse of power. Through his power to arrest (or refusal to arrest), Marshal Pratt controlled the "doors" to the federal courts. As a staunch Republican in the latter part of his term, Pratt followed a shadowy course between political partisanship and upright performance of duty. This questionable conduct resembled the murky behavior of many Americans in that era that Mark Twain called the Gilded Age.

The Republican domination of the New Mexico marshalcy did give the office a sense of direction and purpose. Pratt might otherwise have squandered the resources of federal law enforcement in senseless factionalism. Whether John Pratt could leave his office in 1876 "with a clear conscience," as the editor of the *New Mexican* brazenly concluded, is questionable. To perform the marshalcy's tasks impartially in the future, a man of more moderate political views was necessary.[53]

5

The Arizona Marshalcy, 1866–76

Whereas John Pratt had been concerned with territorial politics when he became marshal of New Mexico, Edward Phelps, the newly appointed lawman to Arizona, in 1866 was concerned with surviving. Marshal Milton B. Duffield, the zealous Black Republican who pressed the confiscation of rebel property during the Civil War, had left a decidedly inquiet legacy. The office itself was a "war baby" and had not been tried in peacetime. The small income discouraged competent men from seeking the marshalcy. Settlements were scattered and isolated, and in between them warlike Apaches reigned. Mexican and Anglo banditti threatened the citizens. Tardy arrival of communications from Washington, D.C., confused the federal lawmen. Any superior performances in the Arizona marshalcy would depend upon the personalities of the incumbents.

The citizens of Arizona were clustered in three districts, each remote from the other: in the south around the villages of Tucson and Tubac on the Santa Cruz River; in the west, along the Colorado River, at Yuma, La Paz, Ehrenberg, and Gila City, the last three the result of a recent mining boom; and in the north-central region, around the newly built capital of Prescott, and nearby Wickenberg, also a new mining camp resting on the fabulously wealthy Vulture Mine. Aside from the few Anglo miners, a majority of the 5,526 white inhabitants in 1866 were of Hispano descent, residing in and around Tucson. Of the Anglos, most were of Southern Democratic persuasion, and they remembered the bitter defeat in the Civil War. Some Anglos intermarried with the Hispanos.

The marshal and his scattered constituents lived in constant fear of hostile Indians. In the late 1860s, these tribesmen numbered

25,000 persons, far more than white settlers. Fortunately for the Anglos and Hispanos, a majority of the Indians—especially the Papagos, Pimas, Maricopas, and after 1868, the Navajos—were peaceful herders and agriculturalists. Some allied with the whites against their hostile kinsmen. While the various branches of the warlike Apaches could muster only a few hundred warriors, their martial abilities compensated for their low numbers. In 1866, these Apaches endangered travel in central and eastern Arizona and occupied a strip of the southeast—the "Apache corridor." Just as in New Mexico in the 1850s, when the warlike Indians confined white settlement to the narrow Rio Grande Valley, in Arizona only the presence of the army reassured the white citizenry.

Given such unflattering geographic and political conditions, it is remarkable that the marshal's colleagues in government were able to unite the Arizonans. The first Unionist governor, John H. Goodwin, recognized the precarious position of his regime and sought an accommodation with the former rebels and the Hispanos. He enjoined them to cooperate with his followers to exploit Arizona's vast natural resources. Goodwin and his successor, Richard McCormick, also opened territorial offices, including the marshalcy, to former Confederates.

Edward Phelps of California succeeded the colorful Milton B. Duffield. Phelps had been surgeon-in-chief at Fort Whipple, Arizona, when he entered the marshalcy in June 1866. The friendly Prescott *Arizona Miner* noted that the president "reposes special trust and confidence in the integrity, ability and diligence of Edward Phelps, [and] has by and with the advice of and consent of the Senate, appointed him marshal." The fact that both Duffield and Phelps were appointed from California revealed the "colonial" status of the new territory to the Pacific Coast state.[1]

Edward Phelps did little to deserve the title of marshal. A United States grand jury in October 1869, complimented the marshal and United States district attorney for their "attention" to the court, but added that the accommodations which Phelps furnished "were wholly unfit for the secret and rapid dispatch of business." In April 1870, the *Miner* criticized the marshal for failing to begin the census promptly. Phelps began the census three months later.[2]

In late 1869, disgruntled jurors began to question the failure of the marshal to pay them. The *Miner* announced in December that the former jurors "would be more than pleased to hear from" the federal constable. United States District Attorney Converse W. C. Rowell informed the attorney general in August 1870, that "complaints of a serious nature are coming to me of irregularities and misapplication of public monies [by Marshal Phelps]." The office had been in arrears since the formation of the territory, and Phelps had not even paid the census deputies. Rowell inquired about the amount of advances that the marshal had received from Washington, D.C.[3]

The attorney general replied that Phelps had received a $10,000 advance in 1867, but he cautioned Rowell to give the negligent marshal every protection against premature rumors. Meanwhile, the chief clerk of the Department of Justice informed Phelps that someone (Rowell) had charged him with official neglect and that "you have entirely failed thus far to render due account of the expenditures of ten thousand dollars advanced to you in March 1867, an instance of official neglect which this office regards with strong displeasure." Under separate cover the chief clerk sent Phelps a copy of United States District Attorney Rowell's letter of complaint. He also informed Rowell that the Department of Justice had ordered Marshal Phelps to make an immediate return of his accounts.[4]

The federal lawman replied to the charge of official neglect on October 9, 1870. He protested that he had received no authority to advance funds to the census deputies and that outstanding bills of his office could not be paid until they were submitted to the Treasury for inspection. The matter rested there for some time.[5]

Like many officials in the territories, Marshal Phelps regarded the marshalcy as a part-time endeavor. In June 1866, he helped the businessmen of Arizona by persuading the military to pay debts in the territory in coin rather than by check. A few months later, Phelps became an "active, honest miner" by leasing a mine. He also contracted to deliver hay to Camp Crittenden.[6]

Edward Phelps had to resign his commission in the army to become marshal, but he did not forego his medical career. He set up a private practice, as well as his official headquarters, in Tucson. The *Miner* realized that the marshal's office paid very little salary and observed that "Dr. Phelps would think it dull times . . . if he could not make as much [in medicine in] a month as the marshal-ship gives him in six, perhaps in twelve [months]." He paid $100 in taxes in 1867 on an income of $2,000, considerably more than his official salary of $200 and fees per annum.[7]

Many Arizonans continued to complain about Phelps's lack of attention to duty. Pierson W. Dooner, the crusty editor of the *Tucson Weekly Arizonian*, was probably thinking of Phelps when he characterized all federal officials in the territory as "a mob of political beggars without brains." The *Miner*, a defender of Marshal Phelps on most occasions, admitted that the marshal was "not on speaking terms with a large share of our people."[8]

When Marshal Phelps announced in January 1871, that he was taking a "pleasure trip" to Sonora, the Arizonans did not question his decision. He very responsibly left a young lawyer to care for his office. On January 28, the United States consul at Guaymas reported that the vacationing lawman had departed for Mazatlan on an English man-of-war.[9]

By late February, disconcerting reports began to reach Arizona that Marshal Phelps had taken "French leave" and had "skedaddled" with $12,000 of federal monies. The movements of the lawyer-in-charge of the marshalcy confirmed suspicions that Phelps had absconded. The alert editor Dooner reported that the young attorney had "concluded to follow the example of his employer." In March vague reports reached Arizona that the errant marshal was still traveling southward; but in April, Mexican bandits killed Edward Phelps for the money in his possession. Dooner prophetically observed that "there would seem to be a fatality connected with the marshal's office."[10]

At the request of the Delegate Richard C. McCormick, who was embarrassed by Phelps's behavior, Attorney General Amos T. Akerman delayed the appointment of a new marshal for a short time. In mid March 1871, the attorney general informed District Attorney Rowell that he would suggest a successor to Edward Phelps unless a satisfactory explanation of the lawman's actions arrived promptly.[11]

On April 15, 1871, three months after Edward Phelps departed on his "pleasure trip," President Ulysses S. Grant appointed Isaac Q. Dickason as marshal. The Prescott *Arizona Miner* noted that he was a citizen of the territory, a noted Indian fighter, and not an "imported pilferer." Dickason was an "intelligent, hardworking, and successful farmer," who used progressive farming techniques and promoted the farmers in Arizona politics. In 1870, he sold his farm in the remote Leonara Valley and purchased land near Prescott. Later in 1870, when unscrupulous men spread false reports about diamonds in northern Arizona, Dickason joined the rush.[12]

In 1871, the people of southern Arizona had complained that the Apaches were raiding white settlements, but the Indian agent ignored the allegation. On the morning of April 30, William S. Oury and several citizens of Tucson led about one hundred Papago Indians and Hispanos against the Apache camp. An army investigator estimated that the vigilantes killed more than forty Indians.[13]

As in the case of the massacre of Indians by the "Mesilla Guard" in New Mexico many years earlier, public opinion unerringly favored the murderers. Indeed, the leader of the massacre, William S. Oury, was later elected sheriff of Pima County and served concurrently as a deputy marshal.[14]

Washington owed the victims of the massacre justice, but the sluggish pace of federal justice delayed the prosecution of the murderers. District Attorney Rowell reported his efforts to collect evidence against the Oury band and in the process, he indicated that a vacancy existed in the marshalcy. Attorney General Akerman was surprised that Isaac Q. Dickason was not yet engaged in official duties. He instructed Rowell to determine whether the former Indian fighter intended to accept the appointment. On August 14, 1871, the reluctant appointee inquired about the salary of the office and informed the attorney general that the duties of a federal lawman were "very arduous and dangerous." Although he received the commission in April, he said nothing about accepting the position. On September 5, the attorney general redirected Dickason to acknowledge in writing if he wanted the office. Evidently, he complied shortly thereafter.[15]

By this time rumors held that Isaac Dickason had resigned the marshalcy. He denied the story. District Attorney Rowell, who was displeased with the choice of Dickason, accused the marshal of negligence. On September 9, he sent the attorney general a newspaper item which noted that Dickason was supervising a group of Mexican hay cutters on the Verde River. Rowell continued to disparage the marshal, and the Tucson *Weekly Arizonian* later accused him of "slandering" Dickason.[16]

There seemed to be no end to the discontent with the appointment of Dickason. In September 1871, Benjamin H. Bristow, the acting attorney general, informed Marshal Dickason that a complaint of dereliction of duty had been made against him. Bristow added in a censorious tone that the fall term of federal court could not begin without Dickason's presence. Bristow instructed District Attorney Rowell to advise him about the marshal's conduct in the future.[17]

When Dickason learned about these complaints, he took exception to the charges. He protested that he had executed all court process directed to him, except in cases when Rowell erred by issuing process without the approval of the court. Dickason protested that he tried to cooperate with the district attorney and even consulted Rowell in the selection of deputies. Dickason added that when funds for the support of the courts were placed to his credit, the Department of Justice failed to notify him. Two months later, in December 1871, the disgusted marshal complained that he still had received no reply to his letter of defense.[18]

While this long-winded correspondence progressed, the marshal and district attorney prepared for the trial of the Camp Grant murderers. In October 1871, a United States grand jury found 108 indictments against the alleged murderers, and the trial was scheduled for December. Since the murderers were prominent citizens, and were carefully shielding each other, ninety-three of the indictments were entitled *alias*. According to the outraged Prescott *Arizona Miner*, the *alias* warrants gave the marshal freedom to choose his victims, and "any innocent person was liable to be arrested at the caprice of our [federal] officers." Although Marshal Dickason had no funds (at least he was not aware of the money) with which to pay the expenses of the trial, the court opened on December 4 and concluded on December 13. The verdict was a predictable not guilty.[19]

In addition to the service of dozens of subpoenas and warrants in preparation for the trial, Marshal Dickason and his Tucson deputy, John Miller, provided much assistance inside the courtroom. The marshal ensured that the physical needs of the court—lighting, fuel, and seating—were adequate; and, as a consequence of his duty as property agent for the court, he guarded material evidence for the trial. The federal lawman administered oaths to officers, such as the court clerk, when they were called to testify.

The participation of the federal gendarme on the side of the government contradicted his personal sentiments about the murderers. Dickason and his subordinates were constrained "to maintain order among the people" who demonstrated against the trial of patriotic citizens at war with hostile Apaches. Marshal Dickason and other federal officials, including Judge John Titus, clearly sympathized with the accused men. After the acquittal of the defendants, the citizenry gathered with Dickason at a nearby saloon and expressed "great respect" for the court officers for upholding the right of Arizonans to defend themselves against hostile Apaches.[20]

The Camp Grant Massacre caused the federal government to reassure the treaty Indians that Washington would protect them. A few months after the trial of the murderers, the Chairman of the Board of Indian Commissioners, Vincent Colyer, visited Arizona in order to demarcate several new reservations. He negotiated treaties of resettlement with many tribes, and by 1872 several thousand tribesmen resided upon new federal lands. Those Indians who refused to relocate, and a few who later fled from the reservations, were forcibly encamped upon the federal sanctuaries by the determined campaign of General George W. Crook in early 1873.

Once on the reservations, the Apache nations lost their sovereignty, became subjects of the laws of the United States, and, by implication, fell under the jurisdiction of the federal courts. The Apaches were obviously not familiar with these unusual procedures and would have looked askance upon an intruding United States marshal. The Indian agents were empowered to prevent the officer from meddling on the reservations. The agent at San Carlos, the largest agency in the territory, established an Indian police force and a native court which tried minor offenses among the tribesmen. The Apaches "came under the jurisdiction of federal courts" only for major crimes such as murder and robbery. Although controversy raged over the extent of federal court jurisdiction upon the reservations (the territorial courts also claimed certain powers) for many years, the marshalcy of Arizona enlarged its responsibilities considerably as a consequence of the pacification of the Indians.[21]

The favorable publicity that accompanied Marshal Dickason's partisan performance at the trial of the Camp Grant murderers was accentuated by another benevolent service. He was the first federal law officer to pay the expenses of the United States courts in Arizona. He announced this historic moment in January 1872, when he arrived in Tucson to serve the process of the territorial supreme court. The Tucson *Citizen* noted that by paying these expenses Dickason disproved the "slanders" of District Attorney Rowell, who maligned him regularly. "Better keep Dickason in office," concluded the editor. In February the officer further elated many Arizonans by receiving authority to settle the outstanding claims against his absconding predecessor, Edward Phelps.[22]

Dickason's holiday from attack was short-lived. In the spring of 1873, political enemies revived the charges of official neglect. A United States grand jury in Yuma accused the farmer-lawman of many shortcomings, and the *Yuma Sentinel* reported in September that a movement was under way to oust the officer. This opposition was spurred by the irresponsible conduct of the lawman, who had abruptly scurried off to prospect for diamonds. This was not his first absence from office to search for precious stones. He had departed for the wilds during the previous year, 1872.[23]

The chronic truancy of the chief enforcer of the federal laws of Arizona caused his bondsmen some concern; one expressed a desire to withdraw as a surety. In August 1873, the new United States District Attorney, James F. McCaffry, justified this decision of the bondsman by alleging that Dickason was "engaged in no regular business" and that he was absent much of the time on prospecting trips. McCaffry admitted that the marshal "gambles," but "I cannot say to what extent." The following month the attorney reported that the marshal had placed $12,000 with the United States Depository in April of the previous year. Since that time Dickason had spent "a considerable sum" in gambling and prospecting. McCaffry did not allege that the officer had spent the public monies on these shaky ventures although, said the attorney, the "opinion is expressed [in Arizona] that he will not return" from his prospecting trip.[24]

Future events supported McCaffry's prophecy. In mid October the postmaster of Prescott could not find the errant Dickason. He left no forwarding address when he departed for the diamond fields. Indeed, he did not return. The wanderlust possessed him. Five years after his unceremonious departure, an Arizona journal learned that the adventurer-lawman died in Deadwood, Dakota Territory, while working as a barkeeper. The federal government instituted proceedings against his bondsmen to recover lost public funds, but the case dragged on for years. In June 1880, the district attorney assured the editor of the *Miner* that the case, "which has burdened the calendar . . . for so many years, . . . would be disposed of soon." The comment of the skeptical Tucson journalist, Pierson W. Dooner, that "a fatality" was associated with the Arizona marshalcy seems prophetic.[25]

The disgraced office was without an occupant from July 1873 to January 1874, when former sheriff and deputy marshal, George Tyng, a former resident of Texas, was appointed marshal. Tyng was a native of Massachusetts and probably a member of the illustrious family that founded Tyngsborough. In July 1872, Tyng contracted beef to the Arizona army posts and was appointed to fill the unexpired term of sheriff of Yuma County, the source of much criticism of the former marshal. He resigned the shrievalty the following year in order to take a position with the mercantile firm of William B. Hooper and Company of Ehrenberg. He held this private post well into his term as marshal.[26]

When news reached Arizonans that George Tyng had accepted the marshalcy, the editor of the Prescott *Arizona Miner* predicted a turn-around in the office. "We learn from a friend at Washington," said the elated editor, "that Arizona marshals have until now stood in bad repute."[27]

Tyng did little to support the editor's favorable comments. Not until August did he inquire whether he should pay claims against his predecessor's term of office. He added that he had no records from Isaac Dickason's term, but complained that "the uncertainty and smallness of payment . . . are doing much to defeat the ends of justice." The following month Marshal Tyng requested, and was granted, a sixty-day leave of absence for reasons of health. His resignation soon followed, and took effect December 15, 1874.[28]

Francis H. Goodwin, who succeeded George Tyng, had migrated from Georgia to Arizona after the Civil War. In politics "he sided with" Governor Richard C. McCormick, and the *Arizona Miner*, which evidently objected to a Unionist governor consorting with a former Confederate, declared that the marshalcy should have gone "to another [unnamed] gentleman." Former Marshal Milton B. Duffield had once accused Goodwin of being "the most confirmed Rebel in Arizona." Goodwin was clerk of the Pima County Court in 1870, and when George Tyng became marshal,

Governor Anson Peacely-Killen Safford appointed Goodwin to serve Tyng's unexpired term as sheriff of Yuma County. Goodwin (no relation to Governor John H. Goodwin) lost a bid for election to the shrievalty in 1874.[29]

From February 1875, when Francis H. Goodwin made his bond as marshal, to July 1876 when he resigned, an interested participant in federal matters could find few solid accomplishments of the Goodwin marshalcy. Perhaps the most worthwhile commentaries on his office were made by Deputy Wiley W. Standefer and District Attorney Everett B. Pomeroy. Deputy Standefer, unaware that Goodwin had just resigned, wrote in July 1876, that the marshal would not answer his letters. Standefer had two prisoners lodged in the county jail at Prescott, but he had no funds to pay their subsistence. The frustrated subordinate added that other county jails would soon refuse federal prisoners unless the marshal provided funds quickly.[30]

District Attorney Pomeroy informed Attorney General Alfonso Taft in December 1876, that with few exceptions federal court expenses had not been paid in the territory for two years. Federal justice languished. Pomeroy added that a United States grand jury in Tucson refused to find any indictments because the jurors knew that Marshal Goodwin would not pay them.[31]

Given the negligence of Arizona's first marshals, it is no wonder that violence and robbery plagued the territory. In 1857, a visitor to Tucson facetiously characterized the village as a "great place"— only six murders had occurred in the past three months. Another traveler commented in the next year that "the morals of the community have not improved but on account of a cold spell of weather . . . no great number of murders have been committed." Many murderers doubled as highwaymen and horse thieves and preyed upon Mexican pack trains that supplied Tucson.[32]

In the early 1870s, highway robbery and murder reached alarming proportions and provoked the residents of southern Arizona to demand protection. The Tucson *Arizona Citizen* became indignant: "There are no hostile Indians on the lower Gila [River]," said the irate editor, "and yet the settlers there are compelled to abandon their homes to shun the [American and Mexican] assassins." This writer concluded that "there is a worse enemy than the Apache—the outlaw.[33]

As the wave of lawlessness swept the Gila Valley, numerous

appeals for help reached the desk of Marshal Goodwin. The federal officer sympathized, but was hampered by the lack of jurisdiction and resources. Many of the robbery-murders, such as the slaughter of the John Baker family on the Gila in 1871, did not involve the violation of federal laws. Even the crossing of the international boundary by banditti did not contradict the laws of the United States unless the desperadoes crossed the border in "organized" fashion. The marshal entered the case only when quasi-military units (such as filibusters) crossed the border. When Arizonans complained again in 1875, the embarrassed lawman protested that he had no authority to interfere with "unorganized" bands. However, when reports reached Goodwin in December 1875 that a band of 300 Mexican revolutionaries had taken refuge in the Gila Valley, he lacked funds to take action. A unit of United States cavalry investigated, but their quarry fled. The marshal's boast that his office would arrest any "organized" border raiders was proven hollow.[34]

In the absence of an effective federal lawman, the alarmed inhabitants of the Gila Valley turned to the governor for protection. This was not uncommon. The governor's office was one of the few full-time positions in territorial government and a natural clearing house for information. As early as January 1865, Governor Ignacio Pesqueira of Sonora exchanged information with the Arizona executive about criminals along the border. The United States had negotiated a treaty of extradition with Mexico in 1862, although its provisions were not entirely satisfactory. Neither party was obligated to release its nationals to the other. Extradition was voluntary. Extradition between the territories and states within the Union was easier. As early as August 1868, Marshal M. A. Shaffenburg of Colorado Territory inquired of the governor of Arizona about the location of a wanted man. "Please answer as soon as possible," requested the lawman.[35]

As border outlawry increased in the 1870s, Governor Anson Safford assumed the mantle of chief law officer in his territory. Safford, a physically small but dynamic executive, characterized the bandits as a "a scourge of civilization" and vowed to eradicate them. Soon after he took office in 1869, outlaws murdered three Americans near the border. Safford was doubly shocked in 1871 when freebooters massacred the John Baker family in the Gila Valley.[36]

Safford presented several recommendations to the assembly to protect the territory. He asked the legislature to elevate the crime of highway robbery to the status of a capital crime and to permit him to establish a twenty-man police force on the all-important Gila Road, which paralleled the international boundary. Safford also asked for authority to offer rewards for information about, or the capture of, known criminals. The reluctant assemblymen agreed only to the last request—rewards for wanted men.[37]

In spite of the hesitant legislature, Governor Safford spurred the lawmen of his district to greater efforts against the highwaymen. In January 1873, he reported that the reward system worked "admirably." Law officers became more energetic. Later in Safford's governorship, Marshal Wiley W. Standefer and his chief deputy received $300 for the arrest of two bandits. Rumors circulated also that Safford secretly paid $500 for the kidnap of a wanted man from Mexico. Safford justified this illegal action by charging that the governor of Sonora had refused to honor an extradition request.[38]

One last contribution of this energetic governor concerned the establishment of a territorial prison at Yuma. The last act of the assembly in 1875 provided for $25,000 to construct a penitentiary. While this appropriation was much too small, the contractor managed to construct two small cell houses. On July 1, 1877, the first inmates arrived. This prison acquired the most unenviable reputation for brutality in the Southwest, although all frontier jails excelled in barbarities.[39]

This exercise of authority over law enforcement by Governor Safford did not distract the marshals from the routine activities of office. The official accounts of the marshals for 1866–76 indicate an appreciable growth of official business, in spite of the many hindrances to the marshalcy. In 1867, Marshal Edward Phelps's office earned a mere $310.20 (salary included), and $357.52 in the following year. Records of Isaac Q. Dickason's short term are scanty, but he (and two deputies) earned $66.82 for the half year, June 30-December 31, 1871. In his very short tenure, July 1-December 15, 1874, George Tyng and three subordinates received $429.07. A significant increase in business occurred under Francis H. Goodwin. From January 9 to December 31, 1875, Goodwin and three deputies earned $1,456.34. While these figures are not extraordinary, they indicate that business did increase in the 1870s.[40]

The deputies deserve much of the credit for the growth of the marshalcy. These underlings were a mixed group. A Prescott carpenter and farmer, Amasa G. Dunn, served as a deputy under marshals Milton Duffield and Edward Phelps. Dunn worked hard, accumulated property, and consorted with Isaac Q. Dickason in a farmers' association in Prescott. He received a stab wound in 1869 when he helped the sheriff break up a fight. The *Miner* noted that he was "busily engaged in taking the census" the following year. Unfortunately, when drinking, this conscientious deputy had "his worse passions aroused." Such was his condition when he vied with a contender for the favors of a barmaid and was killed in 1870. He left a family in New York State. [41]

For all of his faults, Marshal Isaac Q. Dickason selected some energetic deputies. As a deputy marshal for this diamond seeker, Sheriff George Tyng of Yuma County actively searched out unscrupulous men who sold whiskey to the Indians. Dickason appointed the City Constable of Tucson, John Miller, as a deputy. A local paper described him as "an intelligent and energetic gentleman." After Marshal Dickason disappeared into the "diamond fields," Deputy Marshal T. W. McIntosh of Prescott carried out the chief lawman's duties. District Attorney James McCaffry reported that all of Dickason's deputies conscientiously supported the courts after their superior disappeared. [42]

Among the most energetic deputy marshals, F. D. Parker of Prescott held a prominent place. When Marshal Francis H. Goodwin deputized Parker (he was a concurrent deputy sheriff) in 1875, a Prescott paper considered the selection a "good one." Subsequent events supported this choice. In April he pursued Mexican bandits; and in August he trailed an absconding postmaster into Nevada. In April 1876, Deputy Marshal Parker tracked down an absconding army paymaster. [43]

During the erratic tenure of Marshal Edward Phelps the deputyship languished. His records bear the curt notation, "no deputies served or earned fees." Some improvement occurred under Dickason. In the six-month period, June 30 to December 31, 1871, Deputy John Miller earned $483.66 and Deputy George Tyng received $135.16. When Tyng assumed the marshalcy in 1874, six months of service earned for his three subordinates: E. S. Penwell, $5.50; William S. Osborn, $181.66; and Francis H. Goodwin, $42.66. When Goodwin entered the office of federal lawman, Deputy Osborn (who continued to serve) earned fees of

$169.24 for the period January 9 to June 30, 1875. Deputy T. M. Therringer earned $20.00, and F. D. Parker, $266.89. In the following six-month pay period, Marshal Goodwin was constrained to appoint a special deputy, A. F. Buttner, who earned $125.00 for some unknown service.[44]

The marshals and their deputies often turned to territorial judges for guidance. Beginning in 1863, when the scholarly William T. Howell compiled the first law code for Arizona, a series of industrious and conscientious justices occupied the bench. Henry T. Backus moved to Arizona for the healthy climate and served honorably from 1865 to 1869. In the next decade, Charles A. Tweed and DeForest Porter held terms of eight and ten years, respectively. While other justices were not so widely respected, these few conscientious men provided Arizona with a "reasonably" stable court system during the turbulent 1870s.[45]

Even though Arizona's judges demonstrated a commitment to duty, the residents still complained that many federal officers— including marshals—refused to remain in their districts for the duration of their terms. As early as August 1852, Congress refused to pay any territorial officer who took more than sixty days' leave from his district. Abuse of this law was so great that in 1874 the Department of Justice took action. By a circular of June 20, 1874, the marshals of Arizona, and New Mexico, were directed to reside permanently in their districts and to give full attention to their duties. Only by an official leave—normally sixty days—could they leave their districts. The Prescott *Arizona Miner* made a point of printing the announcement for the benefit of its citizens, and its officials.[46]

Like its sister office in New Mexico, the Arizona marshalcy experienced the centralizing hand of the newly created Department of Justice in the 1870s. While the first incumbents failed to comply with bureaucratic regulations at all—Marshal George Tyng could find no records of his predecessors and accused them of six years of "mal-administration"—some order appeared in the office under Francis Goodwin. In a sober letter to the Department of Justice, dated January 20, 1876, the former Confederate revealed a solemn and humble attitude:

> Sir, I have the honor to transmit herewith my Emolument Return and vouchers for the last half of the year 1875.
> I also transmit herewith Estimate for Funds for the U.S. Courts in Arizona.

I also transmit herewith my Report of Official Postage Stamps
on hand January 1st 1876.
I would respectfully state that Vouchers 1 & 2 [of the] Emolument Return are also included in the vouchers accompanying my Account Current this day forwarded to the First
Auditor while Vouchers 5, 8, 9, & 10, are not included.

*   *   *

I have made large payments to claimants in the 2d and 3d
Judicial Districts, but it is necessary for me to go in person to
those districts to complete payments and shall attend the
March Term of the 2d Dist[rict] Court and the May Term of
the 3d District Court and then complete my payments and
make my proper return to the First Auditor. I have also paid
most of the jurors fees, being an indebtedness incurred by my
predecessor [Isaac] Dickason, and which were ordered paid
under special instructions.[47]

The arrival of the telegraph in Arizona in 1873 reinforced this
very proper attitude. Within four years some thousand miles of
wires spanned the federal lawman's district. The nation's most
remote continental territory was only a few seconds away from the
whims of the authorities in Washington.[48]

Unlike the New Mexico marshalcy, which admitted Hispanos to
the deputyship in the 1850s, Anglos guarded this prerogative
jealously in Arizona. This incongruency was obvious to many
visitors. "In Arizona," observed the astute John G. Bourke, "all
officers of the law were Americans." In New Mexico, Bourke
continued, "they [lawmen] were almost without exception Mexicans."[49]

Some important improvements occurred in the Arizona marshalcy during this troubled decade, 1866–76. When the chief lawmen failed to perform their duties, the deputies assumed many
responsibilities. This tradition of assertive and independent-
minded subordinates soon characterized the Arizona office. This
development fitted the geographic character of the territory,
where settlements were widely scattered. The energetic deputies
of Arizona also moderated another threat to the stability of the
marshalcy—the negative influence of the personality of the chief
lawmen of the 1860s and 1870s. In such a young and unstable
federal office, a constructive personality planted healthy precedents;
an unscrupulous incumbent sowed seeds of disrepute.

6

Marshal John E. Sherman, Jr., 1876–82

To a new marshal in 1876, the New Mexico office seemed well established. For a quarter of a century the inhabitants of the Rio Grande Valley, and to a lesser extent of the outlying counties, had participated in the ritual of the American judicial process. The marshals and their deputies visited hundreds of citizens in the routine service of court process. The presence of Hispanos in many deputyships added strength to the federal law enforcement procedure. Yet, the Santa Fe Ring and its Republican henchmen abused the marshalcy as a rule, an unfortunate condition that caused a good deal of anguish among the citizenry. The Colfax County War had exposed the close relationship of the federal lawman to this clique of businessmen. This "war" was not over when the new marshal arrived in 1876. The pressure of new immigrants in remote settlements demanded more efficient service by the marshal and the courts, not to mention a more impartial treatment at the bar of justice. These problems would test the mettle of any new officer in frontier New Mexico.

The new United States Marshal, John E. Sherman, Jr., possessed an impressive lineage, by eastern standards. A member of the distinguished Sherman family of Ohio, he was the son of a well-known attorney, and a nephew to both Senator John Sherman and General William Tecumseh Sherman. He included among his brothers-in-law, Senator Simon Cameron of Pennsylvania and General Nelson Miles. The marshal rounded out these credentials with a banking partnership that included Frederick Grant, son of the president. [1]

The citizens of New Mexico received the lawman with a notable absence of enthusiasm. He arrived in his district about two months late, his appointment being dated May 24, 1876. On July 20, the

New Mexican entitled an article, "Where is John Sherman, Jr.?,"
and reprinted quotations from the Washington, D.C., *Republican*,
which praised Sherman as "a good Republican" and a strong supporter of presidential contender Rutherford B. Hayes. Obviously,
the editor of the *New Mexican*, spokesman for the stalwart Republicans in the Santa Fe Ring, was not yet sure about the new
marshal. The *Cimarron News and Press* also reacted to the Washington journalist and declared that "Good Republicanism is not the
only criterion" for a public official. "A career of personal merit, and
honesty is the best passport he can bring" to New Mexico, concluded the writer. On the very day the *New Mexican* article appeared, so did Marshal Sherman. "Our sanctum was complimented
yesterday afternoon," noted the newspaperman on July 21, "with a
call from Mr. John E. Sherman, Jr., a nephew of Senator John
Sherman of Ohio."[2]

John Sherman, Jr., assumed office during an alarming break-
down of the law enforcement machinery of New Mexico. In the
first half of 1876, a gory calendar of crimes was compiled, much to
the discredit of the sheriffs and other officers. Vigilantes continued
to terrorize Cimarron, Colfax County, requiring a detachment of
troops to keep the peace. A gunman shot and killed three black
troopers in Cimarron. A dispatch from Abiquiu, Rio Arriba
County, moaned that lynchers kidnapped an accused murderer
from a team of constables and hanged him. This correspondent
added that evildoers had murdered four men in recent months, but
that law officers of Abiquiu did nothing. A grisly postscript was
added to this list of killings when an Albuquerque mob took three
prisoners from the sheriff and lynched them.[3]

Highway robbers and cattle rustlers were numerous in the
southern counties, where the population was expanding along the
old Gila Trail, in Grant County, and in the southeast in recently
created Lincoln County. Freebooters looted stagecoaches near
Pajarito, just south of Albuquerque, in late November 1875, and in
Cook's Canyon, east of Silver City, the following January. One of
the victims of this latter robbery was John Chisum, cattle baron of
Lincoln County. Chisum managed to conceal most of his funds
from the outlaws, although they took $100 from him.[4]

John Chisum and his fellow ranchers complained bitterly about
the increase of cattle rustling in their county. The sheriff did little
to remedy the situation. After rustlers raided the Mescalero

Agency's stock at Blazer's Mill in February 1876, the army entered the pursuit. The cattlemen were so dissatisfied with the negligible results of the cavalry, however, they they took matters into their own hands. In July, masked men confronted the sheriff, forcibly seized alleged horsethief Jose Segura, and hanged him. The sheriff and his posse were only three miles from Fort Stanton when the incident occurred.[5]

"A virtual reign of terror" gripped the territory in 1876, and respectable citizens were "paralyzed" in "fear of their lives." The new Chief Justice Henry L. Waldo concluded that the vital organs of justice were diseased. Only military units kept the peace in Colfax County and pursued rustlers in Lincoln County. The civil authorities of Colfax County watched in humiliation as their legal business continued to go to Taos. The complaint of Acting Governor William F. M. Arny a decade earlier, in 1866, was again valid—the sheriffs and other peace officers were failing to perform their duties.[6]

Judge Waldo was determined to restore law enforcement and the jury system. In his charge to a Santa Fe grand jury in July 1876, the very month that John Sherman assumed the mantle of federal lawman, the angry justice lashed out at negligent lawmen, "There is a total failure in the performance of . . . duty by those who are required to aid in executing the laws," he said, and "an entire want of efficiency in the administration of justice." Waldo concluded his charge by urging that all law officers be "prompt and vigorous" in the "execution of the laws" and that jurors avoid "weak and loose-minded" decisions.[7]

Marshal Sherman was fortunate to have such an ally. Not only did Waldo desire to enforce the laws vigorously, but he possessed a gifted facility to conciliate the quarrelsome political elements of New Mexico. In the young and violent frontier districts, the scales of justice were often balanced by weighty political considerations. The previous Chief Justice, Joseph G. Palen, was a partisan of the Santa Fe Ring, as was Sherman's predecessor John Pratt. Waldo was a Democrat, but was "respected by friend and foe alike." The *New Mexican* reported that the governor, secretary, United States District Attorney Catron, and Marshal Pratt, "in fact all of the federal officials" in Santa Fe, had unanimously endorsed the nomination of Henry L. Waldo for the chief justiceship.[8]

This enthusiastic endorsement did not mean that the institution of justice would be freed from the clutches of selfish interests. In the 1870s, the Santa Fe Ring flourished as never before, and its members hoped to continue to manipulate the marshalcy and courts for private gain. The Ring expanded its operations beyond the exploitation of disputed land grants—into mining and cattle investments. Still led by Thomas B. Catron, the United States district attorney since 1872, the Ring had achieved a high degree of sophistication: with a press, the Santa Fe *New Mexican;* eloquent spokesmen, usually the governor or a territorial justice; and exclusive places to fraternize, the Masonic lodges. The Ring also constituted an unofficial "bureaucracy" which reached into all parts of the territory and administered not only economic but political matters of New Mexico. Unwanted presidential appointees were frequently bypassed by a silent conspiracy of the clique. In 1878, Governor Lew Wallace concluded that he was powerless before this informal governmental network of the capitalists and that his office was merely honorific.[9]

Marshal Sherman was aware of the Ring's activities, but crime demanded his immediate attention. On November 20, 1876, three bandits robbed the mail stage eighteen miles north of Las Vegas. Sherman took charge of the pursuit and obtained troops from Fort Union to support his posse. Post Office Detective Charles Adams also cooperated. Adams and a deputy marshal led the posse into Lincoln County, where they captured several bandits and placed them in a military guardhouse. Sherman soon transfered them to the Santa Fe jail to await trial. In the meantime, Agent Adams learned that Nebraska authorities wanted the leader of the robbers, one Bass, for murder. On January 8, 1877, Adams and the Nebraska sheriff arrived to extradite Bass, whereupon the officers learned that Bass had escaped from jail two days earlier. The "officers were rather disgusted," reported the editor of the *New Mexican*, "when they heard of his escape." Marshal Sherman's first important duty ended in failure. It would not be his last regrettable experience in New Mexico.[10]

The violence of the Colfax County War had subsided, but the federal lawman became embroiled in its aftermath. The Reverend Oscar P. McMains succeeded Tolby as spokesman for the squatters in Cimarron, and the territory soon charged him with murder. In

March 1877, McMains protested to Attorney General Charles Devens that the Santa Fe Ring caused him to be tried illegally.[11]

Devens made immediate efforts to prevent any violation of the minister's rights. Devens first directed territorial Attorney General William Breeden to suspend the proceedings against the angry minister. Breeden ignored the order and declared that the Washington official had no authority over territorial cases. Devens responded with instructions to Marshal Sherman, and District Attorney Catron, to intervene immediately. Just what he intended the marshal to do is not clear. Devens also apprised Governor Samuel Axtell of his rebellious underling, Breeden. Axtell quickly interfered, and Judge Henry L. Waldo granted McMains a change of venue to Mora County. McMains's case was dismissed in 1878.[12]

No sooner had the flurry of unrest subsided in Colfax County than trouble erupted in Lincoln County. Although created in 1869, the county failed to attract many migrants. By 1880, the population reached only 2,513. However, Lincoln soon became the largest county, in 1878, when part of Dona Ana was annexed to it. This massive district included some 20,000 square miles of waterless plains in the east, rich grazing land in the Pecos Valley, and potentially valuable mining property in the mountains of the west. Cattle interests headed the list of assessed property, with about 81,000 head in 1883. A few persons, mostly of Hispanic origin, attempted to farm in the valley, although in 1880 only sixty farms were enumerated. During Marshal Sherman's term as federal lawman, the county seat of Lincoln (Rio Bonito) claimed 628 residents and the growing mining community of White Oaks in the west listed 268 inhabitants. Nearby Fort Stanton, on the Rio Bonito, provided protection for the population from any Mescaleros who might roam from their reservation on the edge of the White Mountains.[13]

Like Colfax, where several newly arrived interest groups collided, Lincoln became the home of diverse groups of immigrants. In addition to the Hispanos, several former soldiers from the conquering California Column made their homes in the region in the late 1860s. The lush grasses of the Pecos attracted Texas cattlemen. The mixture was explosive, and in December 1873 a bloody incident followed. A family of Texas ranchers engaged in a gunfight with citizens of Lincoln. Ben Harrold, the family patriarch, was killed. The Harrolds then murdered four citizens, and the following February the local vigilance committee drove the Harrolds from the county.[14]

Among the federal offenses committed in Lincoln County, the theft of government stock attracted Marshal Sherman's attention. The chiefs of the rustlers were George W. ("Buffalo Bill") Spawn and Serefin (Seraphone) Aragon who, in September 1877, stole several mules from the Mescalero Indian Reservation. Deputy Marshal E. A. (O. ?) Dow, a merchant in Lincoln, and Deputy Sheriff Morris Bernstein delivered the two men to United States Commissioner John S. Crouch. Buffalo Bill Spawn was convicted of stealing government mules, sentenced to five years in prison by a Mesilla court, and transported to the Missouri State Prison by Marshal Sherman in December.[15]

During this same period Lincoln County was dominated by a few powerful men—Lawrence G. Murphy and rancher John S. Chisum. Murphy and his younger partners, James J. Dolan and John H. Riley, who were closely associated with the Santa Fe Ring, were the primary contractors of beef to the local Indian reservation and the army posts in the county. John Chisum's ranching enterprise was experiencing some financial difficulty and did not greatly concern the Murphy interests until the arrival of an enterprising Kansas lawyer, Alexander A. McSween, and an Englishman with money, John H. Tunstall. Tunstall opened a store to compete with Murphy's and also established a ranch. McSween broached the prospects of a bank with Tunstall and John Chisum as partners. The indiscreet attorney, strongly religious and self-righteous, threatened to expose the Murphy company for defrauding the government by selling second-rate goods to the Indian reservation.[16]

In 1877, Murphy retired and Dolan took over the firm. He began to lose money, associated with known rustlers (including the Jesse Evans band), and contrived a plan to get rid of his business competition. He placed a claim for debts against the estate of Emil Fritz, former partner of Lawrence G. Murphy. Alexander A. McSween, administrator of this estate, considered the Dolan claim exorbitant and incapable of being proved since the company would not let the attorney examine records on which Dolan based his claim. McSween refused to honor the claim. Acting on the erroneous assumption that Tunstall and McSween were partners (the partnership was to be completed in the spring of 1878), James J.

Dolan obtained the necessary legal papers and had Sheriff William Brady attach the Tunstall store and some stock which McSween was grazing on the Englishman's ranch. On February 18, 1878, a Brady posse overtook John H. Tunstall and some employees who were driving McSween horses to Lincoln. According to the deputies, many of whom were known outlaws, Tunstall resisted arrest and was killed by deputy sheriffs Jesse Evans, Frank Baker, Tom Hill, and others.[17]

Marshal John Sherman was already interested in several participants—outlaw Jesse Evans and his comrades—in the murder of Englishman Tunstall. Sherman held warrants for the Evans band in connection with the theft of government stock and jail breaking. However, the lawman's staff was limited in that remote county, including only Sheriff William Brady (a concurrent deputy marshal) and a young easterner, Robert A. Widenmann.[18] Deputy Widenmann acquired the duty of arresting Jesse Evans and the "Boys" after they escaped from the Lincoln jail in November 1877. Upon receipt of information that they were hiding at Lawrence G. Murphy's ranch, the deputy took a cavalry patrol to the ranch only to find the wily bandit gone. On February 13, 1878, Widenmann found Evans in Sheriff Brady's posse (now in search of Tunstall) and attempted to arrest him. The testy outlaw threatened to kill the deputy marshal if he should ever try to place him under arrest. Widenmann then acquired troops to surround the Dolan store, which he believed to be the temporary hideout of the Evans band. Again the outlaws eluded the deputy. Marshal Sherman, who now wanted Jesse Evans and his friends for the murder of the English citizen, John H. Tunstall, asked the attorney general for permission to use troops in further pursuit of the outlaws. His superior replied from Washington, "It does not appear why the arrest of four men cannot be made without troops" and denied the request.[19]

When he could not find Jesse Evans in the Dolan mercantile house, Deputy Marshal Widenmann arrested Sheriff Brady's deputies who were still occupying the deceased Tunstall's store. The reckless deputy, with troops again behind him, allegedly proposed to the deputy sheriffs that they fight to a finish on the streets of Lincoln. The lieutenant-in-charge of the posse of soldiers wisely refused to allow his troops to participate in such an affair. Sheriff Brady retaliated by arresting Widenmann and his deputy marshals, among them a young killer and rustler, Henry McCarty

—alias William Bonney, alias William Antrim, alias Billy the Kid. They were bound over for trial and charged with rioting.[20]

The impetuous deputy marshal went far toward inflaming the already explosive conditions in Lincoln County. In order to place pressure on the authorities in Washington, D.C., he wrote letters to the British ambassador in the capital and to a prominent San Francisco lawyer, a friend of Tunstall. In the latter piece of correspondence, Widenmann charged that the murder of John H. Tunstall was in the interest of the Santa Fe Ring, of which Sheriff William Brady was a member.[21]

To the surprise of many New Mexican officials, especially Governor Samuel B. Axtell, the deputy marshal's letter obtained results. Tunstall's friend in California sent the Widenmann letter to Axtell who, in turn, published it in the *New Mexican*. When Marshal Sherman saw the letter, he promptly revoked Widenmann's commission as a deputy. The governor, who had been a definite Dolan partisan in a visit to Lincoln in March 1878, and who had experienced Widenmann's denouncing tongue, confirmed the removal of the deputy in a public proclamation against the warring factions in Lincoln County.[22]

As the controversial deputy marshal went about his provocative routine in Lincoln County, he inspired heated editorialism in the *New Mexican*, the organ of the Santa Fe Ring. Widenmann's letter to the British ambassador, according to the angry journalist, was a "Disgraceful Exhibition":

> Widermann [*sic*], a U.S. officer paid with U.S. money, sworn to uphold the laws of the United States, and presumed from his position, to have the honor of the United States at heart, seeks aid from the British government to enforce the law in this Territory; goes to the British Minister resident at Washington with his complaint that a murder has been committed [Tunstall], and declares [that] he is powerless to enforce the laws.

The outraged writer asked if "this renegade American" deputy marshal desired to see "British tribunals . . . try the murderers of Tunstall?" The editor closed with a wish—to see a judge "lay him [Widenmann] by the heels in jail till he is purged of this infamous comtempt" of New Mexican justice.[23]

This controversy over Deputy Marshal Robert Widenmann

provoked a running argument between the editor of the *New Mexican*, a supporter of the Ring, and the *Cimarron News and Press*, a long-time enemy of the clique. In a confused twist of logic, the *New Mexican* accused Widenmann of causing John H. Tunstall's death by failing to arrest Jesse Evans and his band before they joined Sheriff Brady's posse as deputies and killed the unfortunate Englishman. The *News and Press* delighted in pointing up the "fallaciousness" of this argument, reasoning that the deputy marshal would have had difficulty in arresting Evans, since Governor Axtell's proclamation had declared Sheriff Brady's deputies to be the only legal law enforcement body in Lincoln County.[24]

Once Marshal John Sherman learned that many of the charges against Robert Widenmann were politically inspired, he demonstrated a strong sense of independence by promptly reappointing the young man to the deputyship. On March 30, 1878, the *New Mexican* announced that "U.S. Marshal Sherman has reappointed him [Widenmann]." As an additional motive for the reappointment, Sherman may have resented the interference of Governor Axtell, whose proclamation indirectly accused the marshalcy of partisanship in the Lincoln County War.[25]

Marshal Sherman's determination to uphold the integrity of his office—not necessarily his fractious subordinate—spurred the rival editors in Santa Fe and Cimarron to further editorializing. The *New Mexican* characterized the reappointment of Widenmann as an endorsement of the deputy's "ignorant and slanderous utterances" against the respectable citizens of the territory and asked "if the United States Marshal . . . is disgusted with the territorial government? . . . The day has been when United States officials at least . . . considered the government of this country as good as that of England," continued the journalist.[26]

The *News and Press* was delighted: for once a federal lawman possessed the courage to uphold a position against the Santa Fe Ring. The Cimarron editor asserted that Sherman's reappointment of Widenmann added "great weight" to the deputy's charges against the Murphy-Dolan faction in Lincoln. To the Santa Fe newspaperman's question whether Sherman was "disgusted" with the territorial government, the editor of the *News and Press* replied that the federal lawman, as well as "a very large number of the people in the territory," were dissatisfied "and join the *News and Press* in the opinion that in this respect Marshal Sherman exhibits remarkably good taste and good judgment."[27]

In an effort to have Widenmann removed from their midst, the Murphy-Dolan partisans levied charges of robbery and murder against him and several other followers of McSween. On April 1, 1878, Deputy Sheriff George W. Peppin arrested Widenmann, William H. Bonney, and others, for the recent murder of Sheriff William Brady and Deputy Sheriff George Hindman. The deputy marshal and his companions were released soon after.[28]

One week later, the enemies of the deputy marshal and the McSweens made another attempt to remove the troublesome federal lawman. After Judge Warren Bristol appointed John Copeland to fill the unexpired term of William Brady, the new sheriff arrested several McSween partisans, including Widenmann. The charge was resisting an officer of the law. A grand jury refused to return indictments against them. Believing this action to be a miscarriage of justice, Colonel George A. Purington, the Commander of Fort Stanton, now interfered. He constrained Sheriff Copeland to rearrest Widenmann and his friends. Purington accused Widenmann of abusing his authority when he urged the soldiers of his posse to kill Sheriff Brady's posse. However, the deputy marshal and associates were released two days later.[29]

After so many attempts to remove Widenmann, people were not surprised to hear in May 1878, that the Dolan faction had killed the meddlesome deputy marshal. The elder Widenmann, living in Michigan, read the newspaper reports and asked Attorney General Charles Devens to investigate. On June 1, Marshal Sherman telegraphed his superior that there is "no truth in reported death of Widenmann."[30]

With his inflammatory subordinate in and out of jail so frequently, Marshal Sherman and Chief Deputy David Montgomery were required to support personally the federal court which opened in Lincoln on April 14. The atmosphere of the courtroom was tense, and Judge Warren Bristol requested the protection of troops. The United States Grand Jury returned indictments against several McSween followers for the murder of Andrew L. "Buckshot" Roberts on the Mescalero Reservation (that is, on United States property). Sherman and Deputy Montgomery evidently performed their tasks efficiently in this atmosphere of ha-

tred, since a local journal applauded them: they "are acting splen-
didly and deserve great credit." In June Sherman and Montgomery
returned to Lincoln to remove additional prisoners, including the
dangerous Jesse Evans, who had since been arrested.[31]

But the recklessness of Deputy Marshal Widenmann and other
individuals had agitated the public to such a degree that confidence
in all law enforcement had greatly deteriorated. In May a former
resident of Lincoln wrote an anguished letter to a Silver City
newspaper in which he charged that Widenmann had "crowded
down every body who was not in favor" of John H. Tunstall and
Alexander McSween. "If it hadn't been for [Sheriff] Brady he
[Widenmann] would have had everybody in his own hands." The
writer maintained that he tried to avoid the feud, but

> Widerman [*sic*] says to me that he killed a lot of my friends.
> . . . . I told him they were no friends of mine nor no
> particular enemies. Then Widerman says why don't you come
> in with us [McSweens]. . . . And I said it was no fight of
> mine. . . . A day after [this meeting] a friend of mine come
> out to the ranche . . . and said, you better leave because
> Widerman and his party think you are no friend and say they
> intend to put you out of the way.

This terrified writer sold his ranch on May 7, even though he had a
good crop in his fields. He was afraid, he said, that "Widerman
might send some one to kill me in the dark."[32]

As this anonymous refugee fled down the road to Mesilla, he
encountered a party of McSween men who carried a message from
Deputy Marshal Widenmann. They

> told me to come to Lincoln. Widerman . . . wanted to know
> what Murphy and Dolan's party intended to do. I said I knew
> nothing about it, and they let me go. . . . on the road [I] met
> two other men who were afraid for their lives from Widerman
> and his party. . . . I found out that John Chisum, who before
> [the outbreak of hostilities] hated Widerman, was making a
> job [cooperating] with him and McSween to go together and
> clean out the whole country [of the Murphy partisans]. . . .
> [Many people] say that McSween and Widerman and Chisum
> are paying four dollars a day for a man and his rifle."[33]

By late spring 1878, many letters of complaint about Deputy Widenmann and other participants in the "war" had reached the Department of Justice. These accusations, added to the recriminations dating from the Colfax County War, persuaded Attorney General Charles Devens to investigate both outbreaks. Devens dispatched Judge Frank Warner Angel of New York to examine the conduct of the federal and territorial officials. In a letter of April 16, 1878, the attorney general introduced Angel to Marshal John Sherman.[34]

Judge Angel questioned many officials and recorded a confidential assessment of each person in his "journal." About Marshal Sherman, Angel wrote: "means to tell all he knows [about the Lincoln County War]—reliable—but not much back bone unless 'braced up.' Use him through E. A. Fiske." Eugene A. Fiske was an influential lawyer in Santa Fe. When John Sherman arrived in 1876, the two men shared an office in the Palace of the Governors. Sherman trusted Fiske with the affairs of the marshalcy when he took leaves. Judge Angel concluded that Fiske was "shrewd—honest—reliable." He can be "of great service—He controls the U.S. Marshal—Has been of great service to me—well posted as to the people and the frauds in the territory."[35]

The judge quickly assessed the character of Deputy Marshal Widenmann. When Angel found Widenmann, the deputy had taken refuge in Mesilla. Angel concluded: "Great friend of McSween—given to boasting—veracity doubtful when he speaks of himself—well connected in the east & well educated." This judgment could not erase the fact that Deputy Widenmann, the self-proclaimed spokesman for the McSween faction, courageously urged anyone with facts about the Lincoln County problem to assist the government agent. Widenmann published this invitation in the *Cimarron News and Press.*[36]

On May 16, 1878, Judge Angel mailed his report to the attorney general. From his vantage point in Lincoln, Angel declared that the county was very disturbed. Governor Axtell did little to compose the heated tempers. He, said Angel, screened the murderers of John Tunstall, a policy that "has served to discourage and demoralize the honest portion of the community." Angel placed much faith in Marshal Sherman. The "only gleam of hope" for Lincoln, he added, "has appeared in the conduct of the U.S. Marshall [*sic*] who, in spite of the perfidious influences at Santa Fe, has had the courage to reappoint the deputy marshal (Mr. Widen-mann) whose appointment as such, at the first news of Mr. Tunstall's murder, he had been induced to revoke."[37]

While the New York judge sifted the contradictory testimony of the warring factions, Marshal John Sherman sought an additional deputy in Lincoln. The Murphy-Dolan faction had convinced Governor Axtell that Sheriff Copeland lay within the influence of the McSween party. The executive promptly removed Copeland and selected George W. Peppin, a Murphy-Dolan follower. Sherman appointed Peppin as a deputy marshal.[38]

Deputy Marshal Peppin attempted to arrest several McSween men and obtained authority to employ Fort Stanton troops in his posse. However, several obstructions frustrated the employment of the bluecoats. In June 1878, when he attempted to incorporate a unit of cavalry into his posse, the regulars suddenly refused. They discovered that John Kinney, a notorious killer, was a deputy marshal in Peppin's posse.[39]

A few days later, on June 18, Congress permanently severed the link between the marshalcy and soldiers by forbidding the use of bluecoats in any federal posse. This abrupt act not only removed the marshals' access to disciplined and organized forces for their posses, but forbade access to an inexpensive source of possemen since harea have to pay the regulars for service. The national lawmakers did not have the Lincoln County War in mind when they passed this legislation, but, instead, the excessive use of troops at the polls in southern states. This law, commonly called the Posse Comitatus Act, overturned the decision of Attorney General Caleb Cushing rendered in 1854. In 1880, the Democratic majority in Congress reinforced this act by forbidding deputy marshals at the polling places.[40]

Adjutant General of the Army R. C. Drum issued General Order No. 49, dated July 7, 1878, and apprised the New Mexicans of this decision. The outcry was immediate once the New Mexicans realized that military assistance was no longer available in Lincoln County, or anywhere in the territory. A Santa Fe correspondent informed the Pueblo *Colorado Chieftain* that Sheriff Peppin of Lincoln County, with a posse of soldiers, "was at one time within two miles of them [feudists]. . . , when by an order [of the Posse Comitatus Act] they were recalled. . . . The military are anxious to act but they cannot as their hands are tied." The writer added that "the most they [the troops] will attempt to do is to protect the women and children and prevent the wanton destruction of [government] property, by means of guards stationed around."[41]

The Posse Comitatus Act undermined official authority in that remote country. United States District Attorney Thomas B. Catron, who possessed property in Lincoln County, informed Governor Axtell, in late May, that "there is no power . . . that can keep the peace in that country, except the military, of whom both parties have healthy dread." Postal Agent Charles Adams found the mail service of Lincoln completely disrupted. The McSween faction drove the present postmaster, evidently James J. Dolan, from his office. Adams noted that Dolan discharged his duties only with the protection of troops. The agent added that, as a consequence of the Posse Comitatus Act, "the whole County of Lincoln has virtually been turned over to a gang of cut throats."[42]

While the Posse Comitatus Act clearly forbade the employment of troops in posses, Fort Stanton soldiers played an important part in the final destruction of the McSween faction. On July 15, 1878, Deputy Marshal Peppin and a posse of Dolan followers besieged the McSween party in Lincoln. Peppin asked the new post commander, Colonel Nathan A. M. Dudley, for help. The colonel refused, but Peppin, anxious for assistance, replied that one of the besieged party had fired upon Dudley's messenger. This attempt upon a courier sufficed for Dudley to ignore the Posse Comitatus Act. Troops marched into Lincoln.[43]

While Colonel Dudley professed a desire to protect "helpless women and children, . . . the arrival of the military . . . marked the beginning of the end for the McSween side." Dudley shrewdly placed his troops between buildings that the McSweens occupied and threatened them with destruction if they fired upon his troops. With the McSweens effectively divided by the soldiers, part of the lawyer's followers retreated from the village. The Dolans (the possemen) set fire to the main house which McSween and a few men occupied. As the lawyer and his men fled the burning structure, the Dolan faction shot and killed several, including McSween. Others, including Billy the Kid, escaped successfully.[44]

This bloody finale in Lincoln ended the Lincoln County War, although hatreds endured for years. Deputy Marshal Robert Widenmann who had discreetly departed Lincoln weeks earlier, remained a controversial character. The editor of the *New Mexican* still accused the deputy of provoking the Lincoln County War. The journalist declared that "that scrub" Widenmann was "to a great degree responsible for the disturbed conditions . . . in Lincoln County." After Widenmann testified against some of the Murphy-Dolan faction, the *New Mexican* charged that he had given perjured testimony. "We are neither surprised nor disappointed," wrote the angry editor, "as we have long since . . . pronounced him an unmitigated liar and scoundrel . . . [and] murderer. His conduct in Lincoln County shows him to be in every way a villain."[45]

After a brief visit to England, where he attempted to interest John H. Tunstall's father in some shady business ventures, Widenmann returned to Ann Arbor, Michigan, to work in his father's hardware store. He lived out his life in obscurity, playing the role of retired gunfighter to all who would listen and imagining that Thomas Catron's spies were watching him. He died in 1930.[46]

In August 1878, Judge Frank Warner Angel presented a far-reaching report about New Mexico to President Rutherford B. Hayes. Angel accused Governor Axtell of partisanship on the side of the Murphy-Dolans; and decried his attempt to suppress the Colfax County War, by employing troops recklessly. The president, who was already upset by Axtell's insistence upon the use of troops in Lincoln County (in spite of the Posse Comitatus Act), removed Axtell in September 1878.[47]

Judge Angel also leveled charges against United States District Attorney Catron. Ironically, it was not his partisan behavior in the Colfax or Lincoln County wars that New Mexicans found most distasteful, but his failure to prevent the sale of liquor to the Indians. Angel added that Catron manipulated juror and witness certificates of the United States courts. The marshals often issued a certificate of "payment due" jurors and witnesses, since the lawmen seldom received timely payments from Washington. Jurors and witnesses often sold these papers at a discount, and the marshals then paid the new holder the full amount. Judge Angel discovered that Deputy Marshal Mariano Barela of Mesilla had participated in this questionable enterprise. Catron borrowed money for Barela and the deputy marshal used these certificates as collateral. These revelations convinced the president to ask for Catron's resignation. Catron complied on October 10, 1878. Sidney A. Barnes of Little Rock, Arkansas, succeeded him. Marshal John Sherman's position remained secure.[48]

In early October the successor to Governor Samuel B. Axtell,

Lewis (Lew) Wallace, arrived in Santa Fe. Using the Angel report he began to study turbulent Lincoln County. On October 3, he requested a report from Marshal John Sherman. The exasperated lawman replied frankly that he held nine unserved murder warrants for the hostile county and that "the disturbed condition of affairs" prevented him from executing any process of the federal courts. He noted that "a desperate class of men," including some outlaws, controlled the county. Two groups were "committing murder in its most revolting form in cold blood and with a reckless disregard of human life that would disgrace savages." The peaceable citizens were "driven out of that country or frightened into abject submission."[49]

Sherman anxiously explained the failure of the marshalcy to enforce the laws in that bloody county. He recalled that "one of my deputy marshals, William Brady, who was also Sheriff of the county of Lincoln was deliberately assassinated at midday while passing along the public street within fifty yards of the court house." Sherman added that he "personally visited the seat of these outrages," but that "the civil power under my control" is insufficient to enforce the laws. He could not "find a reliable deputy who . . . will risk his life" to make arrests, especially with "the feeble force I can place at his disposal." Sherman concluded that, if possible, the new governor should employ federal troops to enforce the laws in Lincoln. Sherman ruled out the territorial militia, since it was "wholly without organization." The marshal discreetly avoided the subject of his former deputy, Robert Widenmann.[50]

Governor Wallace accepted the recommendation of John Sherman, Jr., to employ troops although the executive regretted the need. If President Hayes agreed, he would be required to follow a long procedure, to include a proclamation against the insurgents in Lincoln County. The presidential proclamation placed the county in a state of rebellion and permitted the chief executive to place regular troops at the disposal of the governor. In this way the Posse Comitatus Act, which forbade troops from serving as possemen, was circumvented. On October 7, 1878, Hayes issued the proclamation and General Edward Hatch, the commander of troops in New Mexico, provided the marshal with bluecoats for two months. They could not serve as possemen, but could help the lawmen restore peace. As an additional measure,

Governor Wallace issued a proclamation of amnesty to the feudists.[51]

While the patrols in Lincoln County reassured the peacefully inclined majority, the troops failed to daunt the passionate minority. Mrs. Alexander McSween, a fiery and anguished woman, employed attorney Houston I. Chapman to recover the property of her deceased husband. Chapman became "obsessed with the idea that he was called" to protect the people from the local army garrison, which, he alleged, was a partisan of the Murphy-Dolan faction. James J. Dolan and Jesse Evans murdered the visionary lawyer in February 1879.[52]

This murder infuriated Governor Wallace, who decided to visit the troublesome county. On February 25, Marshal Sherman informed the attorney general that the "necessity for decisive action has just arisen in Lincoln County," and that the governor had "officially" requested him to accompany the official party to Lincoln. Sherman reiterated that he could find no deputy willing to risk his life in that unfortunate region.[53]

Governor Wallace, the federal lawman, and the official party arrived in Lincoln on March 4, 1879, and directed the military commander to arrest thirty-six desperadoes. Secretary of Interior Carl Schurz informed Wallace that, if necessary, the military was empowered to make arrests without warrants since the county was officially in a state of rebellion. The Fort Stanton garrison arrested the elusive Jesse Evans, but he again escaped on March 19 and promptly departed the territory. When Governor Wallace learned that Chapman's complaint about military partisanship was valid, the executive organized a company of territorial militia, the "Lincoln County Mounted Rifles." He assigned the Mounted Rifles the task of assisting the "civil authorities in represssing violence and restoring order." Wallace rightly concluded that the Posse Comitatus Act did not forbid the use of territorial militia, only regulars, in the posses of the marshal.[54]

No sooner had Marshal Sherman returned to Santa Fe, than several new crises occurred. In the summer of 1879, an outbreak of mail robbery and lawlessness erupted in Las Vegas, forty miles east of Santa Fe, in San Miguel County. In July the first locomotive of the Santa Fe Railroad steamed into Las Vegas, and behind it unsavory frontier characters plied their various trades. Sometimes this assortment of infamous desperadoes were called "sporting men"; at other times, the "Dodge City Gang," since many of them won notoriety in the violent Kansas cowtowns.[55]

Several members of the Dodge City Gang worked their way into various law enforcement posts in the Anglo section of Las Vegas, called New Town. An infamous Great Plains character, Hyman G. Neill, alias Hoodoo Brown, became a justice of the peace. He placed his followers in several police positions in New Town—chief of police, Joe Carson; assistant, David Mather, alias Mysterious Dave, a first-rate gunman; and, policeman, David Rudabaugh, a known train robber. Between August and October 1879, the Dodge City Gang, aided and abetted by Hoodoo Brown and colleagues, robbed two stagecoaches and one or possibly two Santa Fe trains.[56]

With Las Vegas in the grips of hardened criminals, Marshal Sherman searched for a man of courage and honesty for the deputyship of New Town. James H. Dunagan applied in August. He informed the federal lawman that he was a Union veteran and a deputy sheriff of San Miguel County (Las Vegas), but he added that he was also familiar in "perticular [sic] with this Teritory [sic] and know almost ever [sic] caracter [sic] in the Teritory [sic]." Dunagan soon disqualified himself; on August 18 he participated in a stagecoach robbery.[57]

Instead of outlaw Dunagan, Marshal John Sherman deputized Mysterious Dave Mather, whom some persons considered equally untrustworthy. Several persons accused him of train robbery, although a Las Vegas editor replied that Mather's enemies charged him maliciously. While this consideration may have influenced Marshal Sherman, by employing a known tough, the lawman profited from the experience of the city fathers of the Kansas cowtowns. These city councils paid the sporting men high salaries as policemen to enforce the laws against their own kind.[58]

During the fall and winter of 1879, John Sherman and his staff, assisted by railroad detectives and Post Office agents, scoured Las Vegas and vicinity for mail robbers. Some bandits operated in aristocratic fashion by traveling in buggies. When Sherman did not personally command, Chief Deputy Charles Conklin or Deputy Mather directed the pursuit. One journalist noted with amazement that, in October, the federal lawman had placed "eleven deputy U.S. marshals in Las Vegas, looking for train robbers." The extraordinary effort paid. The deputies and postal agents arrested a dozen suspects, among them policeman David Rudabaugh.[59]

Among the lesser United States officers involved in these cases was Commissioner Samuel Ellison of Santa Fe who worked closely with Marshal Sherman. Federal statutes required that the marshal's office take all prisoners to the nearest commissioner for examination. If the evidence incriminated the prisoner, this officer bound over the suspect for trial. He was empowered to decide matters of jurisdiction—whether a case should be tried in a federal, or other, court. He also issued warrants, subpoenas, commitments to jail, and he admitted persons to bail. The commissioner was a federal counterpart of the justice of the peace.[60]

The New Mexico marshalcy was hindered by the failure of Congress to appropriate funds for the support of all marshals for fiscal year 1879. Attorney General Charles Devens advised the marshals to negotiate personal loans for their offices, but with no absolute assurance that the government would reimburse them. Devens was gratified when the marshals "faithfully performed their duties" and worked with "zeal and fidelity, . . . notwithstanding the embarrassment under which they labored."[61]

The absence of funds contributed to the failure of Marshal Sherman to halt the illegal traffic of whiskey to the Indians. In November 1880, the Santa Fe *New Mexican* reported several outrages committed by drunken Navajo Indians and added that the tribe could mount three thousand warriors and do "ten times the amount of injury to New Mexico which was inflicted by [the Apache] Victoria [*sic*]." The chief of the Navajos informed the authorities that he could not restrain his braves, unless the whiskey traders were stopped. This statement caused the *New Mexican* to implore the federal officers to take immediate action. "Here is," said the editor, "a rich and powerful tribe of Indians which . . . are almost invited to make war upon our people by the neglect which has been shown by our officers of the law."[62]

In the summer of 1879, the attorney general instructed District Attorney Sidney A. Barnes to investigate the liquor violations. In June 1880, the attorney reported that many problems interfered with the enforcement of the intercourse and revenue laws. Long distances and witnesses' fear of testifying against the illicit traders contributed to the difficulty, but, even more, Marshal Sherman refused to furnish a deputy or detective to work in the Navajo country against the peddlers. Sherman maintained that he had exhausted his funds. In the same month, Barnes reported that he could take no action against the liquor traffic until Marshal Sherman returned from a leave of absence. "He has been absent," moaned the attorney, "for thirty days."[63]

After Congress made a belated appropriation for the marshals in 1880, Sherman quickly joined with the district attorney to prosecute whiskey traders. Under the broad powers of the Department of Justice, the marshals were permitted to exercise powers of detection. Sherman quickly assigned a detective to Navajo County, although Barnes questioned the dependability of Sherman's employee and explained to the attorney general that "it is difficult to secure the services of honest and competent men as detectives." He also added a jab at the officers who evidently recommended this detective. They are "plundering the government," he said in dismay. "Hence it is an uphill business to get anything done promptly and faithfully." In May 1881, Barnes successfully prosecuted several cases of illegal liquor traffic in Albuquerque, and Marshal Sherman informed the *New Mexican* that the session was "a very successful one."[64]

While Sherman worked to stop the illicit peddlers, he was still preoccupied by the Lincoln County War. As the people of the southeastern county returned to their daily routines in late 1878, outlaws from both factions joined forces to prey upon their former employers. Their criminal escapades soon spread across the territory and into western Texas. One group led by Billy the Kid, rustled heavily from John Chisum's herds; the Kid claimed that the baron owed him back wages. The Kid extended the "long rope" into the Texas Panhandle. Another band, the "Wrestlers," (Rustlers?) committed senseless outrages—brutal murders, rapes, and cattle theft. Early in September 1878, badman John Selman assumed leadership of these outlaws, and newspapers sometimes called the Wrestlers the "Selman Scouts." A ring of counterfeiters, led by Tom Cooper, a Lincoln ne'r-do-well, complemented the bands of Bonney and Selman.[65]

Marshal John Sherman anticipated support from the army and militia in Lincoln County, but the troopers failed to capture these outlaws. "I have no faith in the military," wrote Ira F. Leonard, the governor's personal representative in Lincoln County in late March 1879. The army was "too slow" and bound in "too much red tape." Captain Juan Patron's militia failed to assist the new Sheriff and Deputy Marshal, George Kimball. These militiamen trailed banditti furiously but backed off when a battle appeared likely. Governor Wallace deliberately refused to impose martial law—he did not want to humiliate Lincoln County—but strongly considered this measure after these disappointments. "These outlaws cannot be made to quit except by actual war," he informed Secretary of Interior Carl Schurz in April 1879.[66]

When the military failed, Governor Wallace, Marshal Sherman, and other officials, renewed civilian efforts against the freebooters. In April 1879, Wallace informed Secretary of the Interior Schurz that he planned to visit El Paso, in order to cooperate with Texas officers against the outlaws. Post Office and Treasury agents would also assist the local lawmen. While the Texas Rangers were occupied elsewhere, Marshal Stilwell Russell of the Western District of Texas evidently established an office at Fort Stockton and worked with the New Mexico officers. Stilwell deputized at least one, possibly more, citizens of Lincoln County, and permitted them to serve warrants in New Mexico and Texas. One Lincoln pioneer, Lily Klasner, recalled that her fiancee, Robert A. Olinger, became one of Stilwell's deputies. The Texas lawman justified these irregular commissions, Klasner noted, because of the "uncertainty as to the location of the state line between New Mexico and Texas." No doubt Marshal John Sherman approved of this unusual practice, since this remote border area was difficult to police. Klasner added that "the Post Office Department procured the appointment of several United States deputy marshals" at Fort Stockton and that they pursued stagecoach robbers, counterfeiters, and moonshiners along the border of Lincoln County.[67]

As the various police agencies converged upon Lincoln County, Marshal John Sherman strengthened his office there. When Sheriff George Kimball, whom Sherman deputized soon after he assumed the shrievalty early in 1879, "showed little inclination to risk his life chasing outlaws," Sherman employed an additional deputy, Robert A. Olinger, a former Murphy-Dolan partisan. The date and circumstances of this appointment are uncertain, although Sherman probably coordinated the commission with Marshal Russell at Fort Stockton. Lily Klasner recalled, perhaps erroneously, that Olinger received his badge at the Texas post soon after the burning of the McSween house in Lincoln, in July 1878. Just when John Sherman added his commission is uncertain, although Olinger participated in Deputy Marshal Pat Garrett's posse in November 1880. One historian says that Olinger's commission occurred on January 21, 1881, but this was merely a reappointment by Sherman. Whatever the circumstances, the selection of Robert A. Olinger provoked anger in Lincoln. He was a highly controversial man. In March 1880, Deputy Marshal Olinger ran down one band of rustlers, killed outlaw Frank Hill, and delivered Dan Lemons to Fort Stockton. "When a warrant was placed in his hands," recalled Lily Klasner, "he did not hesitate to attempt an arrest, regardless of how desperate the man might be."[68]

In October Treasury Secret Service Agent Azariah F. Wild collect evidence of counterfeiting against associates of Billy the Kid—Tom Cooper and William Wilson. According to Wild, when he asked Sherman for assistance, the lawman refused. In the words of Wild, the marshal replied curtly, "I prefer not to do so." Wild immediately returned to Lincoln County and solicited the aid of Deputy Marshal George Kimball, cattleman J. C. Lea, and a former buffalo hunter, Patrick Floyd Garrett. Garrett assured Wild that he, and several citizens, were willing to form a posse without pay (they were probably thinking about rewards). Wild then approached Marshal Sherman, who, no doubt reassured that there were men of courage in Lincoln County, quickly provided the commissions.[69]

Wild's reports would lead one to believe that he waged a singlehanded campaign against the banditti, but efforts were under way before he arrived in Lincoln County. As early as April 1879, cattle baron John Chisum contacted the governor for aid against Billy the Kid. Chisum regarded the 1880 election for sheriff of his county to be most important in the war on crime. Not only would the new sheriff be a county lawman, but a deputy marshal as well. Chisum supported Patrick Garrett, a Democrat, against Kimball, the incumbent Republican. Garrett won. With Garrett as sheriff, Marshal Sherman would have deputized him without the solicitations of Agent Wild. In his recollections, Garrett does not accord the Treasury man nearly so much credit as Wild bestows upon himself. In fact, the less-than-nimble Secret Service agent became a laughing stock in Lincoln County. A correspondent in White Oaks noted that Wild "told everyone of his [secret] business" in Lincoln County and concluded that Wild was "a rank coward."[70]

Whatever the merits of Secret Agent Wild, Deputy Marshal

Patrick Garrett's posse, with Robert Olinger among them, entered the field against Billy the Kid's band in November 1880. Sherman gave Garrett federal murder warrants for several survivors of the Lincoln County War, including Billy the Kid. Garrett also received assistance from the Texas ranchers who wanted Billy removed. Cattle Detective Charles Siringo represented the LX Ranch and Frank Stewart led a group from the Canadian River Cattleman's Association. Marshal Sherman deputized Stewart and possibly the entire body of men. However, Garrett still directed the pursuit. [71]

The selection of Patrick Garrett to lead the posse of deputy marshals against Billy the Kid proved to a wise decision, although Garrett possessed a streak of remorseless brutality. On the night of December 19, 1880, his posse ambushed the Kid's band in Fort Sumner and killed one member, Tom O'Folliard. The death of the young rustler, the first casualty at the hands of a federal posse in New Mexico, brought home the fact that Marshal Sherman and his deputies were determined to enforce the laws of the United States. Garrett later recalled that O'Folliard lingered several minutes. In hysterical cries the dying bandit shouted: "Don't shoot any more, for God's sake, I'm already killed." One of the deputies bluntly replied, "Take your medicine." [72]

As Garrett closed in on the Kid's band, other posses and cattle detectives joined the pursuit. Then Garrett, who was anxious to complete the task, suddenly realized that the commissions of his posse would expire on January 1, 1881. He quickly dispatched two men to Santa Fe for the renewals, only to discover that Marshal Sherman was in Washington, D.C. District Attorney Barnes frantically telegraphed the attorney general to be to instruct the marshal to wire the commissions. Barnes commented that the people of Lincoln County were "now willing to aid" the federal authorities and that the government should not lose the confidence of the people through a petty oversight. The outraged district attorney could not ignore the opportunity to add an oblique criticism of Marshal Sherman. "I must have prompt assistance to enforce the laws," he said. Barnes need not have worried. On December 23, Deputy Garrett and his posse captured Billy the Kid. [73]

The young outlaw became the center of attraction in the Santa Fe jail, and Marshal Sherman enjoyed taking wide-eyed spectators to gape at the young killer. The Kid finally complained to the governor on March 4, 1881. "I am not treated right by Sherman," he wrote. "He lets every stranger . . . see me through curiosity . . . but will not let a single one of my friends in." The Kid was so distraught that he and train robber David Rudabaugh attempted to dig their way to freedom. Had not Chief Deputy Marshal Tony Neis and Sheriff Romulo Martinez caught them in the act, they would have escaped.[74]

Tony Neis was given the unpleasant job of escorting the Kid and counterfeiter William Wilson to trial at Mesilla. Armed with a shotgun, he and a guard began the journey on March 28, 1881. At the village of Rincon, Neis encountered a mob that demanded that he turn over the Kid. As the ringleaders approached, the deputy marshal took refuge in a saloon and shouted, "You don't get them [prisoners] without somebody being killed." Neis added that he would kill the Kid before he would allow the toughs to take him. The crowd dispersed. "From all accounts," said the Santa Fe *New Mexican*, "Neis bore himself well throughout the trip, but he says he doesn't want to undertake the job again."[75]

The deputy marshal had protected the Kid from probable death, but the outlaw was not so charitable. The Kid was to be tried in a federal court for the death of William "Buckshot" Roberts on the Mescalero Indian Reservation in April 1878, but his defense attorney proved that the house in which Roberts was killed was merely on, not a part of, federal property. He was, therefore, tried on the territorial side of court and sentenced to hang in Lincoln. The Kid remained under federal protection until the date of execution, and Marshal Sherman assigned Deputy Marshals Robert Olinger and James W. Bell to guard him. The Kid hated Olinger, and killed both men in a jailbreak at Lincoln on April 28, 1881.[76]

For several months the Kid eluded federal lawmen and threatened to kill several prominent men, including Marshal Sherman. On May 5, the *New Mexican* reported that the Kid intended to leave the territory, but not before he paid his "respects to Governor Wallace and U.S. Marshal Sherman." The bandit failed to keep his promise since, on the night of July 14, Deputy Marshal Garrett killed him at Fort Sumner. The young bandit had killed, or participated in the deaths of, three of Sherman's deputies.[77]

While Marshal Sherman and his deputies concluded the pursuit of the last Lincoln County freebooters, a violent disturbance erupted in the opposite corner of his district. In the late 1870s, migrants erected isolated settlements—Farmington, Aztec, and Bloomfield—in the San Juan River Valley in the western corner of

Rio Arriba County. Bandits and rustlers, most notably a wild gunman from Colfax County, William Porter (Port) Stockton, became very troublesome. On January 10, 1881, the vigilantes of Farmington—some were refugees from faraway Lincoln County—killed the rustler. Isaac Stockton, brother of the deceased outlaw, vowed revenge and conducted raids against these isolated communities from the safety of Colorado. By late March the feudists had constrained peaceful citizens to take sides, and Governor Wallace instructed Marshal Sherman to take action. After an examination of the crimes committed, Sherman and the territorial executive concluded reluctantly that the marshal did not have authority to interfere. The brigands had not violated the federal laws. On April 8, Wallace explained this decision to the secretary of the interior, but he expressed a willingness to cooperate with the marshal if a legitimate charge could be found against Ike Stockton.[78]

The order to probe the San Juan County War revealed the peculiar position of Marshal Sherman, as well as that of his colleagues in other territories. While the jurisdiction of his counterparts in the states was clear, the marshal in the territories often participated in trouble not definitely within his purview. Washington could justify a directive to interlope on several grounds. Since the territories were wards of Congress, and not sovereign states, the federal government provided them with extra protection. Furthermore, the law enforcement agencies of the territories—especially the county shrievalties—lacked resources. They were apt to falter, fail, or become hopelessly partisan (as in Lincoln County). In the absence of a territorial law enforcement agency equivalent to the Texas Rangers, the United States marshals had to interfere. If a pretext were required, the federal lawman merely "investigated" the disturbance to determine whether federal laws were violated.

Since Marshal Sherman could not interfere in Rio Arriba, Governor Wallace went elsewhere for support. In March 1881, the executive ordered Adjutant Max Frost to organize two companies of militia in the turbulent county, a procedure that circumvented the Posse Comitatus Act. The energetic governor also asked the executive of Colorado, where outlaw Isaac Stockton resided, to deliver him to the New Mexican authorities. But Stockton soon resisted arrest at Durango, Colorado, and died of wounds on September 27.[79]

Not all of Marshal Sherman's duties were as violent as the county wars. In August 1881, while the San Juan County War raged, Marshal Sherman informed his superior in Washington that he had just "declined" to execute a writ of replevin in the case of the *U. S. v. Watson and Levy.* The defendants had illegally cut public timber, in order to make railroad crossties. They valued the timber at $90,000. Sherman noted that before he could seize the timber he must, according to territorial law, post a bond twice the value of the replevined property. Although District Attorney Barnes advised him to serve the process without a bond, the uneasy lawman reiterated to the attorney general that he would "continue to decline until a proper bond is tendered me" by the United States government. [80]

The attorney general could not understand the qualms of the marshal and bluntly directed him to "proceed with the execution." "You will incur no responsibility," he assured the lawman, "for the law does not require United States [officers] to give bond." With this reassurance, Sherman complied quickly. On August 30, he notified his superior, "I have seized one hundred thousand railroad ties." This incident, seemingly minor, illustrated the great gulf between the marshal and his chief in Washington. Sherman was well aware of the hostility of many New Mexicans to outsiders, such as himself, and more especially to federal officers. Before he would risk a suit in a territorial court, he desired the reassurance of the attorney general. [81]

By 1880, the range of the marshal's duties had expanded all over the nation and the number of complaints about the officers had increased correspondingly. A House Committee on Expenditures, which investigated the Department of Justice, found that the lawmen and their subordinates "charged for arrests that were not made; for travel that was not performed; for expenses that were not incurred; [and] for guards that were not employed." The list of abuses also included misappropriation of public funds and "fee making." The report of this committee concluded with a ringing admonition: "We cannot expect the people to have an affection for the Government . . . when the officers [of the courts] . . . convert the machinery of the courts into an engine of oppression."[82]

These disclosures affected the future of the United States marshals' offices. A permanent corps of examiners, sponsored by the Department of Justice, soon visited each marshal regularly, examined his books, and issued detailed reports to the attorney general. They recommended reappointment or dismissal. In 1882, Examiner Joel Bowman visited Marshal Sherman but evidently found his office acceptable.[83]

Bowman did find, however, a great deal of dissatisfaction with the marshal on the part of the people. In June 1879, a Dona Ana County panel had accused Sherman of "habitually" neglecting to serve process and summon witnesses. Further, he permitted arrested persons to walk about freely with their firearms. A Santa Fe grand jury censured the lawman for failure to do his duties in court. In November 1877, the Mesilla *News* reported that the marshal failed to pay jurors, while Singleton M. Ashenfelter of the *Grant County Herald* accused the lawman of being drunk in court.[84]

The failure of the marshal to curb the liquor traffic among the Indians aroused the most criticism. "Pretty nearly every paper in the territory has at one time or another had its say on the subject of liquor selling to the Indians," observed the Albuquerque *Evening Review:*

> this subject is one of the most important that has ever attracted the attention of the press of the territory. The Navajo Indians have in the past two years committed murders, robbed the mails and indulged in other outrages which could be directly traced to their use of liquor and neither they nor those from whom they obtained the crazing poison have ever been punished. . . . *The Review* can explain it in a few words.
>
> The prosecution and punishment of those who violate the law . . . rests entirely in the hands of one man, U.S. Marshal John Sherman, who . . . has positively shirked the necessary trouble that would attend the arrest [of the malcontents].

Elsewhere in its pages, the *Review* grumbled, "U.S. Marshal Sherman can arrest an unresisting woman but he is not duty-lover enough to go out to Gallup . . . and arrest the scoundrels there who sell the Navajoes whiskey."[85]

These charges, with many others, persuaded the Department of Justice to consider removing the marshal. Within the Republican party some discontent had been expressed against him. The editor of the Albuquerque *Evening Review* charged that Sherman was disloyal to the party. He "belonged to a certain clique of [liberal] republicans, who wanted to reform the party by appointing democrats to office." The editor was thinking of the appointment of the controversial Deputy Marshal Robert A. Widenmann, an active Democrat. Furthermore, a scandal occurred involving the marshal's influential uncle, Secretary of the Treasury John Sherman, with an accompanying loss of patronage. On March 2, 1882, Marshal John E. Sherman, Jr., resigned.[86]

It is unfortunate that John Sherman, Jr.'s, reputation rests upon his failure to field effective posses in the Lincoln County War. Many obstacles frustrated him. The attorney general possessed few funds for the expense of posses (the Department of Justice remained a judiciary and not a detective agency). The suppression of rebellions, and Lincoln County was in rebellion in 1878, was a matter for the president and the army. Marshal Sherman was sincere when he informed Governor Wallace in October 1878 that he could field only a "feeble force" against the insurrectionists. After the feud had quietened, the marshalcy resumed its presence in Lincoln County in the form of Deputy Marshal Patrick Garrett's posse.[87]

Many of Marshal Sherman's problems in Lincoln County arose because of events beyond his control. The Democratic-controlled Congress struck directly at the marshalcies through partisan legislation—the Posse Comitatus. Act, the failure to pay the marshals one year, and stringent budgets for the Department of Justice. In New Mexico, the federal lawman groped with numerous outbreaks of lawlessness—not just that in Lincoln County. Every region of his district experienced serious violence. Time and distance also defeated Sherman's efforts to place posses in the field in a timely fashion.

In spite of these handicaps, John Sherman, Jr., introduced a measure of independence and professionalism into the New Mexico marshalcy. In a show of some fortitude, he refused to follow the lead of the Santa Fe Ring during the Lincoln County War. Sherman assumed this position, even though United States District Attorney Thomas B. Catron led the Ring. When the marshal reappointed Deputy Marshal Widenmann over the objections of Governor Samuel Axtell (also a member of the clique), Sherman acted very courageously. Sherman's behavior surpassed that of his predecessor, John Pratt, who had acted partisanly in the Colfax County War. By rising above political considerations, Sherman set a healthy precedent for his successors.

7

The Arizona Marshalcy, 1876–82

When Francis H. Goodwin stepped down from the Arizona marshalcy in August 1876, many Arizonans hoped that the turbulence and instability characteristic of that federal post had ended. Unfortunately, the problem of concerted lawlessness that plagued neighboring New Mexico was not unique. Arizona's federal lawmen encountered similar disturbances. In the decade after the Civil War, the population and wealth of Arizona grew considerably. New settlements of miners and farmers sprang up overnight in the 1870s, much to the dismay of the marshals who lacked financial resources to protect them. Conflicts also occurred between new arrivals and marshals, especially when the lawmen attempted to protect the Indians. The spectacle of the ludicrous trial of the Camp Grant murderers was still fresh in the minds of the Federal officers. By the mid 1870s roving bands of highwaymen, who always accompanied the law-abiding frontiersmen, threatened to sever Arizona's communications with the outside world. The haphazard enforcement of the laws by marshals Edward Phelps, Isaac Q. Dickason, and Francis Goodwin was partly responsible for this development.

The growth of Arizona's population and wealth in the 1870s was revealed in the addition of two new counties, Maricopa and Pinal, to the original counties—Mohave, Yuma, Yavapai, and Pima. Just north of the Gila River, and astride the Salt River, Maricopa County was created in 1871. Phoenix, laid out around an ancient Indian irrigation system, was the county seat. In the western portion of the county, an important mining district already existed around the Vulture Mine. The legislature provided for Pinal

County, to the south of the Gila, in 1875. While it also contained potential farming lands, this district, with its seat at Florence, consisted of wealthy mining properties. Some of these mineral lands were, however, a part of the San Carlos (White Mountain) Indian Reservation.

In spite of this growth, Arizona's settlements remained terribly isolated, and "the problem of transportation" was "a key factor" in the welfare of the territory. Great freighting firms, such as the company of Pinckney Randolph Tully and Estevan Ochoa, and the impressive operation of Dr. Charles H. Lord and W. W. Williams, not only provided links with the outside but also exercised extraordinary political influence. These men, and their lesser competitors, were especially sensitive to any disruption of their business empires. They became very vocal when bands of highwaymen began to disrupt communications in Arizona.

If ever banditti were accused of disrupting a young economy, the highwaymen of Arizona Territory from 1877 to 1882 earned that distinction. A precise count of the stagecoach and mailcoach robberies is hardly possible, but thirty-six holdups is a conservative figure. The loss in currency and bullion (a five-hundred-pound bar of gold on one occasion) totaled thousands of dollars. Many of these highwaymen were Mexican citizens who sought refuge in Sonora. Others were Americans who had been driven from nearby states or territories.[1]

They were a motley group of misfits—atypical of the sturdy frontiersmen—who had failed to meet the standards of the West. Among Arizona's badmen was William Brazzleton, a hoodlum and killer at fifteen. He entered Arizona from California in 1876 as the proprietor of a show troupe; he claimed that he could swallow a wagon wheel. With disguises he had learned as an actor, Brazzleton began a series of stagecoach robberies in 1878. He was killed in August after betrayal by one of his comrades. It was said that Brazzleton looked dangerous even in death.[2]

Such brigandage brought loud outcries from Arizona's business community. In May 1877, the "official" Republican newspaper, the Prescott *Arizona Miner*, complained that stage robberies were occurring as frequently as had "Indian murders" a few years earlier. The newspaperman lamented that "travel in Arizona will be entirely suspended by capitalists." Associate Justice Charles Silent reiterated these forebodings to the attorney general when he observed that "this lawlessness . . . is paralyzing business." Crawley P. Dake, who became marshal in 1878, noted that these robberies "have caused much inconvenience . . . to the businessmen," while William M. Griffith, superintendent of a local stageline, observed a businessman cancel a trip to Arizona, when he learned that three robberies had just occurred on his route. Said one downcast editor, "This is only [one] instance of the injury resulting to our territory" from banditry.[3]

This problem preoccupied the marshals in the late 1870s and early 1880s. The outbreak occurred in the marshalcy of Wiley W. Standefer, a former deputy marshal, who succeeded Francis H. Goodwin on August 15, 1876. Standefer was a Georgian who had ranches in California before moving his herd to Arizona. He dabbled in mining and accepted the post of undersheriff of Yavapai County. No doubt the selection of Standefer as marshal was a result of his close association with Marshal Francis H. Goodwin, also a Georgian, and Goodwin's friendship with Governor Anson Safford.[4]

After two years in office, Standefer was replaced by Crawley P. Dake, who was appointed on June 12, 1878. A native of Ontario, Dake grew up in New York and moved to Michigan in 1855. He opened a general store, and when the Civil War erupted, raised a company of volunteers for the Union Army. He served until he received a serious leg wound; he suffered repeatedly from this injury throughout his life. Dake had held public office in Michigan and had been an unsuccessful candidate for Congress. Just before accepting the marshalcy of Arizona, he served as chief deputy marshal in Detroit. Although Governor John P. Hoyt of Arizona objected to the appointment of Dake, the influence of Michigan's delegation to Washington (Senators Zachariah Chandler and T. W. Terry, among others) won the day.[5]

Marshal Wiley Standefer, who first experienced the outbreak of banditry, pursued the highwaymen energetically. Standefer was noted in the field in February 1877, with the famous Indian scout Al Sieber as a guide. The pair was again on the trail of outlaws in April and May. On one occasion Marshal Standefer and his posse met bandits in a violent encounter in Ehrenberg. The lawmen wounded one outlaw and captured a second man who, much to the amazement of Standefer, was found to be an undercover agent for the Post Office Department.[6]

The active marshal took time out to officiate at the execution of convicted murderer James Malone on March 15, 1878. This task, another of the unpleasant duties of a federal lawman, was the first such official execution under a federal court order in Arizona. The editor of the *Miner* admitted that "the punishment seems almost barbarous, but . . . he [Malone] committed a most brutal and inhuman murder."[7]

The energy with which Wiley W. Standefer pursued the high-waymen gratified many Arizonans. Then his office became involved in the case of Jack Swilling. Swilling, who was accused of mailcoach robbery near Wickenburg on April 19, 1878, was one of the territory's best-loved pioneers. In May the territorial authorities arrested Swilling and Andrew Kirby, but soon dropped charges so that the federal courts could assume the case (and the costs). Deputy Marshal Joseph W. Evans presented the sheriff at Prescott with warrants for the two men and escorted them to Yuma.[8]

Friends of Swilling were incensed when they learned that Deputy Evans obtained custody of Swilling and Kirby with warrants authorized by a United States commissioner, a very lowly official in the eyes of the Arizonans. Outraged by the highhanded manner in which the federal authorities had overridden the territorial officers, the editor of the *Miner* observed that in the future "all that will be needed to release a person under [territorial] indictment . . . will be to have him charged with some offense before a U. S. Commissioner."[9]

In spite of these objections, Deputy Joseph Evans delivered his prisoners to the Yuma jail. In August the two men were bound over by the commissioner for trial in October. However, the unsanitary conditions of the jail and the intense desert heat aggravated Swilling's chronic ill health. He died in his cell on August 12. To his friends, Swilling was a martyr to the oppressiveness of federal justice. An official statement left by the alleged outlaw stated that, at the age of twenty-three, he had been hit on the head and shot and that recurring headaches drove him crazy on occasions. After commenting about Swilling's "prostrate condition" when he arrived at the local jail, the Yuma *Exposition* maintained that the old pioneer was innocent of the federal charges. On October 5, Deputy Marshal Joseph Evans authorized the Yuma jailer to release Swilling's cellmate, Andrew Kirby, who was also innocent of the robbery charge. Said the editor of the *Arizona Sentinel*:

Now, what compensates this man for his six months weary confinement, and for the long days of such anguish as is always suffered by an innocent man accused of crime and treated like a felon?. . .All the evidence against these men was circumstantial though it was strong. This case should forever be a warning against hasty convictions of guilt, except upon the clearest direct evidence.[10]

Entering the marshalcy under the shadow of Jack Swilling's death did not comfort Crawley P. Dake, who succeeded Wiley W. Standefer in the summer of 1878. Many citizens wanted some sort of retribution for the unsavory affair, and they demanded that Dake fire his ambitious deputy, Joseph W. Evans. When the new lawman informed newspapers that he would retain Evans, the *Miner* commented: "We question very much the veracity of the statement." Yet, Dake stood his ground against the hostile public and appointed deputies in whom he had confidence—J. E. Anderson, the assistant secretary of the territory; Andrew Tyner, sheriff of Yuma County; and Edward F. Bowers, sheriff of Yavapai County. In the last instance, it was noted that this appointment would "enable the sheriff to make arrests where the United States is a plantiff." Dake appointed eight deputies in all.[11]

The new marshal took a keen interest in the physical organization of his office. He quickly made his official bonds, having acquired the signatures of several influential men. He brought with him two men who were qualified to set up the books and the bureaucratic procedures of a marshal's office. These efforts persuaded one editor to conclude that the marshalcy would finally "amount to something." Previously, the marshal was regarded as "a rather small personage." In September the *Miner* noted that Dake, "efficient in his various duties," had opened his office in the "octagonal building occupied by Dr. W. E. Day."[12]

Dake had entered his district under the pressure of a letter from Acting Attorney General Samuel F. Phillips who, in June 1878, informed him that the examination of a band of mail robbers could not begin until he disbursed the necessary funds. A Yuma editor responded to this news with the pertinent question, "How can a new Marshal do anything till he gets money? An Arizona Marshal's jawbone has become rather poor currency." However, Dake was unexplainably delayed until August 18. He found the situation most alarm-

ing—five robberies had occurred that month. The banditti, wrote
Dake, seemed to be organized, divided into bands, and stationed on
the principal routes of transportation. Would the Department of Justice, he queried, allow him to incur the expense of a posse? The acting
attorney general agreeably allowed "reasonable" expenses.[13]

The bureaucratic procedure involved in acquiring permission
and financial support for the arrest of bandits hampered Marshal
Dake throughout his term. Since the Department of Justice
considered the occurrence of highway robbery an exception to the
rule of law and order (obviously not the case in Arizona), the
lawman was required to ask for special funds for the pursuit of
bandits after each robbery. In October 1881, Deputy Marshal
Joseph W. Evans explained this regulation to governor Luis Torres
of Sonora when he advised the Mexican that he could do nothing
against highwaymen without "special instructions" from Washington. Though telegraphic communications were rapid, the loss of
even a few hours permitted highwaymen to flee to the mountains
or into Mexico.[14]

Marshal Dake refused to wait for instructions in September
1878, when bandits struck a stagecoach. He posted a $500 reward,
a procedure that Governor Anson Safford had earlier found effective. Realizing that he was without the authority to offer rewards,
he wrote his superiors in Washington: "If I am to protect the
people, I must have funds to do it." The success of the marshal in
causing the arrest of these bandits did not move the officials in the
national capital to ease the restrictions upon Dake; the outmoded
method of administration continued, although Associate Justice
Charles Silent implored Attorney General Charles Devens to allow
Dake "some extraordinary discretion" in the pursuit of bandits.
The attorney general likewise ignored similar requests by Governor John P. Hoyt and the editor of the *Miner*.[15]

By fall 1878, the marshal, the territorial authorities, and the
Mexican government began to cooperate against the banditti. In
late September the *Arizona Miner* congratulated Marshal Dake
and Governor Hoyt for their attempts to extradite outlaws from
Mexico; and the editor praised Governor Marisal of Sonora "who
has ever shown the kindliest disposition toward the United States."
Dake dispatched a deputy to Sonora for several of the marauders,
while, with or without permission of the Mexican governor, his
posse comitatus crossed the international boundary in pursuit of

highwaymen who had stolen five hundred pounds of silver bullion. These successes were marred only by the tragic loss of two deputy marshals, J. H. Adams and Cornelius Finley. A band of outlaws murdered them south of Tucson on September 2. Marshal Dake had appointed them only ten days earlier at the insistence of Judge Charles Silent, who considered Adams "one of the bravest and coolest men" in the Southwest. Dake informed one journalist that he had "lost a very valuable assistant and the government an officer whose like cannot readily be met with."[16]

Like his colleague John Sherman in New Mexico, Crawley P. Dake encountered the nagging restrictions of the Posse Comitatus Act in a time of crisis. The act imposed severe limitations upon the freedom of the marshal to employ regulars for the pursuit of freebooters in Arizona. The editor of the *Arizona Citizen*, John P. Clum, voiced the disgust of many inhabitants of the territory:

> At least 500 cavalry are stationed in Arizona. We have no Indians to fight now; no trouble in the territory except that caused by the whosesale operations of highwaymen. . . . But alas! here is the same old story—an emergency . . . and yet the army can't come. . . . What a protection.[17]

The residents of other territories—especially Wyoming—shared the dismay of Arizonans and wrote angry letters to Washington. After the president of the Union Pacific Railroad, Jay Gould, complained in Washington about train robbers on his line, the cabinet met in a hasty session. This august body concluded that, indeed, regular troops could be employed to patrol mail routes and to defend government property, but that the Posse Comitatus Act forbade the participation of the army in offensive, or pursuit, activities. With this new construction of the controversial act, General Orlando G. Willcox authorized his forces to assist Marshal Dake in the protection of the mails. Some alarmists expressed concern that Willcox was usurping civilian powers. The *Miner* reassured them that the military had no desire to take away the authority of Marshal Dake and that, on the contrary, "the United States marshals . . . have accomplished a great deal more lately [against the brigands] than the public is yet aware of."[18]

Although the pursuit of the banditti along the international boundary promoted some cooperation between Marshal Dake and the Mexican authorities, the two forces were soon at odds. In

1879, the Mexican government refused to release fugitives the marshal wanted for the murder of deputies Adams and Finley. Later, Dake notified the attorney general that his deputies had recently captured two stagecoach robbers but that two others fled to Mexico. "Shall I go after them?" asked the officer, anxious to clean this humiliating blot from his office. "No!" replied his superior, "do not cross into Mexico." In mid summer the miffed lawman vented his anger on Washington, after bandits robbed three coaches and again escaped to Mexico. The marshal protested that he was cooperating with the several agencies—Wells, Fargo and Company detectives and local law officers—but that the Sonoran officials were protecting the raiders.[19]

Among the many problems that hindered Crawley Dake, none was as irksome as the frustration of an inadequate budget (Congress failed to fund the marshals in 1879.) In connection with his complaint about uncooperative Mexican authorities, Dake wrote that the cost of pursuit of the road agents was enormous. "It is disheartening to me to expend much more money," he wrote, "not knowing whether it will meet with the approval of the accounting officers of the Treasury [Department]."[20]

The reply of Attorney General Charles Devens was not encouraging. Devens informed Dake that only funds for actual court expenses would be furnished. He added that the postmaster general was authorized to pay the actual expenses (a policy not calculated to recruit possemen) of the marshals who pursued mail robbers. Marshal Dake must have been gratified to hear that his close friend and patron in Congress, Senator Zachariah Chandler, proposed to advance the attorney general $100,000 to pay the expenses of the marshals. (The failure of Congress to appropriate money for law and order had outraged the Michigan politician.) In June 1879, the marshal received instructions to apply his remaining funds to the trial of prisoners then in jail, and a few days later the lawman directed his deputies to incur no expenses on the credit of the United States courts. To publicize the deplorable condition of the marshalcy in Arizona, Dake permitted the territorial newspapers to reprint his correspondence with Washington.[21]

New problems arose on the international boundary in the summer of 1880, when unsuccessful bands of Mexican revolutionaries began to seek refuge in southern Arizona. Led by Brigido Reyes and Manuel Marquez, "the noted Pronunciado [revolutionary]," the agitators from south of the border hoped to reorganize and recruit new members. This violation of the American neutrality laws was rather serious since the revolutionaries could have provoked war between the two nations. General Orlando B. Willcox "requested" that Marshal Dake investigate the matter. Dake informed Attorney General Devens about Willcox's appeal and appended a request for funds for the purpose of arresting the band of Reyes and Marquez. By mid August, the resourceful Deputy Joseph W. Evans had captured nine of the Mexican dissidents.[22]

In an effort to direct the pursuit personally, Marshal Dake put in an appearance in Tucson. The *Citizen* noted the arrival of the lawman on August 28 and added that Dake planned to take measures to prevent Brigido Reyes from leading any future raids into Sonora from Arizona. The lawman was pleased with his deputies, who had cooperated closely with Governor Luis Torres of Sonora. Torres congratulated Evans and his comrades for the arrest of the nine dissidents and added that he would not initiate extradition proceedings if they had to be punished in the United States. On September 11, Dake's subordinates captured one Martinez, another leader of the rebels. Five of the Mexicans, including Martinez, were tried in federal court and sentenced to prison. In early 1881, the marshal's brother, Deputy Albert Dake, delivered them to prison in Detroit, Michigan, then the place of confinement for Arizona's federal charges.[23]

The storm of events on the international boundary left no time for the marshal to rest on his laurels. In December 1878, and again in the next year, the Mexican government complained about American outlaws who stole Mexican cattle and sold the stock in Arizona. Secretary of Interior Carl Schurz informed John C. Fremont, Governor of Arizona, who, in turn, investigated the charges. Fremont denied the imputations and accused the Mexican government of permitting outlaws to use Sonora as a lair from which to raid Arizona. Some months before Fremont's report, the *Arizona Citizen* noted that both Mexicans and Americans were stealing horses from the Santa Cruz Valley and driving them into Sonora. The editor admitted that some of these looters probably stole Mexican stock on their return trips to Arizona.[24]

These Anglo raiders, later called the "Cowboys," troubled the officers of both governments for several years. In January 1879, Governor Fremont reported that the American outlaws numbered about a hundred and were led by Robert Martin. His name soon disappeared from this roster of rogues, however, and Newman H. (Old Man) Clanton became the alleged leader of the rustlers. His sons, Phineas (Phin), Isaac (Ike), and William (Billy), figured prominently in the band, along with the brothers Thomas and Frank McLaury, William "Curly Bill" Brocius, Johnny Ringo, and many others. While these men confined their lawless activities to rustling, other Cowboys specialized in stagecoach robbery around the new boom town of Tombstone in southern Pima County. It is difficult to determine whether these brigands were members of the same band and answered the dictates of Old Man Clanton. The most unfortunate aspect of this Cowboy outbreak was that the newspapers failed to distinguish the common, hardworking drovers from the outlaw "Cowboys."[25]

By 1880, the depredations of the Cowboys were seriously menacing the inhabitants of the southern portion of Pima County. Cattlemen grumbled that lynch law might have to be applied. Sheriff Charles Shibell of Tucson exercised little authority in that district, and the residents of the new mining camp of Tombstone soon demanded a separate county. One of the promoters of Tombstone, Councilman William Kidder Meade, successfully introduced a bill into the assembly to provide for a separate county—Cochise. In January 1881, Governor Fremont appointed as sheriff John H. Behan, a Democrat and son of a former Missouri slaveholder. Behan had served as sheriff of Yavapai County (Prescott) from 1871 to 1873 and earned a reputation for bravery in several manhunts.[26]

The appointment of a Democrat to the sheriff's office of Cochise County would cause problems later. Wyatt B. S. Earp, a Republican and an aspirant to the shrievalty, was among the losers. Earp possessed a reputation as a peace officer, as well as that of a professional gambler and saloon man. Born in Illinois in 1848, Earp served as constable of Lamar, Missouri, and as a policeman in Wichita and Dodge City, Kansas. His political aspirations caused him to lose the Wichita position, since he attempted to influence the outcome of the election for city marshal and to place his brothers on the police force. The fact that he had been arrested for horsetheft in the Indian Territory did not prevent him from serving as a shotgun messenger for Wells, Fargo and Company in the Dakota Territory, New Mexico, and Tombstone. One authority asserts that Wyatt and his brothers moved to Tombstone to open a stagecoach line. Whatever their motives, the brothers devoted much time to gambling and to investment in mining property and real estate.[27]

Although Wyatt Earp was the most conspicuous of the brothers in Tombstone, his older brother Virgil, already a deputy to Crawley P. Dake, provided the official capacity for much of their aggressiveness. A Civil War veteran, Virgil drove a stagecoach in Nebraska but soon followed Wyatt to Dodge City. Then in 1877, he moved to Prescott, Arizona, where he drove a mail wagon and worked some mining and timber property. He acquired a reputation for bravery when he assisted the city marshal in the arrest of some Texas desperadoes. The Prescott *Arizona Miner* noted that Virgil's Winchester rifle was the most effective weapon in the city force. He killed one of the outlaws. From September to December 1879, he was nightwatchman for Prescott. In November, Marshal Dake deputized him for Tombstone.[28]

Tombstone was hardly the place for an aspiring deputy marshal to take roots, but Virgil Earp moved his family to the silver town in December 1879. Wyatt and Morgan, a younger brother, accompanied him. Deputy Virgil Earp served actively. In March 1880, he arrested a suspected counterfeiter, only to see him escape from the flimsy jail. The following year he informed Governor John C. Fremont by military telegraph that one of his colleagues, Deputy A. F. Burke, was in desperate need of extradition papers at Hermosillo, Mexico. Burke had trailed a violator of the revenue laws to that place. When Tombstone authorities required assistance, Virgil Earp was always willing to aid. In October 1880, after "Curly Bill" Brocius killed city Marshal Fred White, Virgil, Wyatt, and Morgan Earp escorted Brocius to Tucson in order to avoid a lynching. Virgil Earp was also appointed an assistant city marshal, to hold office until a special election on November 13, 1880. Virgil stood for election to the vacant post, only to lose by about fifty votes. At the regular election in the following January, Virgil again lost.[29]

The Cowboys had little to fear from the authorities in Cochise County, in spite of Virgil Earp's attention to duty. Mutual hostility had arisen between Sheriff John H. Behan and Wyatt Earp when the latter failed to receive the appointment as sheriff. (Wyatt did serve a short stint as deputy sheriff.) This hatred affected Virgil's views as well. Numerous stage and mailcoach robberies occurred in the stricken county as a consequence of the division between the local and federal lawmen. Robberies were carried out in March, September, and October, 1881, and also in January of the following year. Having lost $9,000 to the banditti, Wells, Fargo and Company temporarily closed service between Tombstone and Benson. Deputy Virgil Earp did not let the robberies go unnoticed. After the March 1881 holdup, he and his brothers took to the field:

> Tres Alamos, Arizona
> March 21, 1881
>
> C. P. Dake, U. S. Marshall [sic]
> I left the night the stage was stopped with two of my brothers and Bill [Bat] Masterson. Have not lost a foot print [of the bandits]. Have caught one. Will follow as long as I can find a track.
>
> V. W. Earp
> Deputy Marshal

This chase was frustrating for Deputy Virgil Earp, who led his posse over one thousand miles and made only one arrest. The *Miner* reported that they "fasted" over one hundred and six hours on this jaunt into the desert. "Their intention was good," commented the editor, "but their luck was bad." The journalist nonetheless praised Virgil Earp as "an active officer" who was after "the blood of the highwaymen."[30]

The Cowboys did not confine their raids to Cochise County but continued to maraud nearby Mexico. In a letter to the American secretary of state, dated April 1881, Mexican Ambassador M. de Zamacona enclosed newspaper clippings from Arizona newspapers to confirm the "outrages" by American bandits on Mexican soil. One item reported an alleged raid into Mexico by Billy the Kid. In July the ambassador protested an illegal arrest on his native soil by the sheriff from Tombstone, evidently meaning John H. Behan. An English employee of a mining company in Sonora reported a Cowboy attack upon Mexican traders, probably referring to the ambush and murder of four Mexicans about August 1 and the theft of $4,000. A few days later, the highwaymen murdered a representative of Governor Pesqueira of Sonora as he was en route to Tombstone.[31]

The Mexicans retaliated vigorously. In June 1881, citizens of

Charles P. Clever, Marshal of New Mexico (1858–62). Courtesy the Photographic Collections, Museum of New Mexico, Santa Fe.

Albert W. Archibald, Marshal of New Mexico (1861), did not serve. Courtesy Library: State Historical Society of Colorado, Denver.

The Romero Brothers, Las Vegas, New Mexico. Seated, left to right: Hilario, Trinidad, Eugenio. Standing, left to right: Benigno and Margarito. Courtesy Denver Public Library, Western Collection.

Creighton M. Foraker, Marshal of New Mexico (1897–1912). Courtesy Miss Mary Foraker, Albuquerque.

Creighton M. Foraker and staff (ca. 1908). Foraker, seated center; Fred Fornoff, seated left; Frank Hall, standing right. Courtesy Miss Mary Foraker, Albuquerque.

Secundino Romero, Marshal of New Mexico (1912, 1921–26). Courtesy Denver Public Library, Western Collection.

Milton B. Duffield, Marshal of Arizona (1863–66). Courtesy Arizona Historical Society, Tucson.

George Tyng, Marshal of Arizona (1874), seated left. Courtesy Laurence P. James, Denver.

Francis H. Goodwin, Marshal of Arizona (1874–76). Courtesy Arizona Historical Society, Tucson.

Crawley P Dake, Marshal of Arizona (1878 82). Courtesy Arizona Historical Society, Tucson.

Zan L. Tidball, Marshal of Arizona (1882–85). Courtesy Arizona Historical Society, Tucson.

William Kidder Meade, Marshal of Arizona (1885–90, 1893–97). Courtesy Arizona Historical Society, Tucson.

Robert H. Paul, Marshal of Arizona
(1890–93). Courtesy Arizona Historical
Society, Tucson.

William M. Griffith, Marshal of Arizona (1897–
1901). Courtesy Arizona Historical Society, Tucson.

Myron H. McCord, Marshal of Arizona
(1901–5). Courtesy Arizona Historical Society,
Tucson.

Benjamin F. Daniels, Marshal of Arizona
(1905–9). Courtesy Arizona Historical Society,
Tucson.

Charles A. Overlock, Marshal of Arizona
(1909–14). Courtesy Arizona Historical Society, Tucson.

Fronteras, Sonora, killed four American bandits. A few weeks later, Mexican soldiers killed outlaw leader Newman H. Clanton along with bandit Jim Crane and two unidentified Anglos. The Mexican government also dispatched a claims commission to repossess stock stolen by the Papago Indians of southern Arizona.[32]

Influential Arizonans soon demanded that Marshal Dake make a stronger contribution to the war on banditry. In March 1881, the editor of the Tucson *Daily Arizona Journal* asked how a hundred bandits could terrorize the best system of government in the world and queried, "Can not the marshal summon a *posse* [*comitatus*] and throttle those ruffians?" The *Miner* reported that the stock association of southern Arizona was so hard pressed by losses to the rustlers that its members were considering "summary measures." A few days later, the same newspaper characterized the efforts of all law enforcement agencies as "feeble" and pleaded that someone call the attention of the president to the situation. The *Tombstone Epitaph* urged vigilante action.[33]

These many complaints slowly filtered through the administrative machinery in the national capitol, and eventually back to Marshal Dake. In May 1881, Acting Governor John J. Gosper reported to Secretary of Interior Samuel J. Kirkwood that the marshal urgently needed funds to pursue the Cowboys. Word evidently reached Attorney General Wayne MacVeagh who, in June 1881, instructed the marshal to "arrest the Cowboys," but said nothing about the request for funds. In August, Dake again requested financial assistance; however, his superior refused and added that the marshal must reduce his official debt below his penalty bond of $20,000 before an appropriation could be made.[34]

In a valiant effort to comply with this stipulation, the marshal asked for and received permission to raise an additional bond while his current accounts were being processed and approved. Although Territorial Chief Justice Charles French approved the second bond, as late as December 2, 1881, the marshal had received no additional funds. Furthermore, Justice French's independent approval of Dake's bond was not strictly legal since the entire territorial supreme court was required to review the application.[35]

While the marshal arranged for a new bond, acting Governor Gosper investigated the troubles of Tombstone. In September 1881, he informed Secretary of Interior Kirkwood that Arizona contained "a small army of outlaws well armed and fully able to cope with the ordinary civil power of our counties." He asked that the Posse Comitatus Act be repealed so that the army could assist local lawmen. He added that, while the governor had the power to organize a militia, the territory did not possess the funds with which to support such an organization.[36]

In a separate report to Secretary of State James G. Blaine, Gosper revealed an alarming situation among law enforcement officers in Tombstone, one in which the marshalcy appeared in a dim light. The rivalry between Sheriff Behan and Deputy Marshal Virgil Earp and his brothers prevented any cooperation against the bandits; the "best" citizens, said Gosper, informed him that both factions were in league with the outlaws. These respectable informants had reportedly organized a vigilante force. To aggravate this threatening situation, the two newspapers in Tombstone, the *Nuggett* and the *Epitaph*, were aligned behind Behan and the Earps, respectively.[37]

Had he known the full extent of this rivalry between federal and local officers, the acting governor would have been even more shocked. In addition to the competition for the sheriff's office, John H. Behan and Wyatt Earp were vying for the charms of a young dancer with a traveling troupe. Wyatt also accused Behan of being in alliance with the Cowboys and of having deliberately allowed a federal prisoner to escape. In pursuing stagecoach robbers, the sheriff and the deputy marshal fielded separate forces. Sheriff Behan was considerably embarrassed when an Earp *posse comitatus* arrested his deputy, Frank C. Stilwell, for stagecoach robbery. Virgil and Wyatt Earp were likewise indignant when the sheriff arrested their close friend, gambler-dentist John H. ("Doc") Holliday, for robbery and murder.[38]

Still in search of political recognition, Wyatt Earp sought out Ike Clanton with a proposition that would ensure that Earp would win the upcoming election for sheriff of Cochise County. Since the death of his father, Ike Clanton was the reported leader of the Cowboys. Wyatt Earp asked Clanton to lure the stagecoach robbers, whom Earp suggested to be Clanton's friends, into a trap. The Earps would kill or capture them and pay the reward money to Ike Clanton.[39]

Whether or not Ike Clanton agreed to Wyatt Earp's proposal is not known. However, rumors spread that the rustler leader had sold out to the Earp brothers. When he learned that the plan had surfaced, Ike accused Wyatt Earp of revealing the conspiracy (or the conversation about the plan) in order to embarrass him. He threatened to kill Wyatt Earp, as well as Virgil and Morgan. On October 26, 1881, several Clantons, with their friends Tom and Frank McLaury, appeared in Tombstone and threatened the Earp brothers. Wyatt Earp was determined to seize the initiative and to remove these adversaries before they could carry out their plans. Deputy Marshal Virgil Earp, who was a concurrent city marshal, was the only brother clothed in official armor. He deputized Wyatt, Morgan, and Doc Holliday as city policemen with the intent to arrest the Cowboys. City Marshal Virgil Earp and his deputies confronted the Clanton party with the command, "Throw up your hands," drew their weapons as Virgil shouted the command, killed three of the outlaws, and frightened Ike Clanton from the field. The dead victims were sixteen-year-old Billy Clanton and the two McLaurys. Virgil and Morgan Earp and Doc Holliday were slightly wounded.[40]

Although this confrontation—soon called the Gunfight at the OK Corral—did not involve the Earps in their capacity as deputy United States marshals, this engagement degraded the already tarnished reputation of the marshalcy. The Democratic press took great delight in the embarrassment that the Republican deputy marshals had bestowed upon their party. The Prescott *Democrat* called "the attention of Marshal Dake to the impropriety, to say the least, of appointing one of the Earps to the position of Deputy United States Marshal." The angry journalist declared that since "those distinguished swashbucklers honored Prescott with their presence some two years ago, . . . the odor of their unsavory reputation still taints the nostrils of our citizens." The *Miner*, which maintained a close relationship with Marshal Dake, was shaken by the deaths of the Clanton party and admitted that the deputy marshals had acted "hastily and without provocation." However, the editor stood by Marshal Dake and maintained till the expiration of his term that, aside from a few indiscreet appointments (the Earps), he had made a "good officer."[41]

The news of the Gunfight at OK Corral stunned Acting Attorney General Phillips who, on November 17, 1881, ordered Marshal Dake to take immediate steps against the Cowboys. He added a note of caution, "Your deputy, Mr. [Virgil] Earp, is more disposed to quarrel than to cooperate with local authority" in Tombstone. Dake did not take seriously this obvious hint to remove Virgil Earp. When the marshal failed to take measures to subdue the Cowboys, Attorney General Phillips reiterated the order in the name of the president.[42]

Shaken into action by this stern reprimand, on November 28 the marshal asked Acting Governor Gosper for suggestions about the suppression of the Cowboy lawlessness.

> I am in receipt of communications . . . urging the necessity of taking some steps to stop the raiding and lawlessness on our boarders [*sic*] by the desperadoes called "Cow Boys" also calling my attention to the rivalry existing between the Federal and County officers: knowing of your recent visit to the Southern part of the Territory. . . , I wish you would give me your views. . . . I wish to know the cause of the difficulties . . . and your recommendations that some steps should be taken at once by the Department of Justice.

Dake also requested "your judgment expressed to me in writing," since the governor's letter "will have great influence in bringing about the proper authority for me to act." Gosper complied with Dake's request quickly and suggested that the marshal should request funds for the support of "a man of well-known courage and character" as a deputy with authority to field a *posse comitatus* to investigate the outrages of the Cowboys. He added that "it might be wise to remove" his deputy marshals in Cochise County. (Gosper also desired to remove Sheriff John Behan, but did not have the power.)[43]

The anxious federal policeman presented Gosper's proposal for a special posse to Acting Attorney General Phillips, but neglected to entertain any thought of the removal of Deputy Marshal Virgil Earp. Dake defended his deputies in Tombstone, although the Earps did not kill the Cowboys under federal warrants. "My deputies at Tombstone have struck one effectual blow to that [Cowboy] element killing three out of five." He added that there were "no braver men in Arizona" than the Earps, and he was confident that they would drive the outlaws from the border. However, when he concluded his defense of Deputy Virgil Earp, he still faced the problem of what to do in Cochise County. Dake requested permission to field a special posse, evidently with Virgil

Earp in command, but added that "a special [financial] allowance for this particular purpose should be made," one that would include the "actual" expenses of the *posse comitatus*. On that same day, December 8, 1881, Acting Governor Gosper informed the attorney general of his conference with Marshal Dake and urged Phillips to authorize funds for the marshal to proceed against the Cowboys.[44]

While the federal lawman groped for aid against the outlaws, the Earp-Cowboy vendetta erupted into more violence. On November 8, even before Dake's letter to Washington, Deputy Marshal Virgil Earp telegraphed General Orlando B. Willcox for military protection for himself and his brothers during the hearing over the deceased outlaws. The general was bound by the restrictions of the Posse Comitatus Act and referred the matter to Acting Governor Gosper. The territorial executive was not alarmed since he was aware of the existence of the Committee of Public Safety (vigilantes) in Tombstone. Sheriff Behan also notified Gosper that, in spite of Deputy Marshal Earp's fears, the village was quiet.[45]

Virgil Earp had cause for alarm, although Governor Gosper could not have known the reason. On the night of December 28, several assassins attempted to kill the deputy. He miraculously survived the blast of shotguns, but permanently lost the use of one arm. Wyatt Earp telegraphed Marshal Dake the following day:

> Virgil Earp was shot by a concealed assassin last night. The wound is considered fatal. Telegraph me appointment [as a deputy marshal] with power to appoint deputies. Local authorities have done nothing. The lives of other citizens have been threatened [by the Cowboys].

Although Marshal Dake evidently complied with Wyatt Earp's request, the exact date and nature of this commission is unclear. Deputy Marshal Wyatt Earp was noted in the field soon after against robbers who held up a coach on January 6, 1882.[46]

All attempts to supervise his deputies from faraway Prescott proved ineffective, and Marshal Dake was soon forced to travel to Cochise County. An urgent telegram from former Governor Anson Safford persuaded the federal lawman, and Governor Gosper, to make the trip. Safford informed the two officers that their presence was desperately needed to protect life and property in the mining town. Dake and Gosper arrived in Tombstone on the night of

January 26, 1882. George Whitwell Parsons, a resident and diarist, met the marshal and was reassured to some extent. "At last the national government is taking a hand," said Parsons. "It looks like business now when the U.S. Marshal takes a hand under special orders [from the attorney general]." Dake, who had somehow acquired funds, deposited $3000 to the account of Deputy Marshal Wyatt Earp and authorized him to employ a posse against the Cowboys. In all likelihood, Governor Gosper did not "supercede" Sheriff John H. Behan "as a peace officer" and "invest" Wyatt Earp "with complete powers of law enforcement," as Earp later informed his biographer. Nor did the seven men whom Earp deputized conform to the recommendations of the local vigilantes. The deputy marshals were hardly savory characters—two were suspected of stagecoach robbery, and the remaining men were gambling friends of Wyatt Earp.[47]

The Cowboys did not desire another violent confrontation with Earp and his professional gunmen. They attempted instead to have the Earps tried for the murder of Billy Clanton and the McLaury brothers. Ike Clanton had warrants sworn out for Wyatt and Morgan Earp and Doc Holliday from nearby Charleston. The citizens of this small camp became terribly alarmed at the prospects of a continuation of the feud and begged the escorting officers to return the Earps to Tombstone as quickly as possible. As the Earps reentered the streets of Tombstone, on January 14, 1882 (some days before Marshal Dake's visit), George Whitwell Parsons observed the armed and sullen partisans of both factions facing each other across the streets.[48]

It became evident to the Cowboys that legal means could accomplish little against the Earps, and the Clantons turned to violence once more. On the night of March 18, 1882, assassins opened fire on deputy marshals Wyatt and Morgan Earp who were playing billiards in a local hall. Wyatt escaped injury, but Morgan died in agony on a billiard table. With his "body guard," as the enemies of Wyatt Earp now called his posse, Wyatt escorted the body of Morgan and their invalid brother Virgil as far as Tucson, then sent them by train to Colton, California, where their father resided. While at Tucson on March 20, the deputy marshals spotted Frank C. Stilwell, whom they suspected of being one of the assassins. They shot him to death near the depot. This brutal murder caused much indignation, and Sheriff Robert H. (Bob) Paul of Pima County (where the killing occurred) was given warrants for the arrest of the Earp party. The deputy marshals had already returned to Tombstone.[49]

By now Deputy Marshal Wyatt Earp was bent on a remorseless vendetta against the Cowboys. He would allow nothing, not even his deputy marshal's badge, to stand in his way; Sheriff Behan, who also held warrants for the federal posse, carefully avoided these violent men. One of the suspects in the murder of Morgan Earp was a woodcutter called Indian Charley (Florentio). The deputy marshals shot him to death on March 22. The Earps also claimed that William ("Curley Bill") Brocius fell before their guns, and many years later, Josephine Earp, wife of Wyatt, declared that Wyatt returned to Arizona some time later and killed Johnny Ringo.[50]

The vendetta had run its course. As the local authorities under Sheriff Robert H. Paul mustered their forces against the Earps, the deputy marshal quietly departed Arizona. It was a unique spectacle; a posse of federal lawmen forced from their district. The Earp party boarded a train in Silver City, New Mexico, was observed in Albuquerque on March 26, and later rested at Pueblo, Colorado. The editor of the Pueblo *Chieftain* sought an interview with the notorious partner of Wyatt Earp, Deputy Marshal Doc Holliday, who jumped at the opportunity to defend himself. Holliday averred that he

> had nothing to fear from that quarter [Arizona], as he had received full pardon from the governor [of Arizona] for his bloody work, in consideration of the effective services he had rendered the [federal] authorities. . . . He said that he had never killed anyone, except in protecting himself. . . . He had left Arizona for the single purpose of being at peace with every one [*sic*] around him, and he hoped his enemies would allow him that privilege.

A few days later, Doc was arrested in Denver, but former Deputy Marshal Bat Masterson (now city marshal of Trinidad) obtained his release on a writ of habeas corpus. Sheriff Paul of Tucson attempted to extradite the entire Earp party but for reasons never adequately explained, the case was dropped.[51]

With the departure of the renegade deputy marshals, Governor Frederick A. Tritle, who had recently succeeded the negligent

John C. Fremont, prepared to restore order in Tombstone. After a visit to the unsettled community, Tritle informed President Chester A. Arthur that an "insurrectionary condition" existed in Cochise County and that Marshal Dake needed troops. Tritle also asked for authority to remove Sheriff John H. Behan. However, the Posse Comitatus Act forbade the use of bluecoats in the marshal's posses, and the governor found himself in the same predicament that had beset Lew Wallace during the Lincoln County War. General William T. Sherman, who visited southern Arizona in the spring of 1882, confirmed Tritle's report and expressed disgust with restrictions of the Posse Comitatus Act. Arthur desperately beseeched Congress to make both territories, Arizona and New Mexico, exceptions to the restrictive law, but the lawmakers refused.[52]

In this predicament President Arthur and the officials of Arizona had no choice but to follow the procedures that Governor Lew Wallace had employed in Lincoln County. On May 31, 1882, the chief executive issued a proclamation against the Cowboys and declared the area in a state of rebellion. This step qualified Arthur to dispatch troops to Cochise County in spite of the Posse Comitatus Act. Governor Tritle, however, concluded that the presence of regulars would embarrass the Arizonans and, instead, merely asked for funds to support a company of militia. The nucleus of a disciplined organization already existed in Tombstone in the form of a vigilante committee headed by liveryman John H. Jackson. Tritle persuaded Marshal Crawley P. Dake to deputize Jackson and to form a new posse, now that the Earps had departed. This posse probably consisted of many former vigilantes, since they would be less partisan. In a peculiar procedure, never adequately explained, Governor Tritle declared that when Jackson's posse reached thirty in number, he would incorporate it as a militia company. While no further violence occurred, and tensions relaxed among the feudists, the Jackson posse helped to restore some faith in federal law enforcement in Cochise County.[53]

Now that the vendetta between Deputy Marshal Wyatt Earp and the Cowboys had run its course, the full political implications of the feud became more apparent. The Democratic editor of the *Daily Star*, Louis C. Hughes, declared "that the lawlessness of the federal deputy marshals" must be "shouldered by the Republican party." Hughes pointed out that the Republican "organs are engaged in a persistent effort in their ⌊Earps⌋ defense." When the Republican *Arizona Citizen* defended the deputies, Hughes chided them for assuming "that public sentiment is in favor of the Earps." And, when the *Miner* of Prescott suddenly deserted Marshal Dake and his subordinates, Hughes poked fun at the turncoat journal. The *Miner* "should be read out of the Republican party." Said the editor of the *Star*, "It has gone back on the Earps."[54]

The *Virginia City Enterprise* dismayed many Arizonans by characterizing the Earps as men of law and order. This Nevada journal concluded that the acute "character of the depredations" of the Cowboys demanded a forceful "exhibition by a few determined officers." "The Earp brothers nearly succeeded," continued this editor, "and had they been backed by the sentiment of the community, their success would have been complete." Predictably, a Democratic newspaper, the *Arizona Democrat*, sprang to the defense of the citizens of Cochise County and expressed contempt for the Nevadan.[55]

While the Earps blackened the reputation of the marshalcy in southern Arizona, other deputy marshals earned the regard of the citizenry. In the northeast Deputy Corydon E. Cooley helped rid Springerville of a notorious band of desperadoes in 1877. In November Cooley and a posse of soldiers (this event occurred before the Posse Comitatus Act) arrested outlaw William Snider, alias Bill Caveness, and one henchman, near Springerville, much to the relief of the local populace. In December the people publicly thanked Cooley and his colleagues "for the gentlemanly, carefull [*sic*] and impartial manner in which they conducted their investigations and established peace in the eastern portion of Yavapai County." In the meantime, a terrible fate overtook the Caveness band. In the quaint words of one newspaperman, "Judge Lynch took them and cut them to pieces with knives." When the Springerville area became Apache County in 1879, Corydon E. Cooley became a county supervisor.[56]

At this very time, when the marshalcy was struggling to bring federal law to remote camps in Arizona, technology, in the form of the railroads, was coming to the aid of the lawmen. As the Atlantic & Pacific Railroad slowly inched from New Mexico into eastern Arizona, the Bill Cavenesses had to seek other sanctuaries. In the south, the Southern Pacific spelled a similar doom for wrongdoers.

Two of Crawley P. Dake's subordinates, Deputies Joseph W. Evans and Robert H. Paul startled Arizonans in early 1881 by using the rails to make arrests in Yuma. In February and March, each officer descended upon the tiny community in steam locomotives in order to occupy stores for bankruptcy. In the Evans raid, the deputy and his posse impounded the Isaac Lyons establishment before the people of Yuma were aware of their presence. The *Sentinel* protested the presence of shotgun-armed deputies on the streets, but this complaint could not erase the fact that federal justice could occur rapidly during Crawley P. Dake's term. Dake also used the expanding telegraph network more fully than any predecessor.[57]

A corresponding growth in the staff and business of the marshalcy occurred during Marshal Dake's term. Dake's biannual Emolument Returns, which exist for August 1, 1878, to December 31, 1880, reveal this increase. The steady growth of federal business is unmistakable. In the first five months of his term, August 1 to December 31, 1878, the outbreak of banditry constrained him to deputize nine men. He hired nine more men during the following six months. As highway robbery subsided, the federal officer reduced the number of employees—to six from July 1 to December 31, 1879; five in the next half year; and four in the period from July 1 to December 31, 1880. These numbers do not reflect the state of the marshal's staff absolutely, since the deputies at Tombstone failed to file returns in 1880. At least three men held deputyships in that community—Virgil Earp, Leslie Blackburn, and A. F. Buttner.[58]

Dake's staff experienced a heavy turnover. The deputyship was unattractive and served only to supplement the income of some ambitious persons. Joseph W. Evans earned the largest income in that two-and-one-half-year period—$1602.32. However, under the contractual arrangement twenty-five percent of this amount returned to Marshal Dake, leaving Evans only $1201.74. The deputy was an employee of the marshal, not of the federal government. The marshal reasoned that persons deputed to serve his process of court owed their employment to the chief lawman. The deputies were also required to relinquish any claims to rewards to the marshal. Only if the marshal consented could the employee receive the bounty.[59]

The niggardly financial policy of the authorities in Washington also hindered the improvement of the deputyship. In a revealing letter of September 14, 1881, Dake complained to Attorney General Benjamin Brewster that the Treasury had disallowed some of his expenses for deputies in the pursuit of mail robbers. He pointed out that the usual fees for the service of process were inadequate for the pursuit of hardened criminals. "It is impossible to get competent deputies," Dake declared, 'to act without [adequate] pay especially in that [lawless] state of affairs now existing in Arizona." He continued:

> Heretofore I have paid my deputies $2.00 per diem [in violation of the fee list] for serving all process and have charged the same in my accounts rendered to settlement and which charge has been disallowed by the Department [of the Treasury] as unauthorized; if this can not be corrected in some way it is impossible for the Marshal to serve any process out of the immediate vicinity of the towns where the courts are held without paying the expense . . . out of his own pocket.

The fee list applied to the settled and peaceful towns of the East, not the violent and robber-ridden territories.

> If it is expected of me to serve process and arrest mail robbers and outlaws, . . . reasonable compensation must be paid to secure competent men [as deputies] otherwise, I am powerless to act in emergencies. . . . It is unfortunate that we live in a country where the law does not seem to provide for such emergencies, for the fees allowed marshals for the service of process will go but a little way towards paying the actual expense incurred.

He recalled a recent stagecoach robbery in which three persons were killed. Outraged citizens asked him to dispatch two deputies with volunteers to run down the banditti. "I could not hire efficient deputies," he explained "to take the chance and responsibility for fees and actual expenses under the [present] law—$5.00 per day and actual expenses is the least I can get men to risk their lives for." These entreaties may have influenced the attorney general, who, in spite of Dake's lack of popularity in Washington, soon made generous sums available for the pursuit of mailcoach robbers. On April 12 and May 4, 1882, Dake received $2,000 and $3,000 respectively.[60]

Among many problems, housing prisoners perplexed Crawley P. Dake, who continued to rely upon the county jails or makeshift structures. In June 1880, a grand jury in Prescott criticized Dake for shackling convicted murderer John J. Chapman in an open space, while the lawman awaited funds for transferral of the charge to prison. The funds did not arrive for eighteen months. The shocked jurors directed the district attorney to report the case to Washington "as an act of humanity." Judge Charles Silent sprang to the defense of the lawman, and reported that he could "truly say that Marshal Dake has in all cases been kind to the prisoners under his authority."[61]

The custody of long-term prisoners became a more serious problem. When Dake entered Arizona in 1878, the territorial prison at Yuma had just recently opened. The warden assumed that the new federal policeman would contract with Yuma Penitentiary to house federal prisoners. In this way the penitentiary would earn income, and the marshal would possess a convenient jail for his wards. Dake decided otherwise. In a letter of October 31, 1878, he explained to Attorney General Charles Devens that the prison was characterized by excessive heat—"filthiness and [an] overcrowded condition." "*Humanity* [his italics] cannot be observed," concluded the marshal. Dake added that the facility was "not considered safe" and that Judge Charles Silent had to order "an extra guard" over federal charges in the prison. It was not the unsafe condition of Yuma prison that convinced Marshal Dake to reject that facility; the warden demanded exorbitant subsistence—$1.62 per person per diem. And when the marshal recommended that he be permitted to transport his prisoners to the Michigan State Penitentiary (his home state), which charged only $.40 per day,[62] Attorney General Devens agreed, with some reservations. Federal prisoners under sentence to two or more years should be housed in the Michigan prison; from six months to two years, in the federal penitentiary in Laramie, Wyoming; and under six months, to the county jail in Prescott, Arizona.[63]

These constructive efforts could not overcome the adverse publicity of the Earp Vendetta and, in the spring of 1882, the Department of Justice began a serious investigation of Dake's marshalcy. Examiner Joel R. Bowman and Treasury Agent S. R. Martin conducted the inquiry. Bowman was effectively stymied by the absence of any records in Marshal Dake's office. Martin, who investigated the "standing" of the lawman in the territory, learned that few citizens considered Dake "fit" for office. The marshal failed to serve writs and other process and had held no sessions of court since September 1881. Martin added that Dake seldom had funds for office and had retained as a deputy a known outlaw, Wyatt Earp.[64]

The marshal defended himself as best he could. When Bowman expressed concern at the absence of records of fee collection by his deputies, Dake replied (in a letter to Attorney General Benjamin Brewster):

> I am endeavoring to get my accounts as Marshal closed up as fast as possible. Some of my deputies . . . were driven out of the Territory and scattered all over the country before I could get vouchers from them. . . . I have been using all due diligence to do so.
>
> I enclose a letter, which I received yesterday [May 6, 1883] from my chief deputy, who left me abruptly and accepted a position . . . in the navy. . . . he states that he will forward to me from Peru the vouchers (amounting to some $4000) for which I had written. I have also some vouchers in Colorado [with Wyatt Earp] for similar amounts which I am expecting daily.

The desperate lawman added that he had been incapacitated for two months with "an old wound received in the service during the [Civil] war." "All I ask," he implored the attorney general, "is that you will be patient with me for the present." The marshalcy, he had said in a previous letter, is "thankless & unprofitable."[65]

The ability of Crawley P. Dake to retain his office in spite of his failures was a glaring example of the shortcomings of the territorial system of government. "We want Major Dake retained in office until after the November [1882] election," insisted Acting Governor Hiran M. Van Arman of Arizona. "His retention is important for Republican success in electing a delegate." Senator T. W. Terry of Michigan, upon whose recommendation Crawley P. Dake had been made marshal, urged that he be retained in view of his "peculiar service" in the Civil War. Terry admitted that the marshal may have neglected his accounts while pursuing the Cowboys.[66]

On August 5, 1882, the attorney general directed the marshal to submit his accounts immediately and informed him that his successor, Zan L. Tidball, would assist in the computation. However, Marshal Dake refused to cooperate with Tidball, who, in turn, complained to his superior. Attorney General Brewster's suspicions were now greatly aroused, and a letter from Wells, Fargo and Company confirmed his fears about Crawley P. Dake. The express company revealed that, during the Cowboy outbreak in Cochise County, Dake had borrowed three thousand dollars from Wells, Fargo for the Support of Wyatt Earp's posse. Dake assured the company that the Department of Justice would honor the loan. However, the marshal failed to notify the attorney general about his irregular procedure. With all the evidence in, Brewster ordered one final examination of the Dake case in preparation for a legal suit against the former marshal and his bondsmen.[67]

In August and September 1885, examiner Leigh Chalmers, who made this last inquiry, submitted his reports in Washington. The agent reported that the former Marshal Dake admitted to having "feloniously converted" over $50,000 in federal monies to his private account and that he had drawn "upon it as his individual money." In regard to the $3,000 Wells, Fargo loan, the agent found that the former marshal had obtained it under "false and fraudulent representations." Dake had deposited the money to the account of Deputy Marshal Wyatt Earp in Tombstone. While Earp evidently spent most of the money in the pursuit of the Cowboys, Dake spent some $300 of that sum in a drunken celebration with the posse in the sporting houses of that notorious community.[68]

In January 1885, United States District Attorney James A. Zabriskie pressed charges against Crawley P. Dake and his bondsmen. The district attorney expressed concern about the prosecution, since the former marshal was very ill. The public felt a "deep sympathy" for him, and Zabriskie concluded that many people believed that Dake was the "victim" of an oppressive federal government. The case dragged into 1886 when, in June, Dake entered a demurrer, and the Prescott *Miner* reported that a settlement of his accounts was under way in Washington.[69]

Not all Arizonans accepted the exoneration of Marshal Dake, and some regarded him as a part of Governor John C. Fremont's ring of economic exploiters. Both men were proteges of powerful Michigan Senator Zachariah Chandler. In addition, the "mysterious"

Judge Charles Silent, a "entrepreneur-politician," was a close associate of the marshal and the governor. This Republican machine was aggressive, and during Fremont's term the party invaded the traditionally Democratic stronghold of southern Arizona. The goal was land, minerals, and political offices in and around Tombstone.

The presence of arrogant Republican deputy marshals merely added to the political factionalism in Tombstone. The struggle for control of the shrievalty of Cochise County between Democrat Behan and Republican Earp was merely the surface manifestation of a deeper struggle. The outlaw Cowboys played in between these rival factions.[70]

This period in the frontier marshalcy might be called "the era of the deputyship." At no other time did the deputy marshals exercise so much influence—positive and negative—over federal law enforcement in the Southwest. The lax policy governing the selection and service of subordinates permitted a deputy to conduct the affairs of office according to personal whim. Marshal Dake certainly experienced this frustrating problem with Virgil, and more especially, with Wyatt Earp.

These events resembled the conditions of federal law enforcement in New Mexico. In Lincoln County Marshal John E. Sherman, Jr., encountered a district perplexed by rivalry between outside interlopers and inside vested interests. Deputy Robert Widenmann inflamed passions much as the Earps had in Tombstone. Deputy Marshal Pat Garrett's posse played a role similar to Wyatt Earp's deputies and Garrett resembled the Arizona lawman in the degree of remorseless violence meted out against the outlaws. These strong-willed deputy marshals of Arizona and New Mexico also won nationwide publicity for the frontier federal marshalcy, and the deputies soon became a part of the image and lore of the "frontier marshal." Pulp writers no longer confined their writing to the city marshals of Kansas cowtowns, but turned to Lincoln and Cochise counties for material.

The lordly behavior of these deputies embarrassed their superiors, and even supporters of Dake and Sherman admitted that the marshals possessed one singular shortcoming—indiscreet appointment practices. The successors of Dake and Sherman would devote special attention to this problem.

8

The New Mexico Marshalcy, 1882–96

During the period from 1882 to 1896, New Mexico experienced remarkable, but troubled growth. The construction of railroads, the influx of new settlers, the expansion of the economy, the demands of the Hispanos for more equitable treatment, and a renewed congressional interest in frontier reforms, all concerned the marshals of New Mexico during the fifteen years after the departure of John E. Sherman, Jr. The harried United States lawmen also confronted problems within their office, among them the control of errant deputies, the elevation of deputyship to a respectable position in society, and the reduction of the marshalcy's role in politics. To overcome such problems required a great deal of determination.

When John E. Sherman, Jr., turned in his resignation in 1882, his district contained a mere 119,000 persons. In 1890, the census revealed an increase to 160,000. Ten years later, the figure had climbed to 195,000. Anglo migrants accounted for much of this increase, though the Hispanos still constituted a majority of the population. The Indian population had seldom concerned the marshals, but this changed in the 1880s. Of the 28,000 Indians in New Mexico in 1880—16,000 Navajos and 9,000 Pueblos—most were peaceful. These people were pulled into the mainstream of federal justice.

Many of these social changes resulted from the completion of several railroads: the Atchison, Topeka and the Santa Fe in 1881; the Southern Pacific, in 1882; and the Atlantic and Pacific in 1883. The Santa Fe Railroad generally followed the well-traveled commercial routes. The steam locomotives, meanwhile, introduced many changes. "New towns" of anglos sprang up alongside "old towns" of Hispanos to enlarge Las Vegas and Albuquerque. The railroads opened the remoter districts in the South and the West. Not only would "new political alliances and configurations" result, but also new and sometimes vexing duties for the federal law enforcers. Just as the politicians incorporated these new interest groups by creating new counties, the federal judiciary added new judicial districts.[1]

New political tensions became apparent in the early 1880s. The southern wing of the Santa Fe Ring, located in Dona Ana County, demanded a larger share of the patronage. William L. Rynerson, boss of Dona Ana County, caused a schism in the Ring when he rebelled against the domineering leadership of William Breeden of Santa Fe. The Democratic party cleverly insinuated itself into this cleft and was surprisingly strong in the delegate election of 1882. Much of this strength came from the Hispano population who saw an opportunity to regain lost power in their homeland. The "Democracy" received an added boost in 1884 when Grover Cleveland was elected president. By the 1890s, Governor William T. Thornton, a Democrat, could observe publicly that since the Spanish-speaking people constituted sixty percent of the New Mexico populace, they were "entitled to fair consideration."[2]

In this struggle, the Republicans of the Santa Fe Ring regarded the marshalcy as one of their goals. On March 2, 1882, President Chester A. Arthur appointed Alexander L. Morrison, Sr., to succeed John E. Sherman, Jr. Morrison was a strong and outspoken Republican, and the Ring considered him a stalwart, not a "liberal" like John Sherman. Born in Ireland, in 1832, Morrison immigrated to the United States in time to see action in the Mexican War. He served in New Mexico, a land that enthralled him. He settled in Chicago, served in the Illinois Legislature, and won favor with the Irish immigrant bloc. Senator John A. Logan became his patron; Senator William McKinley of Ohio befriended him. Morrison's sensitivity to the wrongs done to his own people made him deeply sympathitic to the Hispano population of New Mexico. His regard for the latter minority was reinforced by his strong Catholicism. When he arrived in Albuquerque in 1882, he wisely chose this growing community as official headquarters.[3]

It came as no surprise when a Democrat succeeded Alexander Morrison to the marshalcy in 1885. The Americans had elected Grover Cleveland to the presidency, and he, in turn, had appointed a Radical Republican-turned Democrat, Edmund G. Ross, to the governship of New Mexico. For the marshalcy, Cleveland not only chose a Democrat but, to the surprise of many, a native Hispano, Don Romulo Martinez. In doing this, Cleveland rejected two mainstays of the older marshalcy—Republicanism and outsiders. Perhaps the reformers of the Cleveland administration concluded that New Mexico needed more than "a radical reconstruction of its economy and its politics." The territory needed a reform within its federal law enforcement office.[4]

Don Romulo possessed considerable credentials. He had served as a commissioner of Santa Fe County and, from 1881 to 1884, was sheriff. His family was most distinguished; the elder Martinez was probate judge of Santa Fe County. The new marshal considered himself the champion of his people. Some New Mexicans, however, expressed concern that he was too close to the Santa Fe Ring. Charles H. Gildersleeve, chairman of the Democratic party in the territory and a member of the Ring, was a patron of Don Romulo. The federal lawman also was a member of the trading firm of J. L. Johnson and Company and was its representative to the Navajos at Fort Defiance. Although Don Romulo received the appointment as marshal on June 8, 1885, some time elapsed before the Senate confirmed the selection. In June 1886, Governor Ross urged Senator John Ingalls of the Senate Judiciary Committee to confirm Martinez. "I consider [him] the best qualified native Mexican . . . for that place," said Ross, "and among the most thoroughly Americanized Mexicans I have met." Upon confirmation, supporters of Martinez, and the newly appointed Chief Justice, William A. Vincent, gave them a "complimentary serenade" in Santa Fe. The new marshal took much pride in his appointment and sported a fine suit, studded pistol, and studded badge. When some disrespectful pilferer stole the badge, he published a notice of reward in the *New Mexican*. The editor commented that it was so well known in the territory that the thief could not sell it.[5]

The reign of the Democratic marshal was short-lived. In the election of 1888, the Americans returned the Republicans to the White House. Complementary changes occurred throughout the territorial judiciaries. President Benjamin Harrison wisely followed the precedent of the Democrats and appointed another distinguished Hispano, Trinidad Romero, as marshal. On

November 7, 1889, when he received the appointment, Don Trinidad was fifty-four years of age. He was an enterprising capitalist, with interests in freighting, cattle, and a mercantile house in Las Vegas. Don Trinidad served as the probate judge of San Miguel County, as a member of the territorial legislature, and as a delegate to Congress in 1877–79. In family tradition, he is remembered as somewhat "arrogant," but as one who ran in "high political circles."[6]

Many New Mexicans were overjoyed at this concession to the Hispanos by the conservative party, and *La Voz del Pueblo* (The Voice of the People), a Spanish-language journal, expressed this gratitude. The *New Mexican* recalled that the Democrats had charged that the Republicans "would not recognize the native citizens of New Mexico" in the Harrison administration. "No Catholics need apply" either, said the Democrats. "It makes no difference to the Republican party," said the *New Mexican* "where a man is born, what blood flows in his veins, [or] what his religion is." The Grand Old Party had turned over a new leaf in New Mexico, and the marshalcy was part of the new master plan.[7]

Many New Mexicans assumed that the dons would continue to dominate the marshalcy when Democrat Grover Cleveland returned to the White House in 1893. Family domination of public offices was traditional in Hispanic culture. Delegate Antonio Joseph recommended Felix Martinez of Las Vegas to succeed Trinidad Romero. However, Cleveland feared the second Martinez, since he associated with the radical left wing of the Democratic party, the People's party. This faction was New Mexico's contribution to the Populist Movement of the 1890s. The Anglos of the New Mexican Democratic party, wary of Felix Martinez, promoted Edward L. Hall, a Grant County rancher, who announced his candidacy at the end of his term as councilman in 1892. Democratic politicans exerted decisive influence in Washington through Senator William Jackson Palmer, the western railway baron. On May 16, 1893, Hall received the appointment as marshal, much to the joy of partisan journals in New Mexico. The Democrats of the southern counties, according to the *New Mexican*, regarded the appointment of Hall to be the first "knockout" in the struggle of the those neglected counties against the northern "Holy Trinity" within the party—Antonio Joseph, Harvey Fergusson, and Jacob Christ. These three, sometimes called the triumvirate, had supported Felix Martinez. The Silver City *Enterprise* noted, however, that some Democrats had not wanted a "native son."[8]

When Edward L. Hall received his appointment, he represented a momentary return to antebellum days when Missourians had dominated the territory. The new governor, William T. Thornton, and several lesser officials were natives of that state. The Hall family of Chillicothe, Missouri, was noted for public service. U. S. Hall sat in the House of Representatives, William was in the cavalry, John was a naval surgeon, and Edward had just completed a term in the New Mexico Council. Edward ranched in Colorado and then, in 1885, moved to Grant County, New Mexico, where he made an "excellent record" as a businessman.[9]

Many of the duties that engaged the marshals of New Mexico in the 1880s and 1890s were a consequence of reform-minded congressional policy. These lawmakers—Republican and Democrat—embarked upon a crusade to prepare the "lowly territorials" for statehood. Among the reforms that Congress considered essential, the reduction of the liquor traffic among the Indians held a high place. In addition, the legislators desired to ensure every citizen an equal opportunity to acquire inexpensive public lands, to resolve the complex issue of Spanish land grants, and to constrain the territorials to abide by the moral code of the middle class—especially to practice monogamy. Congress even desired to prevent unsightly public exhibitions, such as bullfighting and prize fighting, although the national legislators regarded the threat of bullfighting to be more serious in Arizona.

By spring 1882, when Alexander Morrison occupied the marshalcy, many journalists were expressing hysterical fear of the "drunken Navajos." The *Albuquerque Evening Review*, which spoke for many New Mexicans, berated John Sherman, Jr., and District Attorney William Barnes, for failing to suppress the whiskey peddlers. When a *Review* reporter asked Chief Manuelito of the Navajos about the illicit trade, he replied, "Bad white men are too powerful for me." This journal concluded dejectedly that an Indian uprising could be expected in the summer if the federal lawmen did not act.[10]

Marshal Alexander Morrison devoted special attention to the enforcement of the Indian Intercourse Act and the revenue laws. In May 1882, his deputies broke up a ring of illicit whiskey sellers in the vicinity of the Navajo Reservation. Through their control of the whiskey trade, Thomas Dye and his band of unscrupulous men had acquired considerable influence over the Indians. In fact, Dye threatened to persuade the Navajos to attack a crew of workers on the Atlantic and Pacific Railroad when the construction boss tried to have Dye arrested. When deputy marshals surprised the outlaws in Gallup, and placed them in the Albuquerque jail, enraged friends of the whiskey leader threatened to release Dye by force. Morrison quickly assigned extra guards to the shaky structure. After trial, the elated marshal transported Dye and his partner to the Missouri State Penitentiary.[11]

White dealers not only sold liquor to the Indians, but corrupted the work crews on the Atlantic and Pacific Railroad with their illicit brew. The *Evening Review* lamented the absence of the lawman to prevent this destructive trade:

> All along the line of the Atlantic and Pacific Railroad gangs of roughs make their temporary dwelling place and at present there is no restraint imposed upon their actions save the fear of a lynch-law uprising of exasperated people. . . . One or two deputy marshals can be found between this city and Winslow, [Arizona,] but as a general thing these officers of the law amount to but little.

Colonel I. P. Bradley, commander of Fort Wingate, proposed a novel solution to the problem—to place "the country along the line and on either side of that [rail]road . . . under their control, with power to prevent, by force, the introduction of whiskey." Not even the editor of the *Evening Review* regarded this plan as practical, but the journalist urged the appointment of deputy sheriffs and justices of the peace to see to it. After the first appearance of Marshal Morrison's deputies in Gallup in May 1882, his subordinates made regular stopovers in the turbulent region.[12]

In addition to the prosecution of whiskey sellers, Washington made a serious effort to protect the public lands from great land barons. Abuses of the public domain took many forms: fraudulent land titles; enclosure of grazing lands; and timber trespass. Congress encountered many difficulties as it formulated laws to ensure all citizens a fair chance to occupy land, since stringent laws would retard westward expansion. The frontiersmen concluded that since they took the risks, they should be permitted to take up more land than they could possibly use. Among the exploiters of the domain, the marshals participated just as aggressively as the average citizen.[13]

In December 1881, the Receiver of Public Moneys in Santa Fe, Elias Brevoort, suggested to the attorney general that many fraudulent land titles existed in New Mexico and that the Department of Justice should investigate. Brevoort cautioned that the special agents should be men of "firm and resolute" character, willing to risk their lives, and able to resist bribery. In the following three years, seven investigators found ample evidence of illegal land claims. Between 1882 and 1891, the federal district courts of the territory docketed 3,633 criminal land cases, including: 641 for land fraud; 442 for perjury in connection with these cases; seventy-eight for unlawful enclosure; and sixty-four for timber trespass.[14]

As the marshals served the process of court in these land cases, they encountered a surprising amount of resistance, although much was passive. In eighty-two cases, the deputies could not find the defendants and wrote on the subpoena, "after diligent search could not find the defendant." Indeed, these officers concluded that the defendants were fictitious and did not exist. As Marshal Morrison searched for the post office addresses of indicted persons, he soon complained that he was "never in a place where so many men were known by the same name [Smith ?]." To add to these frustrations, the marshals noted that the records of 209 cases had "disappeared."[15]

Marshal Morrison and his deputies also encountered overt hostility. Near Silver City, prominent rancher John W. Fleming threatened Deputy Marshal Louis Kennon and his posse with violence. Admittedly, the confrontation was partly the young deputy's fault. Fleming claimed that many new settlers were squatting upon his land. The immigrants said that Fleming's titles were fraudulent.[16]

Deputy Kennon panicked, gathered a posse, and arrested the irate cattleman and seven other property owners. Unfortunately, many possemen were new settlers—"the Gila [River] men"—who hated Fleming. At first Fleming threatened to fight to a finish rather than to submit. Kennon telegraphed Marshal Morrison who replied with permission to summon regular troops (Congress provided this power specially in land cases), but urged Kennon to "act very prudently." These steps were not necessary, since Fleming agreed to submit to arrest if he received immediate bail. The editor of the *Enterprise* became indignant when he learned that the deputy had considered the use of troops. It implied that the citizens of Grant County were rebellious. Kennon "acted impudently," according to the journalist, and added that the lawman "could have made every arrest" without the "Gila men" or the army. Other deputies, such as Miguel A. Otero of Las Vegas, made arrangements with defendants in his area to meet him at the railroad voluntarily. Otero then took them to Santa Fe for a hearing and permitted them to return home immediately on bond.[17]

Some New Mexicans observed that various marshals enforced the land laws more stringently than others. Political allegiance played a part. Republican lawmen enforced the land laws lukewarmly; Democratic officers fervently. The reform-minded Governor Edmund Ross (and his much-hated Surveyor-General George W. Julian) urged Marshal Romulo Martinez to carry out the land laws to the letter. In March 1890, several months after Don Romulo departed the marshalcy, the *New Mexican* suggested that Martinez's conduct in the land cases be investigated. "During 1887," said an angry journalist,

> some 400 indictments for alleged land fraud were found. . . . The record will prove that . . . not ten convictions were had; in fact, only two, and these in the third [judicial] district. There were a few pleas of guilty entered there and nominal fines entered simply to make show.

This writer charged that these cases were fabricated so that the judicial officers could "make fees."[18]

Some of the most bitter memories from Marshal Martinez's term arose in southern Dona Ana County. The *San Marcial Reporter* recalled that in 1885 the "reform administration" of Governor Ross encouraged the prosecution of many land-holders in the south. "The fates portend that we should ever see another such [prosecution]," declared the editor. "A gang of armed U. S. deputy marshals arrived in this city and dragged from their homes highly respected citizens; hurried them to . . . [Las Cruces], subjected them to the indignity of incarceration, making the matter of bail as difficult as possible." In addition, the United States district attorney called "the most disreputable witnesses" and attempted to "blast" the reputations of the defendants. From the perspective of the easy-going marshalcy of Trinidad Romero, the *New Mexican* recalled how, in land cases, Marshal Martinez's deputies "persecuted our citizens" and "retarded development and progress generally." However, a Martinez deputy, Miguel A. Otero, charged that District Attorney Joseph Bell and other court officials, not Marshal Martinez, maliciously prosecuted land cases for fees.[19]

As in the land cases enforcement of the laws against timber trespass was generally unsuccessful. The deputy marshals arrested numerous alleged violators, but they were seldom the large-scale lumber dealers. Instead, the poor Hispano peasants felt the brunt of federal justice. In the Las Cruces area five poor farmers had to walk one hundred miles to stand trial for digging mesquite roots on public land.[20]

After nine years of effort, and few positive results, the federal government concluded that the lawmen could not enforce the land laws. Of the more than three thousand cases, the courts won fifteen verdicts of guilty in land fraud cases, none in the unlawful enclosure cases, and only a few in timber trespass cases. The government soon asked for dismissal of all timber cases.[21]

The federal government approached the disputed Spanish and Mexican land grants carefully. In 1891, Congress established a Court of Private Land Claims for New Mexico, Colorado, and Arizona. The marshal of each appropriate state or territory was required to support the tribunal. Marshal Trinidad Romero, who had to prepare for a December 1891 session of the Land Court, considered his problems very novel. Actually, similar courts had operated in Illinois and California before the Civil War. In a question-filled letter in November, Romero inquired about the routine support of this special tribunal—should the marshal attend in person, or could a deputy qualify; would the court have the same officers as a regular session of United States Court; and did the marshal receive extra compensation? The answer to the last question was a definite "No!"[22]

While most land grant cases that Romero handled were routine, that of James Addison Peralta-Reavis was not. Peralta-Reavis, a former streetcar conductor from St. Louis, claimed 17,000 square miles of land in the Gila Valley of New Mexico and Arizona through his Mexican wife, whom he said was a descendant of the original owner, Miguel Peralta de Cordoba.

The fortunes of hundreds of Southwesterners would be affected if Peralta-Reavis won his bizarre claim. Fortunately, in June 1895, the Court of Private Land Claims rejected it as an outright forgery. "Soon after the rendering of the adverse decision," said the *New Mexican*, "the tall form of James Addison Peralta-Reavis quietly moved out of the court room and down on the shady side of the street of the plaza. As he approached the monument, he was placed under arrest by Deputy U.S. Marshal Page B. Otero."[23]

This case taxed the patience of Marshal Edward L. Hall and his deputies, who kept Peralta-Reavis under surveillance during the entire trial. Deputy Otero cautioned Peralta-Reavis not to leave the city. On June 14, 1895, the "Baroness" arrived to testify on behalf of her husband. Such a large crowd gathered that two deputy marshals were required to clear a path for her to the courtroom. The lady was very unhappy when one of the deputy marshals shadowed her movements about the city. On July 17, 1896, a federal court found Peralta-Reavis guilty of fraud and sentenced him to two years in prison and a $5,000 fine. The marshals continued to serve the Court of Private Land Claims (not to be confused with the trial court) until 1904, when it expired.[24]

As a part of its efforts to prepare New Mexico Territory for statehood, Congress demanded that the morality of the frontiersmen be improved. As early as 1862, the national legislators forbade bigamy in the territories, although this act was not seriously enforced. In 1882, Congress passed the Edmunds Act, directed against the polygamous Mormons of Utah and neighboring territories. However, in a surprising turn of events, the federal government discovered that many non-Mormons lived outside the laws of marriage on the frontier. These persons were not, in most cases, bigamous or polygamous, but had merely failed to obtain a civil marriage license. This was especially true in New Mexico, where the Hispanos were married in the Catholic church.

Public opinion became sharply divided about the merits of these two laws, as well as the place of the marshalcy in their enforcement. In August 1890, after several years of watching attempts to enforce the Edmunds Act, the Silver City *Enterprise* declared that the presence of many persons living together without civil sanction was "becoming a very serious affair. . . . The enforcement of this act [by the marshals] is a sort of advance guard of civilization" in the territories. The Springer *Stockman* scoffed at the "slush sympathy" that some journals expressed for the "poor" women who were often victimized by the Edmunds Act. "If there is any one thing we believe in," said the *Stockman,* "it is the sacredness of the marriage relation." Unfortunately, the Edmunds Act most affected poor Hispano peasants whose Catholic marriage customs did not include a civil ceremony. Influential native leader Felix Martinez maintained that he refused nomination to the marshalcy in Cleveland's second term because he would have had "to lend my signature as a tool for the arrest of poor people under the Edmunds Act."[25]

Serious enforcement of the Edmunds Act occurred rather late in New Mexico, during the Democratic marshalcy of Romulo Martinez. His deputies began to move against violators of the cohabitation law in the spring of 1889. The *Enterprise* noted that deputy marshals arrested twenty-one couples in Dona Ana County. The following year, in April, seventy-five indictments were found in the same county. These indictments were a consequence of the diligent work of Marshal Trinidad Romero's office, staffed by Republicans. One of Don Trinidad's most ardent lieutenants was Deputy Dell Potter of Silver City. In July 1890, the *Enterprise* mentioned that Potter was collecting evidence of illegal cohabitation and learned that he possessed enough evidence to send "scores to the penitentiary." The newspaper added, however, that Potter was "impartial," collecting data about Anglos as well as Hispanos, women as well as men.[26]

This morality crusade prompted many misuses of the laws. In May 1895, the respectable citizens of Phenix, Eddy County, petitioned the United States Court at Socorro to remove its saloon crowd by way of the cohabitation laws. The saloon men lived outside the marriage laws. The promoters of the Pecos Irrigation and Improvement Company persuaded Marshal Edward Hall to deputize a Phenix meat market owner, Dee R. Harkey, to arrest the saloon men. His job also consisted of other duties—keeping the prostitutes and their boyfriends off the streets and out of hacks when "decent people" were about. Deputy Harkey arrested thirty unmarried couples and took them before the federal judge in Socorro. When they were released on bail, several defendants threatened to kill the deputy.[27]

Such laws permitted many deputy marshals and other unscrupulous persons to arrest persons on flimsy pretexts. In April 1895, an anonymous resident of Tularosa allegedly proposed to Deputy Joe

Morgan that he arrest a couple who lived out of wedlock. However, this informant would testify against the illegal cohabitants only if Morgan would deputize him. In this way, both men would earn fees from the case. The only evidence to prove that this couple was cohabiting was the occasional presence of the lady's dog in the man's backyard. "The costs of the trip [to arrest this couple] were charged up to Uncle Sam," said an indignant journalist. Deputy Morgan denied these charges.[28]

In 1896, after Congress wisely placed the marshals on fixed salaries, one editor reflected that "we suspect that the Edmunds Act will cut much less of a caper than in former years." The federal lawmen were no longer encouraged to fabricate charges against unfortunate persons in order to earn additional fees. Fortunately, the United States district attorneys dropped many cohabitation cases in New Mexico on the condition that the accused obtain legal marriage licenses.[29]

Congress went to extraordinary lengths to protect the morals of the territorials in 1896, when sports promoters allegedly scheduled a championship prizefight in New Mexico—the Robert Fitzsimmons-Peter Maher match. Several outraged citizens' and ministers' associations appealed to Governor William Thornton to prevent the bout. "Such exhibitions are universally condemned by the best public sentiment in all civilized communities," said a Presbyterian minister from Raton. Delegate Thomas B. Catron hurried a bill through Congress on February 7, 1896, to prevent prizefighting (and bullfighting) in the territories. The attorney general made unusually generous funds available to Marshal Edward Hall for the employment of extra deputies and informed the secretary of war that the government desired to save New Mexico from this "disgrace." The attorney general asked for troops to assist the marshal.[30]

When the promoters turned to disputed pastures around El Paso, Texas, on the Mexican border, Marshal Edward L. Hall went to the scene. On the night of February 11, 1896, Hall, Adjutant General W. H. Mabry (the commander of the Texas Rangers), and Governor Miguel Ahumada of Chihuahua, held a "council of war" to prepare plans to stop the pugilists. On February 13 Hall, who established his headquarters in the Pierson Hotel, dispatched his subordinates westward along the Southern Pacific Railroad toward Strauss, where the fight was supposed to occur. Tipsters had deliberately misled the lawmen about the location of the match; Maher trained publicly in Las Cruces, New Mexico, and Fitzsimmons in Juarez, Mexico. A carnivallike atmosphere reigned in El Paso, and, on February 19, Marshal Hall, Adjutant General Mabry, and Captain John R. Hughes of the Rangers paid a friendly visit to Fitzsimmons in Juarez.[31]

In the meantime, Hall and Governor William Thornton became preoccupied with a very serious feud between politician Albert B. Fall and Deputy Marshal Ben Williams in Las Cruces, and absented themselves from El Paso. Hall left his deputies in the charge of George Curry, Clerk of the Fifth New Mexico District Court. Curry recalled that he and the deputies, with a party of Rangers, traveled by special train to Langtry, Texas, to prevent the bout. When they arrived, evidently on February 21, they found that the pugilists had located the arena on a disputed island in the Rio Grande. Colorful Judge Roy Bean, "The Law West of the Pecos," sponsored the event, which lasted only ninety-five seconds, with Fitzsimmons the winner. Deputy Curry and his colleagues were bitterly disappointed that they missed the famous match. The El Paso Ministers Union thanked Marshal Hall and the other officers for preventing the bout on American soil. The editor of the *New York Times* regarded the fight to be "a victory for pugilism" and a defeat for law and order. "If a little gang of criminals can defy the laws and outwit the officers of one extremely large country," said the journalist, "the [pugilistic] events which illustrate these surprising facts is [sic] certainly worthy of serious consideration."[32]

Such controversial events as prizefights were not the only sensitive issues to occur in New Mexico during the 1890s. Just as the new railroads speeded up the movements of the elusive pugilists, the locomotives promoted the work of labor agitators. In June 1894, Marshal Edward L. Hall received word that the American Railway Union had gone out on sympathy strike for the employees of the Pullman Palace Car Company in Chicago. Soon an estimated three thousand New Mexican workers along the Santa Fe Railroad and the Atlantic and Pacific refused to work. The strike spread into Arizona as well. The strikers chose the railway town of Raton, in Colfax County, for the center of their agitation in New Mexico. When three hundred coal miners from nearby Blooms-burg joined the ARU force at Raton, some thousand rowdy strikers seized the helpless town. When Governor William Thornton asked Sheriff O. W. McCuiston whether he desired assistance, the county officer replied that the strikers assured him that they would not break the law. On June 30 a newspaper reporter noted that the ARU men acted as though the strike were a mere holiday. "U.S. flags are flying," he reported, "and speeches are being made interspersed with comic songs and patriotic music."[33]

When it became apparent that Sheriff McCuiston was more under the sway of the strikers than he admitted, Judge Edward P. Seeds sent Marshal Hall to Raton. Seeds gave Hall a writ of injunction, ordering the strikers to avoid the Santa Fe Railway yards. In addition, any interference with passenger trains carrying the United States mails would constitute a federal offense. Hall found the town in pandemonium; many men who desired to work were intimidated by the strikers. After the rioters abused a telegrapher, the federal lawman requested permission to employ deputies. Judge Seeds authorized him to deputize two hundred men.[34]

When the ARU men heard about the large number of deputies, and that troops might come as well, the strikers became threatening. They greased the rails to the north and derailed cars to the south of Raton. A party of eighty deputy marshals arrived south of town on July 2, but were forced to walk several miles around these obstructions. Hall recalled later that Sheriff McCuiston "warned" him about entering the town with his subordinates, but that Judge Seeds authorized the marshal to arrest McCuiston if necessary. The angry strikers used abusive language against the deputy marshals, many of whom were unsympathetic ranchers from the southern counties, and refused to permit hotel employees to house or feed the lawmen. When rumors circulated that the labor men planned to blow up the Santa Fe eating house, the deputies occupied the structure. In retaliation, on July 3 the union men released sixteen cars from a hill three miles above Raton and sent them careening into the hysterical village.[35]

The timely arrival of troops on July 4 relieved Marshal Hall and his deputies of some peacekeeping duties, and the lawmen began the task of running special trains—"the U. S. Marshal trains"—for mail and emergency purposes. On July 5 Hall arrested twelve of the obstructionists on charges of violating the mails and for contempt of court. Among them were Robert P. Bland, the local strike leader, and D. T. Medill, the poet laureate of the laboring men. While in jail, Medill wrote a poem about the doomed strike, appropriately titled, "After the Ball." On July 13, 1894, Eugene V. Debs, president of the American Railway Union, called off the strike and the railroad leaders, anxious to resume operations, announced that they did not plan to fire all of the strikers in New Mexico. With this conciliation in mind, the federal court in Santa Fe sentenced the strikers to no more than sixty days in jail.[36]

Many residents of the striking communities resented Marshal Hall and his deputies long after the railroads resumed operations. The lawmen, who were from the conservative and antilabor counties in the south, often handled the strikers roughly. On July 7, in Las Vegas, a deputy marshal attempted to arrest an engineer and force him to drive a train into Santa Fe, when the city marshal interfered. "The episode created bad feeling against the deputies," according to one reporter. As late as July 10 a band of fifty strikers patrolled Raton to prevent the deputy marshals from blaming the laborers for "dirty work" that might occur. The partisan Raton *Range* declared that when the strike began "the general feeling among the citizens of Raton was that no occasion existed for the summoning of these deputies" and that the strikers "scrupulously obeyed the order of the courts in keeping away from the railway company's property." On July 16, 1894, Marshal Hall informed Attorney General Richard Olney that the ARU was "bitter" about his conduct in the strike and that he (Hall) expected the strikers to make "political charges" against him. Hall protested that he had merely done his duty at Raton. "I know you [Olney] will do me justice," said the marshal humbly.[37]

While the federal lawmen of New Mexico had to deal with national issues, local problems continued to take up most of their time. Bands of rustlers continued to ply their trade in the southern counties after the Lincoln County War. Newspapers named John Kinney, a former Murphy-Dolan gunman, the leader of the outlaws. When Governor Lionel Sheldon assumed office in 1881, he launched a campaign—"The Rustler War"—against the outlaws, one that soon involved Marshal Alexander L. Morrison. The governor called upon the regular army for support, only to be told that the Posse Comitatus Act prevented such assistance. Sheldon then followed the precedent of Lew Wallace and organized units of militia. The Doña Ana County contingent, the Mesilla Scouts, commanded by Major Albert J. Fountain, was most active, but the Shakespeare Guards enjoyed the glory of arresting John Kinney in Grant County, in March 1883.[38]

Many New Mexicans objected to the employment of militia in the posses of civil lawmen. The Mesilla Scouts were derisively called "The Greaser Militia" since many members were Hispano. The *New Mexican* sprang to the defense of Sheldon and his militia in January 1883, saying that "Life and Property must be both as safe in the mountains and on the plains of New Mexico as they are in New York and Massachusetts." The governor's task was to elevate the territory to the level of the "civilized East," and the militia was necessary if he was to achieve this goal.[39]

Marshal Morrison, who desired to assist territorial officers when possible, unintentionally blemished the reputations of his office and the governor in the war against the rustlers in Valencia County. In September 1882, John P. Casey and other ranchers in the American Valley formed Company C, First Regiment of Militia, to battle the thieves. Casey, as captain, used his unit to frighten away small ranchers and to obtain choice lands. Marshal Morrison, who had purchased a ranch in the valley, and his political patron, Senator John A. Logan of Illinois, purchased half interest in the sprawling John Casey & William C. Moore Cattle Company. Logan's son-in-law also purchased land, a tract that allegedly infringed on the Zuni Reservation.[40]

On May 6, 1883, two recent settlers, Alexis Grossette and Robert Elsing, were murdered in the American Valley. John P. Casey arrested some alleged rustlers, whom Marshal Morrison (although it was not his duty) escorted to the Albuquerque jail. In a radical turn of events, however, William C. Moore and John Casey's brother, James, were arrested and indicted for the murders. Also indicted were two of Morrison's deputy marshals, Timothy Isaiah ("Longhair Jim") Courtright and James McIntyre. Courtright was a personal friend of Senator John Logan, who had hired him and McIntyre to scout for the Illinois politician during his visit to New Mexico.[41]

On the day of the murders Captain Casey divided his militia company into several groups with orders to scout the ranch and to protect Senator Logan's party. James Casey, the two deputy marshals, and others in the Logan party, rode in the direction of the Grossette ranch. This group encountered Grossette and Elsing and arrested them. James Casey, Courtright, and McIntyre, allegedly took the prisoners from the view of Senator Logan and murdered them.[42]

The repugnant nature of the murders and the subsequent flight of the deputy marshals to Texas placed Marshal Morrison in a most unfavorable light. Governor Sheldon offered a reward of $500 for each of the men. McIntyre was arrested in October 1884, tried, and released, since witnesses for the prosecution were "indisposed." In January 1886, Courtright surrendered to Texas officials, who released him to New Mexico for trial. He was acquitted. The sentiments of many New Mexicans were earlier expressed by the editor of the Albuquerque *Daily Democrat:* "Marshal Morrison can afford to be more careful hereafter in selecting his deputies." The resemblance to the excesses of Deputy Marshal Wyatt Earp's posse in Arizona in 1882 was unmistakable. Maverick deputies plagued both marshalcies.[43]

The struggle for economic and political place, which the American Valley murders revealed, became more apparent in New Mexico in the late 1880s. Factionalism—expecially between Anglo and Hispano interest groups soon erupted into violence. The marshals inflamed these passions when they enforced controversial land and morality laws. The appearance of numerous partisan deputy marshals around the election booths late in this decade embittered many people. "In the severe struggle for political place, New Mexican politics naturally developed a seamy side."[44]

A violent political movement, the White Cap (Gorras Blancas) society, revealed much of this discontent among the residents of San Miguel and neighboring counties. This secret society was made up of Hispanos who feared that the Las Vegas Land Grant was about to be seized by Anglo "land grabbers." The White Caps resorted to nightriding, fence cutting, the destruction of property including that of the hated Santa Fe Railroad, and any other means necessary to intimidate the "landlords" of San Miguel County. In order to acquire "respectability," the White Caps claimed to be affiliated with the Knights of Labor.[45]

On August 19, 1890, after complaints from the Santa Fe Railroad and others, the attorney general ordered Marshal Trinidad Romero to investigate the White Caps. Two days later the lawman interviewed trustworthy persons in Las Vegas about this secret movement. One informant, L. C. Booth, notified Governor L. Bradford Prince that Romero was in the city and that he would "give [the marshal] all the assistance I can." Romero was alarmed by what he learned, and in the following months recommended several measures against the agitators. Since the sheriff and his deputies were "in sympathy" with the Gorras Blancas, the marshal could not rely upon them. Governor Prince estimated that three-fourths of the local people were also aligned with the White Caps. Romero concluded that his deputies, who were well known, would be ineffective in Las Vegas and that he should employ a detective. However, he could station deputies at the polls in the upcoming elections. Romero also urged the attorney general to ask Terence Powderly, grand master of the Knights of Labor, to suspend the organization of new locals in New Mexico. Romero surmised that the White Caps would lose labor's support. The attorney general replied that he could not conduct such negotiations.[46]

Washington quickly accepted Marshal Romero's recommendation to employ a detective and Governor Prince hired a Pinkerton operative, Charles Siringo, who had been a member of Deputy Marshal Pat Garrett's posse in the pursuit of Billy the Kid. Siringo made friends with Nicanor Herrera, who, with his brothers Pablo and Juan, were the reputed leaders of the White Caps. When rumors reached the secret society that their organization had been infiltrated (according to Miguel A. Otero, who resided in Las Vegas during this time), the leaders soon abandoned their nighttime forays. They established a political party instead—the Partido del Pueblo Unido (United Peoples Party). A few weeks after Siringo concluded his investigation, the Herrera brothers killed a man who resisted their efforts to organize a labor union. The White Caps rioted for the last time, and the governor summoned the militia to Las Vegas. Pablo Herrera went into hiding for several years, only to be killed in 1894 by a deputy sheriff in Las Vegas.[47]

This conspiratorial atmosphere spread to neighboring counties and became especially serious in Santa Fe. The Alliance League (sometimes called the Button Gang from its identifying tags), supposedly the secret strongarm of Thomas Catron's Republican League Club, opposed the Democratic machine of former Marshal Romulo Martinez and Sheriff Francisco (Frank) Chavez. In March 1890, the remains of Faustin Ortiz, a Republican ward politician, were found near the city limits. Anonymous informants accused Martinez and Chavez and alleged that the former marshal had publicly expressed a desire to see Catron dead. The two Democratic leaders, with a dozen followers (most of whom were deputy sheriffs), were charged with murder.[48]

Martinez and Chavez obtained their release on bail and, in a show of strength, led a rally of two thousand persons on August 27. Among the demonstrators were a thousand coal miners (whom Martinez had befriended) who regarded themselves as the "true friends" of the Democratic lawmen. "Now the miners and the countryside will stand by them," concluded the *Daily Democrat*. The Democratic Party Convention of Santa Fe County proceeded to elect the two accused men as delegates to the territorial convention in Silver City. While there, Martinez announced that he had since sworn never to associate with a Republican, and he gave the grand jury that indicted him the "Hail Columbia!"[49]

Since Frank Chavez occupied the shrievalty at the time of the indictment of Romulo Martinez and himself, the county court had to find a suitable officer to arrest them. Most, or all, deputy sheriffs and city policemen were either Democratic partisans or indictees. The court summoned Marshal Trinidad Romero, although he did not possess the authority to serve county warrants. However, the prestige of his office gave Romero an official aura. His nephew, Deputy Bernardo Romero, served the warrants on the former marshal and Sheriff Chavez, not in an official capacity but as a "responsible citizen." Democratic supporters of Martinez pointed out that the arresting officer was still a Republican. In August 1891, the case of Don Romulo and Frank Chavez was tried in Albuquerque. Thomas B. Catron prosecuted; Neill B. Field, a prominent Democrat and enemy of the prosecutor, defended. Field won an acquittal on a technicality.[50]

While the former federal lawman and his colleague Chavez struggled to win their freedom from the court, a related feud erupted into violence in Santa Fe. In December 1889, former Chief of Police Francisco Gonzalez y Borrego, a partisan of Romulo Martinez, killed another Democrat, Sylvestre Gallegos. The fight may have occurred over the office of county coroner, which Borrego had lost to Gallegos. After Borrego was jailed, Sheriff Frank Chavez allegedly beat the inmate brutally. Thomas B. Catron won the acquittal of Borrego the following March, whereupon the vindicated man promptly joined the Republican League Club. Two years later, on the night of May 29, 1892, Frank Chavez, who had since resigned the shrievalty, was brutally shot to death by unknown assassins. Four days after that, Francisco Borrego killed a follower of the dead man, Juan Pablo Dominguez, who had accused Borrego of the murder of Chavez. Borrego was jailed to await trial. In the meantime, on the night of February 5, 1891, unidentified persons attempted to assassinate Thomas B. Catron. The shots missed the intended target and wounded Joseph A. Ancheta, a territorial legislator.[51]

The murder of Chavez, and the spread of the secret societies, prompted President Grover Cleveland to appoint the former mayor of Santa Fe William T. Thornton as governor in May 1893. Thornton's first role was that of district attorney and crime fighter, rather than executive. Thornton immediately set up a task force of lawmen, composed of Marshal Edward Hall and the energetic new sheriff of Santa Fe County, William P. Cunningham. One hostile newspaperman charged that Cunningham, a former El Paso lawman, was hired to kill "Mexicans." The governor also employed a noted gunfighter from Las Cruces, Thomas Tucker, as deputy sheriff. Former Governor L. Bradford Prince characterized Tucker as a "professional killer." Cunningham and Tucker also received appointments as deputy marshals.[52]

Among the many secret societies, the "Labor Protection Society" of Bernalillo (near Albuquerque) acquired a reputation for brutality. This confederacy ordered employees of the Santa Fe Railroad to refuse to work until the company increased wages to $1.25 per day. When one employee, Jerry Hickey, refused to comply with the order of the Society, its thugs assaulted him. In January 1894, the "enforcing arm" of this conspiracy wrecked a train near Algodones. When Marshal Hall and his subordinates arrested several members of this ring, they earned considerable praise from the editor of the *New Mexican*.[53]

Numerous political assassinations occurred in the early 1890s, but the murder of the former sheriff of Mora County, John Doherty, was the most senseless. Even though the crime occurred outside his jurisdiction, Governor Thornton assigned Sheriff Cunningham the task of seeking out the killers. Upon learning about the governor's plan, the outlaws murdered one of their number to prevent him from revealing the workings of the oath-bound band. When Cunningham could find no immediate evidence against this society, he, as a deputy marshal, arrested several of the suspects for violation of the Edmunds Act.[54] Once incriminating testimony was gathered against the outlaws, the deputy marshal filed territorial charges of murder. Perhaps the most surprising revelations to arise from the exposure of this secret conclave was the implication of an Anglo attorney and the current sheriff of Mora County, Agapito Abeyta. Said the editor of the *New Mexican* in amazement, "Ordinarily the native people . . . are far too shrewd to harness up with Americans of this stamp."[55]

In Las Vegas, thieves led by Vicente Silva, a saloon owner, began to murder, rob, and rustle under the guise of White Cap patriotism. Silva even went so far as to execute members of his band for disloyalty.[56] In May 1893, when Silva suddenly disappeared, the governor and Marshal Hall decided to pursue him. The following May (1894) Deputy Marshal Cameron telegraphed from Flagstaff, Arizona, that he had arrested the elusive outlaw and his wife. This announcement proved erroneous. Deputy Horace Loomis investigated a rumor about Silva's being in Pueblo, Colorado, but that lead also proved false. Only in March 1895, did the federal lawmen receive definite news about the bandit leader. One of Silva's henchmen, then imprisoned for his crimes, revealed that they (the highwaymen) had murdered Silva after he had killed his own wife.[57]

In scarcely a year, the task force of Governor Thornton broke several dangerous criminal societies. At the spring term of court in Las Vegas, in 1894, thirty-five members of the Vicente Silva band were indicted for various crimes; thirty-two were convicted, fifteen of them for murder. As the campaign for law and order continued, the prison overflowed. In December 1895, the *New Mexican* noted with pleasure that "Since the beginning of the present law and order Democratic administration" the prison had held 206 inmates; cells existed for only 190. The editor concluded with pride that four men had been legally hanged.[58]

The war against lawlessness could end only after the murderers of former Sheriff Frank Chavez were brought to justice. In January 1894, Sheriff Cunningham obtained warrants for the arrest of six suspects, but, in an attempt to arrest the suspects, Deputy Sheriff Thomas Tucker killed one of them, Hipolito

Vigil. Rumors of reprisal spread, and Marshal Hall was constrained to place Sheriff Cunningham and his lieutenants in protective custody. Later, Sheriff Cunningham arrested the remaining five suspects, two of whom—Francisco and Antonio Gonzalez y Borrego—were members of the Republican League Club. These men were also members of the "Alliance League." Some said that Thomas B. Catron was affiliated with the League, although no evidence was forthcoming in the month-long trial of the alleged Chavez murderers. Although Catron vigorously defended the Borregos and their three comrades, the jury rendered a verdict of guilty. They were hanged in 1897. With this execution there began a restoration of faith in the judicial system of New Mexico. The marshalcy played an important role in this campaign.[59]

While the marshals were deeply involved with these problems, substantial changes were occurring in the administration of the office that would promote professionalism among the lawmen. The business of the federal courts and, hence, in the marshalcy continued to increase during the 1880s and 1890s. In August 1883, Marshal Alexander L. Morrison requested permission to increase the salary of his clerk and added that the "business of my office has greatly increased since my arrival here. . . . There is every likelihood," he said, "of a still further increase."

Seemingly minor problems—providing interpreters for court— became more troublesome. In 1879, a few years before Morrison became marshal, the *New Mexican* described the trial of five Indians from Laguna Pueblo for sheep stealing. It was an "extraordinary scene," in which double interpreting occurred—"first from English into Spanish, and then from Spanish into the Laguna language, and vice versa." The complexity of court cases, and consequent crowded dockets, prompted President of the New Mexico Bar Association Neill B. Field to reflect in January 1888, that three years would be required to clear the backlog of cases.[60]

This increase of business was reflected in Marshal Hall's office ledger for the fiscal year 1896. This book, which is organized on the quarterly system, shows that on November 30, 1895, Marshal Hall had "on deposit and on hand as corrected," $17,955.76. Unfortunately, only part of this volume has survived, but the expenses for the three months after November 30 can be reconstructed:

Fees of Jurors	$4,301.85
Fees of Witnesses	3,901.00
Support of Prisoners	3,634.25
Fees & Expenses of Marshals	2,052.26
Pay of Bailiffs and Criers	1,067.80
Miscellaneous Expenses	1,253.67
	$17,955.76

The category, Fees & Expenses of Marshals, was heavily used the year-round. From it Hall paid his deputies, as well as bills for official stationery, juror blanks, deputy fee books, telegrams, railroad tickets, telephone calls, and weapons. Fees of Witnesses and Fees of Jurors came into use at sessions of court. At the December 1895 term of court in Socorro (now part of the Fifth Judicial District), Hall paid $449.20 for seventeen jurors in the petit and grand juries; $308.30 for eighteen witnesses for the first panel and seventeen for the second, and for incidental witnesses for the U.S. Commissioner's Court in Santa Fe. The lawman resorted to Support of Prisoners when he paid $7.70 and $6.60 to Leon B. Stern & Company for clothing for a prisoner, Frank McCoy, who was lodged in the Albuquerque jail. Miscellaneous Expenses accounted for such items as pay for interpreters, who normally received $2.00 per day.[61]

As the official demands of the marshalcy increased in the 1880s, the chief federal lawmen searched for more experienced book-keepers and accountants. Marshal Alexander Morrison employed a clerk, but the preceding marshals usually designated as book-keeper any deputy who had the rudiments of education. In May 1894, Edward L. Hall employed an experienced accountant, I. Neustatter, who came highly recommended from the marshal's office in Arizona. Neustatter "was thoroughly versed in all of the details of the U.S. Marshals office relative to accounts and book-keeping," according to his credentials. Unfortunately, the new employee was rather temperamental. He resigned twice, only to be rehired by Hall, who desperately needed him. When Neustat-ter persisted in his behavior, the marshal reluctantly fired him. The spiteful accountant filed charges against him and provoked an investigation into the marshal's administrative procedures. The hapless lawman survived the investigation and soon employed a new clerk.[62]

The marshals went to such lengths to retain reliable clerks out of fear of federal examiners, who now made annual treks to the frontier districts. Marshal John E. Sherman, Jr., had received the first examiner in 1882. Examiner Howard Perry visited Alexander Morrison in 1883. In May 1892, the Las Cruces *Rio Grande Republican* reported that Examiner S. P. Kercheval made an "exhaustive examination of Marshal Romero's office and finds it in good shape." Leigh Chalmers found Edward Hall's papers in "first class condition" the next year. However, the attorneys general continued to disallow some of the marshals' expenses, and the lawmen resorted to extraordinary defensive procedures—they retained lawyers in Washington, D.C., to represent them to the Treasury. Marshal Hall even retained a lawyer for his deputies.[63]

This constant concern about the condition of official records, and fear of political charges as well, persuaded the marshals to place only trustworthy relatives in important posts. In the 1880s and 1890s, the marshalcies became family affairs. Alexander Morrison appointed his son, Alexander, Jr., as chief deputy. Trinidad Romero, who assumed office in 1889, appointed his son Serapio as chief deputy and his nephew Bernardo as chief clerk. The Albuquerque *Daily Democrat* surmised that Serapio would be more than just a deputy—"the marshal de facto"—a traditional practice among the Hispano politicians. Edward L. Hall took a relative by marriage, his brother-in-law Horace W. Loomis of Silver City, as his chief deputy and chief clerk. Another brother, A. W. Loomis, served as deputy.[64]

But the deputyship, which often attracted inferior or untrustworthy persons, remained a source of concern. Admittedly, this post was hazardous and the income paltry. On August 7, 1882, in an attempt to upgrade the position, Congress belatedly extended the 1853 uniform fee list to the territories and authorized the marshals of Arizona and New Mexico to receive double fees for mileage—that is, $.12 per mile, rather than the usual $.06. However, in 1892, the comptroller of the Treasury discontinued this practice (which had recognized the uniqueness of the vast districts in the West), much to the dismay of the marshal's office in Santa Fe. There would probably be "a wholesale resignation of deputy marshals" one subordinate informed the *New Mexican*. Under the original 1882 act, the deputies did not receive the full $.12 per mile, since, under the contract with the marshal, the chief lawman retained a percentage of each deputy's earnings. Marshal Edward Hall adopted an expediency to circumvent this ruling of the comptroller. He required each deputy to provide a horse and, in the words of Examiner J. H. Campbell, "by allowing them [the deputies] liberal compensation for the use of their horses as actual expense in lieu of mileage, [Hall] secures the services of subpoenas." The examiners concluded that this stopgap was necessary given the adverse decision of the Treasury, but added that Marshal Hall still could not persuade his underlings to do anything extra. The marshals fared better than their deputies since, in 1890, the chief lawmen were permitted to retain up to $6,000 in fees per year, rather than $4,000 as before.[65]

What the reduction of fees actually accomplished was an increase in fee making. Numerous charges were brought against the New Mexican officers, as well as nearly every marshalcy in the nation during the 1880s and 1890s. In his *Annual Report for 1883*, Attorney General Benjamin Brewster observed that "only by a wise readjustment of fees or salaries to United States marshals . . . [can] justice be done and expenses properly curtailed." He admitted that many marshals were guilty of "making fees" by encouraging deputies to support "frivolous prosecutions." In February 1896, an outraged citizen of Deming, New Mexico, alleged that Marshal Hall's office was run for "REVENUE ONLY" [his caps]. He added that the chief lawman and his subordinates traveled on free railroad passes (something forbidden by the Interstate Commerce Act of 1887), and then charged the government for the travel expenses. This anonymous informant declared that the deputies turned in ballooned vouchers for expenses—$.75 for a meal at Harvey Eating Houses—when the meal actually cost $.15. "The Marshal & Deputies are very careful to obtain the signature of the Eating House Clerk," he concluded, "to [the] blank voucher and fill it in to reach 75 cents."[66]

This controversy did not prevent the New Mexico marshalcy from manifesting signs of growth and refinement. Marshal Hall installed a telephone in his home (and presumably in his office). He also purchased a typewriter. Marshal Trinidad Romero received the privilege of moving his office into the new Federal Building in Santa Fe in 1890. This structure, with its "elegantly furnished" offices, symbolized the growing independence and importance of the federal judiciary in New Mexico.[67]

In the 1890s, newspapers resurrected charges of inattention to duty and lack of "esprit de corps among county lawmen." If the governor failed to post a reward for badmen, the sheriffs acted "humiliated" and refused to pursue them. The *Las Vegas Optic* observed that sheriffs had "no personal right to rewards, but did earn some income for hazardous duty in the form of fees. In the East, declared one journalist, "there is a pride of office which leads the different sheriffs to endure every possible hardship." The New Mexico shrievalty was guilty of many shortcomings, according to one complainant who observed the Las Vegas sheriff at a session of court, in March 1886. "I have had a chance to get an insight to one matters [*sic*] . . . ," said the humble writer, R. J. Danials [*sic*]. "The present sheriff and his deputy are man [*sic*] of notorious bad caracters [*sic*]." They "have tried to send everybody to [the] pen just to make fees."[68]

To earn additional income, and to overcome the faulty fee system, federal and local lawmen (sheriffs were on fees also) cooperated to earn rewards for fugitives from justice. In October 1896, Sheriff Holm O. Bursum of Socorro County responded to an inquiry from Chief Deputy Marshal Horace Loomis:

> Yes, I have a warrant from John Hinton, [and] am very anxious to get him. There is a reward of $200 [for Hinton]. I think that by doing a little work [persuasion] we can get it increased to $500. If agreeable [with you] I will try to have it increased and we can divide it.[69]

Within the judiciary of New Mexico, the marshals worked closely with the judges. This association was generally routine, although quarrels began to occur as the number of judges increased. In New Mexico in 1887, the Fourth Judicial District was created and in 1890 a Fifth was added. The marshals were not always satisfied with the bench. In August 1882, Marshal Alexander Morrison complained that Judge L. Bradford Prince was too "lenient" with criminals. Prince fined a chronic violator of the revenue laws only $25 and costs, even though Morrison's deputy pursued the offender one hundred miles. Morrison added that Prince allowed only two weeks for court in Albuquerque, when much more time was required to try persons whom Morrison's office had arrested.[70]

A more serious controversy arose between Marshal Edward L.

Hall's office and Judge Albert B. Fall in Las Cruces, seat of the Third Judicial District. In the late 1880s, Fall constructed a Democratic empire at the expense of the Republican leader of Dona Ana County, Albert J. Fountain, former militia leader and outlaw hunter. Each man sought support among the residents of the county: Fall led immigrant cattlemen from Texas, represented by Oliver M. Lee; Fountain counted many Hispanos among his followers. Fall slowly wooed the native population and successfully defended his ranching friends from Fountain, who prosecuted them for rustling. In 1890 and 1892, Fall also won the assembly seat that Fountain customarily occupied.[71]

Fall regarded the control of law enforcement positions to be essential to the exercise of political power and placed his friends in county offices and in the marshalcy. He persuaded Sheriff Guadalupe Ascarate to deputize Oliver M. Lee and several cowboys: Jim Gilliland, William McNew, Thomas Tucker (who later served in Santa Fe), and Philip Fall, brother of Albert, although these men were suspected cattle rustlers. In April 1893, Fall was appointed judge for the Third Judicial District, over the strenuous objections of Albert J. Fountain. When rumors circulated about a plot against his life, the new judge asked for a bodyguard of deputies. Hall complied with commissions for Lee, Gilliland, and McNew.[72]

Just when the pathway to power appeared clear to Judge Fall, a strongwilled deputy marshal, Ben Williams, suddenly obstructed his way. The date of Williams's commission is unclear. He may have held it from the entry of Edward Hall into office; more probably, he obtained his badge during the railway strike at Raton, July 1894. He was noted as an energetic deputy by observers in Raton. A former salesman for the Singer Sewing Machine Company, Williams also dabbled in other trades, such as butchering. He was a staunch Republican. The first signs of tension between Williams and Fall occurred when he produced evidence of rustling against Fall's henchmen, Deputy Marshals Lee, Gilliland, and McNew. As the November 1894 elections were approaching, Judge Fall feared that Williams might expand his snooping to include an examination of Democratic activity at the polls in Las Cruces. Fall promptly asked Marshal Hall to withdraw Williams's badge. In late October, the stunned deputy consented with regrets, but did so "on account of the opposition and personal feeling of the judge." After observing the ease with which Marshal Hall bowed to Fall, the *Rio Grande Republican* (Fountain's paper) asked pointedly, "Now who is marshal? Fall or Hall?"[73]

With the removal of Deputy Ben Williams, Judge Fall exercised full control of the election. Fall's candidate for the assembly defeated Fountain's son, Albert, Jr. However, the conduct of the judge and his bodyguard of deputy marshals was deplorable. Deputy Oliver Lee paraded around the ballot boxes with a Winchester rifle, while Fall intimidated his enemies. A score of protests reached the desk of Attorney General Richard Olney, among them a letter from Ben Williams. With so many charges of misconduct before him, Olney persuaded Albert Fall to resign the judgeship on January 7, 1895.[74]

This abuse of the deputyship in the November 1894 elections embarrassed Marshal Hall, to the delight of the Fountain party. Soon after the fall elections, the *Rio Grande Republican* reported that charges had been filed against the marshal, "owing to the actions of some of his deputies"—namely, Oliver Lee, Jim Gilliland and William McNew. In March 1895, when an examiner arrived in Santa Fe, the Republicans gleefully declared that former Judge Fall had filed the charges against Hall. Sensing a political ploy, the *New Mexican* countered that "Republican tricksters" desired to blemish the reputation of Hall and to split the Democratic Party by driving a wedge between the Fall and Hall supporters. On March 28, the federal lawman joyfully reported: "I have just had a letter from Judge Fall saying that the story is a malicious falsehood." The examiner also found Hall "straight as a string."[75]

The rivalry between Fall and Fountain continued in spite of the loss of the judgeship, and the Democratic deputy marshals (with concurrent sheriff's badges) continued to enforce the will of the former judge. Ben Williams, who had replaced his deputy marshal's commission with a constableship and the post of cattle detective, resumed the investigation of Deputy Marshal Lee's rustling activities. The Fall deputy sheriffs responded by arresting Williams for carrying arms when not on duty. Williams accused them of the same offense, but nothing came of the latter charges. On the night of September 14, 1895, Albert J. Fall evidently determined to remove the nettlesome cattle detective. Fall, with his brother-in-law, Deputy Marshal Joe Morgan, and one unidentified man, ambushed Williams on a side street in Las Cruces. Williams miraculously escaped serious injury, but managed to wound Morgan in the exchange of gunfire. The two parties then exchanged acrimonious letters in the newspapers, and Williams lost his position as cattle detective. In February of the next year, while serving Marshal Hall in the Fitzsimmons-Maher prizefight controversy in El Paso, Deputy Marshal George Curry observed Ben Williams and three armed men suspiciously board a train behind Albert Fall. Curry and Deputy Marshal Thomas Tucker, both of whom feared for Fall's life, insisted upon accompanying him part way to Las Cruces. Otherwise, recalled Curry, Fall "might not have reached Las Cruces alive."[76]

This bitter feud that engulfed so many people originated between A. J. Fountain and Albert Fall. On February 1, 1896, Fountain and his young son, Henry, were brutally murdered, and another wave of tension swept the political factions in Dona Ana County. Fall's "bogus deputy marshals," as Ben Williams called them, "swaggered" down the streets of Las Cruces. Deputy Joe Morgan was allegedly the most arrogant. One newspaper observed that, as a consequence of the murder of Fountain, "feeling is increasing" and both "factions are heavily armed." Only the Fall Democrats could "legally" carry arms, since they were deputy marshals (or deputy sheriffs).[77]

For Marshal Edward Hall and Governor William Thornton, this feud could not have come at a more inopportune time. In the northern counties, secret societies were spreading lawlessness; in the south, at El Paso, a disputed boxing match demanded their attention. On February 21, 1896, Thornton and Hall held a bipartisan conference of Las Cruces feudists in El Paso (a convenient site in view of the presence of Hall's deputies to prevent the prizefight). When Thornton decided to remove Sheriff Guadalupe Ascarate and replace him with Patrick F. Garrett, Albert Fall stormed out of the meeting. Thornton eventually got his way.[78]

But the removal of Ascarate did not resolve the problem of armed deputy marshals on the streets of Las Cruces. Only Marshal Hall could remove this menace. On February 21, the day of the conference in El Paso, he revoked all deputy marshalships in Dona Ana County (less one to serve the process of court). The *Rio Grande Republican* commented happily that "there have been no six-shooters in evidence" since the marshal's order. While the *New Mexican* appreciated Hall's directive, the editor added that this order would not persuade the feudists to hang up their guns permanently. Yet, the fears of the Republicans were moderated when they realized that the Fall faction could no longer carry guns legally.[79]

A Pinkerton detective assisted Sheriff Garrett in the search for the killers of Fountain and his son, but the new sheriff only succeeded in arousing more hatred as he harassed the Fall-Lee faction with unproven accusations. Marshal Hall, who feared the growing anger with Garrett, refused to give him more than a temporary deputyship for specific tasks. However, Garrett soon appointed Ben Williams, a storm center of the feud, as a deputy sheriff. But the marshal cannily avoided previous mistakes by withholding wholesale commissions.[80]

The Democratic administration of Grover Cleveland changed the direction and purpose of the marshalcy considerably in New Mexico. During the 1880s, the federal lawmen assumed a positive role as reformers, in order to help prepare the territory for statehood. The enforcement of various controversial laws—concerning land, marriage, sporting events—and the participation in a "law and order" campaign pointed to this unusual duty. When Hispanos occupied the seat of chief federal lawman in Santa Fe, this positive tendency was even more fully realized. The office represented the entire population more completely than ever before. Only in a backward area, such as a youthful territory, could such powers be exercised fully by the federal lawmen. Mature states seldom required such radical behavior on the part of their marshals.

This positive role created problems as well. Any controversial activity in the 1880s and 1890s opened the marshalcy to charges of policial partisanship; and the office became a mere extension of the party in power. Sometimes the lawman became a tool of one faction within a party. Occasionally, the chief lawman and his deputies willingly participated in fee-making or other shady devices. If federal court business was slack, the lawmen merely fabricated a fee-making action. If the marshalcy was to win the support of all the people, it would have to be insulated to some extent from the political parties.

9

The Arizona Marshalcy,
1882–97

When Crawley P. Dake vacated the Arizona marshalcy in 1882, he left a badly tarnished badge for his successor. In some instances, Dake had been conscientious and energetic, but he had also exposed many weaknesses in the office—among them, the inept and irresponsible method of appointment of deputies, and the failure of the marshals to insulate the office from political factionalism. In the early 1880s, the marshalcy faced many problems that required a strong hand: social assimilation of the Indians, religious squabbles with the Mormons, and the appearance of the Chinese minority in the Southwest, not to mention widespread outlawry. The growth of rapid communications, more fully developed now, made these social elements collide with the federal authorities. For the federal policemen of this era, hectic and sometimes disconcerting tenures lay in store.

During the 1880s, Arizona's population rose from 40,000 to 90,000. By the turn of the century, it had reached 122,000, and consisted of Anglos, Hispanos, Indians (who represented two-thirds of that number), and some Chinese. Navajos, whose reservation straddled the Arizona-New Mexico border, were not included in the population count.[1] Among the new arrivals were the Mormons, who, by 1884, numbered 2,500 in the northeastern counties. The Chinese immigrants numbered only in the hundreds.[2]

New people demanded new counties and judicial districts, all of which affected the United States marshals. As the ratio of people to marshals increased, a complementary increase in the number of deputy marshals was required. In 1879, there were seven counties;

in 1890, ten; in 1895, twelve. These new districts included Cochise, Graham, Gila, Coconino, Navajo, and Santa Cruz. After many appeals to Congress for a new judge and judicial district for the many new settlers, in 1891 the national lawmakers complied by creating the Fourth Judicial District.[3]

Zan L. Tidball, a former Department of Justice examiner, succeeded Crawley P. Dake to the Arizona marshalcy on July 18, 1882. His credentials were impressive: Senator Edward Platt of New York, who recommended Tidball, characterized the selection "as popular and gratifying," while Senator William E. Chandler of New Hampshire, under whom the nominee had served in the past, described him as "most capable and deserving." Arizonans, however, were not pleased. Several residents of the territory had been nominated, but the president had turned them all down for the New Yorker. Said the Prescott *Arizona Miner* about Tidball, "Why he was appointed is more than we can say."[4]

Under Democrat Grover Cleveland, there were significant changes in Arizona's government. Conrad M. Zulick, a New Jersey politician, became governor in 1885. He had listed Arizona as an official address for more than a year although he managed mining property in Mexico. A most unusual problem attended this selection—Mexican laborers held Zulick under arrest at one of his mines in Nacozari.[5]

This embarrassing predicament did not portend good things for the incoming Democratic officials of Arizona. In conformity with the Democratic party platform, President Cleveland appointed a long-time resident of Arizona, William Kidder Meade, to the marshalcy. Born in Virginia in 1851, Meade prospected in the West before investing in mining property in southern Arizona. In 1879–80, he represented Pinal County (Florence) in the lower house of the assembly and later, as a resident of Tombstone, Pima County, he sat in the upper chamber. As a delegate to the Democratic National Convention in Chicago in 1884, Meade introduced the plank which demanded the appointment of *bona fide* residents to offices in the territories. He visited Washington in 1885 with the hope of receiving the governorship of his territory. On July 8, he received the marshalcy instead.[6]

Perhaps no marshal ever entered upon his duties in such peculiar circumstances. His governor was in the protective custody of laborers at Nacozari, Sonora, who, under Mexican law, could detain a mine manager if all wages had not been paid. Marshal Meade promptly employed a former Indian scout, M. T. ("Doc") Donovan, who spirited the hostage to freedom in Arizona, where he assumed office in October 1885. Marshal Meade rewarded Donovan (Dunnevan) with a commission as a deputy marshal.[7]

With the election of Republican Benjamin Harrison to the presidency in 1888, Robert H. Paul, also a Republican and a noted manhunter, received the marshalcy. A native of Massachusetts and a '49er to the California Gold Rush, Paul had been sheriff of Calaveras County. In 1872 he became an employee of Wells, Fargo and Company. This post took him to Arizona in 1878, when Marshal Crawley P. Dake was stoutly resisting highwaymen. As sheriff of Pima County, Paul pursued the Wyatt Earp party of deputy marshals in 1882. He continued to manhunt (he was one of the few Southwesterners who made it a profession) as a Southern Pacific Railroad detective. In 1888, Paul won nationwide recognition when, with the assistance of Mexican police, he killed several American bandits in Chihuahua.[8]

The appointment of "Bob" Paul pleased many Arizonans, who feared the rising crime rate in Arizona would delay admission to statehood. A Tucson resident wrote Senator Richard Coke of Texas, possibly a member of the Senate Committee on Appointments, that "no single act of the Senate will prove of such importance to the general welfare of Arizona and New Mexico as the confirmation of Bob Paul" as marshal. The *Arizona Daily Citizen* agreed that Paul was "known throughout the Southwest as a fearless man, who has frequently taken his life into his own hands in [the] pursuit of criminals."[9]

The return of the Democrats to power in the elections of 1892 caused another turnabout in Arizona's marshalcy, and in the governorship. President Cleveland appointed to the latter post a strongwilled Democrat, Louis C. Hughes. Hughes supported the reappointment of William Kidder Meade, whom Cleveland commissioned on May 8, 1893. However, many of Meade's Democratic friends were put out with the roundabout way he received the office. Governor Hughes first gave Meade the superintendency of the prison at Yuma and, at the same time, he nominated the former Virginian for the marshalcy. Hughes stipulated that Meade should vacate the prison post if the latter appointment materialized. Hughes's party colleagues tried to persuade him to give up Meade, since the former marshal "was constantly sewing seeds of dissension in the party." Meade, they alleged, was a "marplot." The governor overruled party objections, something he would regret later.[10]

The official activities of the United States marshals of Arizona during the 1880s followed the pattern of affairs of the federal lawmen in New Mexico: they constituted a response to congressional directives. When Congress took a position on a particular issue—the investigation into alleged mail frauds—the Arizona lawmen performed the investigation. When Congress legislated against some wrong, such as Mormon polygamy, the federal lawmen again came into play. The same was true with regard to the legislation against Chinese immigrants and the efforts of the national government to resolve the Indian problem. At the same time, the marshals became deeply involved in the internal affairs of Arizona Territory. In many instances they became serious sources of concern because of their partisan behavior.

In the summer of 1882 Marshal Zan L. Tidball received instructions to investigate a postal route, No. 40113, from Tres Alamos Post Office, in Pima County, to Clifton, in Graham County. This investigation occurred in connection with the spectacular Star Route Case during the Republican administrations of Presidents James A. Garfield and Chester A. Arthur. The postmaster general discovered numerous fradulent contracts, in which "rings" of unscrupulous men contracted at moderate costs to carry the mail in remote districts with the intention of obtaining more lucrative terms in the near future. These speculators bid very low on the first contract, planned to acquire additional appropriations, but intended to provide no more service for the increased pay. This was easy to do on the remote frontier where the risk of close supervision by the Post Office Department was not great. Garfield directed Postmaster General Thomas L. James and Attorney General Wayne MacVeagh to conduct the investigations.[11]

When Tidball began his examination into Star Route 40113, he was appalled. At Tres Alamos, Tidball learned that the postmaster and his assistant had long since departed. Instead, "an embecile [*sic*] old man" was in charge. Only one family resided on the fifty-seven mile stretch to Camp Grant, on the San Pedro River, but in four years, the route had been "upgraded" from a weekly, to a tri-weekly, and finally to a daily mail. With these promotions, the route acquired more appropriations—$2,600, to $14,000 to $28,000 respectively. "The truth is," concluded the federal lawman, "the time never was and will not be in some years to come, when a daily mail will be *required* [his italics] to meet the needs of . . . [that] section of country." The marshal concluded that the contracts perpetrated "a deliberate and outrageous robbery" upon the government.[12]

The investigation of Star Route 40113 was an easy matter compared with the difficulties that the federal government encountered in the prosecution of these violations in an Arizona court. "Evidence had to be gathered in distant and thinly settled localities, and government counsel had to function in courts where juries were more sympathetic with local contractors than with strangers representing far-off Washington." These problems were complicated for Marshal Tidball by misconduct on the part of Judge Wilson S. Hoover, the very person the president had appointed to prosecute the Star Route violators in Arizona. The disconcerted lawman was then required to investigate the trial judge. To add additional misery, rumors appeared that a Department of Justice agent, Henry A. Bowen, attempted to bribe jurors in the Star Route trials in Washington, D.C. Bowen had earlier been "an almost constant companion" of Marshal Tidball and his friends when the agent visited Tucson. Tidball's attempts to investigate thoroughly the Star Route violators, and the efforts of District Attorney James A. Zabriskie to prosecute, came to nothing.[13]

Simultaneously, Marshal Tidball became involved in the investigation of Joseph C. Tiffany, San Carlos Indian Agent. A United States grand jury charged him with perjury, embezzlement, and conspiracy in the management of his agency. Tiffany, a member of the Dutch Reformed Church and former New York City railway engineer, conducted illegal dealings with the freighting firm of Lord & Williams of Tucson and also embroiled the marshalcy to a degree by bringing a deputy marshal (and post trader) at Fort Thomas into his manipulation of agency supplies. The marshal added to this list of crimes in October 1882, when he reported to the attorney general that Tiffany had allowed several suspected Indian murderers to escape and had caused the arrest of innocent natives as scapegoats. On October 26 New York City police arrested Tiffany who was visiting in the East.[14]

The trial of Joseph Tiffany turned into a tragicomedy. When the former agent (Tiffany resigned on June 30, 1882) arrived in Tucson for trial in February 1883, District Attorney Zabriskie and Marshal Tidball were in Washington on business connected with the Star Route cases. When Judge Wilson Hoover was suspended and his jury disbanded, Tiffany's case was rescheduled for September. However, Tiffany's attorney proved that District Attorney Zabriskie, and not the jury foreman, had written the grand jury indictment of the San Carlos agent. This act clearly indicated prejudice. The new trial judge, A. W. Sheldon, permitted a new trial jury to be chosen from the box rather than allow Marshal Tidball to select the panel in the usual fashion, from a venire. (The judge felt that since the United States district attorney and the federal policeman worked closely together, the prejudice of one might indicate the existence of bias in the other.) On December 3, 1883, Zabriskie entered a *nolle prosequis* in the case against Tiffany. The case was dropped.[15]

Marshal Tidball and District Attorney Zabriskie made a vindictive enemy in Joseph C. Tiffany, who soon received an opportunity to reveal his spite. In 1884, a congressional Committee on Expenditures called Tiffany to testify about the conduct of Marshal Tidball and other federal officials in Arizona. Tiffany used this opportunity to charge Tidball with bribing George Smerdon, a witness for his (Tiffany's) defense, and then persuading this deponent to flee to Mexico. Smerdon and a friend (who may have accepted a bribe from Tiffany, not Tidball) soon died of yellow fever in Mexico. Tidball responded that Tiffany had offered Deputy Marshal A. F. Buttner a bribe of $100 if he would fail to locate this witness in Mexico. The outraged former Indian agent replied with a charge that Marshal Tidball had packed his official accounts. The federal policeman only learned about this charge in the newspaper. He immediately asked William M. Springer, chairman of the investigating committee, for permission to testify on his behalf. Springer responded that Tidball would have the privilege if anything came of this charge. The issue died quietly.[16]

In the midst of these allegations, Zan L. Tidball was called upon to participate in an equally heated issue—the prosecution of Mormon polygamists. By the Edmunds Act of 1882, which forbade not only polygamy but cohabitation with more than one female, these stern religionists were liable to fine and imprisonment, their children could be declared illegitimate, and they could be denied the franchise and the right to hold public office. In 1885, the Arizona Assembly added its own antipolygamy law.[17]

Gentile Arizonans admitted that the Mormons were very industrious, but they feared the economic and political
power—especially landholding and the vote—that the new arrivals
wielded. The *Arizona Weekly Journal* approved of strong legal
action against these "radicals," while the St. Johns *Apache Chief*,
which led the most notable resistance to the Mormons, advocated
more stringent measures: "desperate [religious] diseases need desperate remedies," that is, "shotgun and rope."[18]

In the fall of 1884, a federal grand jury meeting in Prescott
indicted six prominent Mormons who resided in new communities
along the Little Colorado River. Among the indictees was Ammon
M. Tenney, pioneer missionary to the Indians and founder of the
Mormon community at St. Johns. Tenney and two colleagues were
convicted of polygamy and sentenced to three-and-one-half-year
sentences in the Detroit House of Corrections, the federal contract
prison. Two others received lesser terms in Yuma Prison. The sixth
indictee, Bishop David King Udall, escaped the charge of polygamy, but fell victim to a malicious charge of giving perjured testimony in the land case of another Mormon, Miles P. Romney. In
August 1885, Udall received a three-year sentence to the Detroit
prison.[19]

The marshals occupied a sensitive position in the prosecution of
these Latter Day Saints and could, by humane treatment of their
prisoners, moderate the anguish of the Mormons. Marshal Zan L.
Tidball's deputies, who served the first papers in St. Johns,
aggravated the Mormons considerably by arousing them in the
middle of the night and causing them to travel 275 miles to Prescott
to post bonds. The prisoners argued that they could post bonds in
their own community. Marshal William Kidder Meade, who
succeeded Tidball in 1885, selected deputies who were more
sympathetic. Bishop Udall recalled that his escorts, Bert Foster
and Mike Hickey, "tried to make [the trip to Detroit] as comfortable for me as they could." When Udall returned to Prescott after
receiving a pardon, the two deputies were genuinely glad to see
him. Other Mormons, such as Miles P. Romney, defendant in a
trumped-up land case, fled to avoid the lawmen. "I . . . have kept
my family moving," he informed a church official, "for the last nine
months to keep them out of the Marshalls [sic] hands. . . ."[20]

Bishop Udall held Marshal Meade in especially high regard.
Before his trip to Detroit prison (which cost the marshal's office

$925.25), Meade permitted Udall to have visitors. And when rumors circulated that Udall might have to face polygamy charges later, Meade quickly informed him that the federal government planned no further prosecution. Judge Richard E. Sloan recalled that rather than humiliate the Mormons by serving process in person, Meade permitted them to appear in court voluntarily. Fortunately for all concerned, the new Democratic administration of Governor C. Meyer Zulick desired the support (rather than the hostility) of the Mormons and, in the fall of 1885, reached an accommodation with them. In December, Bishop Udall received a pardon.[21]

The marshals also kept watch on the growing minority of Chinese in Arizona. Following the precedent of the Californians' anti-Chinese organizations, in 1885 the Arizonans organized the Anti-Chinese Labor Association in Tucson; and in Prescott the Anti-Chinese League, with Deputy Marshal Mike Hickey as a vice-president. More direct methods were often employed by residents of the territory. In December 1882, two Chinese passengers on a stage in southeastern Arizona were brutally shot to death by a masked man, and in the following year, the governor offered a reward for persons who killed several Chinese near Clifton.[22]

Congress placed the power of the federal judiciary at the disposal of these prejudiced persons in May 1882, when it passed the Chinese Exclusion Act. This law forbade Chinese laborers from entering the United States for ten years and charged the collectors of customs to deport any violator to "the country from whence he came." Subsequent legislation required Chinese persons who entered the nation before the 1882 act to obtain a "certificate of residence" and be photographed. The marshals devoted a good deal of time to enforcing the Exclusion Laws until 1913, when Congress removed this duty from the office.[23]

By the late 1880s, the Pacific Coast states had tightened security against illegal Chinese entrants, and the Orientals sought other points of access: the Canadian and Mexican borders. In June 1890, Marshal Robert Paul obtained custody of twenty-four Chinese, whom the customs authorities and Treasury agents had arrested near Nogales. At a hearing before a United States commissioner, the federal magistrate ordered Marshal Paul to escort them to San Francisco for deportation. However, William C. Barnes, the defense for the hapless immigrants, appealed this decision to Judge Joseph Kibbey in Phoenix on a writ of habeas corpus. On July 9 the Phoenix bench ruled that the defendants had no right to habeas corpus (they were aliens who violated the United States laws) and that they must be deported from San Francisco.[24]

On July 11 Marshal Paul, three guards, and the aliens, departed for San Francisco, a tiresome journey of 1,000 miles. Paul and his subordinates delivered their wards successfully, only to find another court action to clarify the status of the unfortunate aliens. A defense attorney persuaded a United States circuit court in San Francisco to remove the Chinese from a steamer just before it set sail for their homeland. He demanded that any deportee be returned to the land "from whence he came," according to the Chinese Exclusion Act of 1882. In this case, that land would be Mexico. However, the San Francisco circuit judge upheld the United States commissioner in Tucson, who had ordered these persons to China. The Tucson *Daily Star* noted proudly that Marshal Paul and his party "stuck" with the twenty-four deportees until the court confirmed the original action.[25]

Since the procedures for deportation of Chinese were new, some confusion occurred. On September 10, 1890, Collector of Customs George Christ penned a highly critical letter to Deputy Marshal John V. Paul, son of the marshal, for secretly deporting two Chinese immigrants into Sonora near Christ's customs office in Nogales. This peremptory act occurred "at the early hour of four o'clock," accused the collector, and "I desire to know why you did not notify this office." Christ added that he and Treasury Agent Jacob Kemple, who was also stationed at Nogales, desired to photograph every deportee so that the United States authorities could "prevent their coming again into the United States." Christ or Kemple informed the Treasury Department, who in turn notified the attorney general. The embarrassed head of the Department of Justice wrote Marshal Paul on September 27 that the Treasury secretary was upset about the "clandestine" procedure of Deputy Paul.[26]

Marshal Paul was disturbed by the complaint of the collector of customs at Nogales and responded to the attorney general's letter very quickly. He explained that his son had been constrained to travel by carriage for twenty-four hours to Nogales because of heavy rains and had arrived about four o'clock in the morning. He promptly escorted his Chinese wards to the border, sent them into Sonora, and went to bed immediately, "being very tired and sleepy." When the deputy received the heated letter from Collector Christ, he presented it to his father, who consulted the United States district attorney and Commissioner Louis C. Hughes, the magistrate who ordered the marshal to deport the Chinese to Mexico. "They both told me that my deputy did his duty," protested Marshal Paul, "and was right in paying no attention to Mr. Christ's letter."[27]

The angry marshal was considerably upset by the collector, and pointed out to the attorney general that his office had taken pains to enforce the Exclusion Act:

Shortly after I entered upon the duties of this office last March [1890] I had a conversation with Mr. Frank P. Clark, Collector of Customs, Port of El Paso, [at that time Arizona was in his District] about the enforcement of the Exclusion Act. Since that time I have had several conversations with Mr. J. C. McCoy, Special Agent of the Treasury Department . . . and at his request I have appointed three special deputies, who live near the Mexican line, to watch for Chinese. . . . All the deputies have special instructions to assist the Customs Officials in every way they can legally do so, and there had been perfect harmony. . . . up to the time Mr. Christ took possession of the Collector's office.[28]

Paul was aware that inconsistencies existed in deportation procedures. He escorted some of his Chinese wards to San Francisco; others were ejected into Sonora. Different courts in Arizona directed him to deport the orientals to various contries. Paul took a parting shot at Collector Christ by adding that the previous deportations at Nogales "were made with the full knowledge of the Customs Officers at Nogales," who "never before questioned our right to do so, nor did they ever intimate that we should report to them" before releasing the Chinese into Sonora. The attorney general accepted the frustrated marshal's explanation, but cautioned him to avoid controversy and to cooperate with the new collector at Nogales. The problem of the destination of the deportees was soon resolved for the Arizona marshals—all illegal Chinese entrants were to be returned to China.[29]

The decade 1887–97 was notable because of a large number of mail train robberies in Arizona. At least twelve passenger trains were halted by the banditti. Like their comrades who had preyed upon stagecoaches a decade earlier, the railway highwaymen fitted no stereotype: two robberies were carried out by former Southern Pacific Railroad employees; others were committed by cowboys or miners; and one was even committed by a blacksmith. One holdup was a product of a Mexican Indian called Geronimo (not to be confused with the Apache leader).[30]

Federal and local law enforcement agencies had different ideas about the most effective methods for detecting train robbers. Wells, Fargo Detective James B. Hume maintained that operatives of private firms were most successful. Hume informed one journalist that he had investigated 353 express robberies in his career, 200 of which involved the United States mail. "I have never known the federal government paying out a cent," complained the veteran sleuth, "to detect robbers." He added that he never observed "United States officers going out to investigate" a robbery.[31]

This unfortunate antagonism helped to prevent cooperation between Marshal William Kidder Meade of Arizona and Wells, Fargo Agent Frederick J. Dodge. The rift between them dated back to the feud between Deputy Marshal Wyatt Earp and Sheriff John H. Behan in Tombstone, where Dodge and Meade had resided. Dodge had supported the Earps, Meade had aligned with Behan. In 1887, when the outbreak of train robberies occurred, the two lawman could not shed their grievances. Dodge disliked Meade because he "shot off his mouth to an extended extent," and the detective "had to call him [Meade] good and hard" on one occasion. Thereafter, Dodge provided this "pussyfoot" marshal with information only in an official capacity.[32]

In spite of criticism, Meade pursued robbers aggressively. He arrested suspects in the robbery of two trains in 1887, and in the following February, the lawman pursued the outlaw band of Larry Sheehan into Chihuahua, Mexico. This unceremonious entry of an American lawman, with posse and Indian trailers, caused a minor diplomatic incident. While Meade maintained that he was destined for the nearest Mexican customs house to report his business, the Chihuahuan authorities arrested his posse "because they carried no permit of the Mexican Government to enter the country in pursuit of criminals." The federal lawman *had* been rather indiscreet; he chose a Mexican port of entry some sixty-five miles inside Chihuahua to make his report. Lieutenant Martinez, chief of the customs section of Janos, where the arrest took place, held Meade and his posse in custody from February 29 to March 13, 1888.[33]

The Democratic friends of William Kidder Meade were outraged by the behavior of the Mexican authorities and feared that the Republicans would publicize the incident. One journalist grumbled that Lieutenant Martinez should have assisted, not arrested, Meade. A friend, and fellow Democrat, Gideon J. Tucker, wrote a letter of appreciation for what Meade had done, and characterized the lawman as "calmly courageous." This letter appeared in several northeastern newspapers.[34]

In a most surprising turnabout of political loyalty, Governor C. Meyer Zulick, whom Meade had freed from detention in Mexico in 1885, abandoned the marshal. In his report to Secretary of State Thomas Bayard, Zulick charged that the prospects of rewards for the Sheehan band (although none had been posted when Meade entered Mexico), prompted Meade to pursue the outlaws and that the federal policeman "could not expect any better treatment than that which he received" in Mexico.[35]

Upon his return to Tucson, Meade issued an official protest on March 20, 1888. His arrest was a "high-handed outrage," declared the marshal.

> As we had proceeded to the nearest Customs House announced our official rank and were identified by [American] acquaintances in the vicinity, had reported fully our business and requested that they [the Mexicans] continue the pursuit and arrest the robbers, offered to pay all the expenses and any duties which might be due and had offered any bonds demanded; we considered our treatment outrageous.

Meantime, Robert H. Paul, a Southern Pacific Railroad detective, obtained the cooperation of Mexican police through official channels. This combined force surrounded the bandits in Mexico and killed the entire band.[36]

Marshal Meade laughed at his predicament after the incident passed. When residents of southeastern Arizona proposed to join neighboring New Mexicans to form the "State of Grant," Meade added his support.

Editor *Enterprise*

My paper just received. Hurrah for the State of Grant! It will include the section of Arizona where train robberies occur, and thus I will not be called upon to go on the chase. There are things I had rather [face ?] than those that carry Winchesters [rifles].

U.S. Marshal [W. K.] M-e[37]

In most pursuits, the federal lawmen merely followed the physical evidence of highwaymen—hoof marks, campfires, or other telltale clues. An occasional case was not nearly so clear-cut. On May 11, 1889, thirteen American outlaws ambushed and robbed army paymaster Joseph Wham near Fort Thomas, Graham County. The bandits wounded eight soldiers. The remainder withdrew or fled, leaving $29,000 to the brigands.[38]

Marshal William Kidder Meade, who still chafed at the loss of the Larry Sheehan band in Chihuahua, took charge of the pursuit. Among the deputies on the scene were Chief Deputy C. T. Dunavan (evidently not the rescuer of Governor Zulick) and William ("Billy") Breakenridge, a former county official in Tombstone and friend of Sheriff John H. Behan. Breakenridge recalled that the marshal "sent me to [Fort] Thomas on the first train" and that he "went from there to the [Cedar Spring] canon where the crime was committed." From his investigation, the deputy "was convinced that the robbers had gone toward the Gila River where the Mormon settlement [of Pima ?] WAS [LOCATED]." At Fort Thomas, Breakenridge found a witness, a black female camp follower, Frankie Campbell, who had observed the bandits constructing mock forts and placing stones in the road.

> She told me that she came through the canon just as the robbers were placing the rock in the road. They were masked, and told her to hurry around the bend in the road ahead and not to look back, and to forget that she had seen anything or they would get her. She said she . . . would deny that she had told me anything if she was subpoenaed, but said she recognized several of them, and some of them were Mormons.

Because of her information Breakenridge arrested M. E. Cunningham, a local "saloon-keeper and gambler." Eventually several Mormons were arrested for the crime—Lyman and Warren Follett, Gilbert and Wilfred Webb, Thomas N. Lamb, and David Rogers. Another shady character, William Ellison Beck, alias Cyclone Bill, was released when he produced an alibi.[39]

The Mormons, who were already agitated by the efforts of the marshals to enforce the Edmunds Act, immediately concluded that these new allegations against their church members constituted persecution. One irate sympathizer accused the deputy marshals of being "over-officious" and of making arrests indiscriminately to earn rewards. Marshal Meade offered $500 for each of the robbers. Other enemies charged the deputies with neglecting to investigate a group of mysterious men who fled Graham County after the robbery and with bribery and brutality in their efforts to obtain evidence. The Mormons also declared that the marshal's men, in order to make arrests, planted part of the recovered gold coin on a prominent member of their church.[40]

As these charges appeared, the Mormons demanded the removal of Marshal Meade. On June 19, 1889, a dispatch from Tucson reported that, since the Republicans had just entered the White House, "friends" of the suspected thieves were attempting to have Meade's successor appointed very quickly. United States Commissioner (and future governor) Louis C. Hughes informed the attorney general that Meade had stepped on many "rich toes" in his investigation. And a special attorney on the case observed that, in an effort to discredit the marshal, the Mormons succeeded in alienating the trial judge, William E. Barnes, from the struggling officer. This attorney added that Meade's performance continued to be dignified and manly. . . . He has stood like a rock." The community of feeling that existed earlier between Marshal Meade and the Mormons vanished in the heated atmosphere of the Wham robbery.[41]

Meade and his subordinates devoted an extraordinary amount of time to the Wham case. The editor of the Tucson *Daily Citizen* observed that this case had "probably furnished more work for the deputy marshals . . . than any previous case in the history of the territory." By October 1889, as the trial approached, "signs of weariness" appeared among the overworked deputies. In addition to the collection of evidence, they served the papers for the preliminary hearing, the subsequent grand jury, and for the long trial. They also guarded the jail (five special deputies were employed for this task). More than one hundred witnesses and some seventy prospective jurors were summoned. Chief Deputy C. T. Dunavan devoted eighty-two days "in hunting evidence" for this case.[42]

The trial of the suspects in the Wham robbery was long and disappointing for the marshal and his colleagues. From November 11 to December 14, the testimony of the witnesses was heard. The alleged robbers employed one of the outstanding lawyers and politicians in the territory, Marcus Aurelius Smith, who, strangely enough, was a friend of Marshal Meade. Smith methodically grilled Major Wham and the military escort, not to mention the nervous Frankie Campbell. These witnesses admitted that they had not seen the participants too clearly. Deputy Breakenridge remembered the day that Major Wham appeared on the stand.

> Major Wham . . . swore that he recognized some of the twenty-dollar gold pieces that were found hidden in a haystack at [Lyman] Follett's farm. The attorney for the defense [Marcus Smith] took some marked gold pieces from his pocket and asked the judge to mix them up with the ones in evidence. He then asked Wham to pick them out, and, of course, he could not do it.

The verdict of "not guilty" was expected. Breakenridge noted drily that "the Government had a good case against them [the robbers], but they had too many friends who were willing to swear to an alibi, and there were too many on the jury who thought it no harm to rob the Government."[43]

The exoneration of the suspects was a defeat for federal justice, and Marshal Meade became the scapegoat. The *Missouri Republican*, an enemy of Meade, characterized the failure of the government to convict "a dozen farmers" as a "stupendous failure" and charged that Meade had made no effort to capture the robbers until a reward was offered. Although a political opponent of the marshal, the Tucson *Daily Citizen* admitted that the lawman made several arrests before rewards were posted and, pointed out furthermore, that the government forbade federal officers from earning rewards. Bryan W. Tichenor, lawyer and court reporter at the trial, attributed the jury's verdict to local prejudices. "Here vice is still rampant," he informed an acquaintance, "as evidenced by the recent acquittal of the 'Wham robbers' by an Arizona jury." "A large portion of the community" expressed sympathy for defendants," added Tichenor, "because the money stolen was government property and the men shot were colored troops." The case transcended mere robbery and became part of a religious crusade by the Mormons against the gentile federal government and its agent, Marshal William Kidder Meade.[44]

When the harried marshal stepped down from his office on March 4, 1890, the former Southern Pacific detective and new marshal, Robert H. Paul, inherited a perplexing problem—how to proceed in the Wham case. The prejudice against the United States government was intense in the Mormon community. When Paul was nominated for the marshalcy, one Tucson resident connected the appointment of this manhunter with the defeat of Marshal Meade at the Wham trial. "The robbery and subsequent acquittal" of the suspected robbers "will have the effect of encouraging the criminal element throughout the West," wrote this Arizonan to Senator Richard Coke of Texas, "but in my opinion no single act of the senate will prove of such importance to the general welfare . . . as the confirmation of Bob Paul."

If the anxious Arizonans anticipated spectacular results from the old manhunter, they were sadly mistaken. He adopted a policy of watchful waiting and did little more than offer a $500 reward for the Wham robbers. When the attorney general authorized Paul to post the reward, he added that the War Department (victim of the bandits) encouraged the Department of Justice to offer the reward. A few months later, in August 1892, the department also instructed the United States district attorney to investigate charges that the Wham jury had been bribed.[45]

While Marshal Paul frittered away valuable time, encouraging news came from the Mormon community. In May 1890, officers of Graham County arrested several men, some of whom had been charged with the Wham robbery, for cattle theft. Among them were M. [Mark] E. Cunningham and Lyman and Warren Follett. The latter two men were sentenced to two-year terms in prison. Wilfred and Gilbert Webb were also charged with defrauding the county school district. Wilfred was a trustee of the school district. "Graham County has scored a victory for good government," said one elated editor, "the conviction of the Follett brothers . . . shows that the criminal class does not control Graham [County]."[46]

The strange twists of political fortune must have befuddled William Kidder Meade. When he departed the marshalcy in March 1890, he did not expect to return to the troublesome post; but on May 8, 1893, with the restoration of Grover Cleveland and the Democrats to the presidency, he did just that. A few months after this reappointment, a band of robbers began to rob stagecoaches in Graham County, and on January 6, 1894, robbed a Southern Pacific train at Teviston Post Office, near Bowie. The marshal employed a noted manhunter, Alexander Ezekiels, to investigate. Ezekiels performed expertly. On January 26 Meade reported that Wilfred Webb, a deputy postmaster at Pima and relative of the suspects in the Wham robbery, had led the raid on the passenger train. Other men were associated in the holdup, Jake Felshaw, Tom Jackson, and one Wisner. No doubt Meade concluded that the conviction of these outlaws, one of whom was related to the Wham robbers, would vindicate the marshalcy, the federal government, and be a victory for justice.[47]

The lawman watched the trial of the bandits in December 1894 with much gratification. Wilfred Webb and two accomplices were sentenced to ten years in prison for robbery of the mails. While pleased with the conviction, Meade would have preferred longer terms. Ironically, the special prosecutor for the federal government was William E. Barnes, the enemy of Meade in the Wham trial. The United States district attorney had shrewdly employed Barnes to prosecute the very persons whom he upheld a few years earlier. Barnes noted after the conviction of Wilfred Webb that "this is the first conviction in an important case for the government" in Graham County. What had begun as a robbery case in 1889 ended in a very important test for federal justice in Arizona Territory, and Marshal William Kidder Meade played a critical part in this struggle.[48]

This problem of banditry was exacerbated by contributions from another source—the Indians. Their situation had changed remarkably in Arizona (and neighboring New Mexico) during the two decades after the Civil War. From once powerful and sovereign tribes, waging war against foreign white invaders, the Indians fell to the lowly position of subjects of the United States government. The military campaigns of the Apaches degenerated into mere raids for booty.

The significance of this transformation occurred to the military leaders of the frontier army in the early 1880s, and they began to look upon the Indian raiders with contempt. In his *Annual Report for 1881*, Brigadier General John Pope observed that:

> The raids of the Apaches into Southern New Mexico for the last two years bear no resemblance to an Indian war or general outbreak. They rather resemble the operations of the cow-boys [white bandits of Arizona] and other bands of robbers on the frontier, or to the parties of train-robbers in Missouri [Jesse James].

Pope's superior, General of the Army William T. Sherman, agreed and noted that, aside from "temporary alarms" of Indian wars, these once threatening natives had been "substantially eliminated" as a "problem of the army."[49]

As the frontier army slowly relinquished control over southwestern tribes, the United States marshals and the federal courts assumed it. The judicial position of the Indians in Arizona was clouded by the uncertain status of the reservations, especially the great San Carlos Reservation (which contained as many as 5,000 Apaches). To what degree were the Indians immune from civil tribunals when they resided upon a reservation? To what degree were they susceptible to the United States or territorial courts when they raided outside the boundaries of the reservations? Were the raiders still a matter of concern solely for the military when they departed the reservations?[50]

In September 1881, an outbreak occurred among the White Mountain Apaches when the army arrested a powerful medicine man. Eleven soldiers and seven civilians (one was a mail carrier) were killed. A few days later, a band of sympathetic Chiricahuas murdered several whites. One victim was Deputy Marshal George Turner, Jr., who attempted to rescue settlers near Globe. The army arrested the White Mountain dissidents and prepared to turn them over to Marshal Crawley P. Dake for trial in civil court. However, the marauding Chiricahuas ambushed the military escort, hoping to free their comrades. On October 3, 1881, the military informed Dake that the Indian prisoners did not escape during the engagement and that the bluecoats would soon place the White Mountain fugitives in his custody.[51]

The question of jurisdiction over the reservation Indians remained a problem. District Attorney E. B. Pomeroy delayed the trial of the Apaches and asked Attorney General Benjamin Brewster if they were on firm legal ground. On February 28, 1882, Brewster directed Pomeroy to hold the trial "at the earliest practicable day," and later reiterated that Pomeroy should "push the prosecution" of the Indians and let the court decide jurisdiction. He added that he had instructed Marshal Dake to provide the necessary funds for the trial and to consult with Pomeroy. Dake also expressed concern in separate letters to the attorney general. On October 8, 1882, the new head of the Department of Justice, Wayne MacVeagh, reaffirmed the position of Benjamin Brewster in the Indian cases. When the natives commited crimes against the United States, they were to be treated like any white criminal. [52]

This congenial relationship between marshal and military failed when the federal lawmen attempted to obtain custody of the wily Apache leader, Geronimo. In the summer of 1883, Marshal Zan L. Tidball held a murder warrant for the chief, who was then in Mexico. When Geronimo expressed a desire to surrender, Lieutenant Britton Davis went to the border to receive the warrior. Tidball and the collector of customs (he wanted Geronimo for smuggling cattle into the United States) confronted Davis at a ranch in the Sulphur Springs Valley and demanded custody of the Apache. Lieutenant Davis was in a dilemma. The chief would refuse to surrender if he learned the purpose of the marshal's visit. Davis, who had promised Geronimo a few days to rest his cattle before traveling to San Carlos, employed a ruse at the expense of the federal lawman. Davis persuaded Geronimo to drive his cattle a few miles north of their present camp; in the meantime the soldier opened a bottle of scotch. By the time the groggy lawman and the collector of customs awakened, the elusive chieftain was en route to San Carlos. [53]

While Marshal Tidball laughed at his gullibility (it seems out of character), Marshal William Kidder Meade refused to see any humor in the subordination of federal justice to the military. But Meade encountered a man of equal stubbornness—General Nelson Miles. In 1885, Governor C. Meyer Zulick promised Arizonans that the civil courts would try Geronimo for murder. In March 1886, when General Miles began new negotiations for the surrender of Geronimo (he had left the reservation again), the renegade fled when he learned the reason for the presence of the marshal at the talks. The squabbles between lawman and military man hindered the establishment of peace on the frontier.[54]

Marshal Meade still anticipated the arrest of the notorious chieftain. In the following September, when the army lodged Geronimo at Fort Bowie, Meade delegated the task of arresting the Apache lord to Deputy William Breakenridge. Breakenridge relished the task of arresting "the wily old scoundrel," but heard that Geronimo "made the general [Miles] promise he would not turn them [the group included other Apaches] over to the civil authorities for trial." When the deputy confronted the soldier, Breakenridge recalled that Miles "refused to let me have them." The disappointed lawman concluded that "there was plenty of proof against them and no doubt they would have been hanged."[55]

Much of this controversy was related to the uncertain place of the reservations in the territory. Since the early 1870s, Congress and the commissioners of Indian Affairs had argued about local and federal courts' jurisdiction over the reservations. On March 3, 1885, the national lawmakers promulgated a law which provided that an Indian, "committing against the person or property of another Indian or other person" any of seven serious crimes (including murder) "shall be subject . . . to the laws of such Territory relating to said crimes."[56]

While this act extended the jurisdiction of the territorial courts over crimes committed by an Indian on or off the reservation, it failed to clarify federal authority. Indeed, an Arizona tribunal immediately concluded that since the United States had given part of its jurisdiction over the reservations to the territories in the Act of 1885, that the federal authorities had given up all authority. In 1891, the Supreme Court yielded some jurisdiction to the territory but the United States courts retained jurisdiction over offenses committed upon reservations by persons other than Indians. The marshals therefore retained some authority upon the troublesome reservation.[57]

The matter of serving the process of federal court on the San Carlos Reservation presented the marshals with many sensitive problems. Not only might the Indians become aroused, but the agents, always jealous of encroachments upon their domain, might refuse to cooperate with the lawmen. William Kidder Meade wavered between maintaining a deputy at San Carlos or using more informal measures. In 1888, he deputized the famous Chief of Scouts Al Sieber. On October 2, Meade mailed five warrants to the new deputy for Apache murderers, but the marshal cautioned the scout to be careful to inform Captain (and Agent) J. M. Bullis before serving the papers. A few weeks later, when the marshal desired to serve more warrants, Deputy Sieber was not available. Meade first considered sending a regular deputy; then he had second thoughts. A strange deputy "might arouse suspicion among the Indians and make arrests more difficult," said the lawman to Bullis, and added: "I have thought best to inclose [sic] warrant for 3 Apaches." Bullis could sign a commission as temporary deputy, serve it, and mail the process to the marshal.[58]

The reservation Indians were not only the subject of warrants, but participants in the federal court. Deputy William Breakenridge, with an office in Phoenix, was assigned the task of escorting thirty Apache witnesses to court. Although Marshal Meade could have authorized transportation by rail, he directed the deputy to escort them by the less-expensive route overland. Breakenridge was relieved when the four-day trip was completed, since the Apaches were a "sulky lot." The marshal adopted a patronizing attitude toward the Apaches because they were untutored in American court procedure. Rather than pay a group of Indians the total amount of witness fees for appearing before a grand jury in October 1886, he permitted their agent to collect their fees. Meade explained that "they might get good and drunk" if they received their allowances.[59]

While Marshal Meade struggled to establish procedures for the San Carlos Apaches, his superior in Washington hesitated to honor the lawman's reservation expenses. From his distant office, the attorney general could hardly sympathize with the problems of serving process on an Indian reservation. In April 1887, the Department of Justice refused to honor some of Meade's expenses in the investigation of several murders at San Carlos. The marshal promptly informed his attorney in Washington, A. J. Falls, that "this new [Indian] business will greatly increase the expenses of our office."[60]

This new responsibility, as well as other duties—the prosecution of the Mormons, Chinese aliens, etc.—constrained the marshal to maintain larger staffs than ever before. During his second term, 1893–97, Meade employed eleven subordinates: in Tucson, Phoenix, Florence, Winslow, Prescott, Williams, Solomonville,

Bisbee, Yuma, Globe, and Tombstone. Meade also demanded that his deputies have some training in paperwork. He explained the reason to an acquaintance in May 1887:

> The "red tape" of the office of marshal is such that I have found it impracticable to appoint deputies until they are well schooled in the manner and form of keeping accounts, taking receipts, etc.[61]

Many deputies were part-time and underqualified. Deputy John H. (Jack) O'Neill, a miner and freighter in Fort Thomas, served in various law enforcement capacities for many years. He was tactless and overbearing. In August 1891, a citizen complained that O'Neill had insulted him. Another resident of Fort Thomas accused the lawman of padding his accounts. Marshal Robert Paul suspended the arrogant subordinate. "Well Mr. Paul," said the unlettered deputy humbly, "I cant imagin or remember when I charged witness fees and not made servis. . . . I am sorry that sutch a thing turned up. But I can not think who the witness es." Paul stood by O'Neill and declared that he was a "good deputy."[62]

Even this large force of deputies failed to cover remote parts of the district, and federal lawmen were constrained to adopt expediencies. In September 1886, William Kidder Meade mailed Richard Harrison of La Marcia a commission as special deputy with expense money and subpoenas to serve upon jurors. The marshal included careful instructions for this procedure:

> You will serve them [the subpoenas] by showing the original subpoena with seal thereon, and deliver to each a copy which is attached to the original and make returns [the deputy's notes] on back of original and send to this office as soon as served. . . . I enclose notices which you will deliver to the trial jurors you can pick up anywhere in the district, whether it be in Pima or Cochise County.

Meade added that Harrison should take the oath of deputy before a justice of the peace "before making any of these services."[63]

Like any political office, the Arizona marshalcy owed its existence to political patronage. In June 1893, when Governor Louis C. Hughes's Democratic administration took office, the executive used Marshal Meade's office to pay political debts. When an aspirant to the superintendency of the territorial prison failed to obtain

that post, Hughes replied that he would do "everything" necessary
to provide him with the deputyship of northern Arizona. A few
days later, Frank H. Hereford, former deputy and established
lawyer, informed Sidney Bartleson of Florence that he "had a talk
with Marshall [sic] Meade and he very much gratified me by
saying, 'Tell Mr. Bartleson that you have spoken to me [Meade]
and his appointment will be made out today.' "[64]

The political nature of the Arizona marshalcy was expressed most
clearly in the assumption of office by William Kidder Meade in
1885. An ardent Democrat and follower of Governor C. Meyer
Zulick, Meade planned to assist the new executive in the reform of
the corrupt Republican government. The "eminent reformer,"
William Kidder Meade, entered upon his duties "with a flourish of
trumpets," according to one Tombstone editor. "To hear some of
his satellites talk," continued this writer, "one would think that a
second Reformation was at hand with the new marshal in the role of
Martin Luther."[65]

The Democratic lawman did not conduct reforms alone, but
resorted to the federal grand juries to investigate wrongdoers. This
"ancient and inherited mode of Anglo-American law enforcement
looked not to permanent officers but to the 'grand jury' of local
citizens" to report "the scandal of the countryside." Meade urged
the federal grand juries to examine the conduct of previous Republican officials closely and attempted to obtain wholesale indictments. However, these excesses discredited the marshal among
some of his friends, and the district attorney was constrained to
drop most of the indictments. Meade's enemies promptly charged
him with "extravagance" in the conduct of his office:

> Meade's grand jury of last fall [1885] exhibit[s] some of the
> farcial [sic] features of a legalized masquerade conducted
> almost solely for the purposes of venting personal and political
> spite at the expense of the United States. . . . The grand jury
> . . . was in session for one month, and they had completed all
> the legitimate work before them in four days' time. . . . From
> the fourth day . . . until it adjourned . . . it became a political
> conspiracy.[66]

In February 1886, shortly after the fall sessions of court, a special
agent of the Department of Justice, D. A. Fisher, arrived in
Arizona unexpectedly. The editor of the Prescott *Arizona*

Journal-Miner observed teasingly that "it is a peculiar coincidence that he arrived . . . very shortly after the vouchers for the expenses of the last term of the United States Court reached Washington." This was Meade's expensive session. When news appeared that the marshal was required to make a new bond, the same writer declared: "We should like to inquire right here, if Special Agent Fisher did not come here to examine Marshal Meade's account." However, the Tucson *Citizen* soon reported that Fisher found the lawman's accounts "correct to the penny."[67]

The examiners, who now made routine annual visits, were unable to grant Marshal Robert Paul such a clean bill of health. In April 1892, Examiner S. F. Kercheval found evidence of dishonesty in his office. The agent noted that Paul "is not . . . a successful businessman" but he "manages . . . to successfully manipulate the business of office . . . to make his maximum fees." Kercheval found per diems charged when no business was transacted in the courts, as well as duplicate charges. Most important, Paul abused the powers of the marshal to select jurors. His juries were composed of "loafers, bar-room bums and the 'ragged reubens' of the community, especially about Tucson where the marshal resides." Critics accused the lawman of placing smugglers on juries trying smugglers and Mormons on panels sitting in judgment upon Mormons. Paul was able to exert this authority in the selection of juries because, unlike New Mexico, Arizona did not yet have United States commissioners to provide this service.[68]

Examiner J. H. Campbell reported favorably on the second term of William Kidder Meade. He especially appreciated Meade's selection of Alexander Ezekiels as office deputy. "I regard Deputy Ezekiels as an extraordinarily efficient deputy," concluded the investigator. However, he added that Meade had "trouble" employing efficient deputies because of the recent decision by Congress to forbid payment of double fees to deputy marshals. Kercheval observed that the new scale for fees did not cover adequately the travel expenses of deputies in the large western territories.[69]

The Arizona marshalcy encountered many stumbling blocks in the 1880s and 1890s, but perhaps political factionalism upset the office most seriously. The marshals often became victims of inconsistent public biases. The same Arizonans who applauded the lawmen for deporting Chinese aliens berated the federal officers for enforcing the laws against the Mormons. The marshals were, in turn, victimized by the Mormons, who regarded them as representatives of an oppressive federal government. In such an atmosphere, the marshals seldom pleased a majority of the population.[70]

A remarkable discrepancy existed between the official activities of the Arizona and New Mexico lawmen during the latter part of the nineteenth century. The congressional laws—cohabitation, land, sporting events—bound both offices equally. However, Arizonans desired more immigrants and economic development, and the governors permitted only a ritualistic enforcement of the antipolygamy law, since the Mormons contributed significantly to the fledgling economy. Lawlessness was also different in Arizona. Sophisticated secret societies contributed significantly to lawlessness in New Mexico, but primitive freebooters (Anglo and Indian) ravaged Arizona. When the Arizona marshals pursued these desperadoes, they resembled the popular conception of the manhunting "frontier marshal." At no other time did the chief federal lawmen approximate this image.

The Arizona post lay under a cloud as a consequence of the bloody deeds of the Earp posse in Tombstone, and Marshal Crawley P. Dake's failure to discipline his subordinates. Zan L. Tidball, William Kidder Meade, and Robert H. Paul were men of some character and integrity, and chose deputies more wisely. Meade and Paul also represented a concession to "home rule" advocates in the territory. All these marshals contributed to unifying Arizona's diverse populace and to bringing the territory that much closer to statehood.

10

Marshal Creighton M. Foraker,
1897–1912

By 1897, the year Edward L. Hall vacated the New Mexico marshalcy, the office had acquired an important place in territorial law enforcement. Hall had demonstrated a capacity for aggressive enforcement of the laws and had made the marshalcy an inseparable part of Governor William Thornton's "law and order" regime. But the marshals of this era also abused their powers and exposed the office to ridicule and hatred. To maintain the confidence of the people, the marshalcy of New Mexico required a disinterested leader, one who could withdraw, to some extent, the marshalcy from political partisanship. As the twentieth century approached, the fee system, which lay at the heart of the problem, required serious attention. Only then could a truly "professional" attitude prevail in the marshalcy.

New Mexico of 1897 differed greatly from that of 1882, and the inhabitants, especially the Hispanos, refused to tolerate the roughshod tactics of the marshals. The crude tactics of the Santa Fe Ring and Democratic bosses, in which partisan deputy marshals "bulldozed" voters, was a thing of the past. Governor L. Bradford Prince, who had observed these arrogant marshals at the voting places, concluded that "rule by coercion" would no longer be permitted by "the native people."[1]

This new political order became apparent as Republican President William McKinley formed a new regime for New Mexico in 1897. While the New Mexicans elected Democrat Harvey Fergusson as delegate to Congress, McKinley placed Republicans in office in the territory. McKinley's selection of the governor was

189

closely bound to that of the United States marshal. Thomas Catron, the lame duck delegate, presented the chief executive a list of candidates for high place in New Mexico: Pedro Perea, influential Hispanic leader and son of an early assemblyman, for governor; Solomon Luna, Republican boss of Valencia County, for marshal; and Catron himself for United States district attorney. In reply to office-seeker Hugh N. Price, Delegate Catron declared that he would "take great pleasure in assisting you to an appointment to any office . . . except that of U.S. marshall [sic]." He had promised his support to a person "of Mexican extraction" [Solomon Luna], who was "one of the strongest politicians in the territory." The wily delegate perceived the very important role of the marshalcy in territorial politics and went on to remark that "in connection with the office [of marshal, Luna] would be able to control more votes than any ten men."[2]

Several men contended for the marshalcy, and it soon became obvious that Catron's influence was not as great as it had been in the past. Miguel A. Otero, former chief deputy to Marshal Romulo Martinez, desired the position. Serapio Romero, son and chief deputy of Trinidad Romero, also entered into the nomination. Creighton M. Foraker, a Grant County rancher and brother of Ohio Senator Joseph B. Foraker, was a strong contender. Catron did not regard these applicants as "a great deal" of competition so long as the Republican Party, with the assistance of Senator Stephen B. Elkins in Washington, maintained a united front.[3]

Solomon Luna and Miguel A. Otero journeyed to Washington to confer with McKinley, only to learn that he had "partially agreed" to appoint Creighton Foraker. When the president urged them to discuss the appointment with the appropriate department in the capital, the two office-seekers decided not to "push" their nominations. Foraker would become marshal.[4]

In New Mexico, the political commentators were already certain that "Creight" (sometimes "Crate") Foraker was the president's choice. In March 1897, the Las Vegas Optic noted that Senator Joseph Foraker "is bringing some powerful influences to bear on the President in favor of his brother." On July 22, when the appointment became official, the Rio Grande Republican concluded that Solomon Luna's fall was a consequence of his association with the Santa Fe Ring. This writer added that McKinley understood the political conditions of New Mexico and would appoint none "but clean, honest and reliable men." He assumed that Foraker would "make a capable and efficient marshal," since he had generally avoided politics during his residency in the territory. In the meantime, Miguel ("Gillie") Otero, who went to Washington to seek the marshalcy, returned to New Mexico as governor.[5]

Otero's appointment meant that the entire judiciary of New Mexico experienced changes. Otero appointed three judges, including William J. Mills as chief justice, while McKinley selected two members of the bench. Otero and Thomas Catron agreed that "Democratic judges then in office should be removed as soon as possible." Catron, however was terribly disappointed when Otero refused to help him obtain the post of United States district attorney. Catron concluded that the new governor was "an ingrate." Otero refused to urge Catron's nomination because the Republican boss had supported Solomon Luna, not Otero, for the marshalcy. The chief executive refused to make a change in the attorney's office when incumbent William Burr Childers diplomatically changed his party affiliation from Democrat to Republican. When the power of Thomas B. Catron could not stem the tide of judicial change in New Mexico, a "new order" had indeed arrived. It would be interesting to observe the marshalcy and United States courts under this new regime.[6]

Among the many appointees in 1897, Marshal Creighton M. Foraker was the least well known. Born in Hillsboro, Ohio, May 8, 1861, he attended the local high school and, in early 1882, prospected in Gilpin County, Colorado. He and an older brother, Charles, soon moved to Grant County, New Mexico, where they mined and invested in a ranch in the Burro Mountains. The *Silver City Enterprise* was impressed with the presence of members of such a distinguished Ohio family and reported the visits of Creighton Foraker's relatives. In October 1887, after several goat ranchers complained about the ravages of a mountain lion, Foraker investigated, only to be treed by the animal. He killed the cat and won the regard of many citizens. The *Enterprise* characterized him as a "model pioneer" who fought mountain lions "like a dime novel hero." Foraker built a reputation for honesty and integrity. In 1895, he married Minerva Eugenia Hall of Silver City. He also joined the Benevolent & Protective Order of Elks.[7]

The transition of office provided journalists an opportunity to assess the performances of the former marshal Edward L. Hall and the new appointee. A Republican editorialist for the *New Mexican* regarded Hall as "a fair man and just in his administration" of the marshalcy, even though a Democrat. "Whenever he could," continued the writer bluntly, Hall "aided his party and his party friends" with deputyships. Hall departed "the office with a clean and honorable record," said the *New Mexican* writer, but added that Creighton Foraker enjoyed an equally "fine reputation." He possessed "all the necessary qualifications, [and] . . . as to his Republicanism, any man from Ohio by the name of Foraker ought to be a stalwart." While the citizens of New Mexico demanded honesty in office, they did not regard patronage through public office to be misconduct.[8]

The new marshal was the first to serve a full term under the newly established salary system, adopted by Congress in May 1896 in place of the antiquated fee system. Section Nine of the Annual Appropriations Act for the Department of Justice provided for salaries for the marshals and office personnel. The salaries were computed according to the amount of business in each judicial district. The marshals of New Mexico and Arizona were given $4,000 per year, some $500 less than attorney General William H. H. Miller had requested.[9] This act also formally divided the personnel of each marshalcy into marshal, office deputies, field deputies, and special deputies for emergencies. The attorney general appointed the office and field deputies, upon the recommendation of the marshal. The marshal could no longer employ the deputy and receive a portion of the subordinate's fees. The New Mexican deputies also lost the "double fees" that they had received under the previous arrangement.[10]

This reform, which, incidentally, occurred in the last year of Marshal Edward L. Hall's term, elated the attorney general. From his perspective in Washington, D.C., he thought the 1896 Act a resounding financial success. When the attorney general computed the expenditures of the federal judiciary for the period from July 1 to September 30, 1896, he projected savings of $2.2 million for the coming fiscal year. In regard to the upkeep of the marshals across the nation, he estimated a decrease in expenses of $400,000 in 1897.[11]

While Creighton Foraker approved of the salary system for himself and office deputies, he felt that the act did not go far enough. Field deputies remained on the fee system, even though the new law withdrew permission to collect "double fees" in New Mexico. Because of the vast distances and high cost of transportation in the sprawling territory, Congress had permitted the deputy marshals to earn twice the mileage fee. Foraker cited an example of the inadequacies of the fee system: the marshal held a warrant for William McCrea for violation of the land laws. McCrea resided near Largo, San Juan County. The trip to Largo would cost a field deputy $64.10 in travel expenses, since he must travel by way of Durango, Colorado, the only practicable rail route to that inaccessible area. But the field deputy earned only $18.02 in fees. The deputy suffered financially if he served the process; the government lost if he refused to serve the document.[12]

The marshal proposed a plan to overcome the failure of the new congressional legislation to provide for salaried deputies. "I can see no way to serve process [of court] in this district under the present fee bill," said Foraker, "except by salaried deputies." He suggested the abolition of all field deputies and the creation of a force of six office deputies and one chief office deputy, all on salaries. The chief office deputy would receive $1800 per annum, two office deputies in the headquarters $1200 each, and office deputies in Las Vegas, Albuquerque, Silver City, and Roswell, $600 annually. (Foraker did not move his official headquarters to Albuquerque until 1899.)[13]

Much to his surprise, the attorney general approved the plan, authorized Foraker to discontinue all field deputies, and agreed to let the marshal maintain a smaller force of salaried office deputies. They would serve the process of court in the field, but reside in permanent offices at strategic points in the district. In a letter of October 13, 1898, Foraker informed Marshal William M. Griffith of Arizona about this new system. "I realized . . . that it would be a serious task to get along under" the single fee system for field deputies, declared the marshal. Foraker added that "It would be cheaper to the Go'vt" if his plans were adopted, "that the service would be improved, and that the position of Deputy Marshal would be elevated to an extent that a Deputy Marshal would not be mixed up in the 'creation of business for the purpose of the creation of fees.' "[14]

As the plan went into operation, Marshal Foraker became convinced that it improved the efficiency of his office. He explained to

William Griffith that he "got permission to appoint 3 office deputies, one at Las Vegas, one at Socorro, and one at Silver City":

> The effect on the business of the Marshal's office was phenominal [sic]; instead of working up cases these men [the deputies] fixed them straight without the intervention of the law, they kept all matters quiet, and as the salary was sufficient, ($900.00) they attended strictly to it [business], made investigations and reports, well, to make a long story short, they killed off 60% of the usual business. . . . The quality of the work done by these men was the best, their expenses were [at] a minimum.[15]

The New Mexico deputies worked so diligently that the business of the courts was soon cleared. The backlog "that was hanging for years" disappeared from the dockets. This so impressed the "heads" in the national capital, according to Foraker, that they reduced his staff by two. The two deputies had worked themselves out of positions. The marshal expressed some disgust for "those that be" in Washington, and added humorously that "tacks also have heads." In spite of this momentary reduction of his force, Foraker declared joyfully that "I have no field deputies, [and] I refused to make any appointments . . . though so requested by the Dep't of Justice." Field deputies worked on the fee system, and they were open to too many abuses. Salaried office deputies now served all process in the field.[16]

Creighton Foraker demanded high qualifications for his staff. When a resident of Washington, D.C., applied for the chief deputyship in 1897, Foraker replied that he had already employed a person "who is familiar with the country." "It is almost absolutely essential," added the lawman, "that deputies here speak Spanish." When the marshal recommended Elmer D. Ewers as office deputy in July 1906, Foraker informed the attorney general that Ewers has "had a large amount of experience as a stenographer and in clerical work." When Chief Office Deputy George A. Kaseman took an indefinite leave of absence, the marshal wanted to promote Deputy William R. Forbes to that post and to add Henry F. Bogh. The lawman explained that Bogh was forty-eight years of age, had been a resident of New Mexico for seven years, and possessed "a large amount of experience in office work and as an accountant." Not only did Foraker have standards, but he assured his employees an opportunity for promotion. The New Mexico marshalcy reflected efficiency and the beginnings of a merit system, although the office did not yet fall under the classified list of the Federal Civil Service.[17]

While he demanded clerical skills, Foraker also looked for men with practical experience. In July 1906, he offered a deputyship to William Smith and apprised Washington that Smith was "well qualified." He had fought with the Rough Riders in Cuba, had been a special agent for the Rock Island Railroad, and was presently city detective in El Paso. Foraker outlined the duties of office to Smith.

> You would have to be away from home probably more than half the time, traveling over different parts of the territory, during which time, of course, you would be allowed your actual expenses, excepting that your subsistence, that is your charge for meals and lodging, would be restricted not to exceed $2.00 per day.

The salary was $100 per month and headquarters were in Albuquerque. "Billy" Smith became a valuable member of the marshal's staff.[18]

Marshal Foraker maintained a close watch upon his subordinates. In April 1898, he scolded errant Deputy Frank W. Hall for serving process in another deputy's district. "Remember this!" exhorted the chief lawman. "You must always send any writ to the nearest deputy in the neighboring district." When Hall failed to locate the subject of his warrant in New Mexico, he promptly crossed into Texas and made a complaint before the authorities in El Paso. "The proper way for you to have done," the marshal declared, "would have been to deliver the warrant to the Marshal of the Western District of Texas." Foraker added a firm rebuff with his instructions. "I again suggest," he said, "that a book of Instructions . . . would be a valuable thing for you to read." When a citizen of Clayton asked for a deputy marshal to suppress some rowdies, Foraker replied that this duty was out of the purview of United States officers. Such problems were a responsibility for city lawmen. "I will not tolerate anyone [deputy]," the marshal asserted firmly, "who seems to be disposed to be a 'bad man'."[19]

As the prestige of the deputyship increased under Creighton Foraker, even the criminal element began to capitalize upon it. In

December 1897, the marshal learned that J. C. Carrington of Elizabethtown had impersonated a deputy marshal. "This kind [of crime] cannot go unheeded," the marshal informed the postmaster of Carrington's community. In February 1907, an Indian, William Posey, presented himself as a deputy marshal and brother-in-law of the marshal of Oklahoma. Foraker became suspicious when Posey asked him to endorse a personal check, and Santa Fe authorities, whom the Indian had already approached, confirmed these suspicions. In January 1910, James Ryan, alias Frank Carpenter, posed as a deputy to obtain food, lodging, and transportation along the Arizona border. To sport the badge of deputy marshal exalted the impersonator in the eyes of the citizenry.[20]

Citizens in remote districts constantly pleaded for the help of deputy marshals. In most instances, the deputies did not have jurisdiction, and Foraker declined to assist them. In January 1898, a resident of Martinez requested protection from one Sigardo, a noted cattle thief. Foraker replied that this offense did not fall under the federal laws. "You are no doubt aware," chided the lawman, "that self protection is the first law of nature." When A. F. Miller of Farmington appealed for a deputyship for himself, and presented a petition of signatures on his behalf, the federal lawman replied that in the applicant's village "any probable violations of the laws would be of the Territorial and not the Federal laws."[21]

While the marshal demanded well-qualified deputies, he nevertheless opened himself to charges of nepotism. In February 1903, he asked the attorney general to approve the appointment of Charles E. Foraker, the marshal's brother, who "has a thorough knowledge of the Territory and its people." J. Benson Newell, nephew of Creighton Foraker, accepted a badge in September 1907. Moreover, New Mexico's federal lawman was not above asking for favors. In July 1900, his nephew Frank Foraker visited the territory and desired to see the Pacific Coast. The marshal asked one of his railroad friends for free roundtrip railway fare as guard for Chinese under order of deportation. Under the arrangement with the marshal, the railroads contracted to provide guards and fare. In this instance, Foraker would use his nephew as a guard at no cost. The tradition of the family marshalship, once practiced so zealously by the Romeros, remained in the modern office.[22]

The staff of the New Mexico marshalcy worked in physical conditions that differed considerably from earlier ones. When

Foraker moved to Albuquerque in 1899—another indication that the "Duke City" was becoming the center of territorial activity—he furnished the headquarters with personal belongings and furniture belonging to Bernalillo County. In 1904, he obtained the equipment of the disbanded Court of Private Land Claims. "Although this is old furniture," he informed the attorney general, "it would help me out very much." Foraker's office was then located in suites 21-26, Grant Building, then at Third and Central above the Golden Rule Saloon, and later in the Post Office Building. In June 1907, the Commercial Club and other interested parties persuaded the Treasury Department to approve a new Federal Building. The structure was not completed until 1910, near the end of Creighton Foraker's marshalcy.[23]

A noticeable improvement in office equipment complemented the physical surroundings. Foraker regarded one typewriter to be insufficient and demanded another. During a hot spell in May 1901, Foraker and his staff suffered intensely, whereupon he requested authority to purchase a water cooler (ice would cost $3 per month) and an electric fan (also $3 per month). "I have not heretofore been supplied with these comforts," he wrote the attorney general, "but am advised that such [are] usually supplied the Department at Washington." Communications improved drastically in August 1907, when Albuquerque received long distance telephone service. Foraker was a firm believer in the telephone. It permitted "the head to save the heels" of his deputies.[24]

Other newfangled innovations were of more immediate interest to Creighton Foraker. On February 6, 1910, the *Albuquerque Morning Journal* announced that the lawman was the "proud owner" of a new Studebaker automobile which, it was hoped, would speed the delivery of court process. On May 26, the marshal was involved in a near accident with a burly teamster at an Albuquerque intersection. For several minutes the two parties glared at each other and refused to give way. All at once "the big federal marshal got out of his machine and started for the teamster." At that point the wagon driver, who thought the hefty opponent (over three hundred pounds) was heavyweight boxer Jim Jeffries, wisely whipped his team into motion.[25]

Many southwestern lawmen foresaw very positive effects of the automobile upon law enforcement. As early as 1907, Foraker used

the new motor busses to serve process in remote villages, and he
supported the New Mexico Automobile Association, which agitated for improved roads. The *Morning Journal* summed up the
impact of the "buzz wagon" upon law enforcement in an editorial
called "The Gasoline Roundup":

> One by one the precious relics of our earlier southwestern
> civilization are disappearing. Nearly extinct is the outlaw. . . .
> the professional train robber has taken to the remote can-
> yons. . . . Now comes the buzz wagon, the benzine buggy,
> the gasoline vehicle and drives forth.

Hardly a month later, in neighboring Arizona, Sheriff Carl Hayden
of Phoenix pursued and captured two teenage train robbers by
automobile. The year 1910 looms rather large in the annals of law
enforcement in the Southwest.[26]

The automobile did not appreciably affect the marshalcy during
Foraker's tenure, and the deputies still carried out their duties
under trying conditions. I "am *stuck* [his italics] unless something
unforeseen turns up," Deputy John M. Wiley informed his superior
during a disastrous flood, in October 1904. He was marooned in Lincoln. "I cant [sic] *start* for Roswell," he added; "The rivers and
creeks are on the boom." A few months later, the hardy deputy was
isolated in Silver City. "The roads around here are almost impassible
[sic]," he judged, and people were packing "grub in to [sic] Pinos Altos." At Espanola, the weather "was something fierce." Snow fell
and the "wind blew about 40 miles an hour." The elements had no
respect for servants of federal justice.[27]

As the new century opened, the growing population of New
Mexico forced the marshal to expand his services. The population
of the territory reached 195,000 in 1900, and in 1904, the territorial
supreme court added a sixth judicial district. The headquarters of
the Fifth Judicial District was moved from Socorro to Roswell, and
Alamogordo became the seat of the Sixth. A Seventh Judicial
District was created in 1909. When the people of Roswell demanded a new judicial district, United States District Attorney
William B. Childers asked the advice of Marshal Foraker. He knew
better than any federal official the amount of United States court
business of the region. Foraker informed Childers that the Pecos
Valley imposed little demand upon his office because the settlers
were so remote from the railroads. He added, however, that many

offenses—timber trespass and land frauds—occurred there but were seldom reported. "I think that in justice to the people who live in the southeastern part of the Territory," urged the lawman, "there should be a court" in Roswell. Of course, the addition of a new district required Foraker to lease new quarters for the court.[28]

The preparation for a session of court still required a good deal of effort on the part of the marshal and his staff. In August 1907, when the office began to prepare for the busy fall session, the *Albuquerque Morning Journal* followed the federal lawmen through their routine. Foraker and seven deputies assumed certain areas of responsibility: the marshal summoned jurymen for the Second Judicial District; Deputies Harry Bogh and J. H. Smith worked Santa Fe, Rio Arriba, and San Juan counties for the First District; Harry Cooper worked the Sixth District for the session at Alamogordo; Chief Deputy Harry Forbes assisted Charles Ballard at Roswell; John Collins confined his activities to Santa Fe and vicinity; and J. Benson Newell (the marshal's nephew) remained in charge of the headquarters. In the absence of field deputies, the demands of six districts taxed the staff of the marshalcy considerably.[29]

Among the servants of the federal courts, the clerk of the Fourth Judicial District Court, Secundino Romero, worked closely with Creighton Foraker. Romero, a nephew of former Marshal Trinidad Romero and brother of Sheriff Cleofes Romero of San Miguel County, served as clerk from 1897 to 1910. When New Mexico became a state two years later, Secundino Romero became United States marshal. A prominent rancher and Republican boss of San Miguel County for many years, "Sec" Romero earned a reputation for fractiousness. One Albuquerque journalist described him as the "noted pugilist from classic San Miguel County," when Romero reportedly assaulted Judge Elisha V. Long in a personal dispute.[30]

Court clerks such as Secundino Romero provided valuable services for the federal judiciary of New Mexico. They were charged with the responsibility to record "the orders, decrees, judgments, and proceedings" of the tribunals. The clerks received fees as their income and were accountable only to the judges. When the attorney general became head of the new Department of Justice in 1870, he brought the clerks under closer scrutiny. Some abuses continued, especially in the fee system, until in 1919, Congress belatedly placed the clerks on salary.[31]

Marshal Foraker and Clerk Secundino Romero cooperated

closely in the routine preparation for court. The marshal could not serve process of court until the clerk issued the papers. For instance, venires for juries issued from the clerk's office only after a judge authorized them. In April 1899, Foraker returned a jury venire to Romero "so that you may state the precinct number of these jurymen." "Otherwise," he continued, "I will have nothing to go by to find these parties." After the jurors had served on the panels, the marshal required the signature of the clerk on their payrolls. The clerk was also custodian of evidence for trial, a duty that could be troublesome. "I discovered yesterday," Romero informed Foraker, "that the guns, etc., in [the] case of US v John Black, et al. [train robbers] had been taken from this office." The clerk accused Deputy Marshal Harry Cooper of taking the weapons, but the marshal replied that one of Romero's subordinates must have been the culprit. The outcome of the dispute is not known. [32]

A community of spirit generally prevailed between the marshalcy and the clerk's office. This comradeship was possible, since Foraker and Romero occupied their posts for more than twelve years. "Say, old socks," wrote Deputy Marshal Frank W . Hall to Charles C. Shirk, deputy clerk of court, "how are you feeling these days? . . . It will not be very long untill [sic] we [deputies] are up there [Las Vegas] attending the court," added Hall, "and then we will have to make up for lost time. . . . Give my regards to the boys [in the office]," concluded the jovial deputy. A few months later, the deputies promised Shirk that they would "buy a small bottle when . . . we meet" even though "you are on the water wagon." The subordinates of Marshal Foraker "wont [sic] stand for any such statement" as abstinence. [33]

The deputies often divulged their private thoughts about the marshalcy to their friends in the court clerk's office. In June 1900, Deputy E. B. Pickard informed Deputy Clerk Shirk that "the president of the gut trust is here [in Albuquerque] and [is] full of business." Evidently, he meant that Marshal Foraker had returned to the office. The marshal is "full of business and is takeing [sic] his spite out on" the staff, but "we are used to that," added Pickard. Three days later, this deputy complained to Shirk that he was "inclined to feel a little stiff" since he had participated in a baseball game on Sunday. This event was an annual affair first begun by Marshal Edward Hall in 1895, in which the "Federals" had challenged the county officers under Sheriff William Cunningham. The game between the "Leans" (federals) and the "Fats" (county officers) became a traditional event. After the big game in June 1900, Deputy Pickard laughingly told Shirk: "You aught [*sic*] to see the other fellows" nursing their wounds.[34]

This humor of "the boys" in the federal offices led to mischievous, if not cruel, tricks. "We will soon have a new man [deputy] up there [in Las Vegas] to make some service," Deputy Hall notified Shirk, "and he is a regular WILLIE BOY [sissy]. . . . You can have a bushel of fun out of him," added Hall, "as he will believe about everything you tell him." The young officer was ordered to serve a warrant on "parties that are wanted for adultery," a case that would provide Shirk with an opportunity to "scare him up a little." The joke evidently went very well, and the "boys" in Las Vegas advised the untried deputy (not named) that the male defendant in the adultery case was very mean and would not permit the federal officer to place him in jail.[35]

This healthy comradship had not always existed between the marshalcy and county officers. Since the Salary Act of 1896, which gave the attorney general the final voice in the selection of deputies, the traditional practice of marshals deputizing sheriffs had been disrupted. Under the old procedure, sheriffs with concurrent deputy marshalships often placed their county loyalty first. After the 1896 Act, Marshal Foraker was freed from much of this local influence, since the sheriffs could only hold temporary commissions as deputy marshals.

The custody of federal prisoners caused many disagreements. The county sheriffs, who housed the marshal's prisoners, were often lax or negligent. When train robbers John Murphy and Jim and John Black were placed in the Las Vegas jail in 1905, they became local heroes. "I think that they have become too familiar with their keepers," complained Marshal Foraker to Attorney General William H. Moody. "The jailer has taken them out of the jail and into saloons and around town." This was not the first complaint about the officers at Las Vegas. Foraker scolded Sheriff Cleofes Romero in October 1901 for "allowing United States prisoners too much liberty."[36]

A most serious breach of official conduct occurred in Alamogordo, Otero County, where the sheriff permitted federal prisoners to work for local businessmen. It is not clear whether the sheriff demanded a portion (or all) of the prisoners' wages. In June 1901, Marshal Foraker confirmed these abuses and urged the government to prosecute the errant county officer. A few weeks later, New Mexicans witnessed a bizarre spectacle—the arrest of the Alamogordo sheriff by the marshal.[37]

This scandal awakened Attorney General Philander Knox to the many inconsistencies in the care of federal prisoners in New Mexico. He was under the impression that all United States prisoners were housed in the territorial penitentiary in Santa Fe. Soon after the scandal at Alamogordo, the attorney general dispatched an examiner to New Mexico, with instructions to clear up this problem The agent discovered that, in 1886, Marshal Romulo Martinez arranged for the warden of the prison to set aside a building as the "United States Jail." However, in 1901, the examiner could find no official contract for this arrangement. Meanwhile, the marshals continued to house short-term prisoners in county jails. The federal lawmen argued that the vast distances and poor transportation in the territory rendered the prison inconvenient.[38]

As the roots of the controversy became clearer, the attorney general resolved to dispose properly of the government's inmates. As early as 1891, Congress provided for the construction of several federal prisons in the territories, but the project moved slowly. Not until 1907 did the Department of Justice fulfill its obligation. On June 1 Marshal Foraker received instructions to escort his prisoners to the federal penitentiary at Fort Leavenworth, Kansas, for permanent disposition. The notorious train robbers, Jim and John Black and John Murphy, were the first inmates from New Mexico. When the *Albuquerque Morning Journal* learned about this directive, the editors regarded it as a slur on the reputation of the territorial penitentiary. Foraker could not change the direction of the federal judiciary.[39]

While Marshal Foraker enjoyed the growing independence of his office from the local authorities, he protested that he still depended heavily upon the sheriffs. He carefully reassured the New Mexicans that the marshalcy would not become a tool of federal oppression. When the attorney general urged Foraker to obtain more economical jail contracts from the sheriffs, Deputy Marshal J. H. Campbell replied: "We have to rely a great deal upon sheriffs and other local officers for information and assistance."

The district is so big, and settlements so widely scattered, that "hold-ups" would get too much start if we could not obtain information and assistance from local officers. It is very profitable [for the sheriffs] to keep U.S. prisoners and the marshal feels that if he took steps to force the price [of prisoner upkeep] down he would antagonize the sheriffs, and thus lose their help.

The marshal confirmed this when he urged the postmaster general to pay quickly the reward for the capture of a postal thief. "When [post] offices located in out of the way . . . places are held up," he declared, "the government must depend largely upon the local officers to . . . capture the robbers." "The interests of the [postal] service," concluded the marshal, "are promoted by prompt payment of the reward offered."[40]

The desirability of cooperation between local and federal agencies became most apparent during the decade of 1896–1906, when an extraordinary outbreak of banditry occurred in New Mexico. Highwaymen victimized numerous railways: two trains were robbed in 1896; three in 1897; three in 1898; two in 1899; one in 1901; one in 1903; and one in 1905. The New Mexico Assembly had taken notice of train robbers in 1887, when it passed a law making train robbery a capital offense. Arizona followed with a similar law two years later, and Congress followed belatedly, on July 1, 1902, with a less stringent national statute against train robbery. This last legislation required the marshal to pursue bandits even if the mails were not rifled and imposed upon the robbers a fine up to $5,000 and a prison sentence of not more than twenty years.[41]

Among the banditti of the railways, the William ("Black Jack") Christian band was especially troublesome. In 1895, Christian fled the Indian Territory after killing a deputy marshal. No sooner had Marshal Foraker's men killed Christian in April 1897, than Thomas ("Black Jack") Ketchum took up where the dead outlaw had left off. Other bands grew from the previous ones: William ("Bronco Bill") Walters's, George Musgrave's, Daniel ("Red") Pipkin's, Henry Hawkins's "Mesa Hawks," and John and Jim Black's.[42]

The Black Jack bands caused the lawmen of the Southwest a good deal of consternation. Marshal Edward L. Hall, during whose term these pillagers first appeared, informed the attorney general that this eruption of violence and robbery was the "most important" problem for the territories. Desperadoes were "a continual menace" to Wells, Fargo Express Company and "the various banks, post-offices, stages and, in fact, all business." When he succeeded Hall, Marshal Foraker quickly agreed. On October 26, 1897, after his posse returned empty-handed, Foraker characterized the Black Jacks as the most "murderous" outlaws that ever "defied the federal authority." They "have robbed no less than 4 U.S. post-offices, . . . three different [railway] mail routes," and other businesses. However, Foraker informed a Montana correspondent that this band was not responsible for "all the develtry [sic]" in New Mexico. Other bandits pillaged under the name of Black Jack. [43]

In the pursuit of these freebooters, the federal lawmen encountered a lack of interest and even obstructionism among the citizenry. Edward Hall complained that he could not rely upon citizen possemen. They were unable to withstand hardships and their horseflesh was unable to endure the pace of pursuit. Both Hall and Foraker, in turn, learned to distrust cowboys in their posses. "The sentiment of the cowboys," said Foraker, is to get "the best of the express companies." He added that the herders "are very slow to aid my officers." When Deputy Marshal George Scarborough of New Mexico asked cowboy James McCauley to guide his posse, the stockman refused. If he aided the deputy marshal, McCauley recalled, his "time would soon be up." The Black Jacks would kill him. Having been a rancher in Grant County, Marshal Foraker sympathized to some extent with the ranchers. They were compelled "as a matter of protection" from the outlaws to divulge the movements of the federal posses. [44]

When he entered the marshalcy in 1897, Foraker found that Edward L. Hall had substituted a less-expensive means of detection for the unwieldy posses. Hall offered known associates of the outlaws reward money if these renegades would lead deputy marshals to the Black Jacks. In April 1897, Deputy Marshal Fred Higgins of New Mexico and Deputy Sheriff Ben Clark of Clifton, Arizona, had ambushed and killed Black Jack Christian as a result of information provided by turncoat James Shaw. Marshal Foraker recommended payment of this informant when he entered office. [45]

Creighton Foraker complemented this procedure with an even more successful tactic—the "still-hunt." This practice was com

monly used by big-game hunters in the Southwest and involved the quiet pursuit, usually by one man, of mountain lions. To still-hunt required stealth, nerve, and patience. In July 1898, the marshal dispatched Deputy J. J. Sheridan "on a 'still hunt' for evidence" along the border o
Arizona. Sheridan would go "on a quiet jaunt to the vicinity of Clifton, Solomonville, [and] Bisbee [Arizona] and north to Cienega, Luna & thereabouts" in New Mexico. In the following months, Foraker assigned Deputy Horace Loomis to still-hunt for Bronco Bill Walters in the same area. To expedite the still-hunt, the marshal directed Loomis to avoid collecting the telltale expense vouchers, which always tipped the outlaws that a federal lawman was in the neighborhood. This tactic paid dividends when Loomis located Walters in eastern Arizona. Foraker informed Marshal William Griffith, who, in turn, dispatched Deputy Marshal Jefferson D. (Jeff) Milton after Bronco Bill. Milton's men killed one bandit, William ("Kid") Johnson, and captured Bill.[46]

When Marshal Foraker employed the still-hunt, he did not rule out completely the noisy and unwieldy posse. He merely waited until the still-hunter located the quarry. Then the posse, like Jeff Milton's party, moved in on the outlaws. These heavily armed posses were easily distinguishable from the average Westerner, who did not normally go about heavily armed or ride his best animal. William French, cattleman and rancher near Alma, New Mexico, encountered a posse in the late 1890s:

> We had scarcely got through [breaking horses] . . . when we were invaded by three tough-looking strangers. They were heavily armed with pistols and saddle-guns, and the size and quality of their horses would have drawn attention in any frontier camp. . . . Those three gentlemen . . . were in pursuit of stolen horses—a grave offense on the frontier and still somewhat prevalent throughout the territory of New Mexico. In this case it was a notorious outlaw who went by the name of "Black Jack."

French accompanied this posse, which captured one of Black Jack's followers.[47]

In some instances, these possemen were as dangerous as the men they pursued. On December 9, 1897, the Black Jack Ketchum

206 CHAPTER 10

band robbed a train at Stein's Pass, New Mexico, and a combined
posse of deputy marshals from New Mexico and Arizona arrested
five men in Cochise County. One suspect, Walter Hovey (Hoff-
man), recalled the deputies with much anguish:

> The appearance of heavily armed strangers was generally the
> giveaway [of trouble]. . . . These posses were usually
> composed of around [a] half-dozen Americans and fifteen to
> twenty Mexicans and Indians. These [posses] were far more
> dangerous at your camp than the outlaws themselves.

Hovey added that Foraker's posse (the marshal was not present)
was composed of "twenty-three breeds" who held a "court of
inquiry" over the captives. The posse yelled and fired their
weapons around the heads of the helpless victims and "insulted"
them. Hovey concluded that only the restraining influence of
Deputy Marshal Cipriano Baca, a noted New Mexico lawman,
saved the suspects from death at the hands of the Foraker party.[48]

Once the arrests were made, the marshal, who desired a victory
over the bandits, began arrangements for a speedy trial. His
problem was to select a site in which the jurymen would be firm.
On December 30, 1897, Foraker consulted the veteran Wells,
Fargo agent Fred Dodge. Both men agreed that a jury of cowmen
would possibly be too friendly to the outlaws, but "Mexicans" were
equally untrustworthy on the panel. The judges often fired the
Hispanos for incompetency (or leniency). The marshal finally
decided that Silver City, his former home (where he knew many
reliable men), would be the best place. "We could select a jury,"
concluded the federal lawman, "without a single 'Cow man.' " He
added that, "I will do all I can to have justice meted out to these"
outlaws.[49]

These were terrifying times for Walter Hovey. Rather than
being tried on a federal charge first, the Territory of New Mexico
charged him and his comrades with train robbery. When a Silver
City jury exonerated the suspects, Marshal Foraker promptly
rearrested them for robbery of the mails and jailed them in Las
Cruces. Hovey bitterly recalled the jury at his second trial. He and
his friends "felt lost" at the sight of the "longhaired, seamy, greasy
faces." "What is the use? [Sheriff] Pat Garrett controls any Mexican
in Dona Ana County," said defense attorney James Fielder. The
jurors, recollected Hovey, could not speak English, but replied to

questions, "Me no savvy." Hovey and two of his colleagues were found guilty and, on September 28, 1898, began to serve a term of ten years each in the United States jail at the New Mexico Territorial Prison. A short time later, outlaw Black Jack Ketchum confessed to the Stein's Pass train robbery, and Hovey and his friends were eventually pardoned in 1904. This miscarriage of justice was most unfortunate for the cause of federal justice in New Mexico Territory. One historian concluded that the wrongful conviction of the three men "was callously engineered by men who, in the main, neither knew nor cared whether the three men were innocent or guilty."[50]

While some deputy marshals may have been callous, others served faithfully and even died in the line of duty. In 1899, Samuel Ketchum, brother of Black Jack, robbed a Colorado Southern passenger train near Des Moines, Union County, New Mexico. Marshal Foraker organized a sizeable force, including railway detectives and Sheriff Edward Farr of Walsenburg, Colorado. (In order to expedite the pursuit, Foraker may have commissioned this posse without immediate authority.) On Sunday evening, July 16, seven of the posse under Deputy Marshal Farr stumbled upon the Ketchum band in an isolated canyon near Cimarron. In a hail of gunfire three of the deputies fell—Farr was killed, and H. M. Love and J. H. Smith were wounded, the latter fatally. Outlaw Sam Ketchum was wounded and captured, but died after an arm amputation. The legendary Black Jack, who did not participate in this engagement, soon attempted to rob a train in the very same spot. The day after this abortive robbery, he was captured. In 1901, the Territory of New Mexico hanged him for train robbery, making him the only victim of the stringent territorial law against train holdups.[51]

Among the many badmen in Creighton Foraker's long marshalcy, none surpassed George Musgrave in notoriety. After the death of Black Jack Ketchum, newsmen erroneously credited Musgrave with most of the lawlessness that occurred in the territory. This outlaw had long since settled his family in Colorado, but Foraker urged the neighboring states and territories to watch for him. In February 1907, the New Mexico marshal erroneously thought Musgrave had been found in Dalhart, Texas. "Musgrave is an outlaw and desperado of the worst kind," said Foraker to Marshal George H. Green, "and I have been hunting him for the

past nine years." Unfortunately, the Texas suspect was not
Musgrave. Not until January 1910 did New Mexican authorities
capture George Musgrave, who was tried for murder and acquitted. The last of the Black Jacks paid his debt to society, but the
payment came in the form of exile for ten years in Colorado, not in
a prison cell.[52]

In the pursuit of these bands, Marshal Foraker sometimes
charged that local authorities were not doing as much as they
should. In October 1897, after Deputy Cipriano Baca's posse drove
the Black Jacks into Mexico, the marshal wrote an angry letter to
the attorney general:

> I notified him [Baca] to return. . . . Further expense in this
> matter was useless, and I do not think I will ever again
> request aid to serve process on this gang and deem it high
> time that the Territorial officials of Arizona and New Mexico
> devoted some of their energies in this behalf . . . . I think
> now that the gang is in Mexico the Government of Mexico
> should be appealed to, to gather them in; for in Mexico they
> usually bring them [the outlaws] in dead, and these men
> should be thusly treated.[53]

Many citizens of New Mexico and Arizona were embarrassed by
the lawlessness, and feared that such criminality delayed
statehood. In 1901, the Arizona Assembly created the Arizona
Rangers, a small corps with powers of arrest throughout the
territory. On February 4, 1905, the New Mexico Assembly
followed with the Mounted Police. In Sonora, the Mexican
government had for some time maintained a force of Rural Police
(*rurales*) under Colonel Emilio Kosterlitsky, a Russian immigrant.
Kosterlitsky worked closely with the marshals of Arizona. The
southwestern sheriffs also began to hold conventions and to discuss
and improve methods of detection.[54]

Creighton Foraker willingly cooperated with these agencies. He
readily agreed to the irregular procedure of deputizing Captain
Burton Mossman and two additional Arizona Rangers. Several of
Foraker's deputies also became mounted policeman, and his
former Deputy Marshal Fred Fornoff became Captain of the
Mounted Police in 1907. The editor of the *Albuquerque Morning
Journal* was a little surprised at the extent of the cooperation
between the federal lawman and Captain Fornoff in September

1908, when the Mounted Police established a camp on Foraker's ranch just north of the city. Realizing that the readers of the *Journal* would wonder, the journalist added in explanation that "it is understood this [camp] is not for the protection" of the marshal. The mounted policemen were attending the territorial fair.[55]

The federal government also improved its methods of detection. In 1895, Congress authorized the Department of Justice to establish a criminal detection system similar to the Bertillon procedure of the French government. Any peculiarities and physical characteristics of offenders were recorded on cards. In his *Annual Report for 1907*, Attorney General Charles J. Bonaparte declared that his department possessed twenty thousand cards and, from them, had made six hundred successful identifications. The following year, the Department moved the file to the Federal Prison at Fort Leavenworth, Kansas. Fingerprinting began in October 1904, and five years later, the Department inaugurated a separate detective agency, the Bureau of Investigation (forerunner of the Federal Bureau of Investigation).[56]

This new detective agency caused some changes in the place of the United States marshals in federal law enforcement. The Bureau represented the conclusion to a trend that began with the Department of Justice in 1870—an increase in the detective powers of the government. Many congressmen feared this agency and preferred that the marshals rely upon the people, in the form of informants or grand jurymen, for assistance against criminals. A large, centralized, detective agency in the Department of Justice boded danger to the Republic. In 1909, the Bureau of Investigation remained purely an "investigative" agency, with the assignment to "aid" federal officers. The attorney general soon issued a circular that defined the limits of the Bureau's jurisdiction in the sphere of the marshalcy.[57]

In the meantime, Marshal Foraker's staff had conducted several important investigations for Washington. At the turn of this century, many Americans became alarmed by the spread of radical or revolutionary movements—anarchism, and socialism. Several events reinforced these fears: The Pullman Strike of 1894; the nationalistic spirit that accompanied the Spanish-American War; and the assassination of President McKinley in 1901. In November 1900, sometime before the death of the chief executive, District Attorney William B. Childers directed Creighton Foraker to investigate anarchists who were recruiting followers in the remote coal-mining camps of New Mexico. Deputy Fred Fornoff undertook the task.[58]

By January of the following year, Fornoff had completed his investigation. He found several radicals but none were threatening: L. Barrigi, an open anarchist, but one who had made no "overt act" against the government; D. Chino, a miner who was presently among those on strike in Gibson, New Mexico; and coal miner Enrico Aira, a subscriber to a radical journal, but noted for "industry and sobriety." The deputy enclosed copies of anarchist periodicals which he found in the camps—*La Questione Sociale: Periodico Socialists-Anarcho*, published in Patterson, New Jersey; and *L'Aurora: Periodico Anarchico*, printed in Spring Valley, Illinois. However, Deputy Fornoff concluded that these persons did not seem to be "engaged in a common purpose of propagating the tenets of anarchy, or in preparing for some concerted action in opposition to . . . [the] government."[59]

While no apparent danger existed in the mining camps, the assassination of William McKinley in September 1901 by a deranged fanatic spurred the federal government to new measures against the anarchists. On September 28, Attorney Childers reported that Marshal Foraker had arrested a known anarchist, Antonio Maggio, for conspiracy. The marshal proceeded to collect evidence and asked Marshal Myron McCord of Arizona to locate witnesses in the Maggio case. The Maggio family, who resided in Baton Rouge, Louisiana, came to the aid of Antonio. A brother pleaded with the marshal to help Antonio get out on bond, but Foraker replied that he could not. Maggio's sister wrote a worried letter to the lawman. Foraker urged her not to fret, since Antonio would probably get off with a light sentence. Probably, the marshal exercised very little control over the case, since the secret service asked him to maintain silence.[60]

If the marshal possessed a personal conviction in such cases, it was definitely on the side of order and property. He expressed these sentiments clearly in early 1904, when laborers struck the Santa Fe Railroad yards at Alamogordo and Santa Rosa. Employees of several local railroads soon followed in sympathy. The marshal repocted that as a tactical measure he recommended that the railroad make "temporary concessions" to the strikers. In this way a crisis was avoided "until such a time when the matter could be better handled." By May the strikers had stopped all rail traffic, and the marshal had to employ extra guards to protect the mails and to assist railroad agents. The agitators obstructed one road in an attempt to derail a passenger train, but an unscheduled freight train knocked the obstructions from the track. The deputy marshals traced the would-be wreckers to the hills where one killed himself. With this incident, the strikers relented and the marshal withdrew his extra deputies.[61]

While the federal lawmen kept an eye on the agitators, they also observed the activities of the Indians. By the turn of the century, the marshals had assumed much of the responsibility for keeping peace on the reservations. Unscrupulous whiskey peddlers still provided the Indians with ample amounts of liquor, and the New Mexicans could not shed their neurotic fears of potential Apache raids. In 1902, N. S. Walpole, Agent of the Jicarilla, reported that several saloons were situated near the reservation. Fortified with such beverages, several Apaches left the reservation to attend the Pueblo feasts in Taos. At the request of the secretary of the interior, Marshal Foraker dispatched Deputy Fred Fornoff to police the festival. Some drunkenness did occur, and Fornoff disarmed several Jicarilla and arrested three Picuris. Similar disturbances occurred at feasts the following year, and the deputies continued to patrol the festivals.[62]

That Creighton M. Foraker was reappointed to the marshalcy on four occasions was a tribute to his popularity. A contemporary of the federal lawman observed that Foraker was "possibly personally known to more people in the territory than anyone." The southwestern newspapers were not above glamorizing the federal lawman. In 1903, an Arizona journal reported the conversation between a correspondent and a "prosperous looking man," possibly a wealthy rancher, who boarded the writer's train at Raton, New Mexico. The journalist introduced himself to the new passenger and added that he (the writer) was from Cincinnati, Ohio. The new arrival replied that he, too, was an Ohioan. The distinguished name of Foraker naturally arose in conversation about that state, and the new passenger interjected that he remembered the name "Foraker." Upon arriving in Albuquerque, the "prosperous looking man" presented the correspondent with his card: "C. M. Foraker, U. S. M. for N. M."

Residents of Albuquerque expressed their respects to the

marshal. At Christmas Hispano and Chinese citizens presented Mrs. Foraker with gifts, while Black townspeople offered the marshal the traditional holiday opossum.[63]

This extraordinary popularity helps explain the many novel appeals for assistance registered in his office. "Well Mr. Foraker," wrote a needy newlywed from Bernalillo in March 1905, "I [would] like for you to do me a favor to see if you can find a job for me." In November 1906, a Tennessean asked the marshal to find a lost sister. "I am personally acquainted with her," replied the marshal. "You can probably locate her by writing the postmaster at Mountainair." A grieving father appealed to Foraker in 1902 to obtain a pardon for his son, George Massagee, convicted of post office robbery. "I think . . . that he is not as bad a boy as pictured," replied the federal officer, "and I shall do what I can consistently to aid him." Surprisingly, men whom Foraker sent to prison requested his aid. "I have no doubt but what you will be surprised," wrote outlaw James Black from Leavenworth Prison. "They have the parole law here now & I and John [a brother] are going to try to get out." Black had a purpose in his letter of October 9, 1910. "A man has got to have work before they will let him out on it [parole]," added the convict, and "you said the last time I saw you when I got out [to] come down & you would give me work."[64]

With all his prestige, Creighton M. Foraker could not survive the political changes that statehood wrought in New Mexico. President William H. Taft proposed to retain Foraker, but during discussions with the Republican delegation of the territory in January 1912, Solomon Luna steadfastly demanded the appointment of Secundino Romero, the former court clerk at Las Vegas. Only by this appointment to the marshalcy could Luna guarantee Taft a solid pro-administration delegation to the National Republican Convention in 1912. Romero brought the complete support of San Miguel County to the New Mexico Republicans who, of course, desired statehood above all things. The possibility of a bolt by some New Mexico delegates (possibly Romero) to Theodore Roosevelt's Bull Moose Party was ruled out by the selection of Secundino Romero as a candidate for the marshalcy. In the words of Ralph E. Twitchell, a participant in territorial politics, the nomination of Secundino Romero for the marshalcy "made a combination possible which otherwise could not have been effected in the interest of the national administration."[65]

Creighton Foraker assumed the baton of federal law enforcement during an era of innovation within the Department of Justice. When Congress authorized the salary system for marshals in 1896, the lawmakers unwittingly opened the way for many unexpected changes. Foraker, who placed his entire staff (not just office personnel) on fixed incomes, elevated the deputyship to a place of respectability. An energetic individual could support a family from this income, whereas in the past, the deputy held other simultaneous employment. The marshalcy no longer had to employ the county sheriffs, who generally experienced conflicting loyalties about their duties. This period of reform coincided with the nationwide movement called Progressivism, which advocated the rationalization of bureaucratic administration and centralization of control. Within the Department of Justice, the attorneys general directed this centralization; within the New Mexico marshalcy, Creighton M. Foraker performed the same function. He also demonstrated an ability to reject the sacred cows of law enforcement to some extent—the *posse comitatus*—especially for the sake of economy and efficiency.

Creighton Foraker quickly abandoned the controversial role of reformer that Congress had imposed upon his predecessors. He returned to the statutory role of ministerial officer to the courts. A man of integrity and energy, he could be tough when the need arose. He made errors—some that may have cost innocent men years in prison. But he demonstrated compassion for the needy, even for persons whom he had helped to send to the penitentiary. In his unofficial role as dispenser of favors to the downtrodden, he was a fitting person to lead the marshalcy into the twentieth century.

11

Theodore Roosevelt and the Arizona Marshalcy,

1897–1912

When William Kidder Meade resigned from the United States marshal's office in Tucson on June 15, 1897, he left a much stronger federal institution than he had found. This did not mean that the marshalcy was fully established in Arizona—far from it. Many of the lawless conditions of the 1880s persisted into the early 1900s. The geographic isolation of the territory and the cultural diversity of the newly arrived settlers encouraged crime. Political factionalism, rather than political parties, continued to flourish. The international boundary remained a sensitive consideration, especially as revolution in the Republic of Mexico began to take shape.

The Arizona Territory of 1897–1912 differed considerably from that of the 1880s. The population had increased from 123,000 in 1900 to 197,000 in 1910. As stimulants to growth, a boom occurred in copper mining in the southern counties and the production of silver remained steady. The public school system improved, something considered absolutely necessary for statehood. The number of counties increased: from ten in 1881 to fourteen in 1909. A Fifth Judicial District was added in 1905.[1]

In 1897, President William McKinley appointed a prominent Arizonan, William M. Griffith, to the marshalcy. Griffith operated the Texas & California Stage Company in the 1870s, which connected Fort Worth, Texas, with San Diego, California. As the railroads replaced the stage, he established many feeder stagelines to the isolated mining camps of Arizona. When he purchased a large ranch near Tucson, Griffith received the title, "Baron of Dripping Springs." A Mason of long standing, he eventually graduated to the thirty-third degree. He became national committeeman in the Republican Party, and McKinley rewarded him with the marshalcy on June 15, 1897. Local Republicans were not entirely pleased. The Phoenix *Arizona Republican* recalled later that McKinley "foisted" Griffith upon the territorial Republicans and helped to provoke a split in the party.[2]

In a strange turn of events, Marshal William M. Griffith was succeeded on June 6, 1901, by his former governor, Myron McCord. Educated at the Richburg Academy in New York, McCord moved to Wisconsin in the 1850s. He represented his state in Congress where he sat next to future President McKinley. The two men became good friends. McCord moved to Arizona in 1893, where he impressed the people with a scientific farm and cattle ranch, and served as a member of the Board of Control (it managed the prison, insane asylum, and reform school). President McKinley rewarded McCord in 1897 with the governorship of Arizona. When the Spanish American War erupted one year later, McCord suddenly resigned to assume a colonelcy in the First Territorial Infantry. His unit did not see action, and McCord became manager of the Phoenix *Gazette*. His rival, the *Arizona Republican*, considered McCord's service commendable and characterized him as an "efficient officer."[3]

Myron McCord assumed that, even though his patron William McKinley was assasinated, he would win reappointment to a full four-year term in the marshalcy in 1902. However, Theodore Roosevelt, who succeeded McKinley in September 1901, appointed Benjamin F. Daniels, a friend and former Rough Rider. A noted frontiersman, Daniels hunted buffalo, gambled, and in the 1880s, served as assistant city marshal of Dodge City, Kansas. He participated in a bloody county seat war (Gray County, Kansas), in which he and several other deputy sheriffs killed one man and wounded three more. After a stint as policeman and gambler in Cripple Creek, Colorado, Ben Daniels enlisted in the Rough Riders in 1898. Theodore Roosevelt praised him for being to the "front in any enterprise." After the war, Daniels invested in mining property around Nogales, Arizona, where he made his home.[4]

The enemies of Theodore Roosevelt looked upon the appointment of Ben Daniels with alarm, and, in order to avoid embarrassment, the president urged the gunfighter not to withhold any compromising facts about his background. Needless to say, when rumors appeared that, as a young man of eighteen, Daniels had served a term in prison for horsetheft, the president was chagrined. In a letter of February 22, 1902, he upbraided Daniels and asked for his resignation. "You did a grave wrong to me," said the president solemnly, "when you failed to be frank . . . and tell me about this one blot on your record." While Roosevelt's political enemies cheered, the dejected president accepted Daniels's resignation. On March 18, 1902, he reappointed Myron McCord to the marshalcy, although it was reported that the appointee had spoken "disrespectfully" about the chief executive during the controversy over Daniels.[5]

For persons who knew the stubborn president best, it came as no surprise when Roosevelt continued to express an interest in Ben Daniels. When he asked for the gunfighter's resignation, the chief executive reassured Daniels that, "if you stand straight your friends will be able to use you in the future." The future was not far away. In 1902, Roosevelt appointed another former Rough Rider, Colonel Alexander O. Brodie, to the governorship of Arizona. In 1904, Brodie made Daniels superintendent of the territorial prison.[6]

By 1906, the president concluded that Ben Daniels had atoned for his shortcomings and should be reconsidered for the marshalcy. Roosevelt, among others, provided letters of reference for the reconsideration of the Senate. Frederick J. Dodge, veteran Wells, Fargo detective and former associate of Daniels, asserted that he had never found the man "wanting" in courage. Another acquaintance of Daniels characterized him as a "gentleman" of "ability" and "nerve." The former sheriff of Ford County, Kansas (at Dodge City), William B. (Bat) Masterson praised Ben Daniels as a courageous officer.[7]

While the comradeship that Roosevelt expressed for his fellow Rough Rider was incomprehensible to many Republicans, the president regarded Daniels as an example of the classic heroic individual. The marshal and his fellow plainsmen were "Vikings," said the chief executive to Senator Clarence Clark. In the "primitive west," he added, Ben Daniels was a "frontier scout" and "ranger" at the age of eighteen. According to Roosevelt, Daniels was a member of that unique class of Westerners, the "two-gun man," whom the "colonel" described to historian George Otto Trevelyan as a man who had exercised "the right of private war [personal encounters] under primitive western conditions." To the admiring president, Daniels and his fellow gunfighters occupied a semidivine place in the frontier West.[8]

In spite of this high praise, the Senate delayed the appointment of Ben Daniels. When news of the confirmation of Daniels was finally received in Arizona in April 1906, the *Arizona Republican* credited the Senate's positive action to the work of Sidney Bieber, former fire marshal of Washington, D.C., and friend of Daniels. Bieber resided a year in Arizona and there made the acquaintance of the gunfighter. He "started out to make easier for Daniels the road he was traveling toward the berth to which President Roosevelt had named him," declared the editor in a confused piece of journalism. No doubt Bieber's friendship with Speaker of the House Joseph G. Cannon helped to confirm the appointment. For the enemies of Roosevelt and Daniels in the Southwest, the appointment merely confirmed what they suspected—the president intended to place his "Soldiers of Fortune" in as many governmental offices as possible. The *Kansas City Journal* (Missouri) computed the number of Rough Riders in the Territories of Oklahoma, New Mexico, and Arizona at eighteen appointees, who earned, collectively, $52,000. As Burton Mossman, influential cattleman and captain of the Arizona Rangers later recalled, "the devastating blight of the Rough Riders was spreading over the Southwest."[9]

When William H. Taft succeeded Theodore Roosevelt in 1909, the future for the anti-Daniels Republicans brightened. On August 7, 1909, Taft appointed Charles A. Overlock to succeed Ben Daniels. Overlock was born in Bangor, Maine, in 1859. He carpentered in Boston and moved to Oregon in 1881, but settled in Tombstone the following year, where he invested in cattle and opened a butcher shop. After a short stay in Bisbee, Overlock and several associates learned that the Phelps-Dodge Company planned to construct a smelter near the international boundary. In 1900, they organized the International Land and Improvement Company and plotted the future site of Douglas near the new company. Overlock and his partners became millionaires. He and his son Harry branched into the lumber business, while the senior Overlock became mayor of Douglas. His biographer declared that the territory owed to him alone "the foundation and business and Civic development on one city," Douglas.[10]

Like its counterpart in New Mexico, the Arizona marshalcy experienced many changes because of the Salary Act of 1896. William Kidder Meade, who served his last year under this legislation, regarded the law as salutary but restrictive. Attorney General Judson Harmon authorized Meade one chief office deputy and one office deputy, at salaries of $1500 and $900 respectively. Harmon also fixed Meade's headquarters in Tucson. The marshals no longer possessed the freedom to choose their place of residence. The attorney general also directed that "the marshal and his office deputies . . . serve all process in and around official headquarters" and "perform all service necessary during sessions of courts at other points." Harmon added bluntly: "No field deputies are to be located" in Tucson, the headquarters city.[11]

Meade, who regarded this last restriction as senseless, quickly appealed to the attorney general. "In the interests of justice and efficiency," he asked for two field deputies in Tucson, Meade's official headquarters.

> The fact that there are four judicial districts . . . , each holding two sessions annually when it is necessary to have both office deputies with me, should demonstrate the necessity of at least two field deputies at Tucson; otherwise, it would be equivalent to saying that the law should not be enforced excepting under certain conditions.

The dismayed lawman pointed out that "smuggling and liquor selling to the Indians is almost a daily occurrence" around Tucson. Deputies were required to perform considerable "police service," and many crimes were "largely prevented owing to their [mere] presence." In view of these considerations, Meade asked for permission to appoint two field deputies to Tucson. Evidently, Attorney General Harmon refused his solicitation, since Meade requested permission to select two additional office deputies a short time later. These men would perform the tasks that Meade had planned for the field deputies in Tucson. While the attorney general permitted field deputies elsewhere in the territory, he refused this second request.[12]

The marshal was restrained in correspondence with his superior, but expressed his inner thoughts about the Salary Act to his lawyer in Washington, R. R. McMahon. Retention of an attorney in the capital became a common means for the marshals to defend themselves against the bureaucracy. In a letter of July 6, 1896, William Kidder Meade revealed doubts about his position under the new law. Whereas marshals of the settled states merely served the process of federal courts, their counterparts in the sparsely settled territories not only performed this duty but also pursued badmen and other lawbreakers. Attorney General Harmon failed to understand this unique condition. Meade put it pointedly. Were his duties "of a supervisory character," as in the East, or "am I expected to be a criminal hunter?" he asked McMahon. The Salary Act provided him and his office deputies with an adequate fixed income, one suited to the duties of a ministerial officer of the courts—the service of warrants and subpoenas. But the new act failed to provide Marshal Meade with adequate resources—funds and authority—to pursue banditti who were presently ravaging his district.

The perplexed lawman asked the unanswerable question—was the marshal merely the ministerial officer of the courts, or was he a detective as well? The Judiciary Act of 1789 designated him an executive (ministerial) officer with the task of serving process in peaceful communities. But the territories were often very lawless, and the marshals became pursuers of badmen. In the absence of a detective force in the Department of Justice, and when sheriffs were ineffective, the marshals performed this task. The answer to Meade's question was that the marshal had to perform both functions—serve process and hunt outlaws—simultaneously and to the best of his ability. In regard to the second duty, he must search out the banditti with inadequate resources. This jerry-built structure persisted until 1909, when Congress authorized the Bureau of Investigation.

In September 1896, the marshal penned a second angry letter to his attorney. The comptroller of the Treasury suddenly revoked the privilege of earning double fees for mileage in Arizona and New Mexico. This practice, a concession to high transportation costs and great distances in the Southwest, had made the deputyship more attractive in the past. The comptroller based this decision upon the Salary Act and assumed that the office deputies did not deserve preferential treatment. But he also struck at field deputies, who were less prosperous. "Every railroad in Arizona, with one exception," declared Meade, "charges six cents per mile." Under the Fee Bill of 1854, which was still in effect after the revocation of double fees, the mileage fee was only $.06 per mile. His deputies simply broke even. Meade could not believe that "Congress would knowingly commit such an outrage," and he was "inclined to look upon it as a clerical mistake." A few days later, the marshal informed his Phoenix Deputy J. M. Pratt that "your per diem is just one half what it should have been" since the comptroller had abolished double fees. Meade's observation was close to the truth; Congress overlooked the double fee provision in the formulation of the Salary Act. Double fees were soon reinstated.[14]

The successors of William Kidder Meade continued to fret about the provisions of the Salary Act of 1896. In June 1901, the attorney general fixed Myron McCord's headquarters in Phoenix, Maricopa County, the territorial capital since 1889. On September 7, McCord quietly informed his superior that he had leased office space in the O'Neill Building and that plans were under way to move the office equipment from Tucson. However, the citizens of Phoenix were so excited about the move that someone circulated a rumor that the marshal had chartered an entire train to move his records to the territorial capital. The *Arizona Republican* quickly killed this story.[15]

While McCord did not object to Phoenix (his residence was there), the business of the federal courts was heavier around Tucson and in the southeastern counties. Transportation and communication focused upon Tucson. Accordingly, McCord made the irregular request that he be permitted to maintain an office deputy in Tucson, rather than to concentrate all of his office personnel in Phoenix. "The amount of business in the southern and eastern ends of my district will keep at least one [office] deputy busy all the time," declared the lawman. The attorney general consented, and Office Deputy Justus P. Welles occupied the Tucson post.[16]

The Arizona lawmen continued to require the services of field deputies in the many isolated camps and villages of the territory. In July 1901, McCord dispatched the appointments of four field deputies to the attorney general for approval. Eventually, he selected a total of twelve field deputies. McCord singled out strategic villages for field deputies—Flagstaff, Prescott, and Kingman in the north; Clifton and Morenci in the southeast; the San Carlos Indian Reservation; Benson and Bisbee in the south; Globe and Phoenix (McCord demanded a field deputy in his headquarters town) in the central counties; and Yuma in the far west. McCord insisted upon a deputy for Clifton because he considered that area a growing problem:

> [Clifton] is a large mining camp, about 8,000 persons being there and in the immediate vicinity. There have been frequent violations of the federal laws . . . and the guilty parties often escape punishment because of the great distance an office deputy must travel from headquarters [to Clifton]. . . . The expenses of such deputy must necessarily be very heavy owing to this distance, over 300 miles.

The fact that a United States commissioner resided there also added weight to the demand for a field deputy in Clifton.[17]

In addition to maintaining effective deputies, the marshal also rented suitable quarters for the courts. It was not always an easy matter. In March 1904, Judge George R. Davis objected to his facilities, although the nature of his objection is unclear. While attempting to please Davis, one of McCord's subordinates inadvertently misplaced the leases to all court accommodations. Finally, the lost papers were found "mixed with a quantity of old papers," and the marshal forwarded them to Washington. "The above explanation is but poor," admitted McCord, "but is in accordance with the facts."[18]

Like his colleagues in New Mexico, Marshal McCord became involved in the agitation for a new federal building. While not necessarily as important as many thought, such a structure symbolized the maturation of the federal power and the growing independence of United States authorities in Arizona. In September 1904, Delegate John F. Wilson proposed a bill for a federal building in Phoenix. The structure would house the post office, marshalcy, and other federal institutions. In that same month, the Treasury Department asked Marshal McCord to prepare "an estimate showing the amount of space required for the present and prospective needs of the United States and courts and officials."[19]

While some court facilities were adequate, others lacked even the minimal graces. In 1900, Frank Hereford, aspiring young lawyer and sometime deputy marshal, described a courtroom in the border town of Nogales.

I have just come from a scene that was as striking as unusual. The court house of this little town [Nogales] is in the middle of a large enclosure, grown with grass. . . . The courthouse is a one story adobe building, unplastered through on the outside [?], and divided into quarters in the center by shalls [shawls ?] running from front to back and from the court room on one side to the jail on the other. The court room is the only large hall in the town, and it is used for all large gatherings. The Republicans voted in it last night and the Democrats the night before. Tonight there was a church entertainment there.[20]

Many of the marshals' duties took them to the border country, where persons of diverse origin and motive sought refuge and new fortunes. Some were attracted by the copper boom of 1900. Some were highwaymen. Others were revolutionaries fighting against the government of Mexican President Porfirio Díaz. This influx of settlers into southern Arizona promoted a resurgence of crime, an outbreak not unlike that around Tombstone in the early 1880s. In June 1900, the editor of the Phoenix *Arizona Republican* complained that "an alarming percentage" of wanted men were never captured. In a blunt editorial entitled "Crime in Arizona," this writer stated the facts:

A few years ago a man murdered his wife under the most revolting circumstances and lingered for months in the vicinity of the crime. A band of desperadoes [led by Burt Alvord], all of them well known, are leisurely wandering about in Cochise and Pima Counties, being interviewed by newspaper reporters and writing jocose letters to the sheriff [Scott White]. Pursuit of them seems to have been abandoned. Four years ago the notorious Black Jack [Christian] gang infested southeastern Arizona and were met almost daily and talked with. Four outlaws who lately committed a murder in this county [Maricopa] seem to have taken themselves out of reach of justice . . . and if they are ever captured the capture will probably be an accident. . . . The trouble seems to be in the disposition of many presumably lawabiding citizens to look lightly on crime and even afford aid to escaping criminals.[21]

Cochise and Graham counties were heavily infested with outlaws and often required the attention of the marshals. In April 1900, three posses and one army unit pursued banditti in Cochise County. Each group hunted a separate band. One newspaper maintained a roster of murders—"Cochise's Bloody List"—for the unfortunate district. Among the most sadistic brigands in Graham County, Augustino Chacon boasted of having killed fifteen Americans and thirty-seven of his own people, Mexicans. After a Solomonville jury convicted Chacon of the murder of a deputy sheriff in 1895, the crafty outlaw escaped jail. County officers pursued Chacon for several years, but the highwayman eluded the lawmen. The inhabitants of this area were, in many instances, "natives of Chihuahua . . . [and] outlaws or refugees from Mexico for political reasons."[22]

As these bandits continued to roam southeastern Arizona, the citizenry began to complain about ineffective sheriffs. In July 1900, a Cochise County grand jury recommended that Sheriff Scott White resign. White was guilty of "gross negligence" and had permitted notorious outlaw Burt Alvord to escape jail. The *Arizona Republican* declared that Sheriff White permitted the canny outlaw to "josh" and humiliate him. When Sheriff Ben Clark of Graham County failed to capture Augustino Chacon, a resident proposed that the local political parties forego campaigning for the shrievalty. Instead, all candidates would receive deputyships and pursue Chacon. The deputy-candidate who captured the free-booter would automatically receive the office of sheriff. This novel proposal did not receive serious attention.[23]

Among these knights of the road, the Arizona marshals singled out Albert (Burt or Bert) Alvord for especial attention. The son of a poor Tombstone justice of the peace, Alvord, in the 1880s, served as a deputy sheriff under Sheriff John Slaughter in Cochise County and later as a constable in Willcox. However, in September 1899, Alvord and another policeman, William (Billy) Stiles, organized a band of outlaws and robbed trains at Cochise and Fairbanks. In the latter robbery, Wells, Fargo messenger Jefferson D. Milton (a former deputy marshal), mortally wounded one of the bandits. Before he died the highwayman implicated Alvord and Stiles.[24]

Alvord demonstrated remarkable deviousness. He helped the territorial authorities capture Augustino Chacon, whereupon the local judge dropped all charges against Alvord. Even Cochise County lawmen became very friendly with the outlaws, and one journalist noted that "the train robbers seemed to have nothing but friends" in Cochise County.[25]

The county officers failed to reckon with the sensitivity of federal authorities to the Alvord case. In July 1903, a United States grand jury indicted Alvord for mail robbery, and District Attorney Frederick Nave prepared his case. Alvord complained bitterly that the territorial officers had misled him with promises of immunity, since he had assisted them against Chacon. Billy Stiles claimed a similar status. In a probing article, "The Alvord-Stiles Case," the *Arizona Republican* asked the question, to what extent is a United States prosecuting attorney bound by the promises of lawmen to criminals? More especially, to what degree is the United States district attorney, who knew nothing about this secret agreement between territorial authorities and Burt Alvord, tied to this contract? The residents of Cochise County, who mistakenly considered Alvord a misguided person, solicited funds for his bail. Former Sheriff John Slaughter, once Alvord's superior, contributed to his bond. The citizens of Cochise County demonstrated a remarkable prejudice against law and order, more especially against federal law and order.[26]

This troublesome case soon involved Marshal Myron McCord. In December 1902, immediately after the county dropped charges against Alvord, McCord had arrested him on federal warrants for mail robbery, and, in July 1903, he went to great expense to transport five former members of the Alvord band from Yuma Prison to testify before the grand jury in Tombstone. The jail in this aging mining camp was a ramshackle affair, which persuaded the marshal to employ several extra guards. When District Attorney Nave concluded that these witnesses from Yuma Prison should be lodged in separate rooms (evidently to separate them and prevent collusion in their testimony), Marshal McCord had to employ five additional guards.[27]

With the examination and indictment of outlaw Alvord completed in July 1903, the federal lawman prepared for the trial in December. At the insistence of the trial judge and District Attorney Nave, McCord obtained authority to employ six guards for the court, because the five Yuma inmates were again to be witnesses. McCord also expressed a fear to the attorney general that there was "grave danger of [an] attempted jail delivery." The marshal's words were prophetic. A few days after the jury sentenced him to a short prison term, Burt Alvord and Billy Stiles led a mass jailbreak from the flimsy Tombstone jail. They were soon recaptured, however, and Marshal McCord had the pleasure of transporting Alvord to the territorial prison. [28]

In his criminal escapades, Burt Alvord embarrassed not only the United States government, but the Mexican government as well. In the fall of 1905, Sonoran officers asked for custody of the bandit upon expiration of his prison term. Marshal Ben Daniels, who entered office in June 1905, was familiar with the Alvord case. As superintendent of Yuma Prison when the outlaw entered the penitentiary, Daniels computed the termination of Alvord's term as October 26, 1905. Daniels was in no rush to present the Mexican warrant to the new superintendent, Jerry Millay. However, in early October, the marshal was shocked to read a newspaper announcement that Millay had released Burt Alvord on October 9, sixteen days before the lawman anticipated the departure of Alvord. J. F. Tener, whom Alvord had robbed of a $7,000 payroll in Sonora, complained bitterly to the attorney general. Tener reported that Alvord's attorney, Thomas E. Flannigan of Tombstone, publicly boasted "that Alvord would never be turned over to Mexico" and "that he [Flannigan] had arranged the matter [of the premature release] with the authorities" at Yuma Prison. [29]

Indications of conspiracy between Cochise County officials and the territorial prison were sufficiently clear to demand an investigation. The marshal had been duped, or at least disregarded, in the release of Burt Alvord. In the spring of 1906, Attorney General William Moody dispatched an examiner, J. D. Harris, to Arizona. Harris concluded that Attorney Flannigan knew in advance that Alvord was to be released before the date established by Benjamin Daniels. In a sworn statement, Jeff Milton, the noted Wells, Fargo messenger, stated that Flannigan bragged in Tombstone that he "fixed" the early release of the outlaw. However, when Alvord sought sanctuary in Mexico, he refused to pay the attorney's fee. Milton declared that Flannigan then turned on the crafty bandit and characterized Alvord as "a damn son of a bitch" for not "treating him [Flannigan] right." As for the roles of Superintendent Jerry Millay and Marshal Ben Daniels, the investigator accused the former of "gross negligence" and exonerated the latter. Although Examiner Harris did not discuss the possibility of political chicanery, it would have been a good opportunity for the conservative Republican enemies of Marshal Ben Daniels, a strong supporter of reformer Theodore Roosevelt, to embarrass the federal lawman. [30]

The efforts of the federal lawmen to capture the Cochise County outlaw implied a struggled between local and federal authorities. The former were determined to prevent the encroachment of the alien federal power. In July 1903, when Marshal Myron McCord attended the federal grand jury investigation of Burt Alvord in Tombstone, Chief Deputy Justus P. Welles wrote him:

> You folks seem to be kicking up a little mess of your own [in Cochise County]. Poor Alvord! and [Billy] Stiles! Good Lord of the Woods! What are you [federal] people trying to do with those poor, persecuted devils?[31]

Burt Alvord and Billy Stiles continued to elude the lawmen of the Southwest and Mexico. Newspapers reported that they were leading a band of Yaqui Indian outlaws in Mexico in 1907. Stiles soon tired of outlawry and asked Marshal Ben Daniels to accept his surrender. Stiles declared that "he was tired of being a fugitive" and his life was in danger in Mexico. He could visit his wife in Arizona only in secrecy and he had lost all his worldly belongings when he jumped from a train to avoid arrest. Stiles added one stipulation to his surrender—the marshal must confine the bond of the outlaw to $3,000. The cautious marshal, who was aware of the extraordinary world of treachery in which Alvord and Stiles played, wisely refused. A Bisbee journalist appreciated the decision of Daniels and declared bluntly that "there was a secret compact between him [Stiles] and the Cochise County Officers." Nevertheless, Billy Stiles returned secretly to the United States, became a deputy sheriff in Nevada, and was killed in December 1908. Burt Alvord reportedly married a wealthy coffee heiress in

Jamaica, where he had nothing to do "but sit around" Kingston and smoke "fine havanas."[32]

These wide-ranging outlaws convinced the Arizona Legislature to create a special police force, the Arizona Rangers, in 1901. Never over twenty-six men, the rangers assisted local as well as federal authorities. Their headquarters were located at various southern border towns—Douglas or Naco—where lawlessness was most rampant. Burton Mossman, former superintendent of the Aztec Land and Cattle Company (The Hash Knife Outfit), was appointed the first captain.[33]

Marshal Myron McCord supported the Rangers enthusiastically. In 1902, he asked for authority to deputize Captain Mossman and two subordinate Rangers. "This I ask," he defended his decision, "for their protection as well as in the interest of the government." He would not pay the Rangers, but the deputyships would "simply clothe them with authority to make arrests" for the United States. Attorney General Philander Knox complied with McCord's request, and Marshal Creighton M. Foraker of New Mexico also deputized the three Arizonans.[34]

In addition to enlisting the Arizona Rangers, the Arizona marshals sometimes took the extreme measure of employing men of questionable reputations. The lawmen concluded that brutal men were required to pursue equally vicious outlaws. In February 1899, Marshal William Griffith deputized John Selman, Jr., the son of John Selman, Sr., Lincoln County outlaw. In 1895, the elder Selman won a reputation for prowess with a pistol when he killed the most infamous mankiller of Texas, John Wesley Hardin. John Selman, Sr., was shot to death, in turn, by George Scarborough, a noted deputy marshal of New Mexico. In an unlikely turn of events —one that resembled a Hollywood western movie—Scarborough appeared in Geronimo in January 1899, shortly before young Selman was made a deputy marshal. The junior Selman confronted Scarborough and "had some angry and ugly words" about the death of the elder Selman. Had not Sheriff Ben Clark stepped between the two mankillers, said one journalist, "some trouble" would have resulted. No sooner had young Selman become a deputy marshal than he threatened to kill an Indian policeman. Marshal Griffith promptly revoked Selman's commission.[35]

Mickey Free, a man of mixed Apache and Mexican heritage, often tracked badmen for the Arizona lawmen. In 1898, Free organized a company of ten Apache warriors for manhunting duties. Marshal William Kidder Meade may have acquired the services of an equally calloused scout, Tom Horn. After the Apache campaigns of the 1880s, Horn became a cowboy and rodeo performer. In November 1896, when the Black Jack Christian band raided southern Arizona, Meade contacted Horn, then a ranch foreman at Aravaipa. In a revealing letter to the federal lawman, Horn refused to accompany his posse. "Any posse you could get," said the manhunter derisively, "could not accomplish any thing [*sic*]." Horn added: "I can stand a better show to get them [the Black Jack band] by going alone." However, he wanted to know "*if there is any thing* [*sic*] *in it for me* [his italics]." But he concluded by saying "No Cure No Pay" was his "mottoe" [*sic*]. If he did not capture or kill the bandits, Tom Horn charged no fee. Horn soon began a career as a paid assassin. In 1903, he was hanged in Cheyenne, Wyoming, for murder.[36]

In the early 1900s, the Arizona border became the sanctuary not only for bandits but for Mexican revolutionaries. These dissidents, members of the Mexican Liberal Party, headquartered variously at St. Louis, Missouri, Toronto, Canada, and in Los Angeles, California. By 1906, the fiery anarchist, Ricardo Flores Magon and his junta had organized many clubs in the Southwest, with "captains" at their head.[37]

The Liberty Club of Douglas, Arizona, soon attracted the attention of Marshal Ben Daniels. In September 1906, Daniels became convinced that "Captain" Tomas Espinosa and his revolutionaries were violating the neutrality of the United States. Deputy Marshal (and Arizona Ranger) Arthur A. Hopkins arrested ten members of the Liberty Club and held warrants for an additional thirty-five. The United States district attorney charged them with "setting on foot" an expedition against Mexico. While the situation was tense in Douglas, Marshal Daniels assured Attorney General William Moody that his deputies and the rangers could control the agitators.[38]

The following December, Tomas Espinosa and his colleagues were tried by a federal court in Tombstone. According to testimony, the Liberty Club planned to steal explosives from mercantile houses in Arizona and to rob the Mexican Customs House at Agua Prieta. From there the Liberty Club would lead a march on Cananea, Sonora, the site of a serious labor strike the preceding May. Evidently, Ricardo Magon, who would lead this crusade, hoped to revive the strike against the mining baron of Cananea, William Greene. Greene had imported Arizona Rangers (some of whom held concurrent deputy marshalships) to suppress the May strike. The Mexican government denied that any relationship existed between the strike and the agitation of the Mexican Liberal Party.[39]

In any event, on December 27, 1906, the federal court at Tombstone sentenced Tomas Espinosa to two years in Yuma Prison. Other dissidents were deported without trial and subsequently were shot by Sonoran officials. Arizona journalists expressed regrets about these summary executions, but refused to countenance conspiratorial *juntas*. The Arizona *Republican* expressed some admiration for Porfirio Díaz's government, since it made Mexico almost as "secure" as most Anglo-Saxon governments.[40]

The presence of Mexican revolutionaries in southern Arizona prompted the United States marshals to cooperate with the Sonoran officers on many occasions. As early as 1904, Marshal Myron McCord joined his counterparts in Sonora against gunrunners. Ben Daniels continued this friendly attitude, although he feared that his political enemies, both Democrats and Republicans, might trump up charges that he sent helpless Mexican prisoners back to their deaths under the evil Diaz. "I am desirous," said Daniels to Attorney General William Moody in July 1906, "of not having anything [occur] which might result in censure of my administration." The lawman was wise, since the Mexican officials permitted few legal restrictions to bind them in the pursuit of labor agitators and revolutionaries. In April 1907, Colonel Emilio Kosterlitsky of the *rurales*, and close friend of Daniels, revealed the desperation of the Díaz regime. When Kosterlitsky failed to keep an appointment with the marshal, the *rural* informed Daniels that "some damn fools of Americans intended to strike [against the William C. Greene Company in Cananea]. He continued, "You know Ben, in our country we can't allow . . . even the Angels or Girls to strike."[41]

That the Arizona marshals were guilty of complicity in these transgressions by the Sonoran officers was obvious to the junta. John Kenneth Turner, an outspoken American socialist and supporter of the Mexican Liberal Party, declared in 1910 that "for the past five years the law of our border states . . . has been very much the law of [Porfirio] Díaz." Turner accused the marshals of permitting resident Mexican consuls actually to direct "posses of United States Marshals" in the suppression of the revolutionaries.[42]

These angry words struck close to the truth. On the night of June 10, 1907, several Arizona lawmen kidnapped revolutionary Manuel Sarabia from the Douglas jail and released him to Mexican *rurales*. As the kidnapper's automobile sped toward the border, Sarabia shouted to bystanders: "Long live liberty, don't let them take me to Mexico; I am a political offender!" This cry saved his life, since several newspapers publicized this flagrant violation of American law. At the very moment of the kidnapping, a dynamic labor agitator, "Mother" Ann Jones, was at work in the vicinity. She quickly telegraphed Governor Joseph Kibbey and the president and organized a protest demonstration in Douglas. This grand lady declared that "the kidnapping of Manuel Sarabia by Mexican police with the connivance of American authorities was an incident in the struggle for liberty." And when she personally confronted Governor Kibbey, he informed her that he had already dispatched Ranger Captain Harry Wheeler to retrieve the abducted Mexican revolutionary.[43]

When the full particulars of the kidnapping became public, Marshal Ben Daniels found himself in an embarrassing position. Sarabia had been the responsiblity of the marshal. On July 6, 1907, Attorney General Charles Bonaparte ordered an investigation of the incident. Sarabia charged that he had been arrested by an unnamed Arizona Ranger who held no warrant for his arrest. The Mexican consul in Douglas, one of those foreign officials so despised by John Kenneth Turner, and several Douglas policemen, were indicted for kidnapping. The court went through the motions of a trial and quietly released the kidnappers.[44]

Other members of the Mexican Liberal Party, including Ricardo Flores Magon, were still at work, although from the safety of Los Angeles, California. In September 1906, when the Douglas grand jury indicted Tomas Espinosa and his comrades, the same panel ordered the arrest of Magon, Antonio Villareal, and Librado Rivera in Los Angeles. While the marshal of southern California arrested them, the trio of dissidents fought extradition to Arizona and appealed their case to the United States Supreme Court. The radical Western Federation of Miners raised funds for their defense. However, in December 1908, Magon and his friends reluctantly abandoned this appeal to the Supreme Court and agreed to stand trial in Arizona. On the night of March 3, 1909, the United States marshal for the Southern District of California turned over the three Mexicans to Marshal Ben Daniels at the Arizona boundary.[45]

On May 12, 1909, the trial of the three revolutionaries began in Tombstone. Family and friends attended. When some of them threatened the life of District Attorney John L. B. Alexander, Marshal Daniels employed extra guards. Magon threatened that "if certain things were not done," reported the lawman, "the officers of the court might expect violence." Members of the Western Federation of Miners created a tumult by clapping their hands and shouting down Attorney Alexander. When the jury sentenced Magon and his friends to two years in prison, the family of Villareal again threatened the life of Alexander. Since the convictions carried light sentences, the jury recommended the mercy of the court.[46]

Though the revolutionaries considered District Attorney Alexander an avowed enemy, he expressed compassion for many of the political refugees and quietly interfered on their behalf with Mexican authorities. In September 1906, Alexander placed stipulations upon the deportation of several dissidents to Sonora. In a letter to General Luis Torres, military commander of Sonora, Alexander remarked that the Mexican secretary of state had assured him that the deportees would be protected by the laws of Mexico. "It was upon these assurances," said the federal attorney, "that I insisted upon their deportation." "I hope," he continued, "that the offenses committed by them will not be so serious as will demand the taking of their lives." Sometime later, in June 1912, Alexander suspected treachery when Mexican authorities charged another political refugee, Santiago Escobosa, with theft of $25 and asked Marshal Charles A. Overlock to deport the prisoner. Alexander informed the marshal that the Mexican "charge bears the earmarks of political activity rather than a genuine effort to take back a criminal to Mexico."[47]

After the trial of the revolutionaries in 1909, the marshalcy continued to investigate the agitators and their American friends, who were now publishing periodicals in support of the Liberal Party junta. In February 1910, the newly created Bureau of Investigation asked Marshal Charles Overlock to locate Effie Duffy Turner who was associated with *The Border*, a leftist journal. Special Agent Marshal Eberstein informed the lawman that the periodical headquartered in Phoenix and that the editors were reportedly Charles E. Babcock and John Murray. He speculated that Effie Turner was related to John Kenneth Turner who wrote insidious articles entitled "Barbarous Mexico" for the *American Magazine*.[48]

The task of investigating Effie Turner and *The Border* fell to Deputy Marshal Bernard Anderson. After some searching, he found that the journal had been published in Phoenix for a short time, then moved to Los Angeles, California. He found one uncommunicative man who knew the intellectual. When the press was located in Phoenix, the editors were Maurice Zalzman and Angelia Newton. Although the deputy did not speculate, these names may have been aliases. When the first issue of *The Border* appeared from its presses in Tucson (not Phoenix), in November 1908, an Albuquerque journalist praised it for its "bright clever stories."[49]

While the marshals engaged in these lively events along the boundary, many of their formerly troublesome tasks became routine. The service of process of the Indian reservations occurred casually. In October 1905, Deputy Walter Gregory asked Superintendent of the Sacaton Agency J. B. Alexander to notify several Indians "to be in Sacaton on a certain day" for the lawman to subpoena them as witnesses. Gregory later informed Marshal Ben Daniels that the agent "assured" him "that these witnesses will be notified by the Indian police and will be on hand." Some Indians even held the deputy marshalship. In 1909, a Yuma Indian policeman, Charlie Escalanta, held this post. However, Mexican outlaws stabbed him to death in May.[50]

Disturbances did occur among the Indians, but the marshals maintained peace without the assistance of the military. Deputy Marshal Charles Utting provoked a near uprising in 1903, when he and two guides killed an alleged Papago Indian smuggler. When the deputy failed to emerge on schedule from the reservation, Marshal Myron McCord assumed that the Papagoes had killed him. McCord promptly prepared a posse of twenty-five men, only to observe Utting arrive safely before the deputies could invade the reservation. A similar false alarm occurred in June 1907, when Sub-Agent W. H. Gill killed Chief Austin Navajo, an Apache chief, at Fort McDowell. Some four hundred angry Apaches reportedly intruded upon the military grounds (the location of the sub-agent's home). While troops were alerted, Secretary of Interior James R. Garfield asked the attorney general to authorize Marshal Ben Daniels to organize a posse and expel the demonstrators from the fort. Daniels was scheduled to eject the interlopers on July 6, but the Indians evidently departed voluntarily. The Apaches were no longer a military problem.[51]

Tension persisted between the Hispanos and the marshals. When Deputy Marshal J. A. Porterie killed a Phoenix Hispano in the performance of his duty, comrades of the dead man charged the deputy with manslaughter. When a jury exonerated Porterie, he resumed his duties. When another deputy searched for a fugitive among Hispano construction workers on a railroad near Kelvin, Marshal Myron McCord reported to his superior that the laborers were "very suspicious and evasive . . . to questions." McCord finally employed a person who spoke fluent Spanish and who was "intimately acquainted with the character of the people." Anglo Arizonans conceded an occasional law enforcement position to Hispanos: in 1907, Don Nabor Pacheco was sheriff of Pima County. But the marshalcy remained predominantly Anglo.[52]

The enforcement of the Edmunds Act, once a serious problem, lessened after the turn of the century, although some hard feelings persisted among the Mormons. In July 1905, a Prescott grand jury secretly indicted Bishop David K. Udall and eight leaders of the Mormon stake in Apache and Navajo counties. Not only was the secrecy unusual, but the Department of Justice filed the charges in a Washington, D.C., court, rather than in Prescott. To his dismay, Marshal Ben Daniels did not learn about these indictments until Idaho Senator Fred T. Dubois, who reportedly visited Arizona to provoke a dispute with the Mormons, confronted the lawman. The Mormons did not oppose the warrants served by Deputy Walter Gregory, but they publicly charged the gentile government of the territory with political persecution. The Mormons opposed statehood, which many Arizonans considered the first priority. At the trial in December, Udall and seven comrades pleaded guilty to polygamy and paid fines of $100. The ninth defendant was acquitted. The marshals continued to arrest an occasional Mormon for violation of the Edmunds Act, but with decreasing frequency.[53]

The marshal also continued to arrest, detain, and transport unfortunate Chinese aliens to San Francisco, California, for deportation. In 1904, Marshal Myron McCord complained that while "the [regular] business of my own department occupies nearly all the time," the federal government had increased his deportation duties. The lawmen leased entire railroad cars and contracted with the Southern Pacific Railroad to provide extra guards. The trip of one thousand miles was tiring and sometimes hazardous. Chinese prisoners escaped on several occasions and, in May 1906, Marshal Ben Daniels's train wrecked. Fortunately, he and the orientals were not injured. These officers escorted nine hundred Chinese and three hundred persons of other Asian nationalities to San Francisco between January 1903 and August 1907. The pace of deportation quickened until the disruptions of the Mexican Revolution reduced the immigration of the orientals after 1911. The Bureau of Immigration relieved the marshals of this difficult task two years later.[54]

The politics of statehood—Arizonans subordinated all considerations to that goal—interfered with the marshalcy more than any other force in the first decade of the 1900s. When Ben Daniels entered the marshalcy in June 1905, the citizens of the territory regarded him as more important as the local voice of President Theodore Roosevelt than as the federal lawman of Arizona. While they were anxious for statehood, they were disconcerted about the president's support for a controversial plan—jointure—in which Arizona and New Mexico would be admitted as one state. Neither territory approved this plan, but Marshal Daniels supported jointure strongly as a favor to the chief executive. When Daniels joined Secretary of Interior James R. Garfield for a "consultation" and trip to the Grand Canyon in August 1907, the press waited anxiously for the federal lawman to reveal the nature of the conference. "Every time a jointist meets a jointist today," said the *Albuquerque Morning Journal*, the first question popped is, " 'What did Garfield tell Ben?' " The tight-lipped lawman refused to say "much."[55]

A change of administration could come none too soon for the people of Arizona, who despised jointure. Hope for this change appeared in the November election in 1908, when conservative Republican William Howard Taft won the presidency. While he professed to follow the pathway of his friend and predecessor, Theodore Roosevelt, Taft soon departed the road of reform that the Rough Rider paved. In Arizona the future of the conservative (anti-Roosevelt) Republicans brightened even more when voters sent Ralph Cameron to Washington as territorial delegate. This victory over the long-time incumbent Democrat Marcus Aurelius Smith reassured the Republicans that they would now have an opportunity to unseat Roosevelt Republicans. This desire motivated them as much as the wish to defeat the Democratic Party and enter the Union.[56]

Conservative Republicans regarded Marshal Ben Daniels, a jointist follower of Roosevelt, as very dangerous. For some time, the "organization," as the conservatives called themselves, had been preparing to unseat the federal lawman. These insurgents included Hoval Smith, Chairman of the Republican Central Committee in the territory; Delegate Cameron; and the new governor, Richard Sloan, a veteran of the territorial bench. They regarded Charles A. Overlock, a strong advocate of separate statehood, to be the most appropriate choice to succeed Ben Daniels. In May 1909, Smith informed Delegate Cameron that he was busily collecting endorsements for Overlock and that he had promised Overlock to work for his appointment as marshal. "It is the one promise," he said, "which I . . . must fulfill in every way possible." Smith declared bluntly that, if Overlock did not receive the appointment, he (Smith) would resign. Overlock "has always been a strong and loyal Republican," added Smith, and furthermore, "is a man of wealth."[57]

As the organization marshaled its forces against the jointist marshal, Charles A. Overlock entered the campaign personally. In a letter of May 12, 1909, to Delegate Cameron, Overlock emphasized the value of the marshalcy to the organization in any eventual statehood elections. He had visited Governor Richard Sloan, whom President Taft appointed to help prepare Arizona for admission to the Union, and obtained an endorsement:

The governor says he is very anxious to have this change [in the U.S. marshal's office] made as soon as possible. . . . We soon expect to enter upon a statehood election, [and] it will . . . take the full strength of our [Republican] party, both financial and influential [to win]. . . . The governor feels that

a Republican U.S. Marshall [*sic*] and his several deputies
would have a great influence over allowing to remain in office
a Democratic marshall [*sic*] with Democratic deputies.

The organization maintained that Ben Daniels was, in spirit, a
Democrat, not a Republican, and that his loyalty to Roosevelt was
personal, not political.[58]

By this time, Delegate Cameron was actively soliciting the help
of influential persons in Washington. Evidently, Postmaster Frank
H. Hitchcock added his prestige to the nomination of Overlock,
and President Taft approved on August 7, 1909. Hoval Smith
expressed his thanks to Hitchcock a few days later and added the
regards "of the Republican organization of Arizona for your
invaluable effort . . . in the U.S. Marshall [*sic*] matter." The
removal of the jointist Ben Daniels, said Smith, removed "the
element of political uncertainty" from the territory and "likewise
the way is paved for continued political control of Arizona" by the
Republicans. The issues of statehood, the marshalcy, and Republican domination, were inseparable in the minds of the
conservative members of the Grand Old Party in Arizona.[59]

The entry of Arizona into the family of states in 1912 altered the
position of the United States marshal's office, although the duties
remained substantially the same. With admission to statehood, the
territorial court, which embodied both local and federal
jurisdictions, became extinct. More precisely, the territorial court,
which possessed jurisdiction over federal cases, was abolished. The
marshalcy of the territory went the same route. The federal
lawman was not the marshal of, but the marshal in, the Territory of
Arizona. Strictly speaking, he did not possess a district, since
Arizona Territory did not have a United States District Court. The
territorial court tried federal cases, and the marshal served the
United States side of that tribunal. But these constitutional
quibbles disappeared with the entry of Arizona into the Union. On
March 2, 1912, the circuit judge at San Francisco, California,
signed an order for the creation of a Federal District Court for
Arizona. This court was separate and independent from the newly
created state courts. With this new United States court came a new
marshal. On March 4, 1912, Charles A. Overlock, former marshal
in the Territory of Arizona, became marshal of the new tribunal.[60]

While this promotion placed the Arizona marshalcy on a par with its sister office in Albuquerque, this elevation did not erase the striking difference between the two. Whereas the New Mexico officer served a district concentrated in the Rio Grande Valley and bound by a unified transportation network, the federal lawman in Arizona still presided over a district of scattered villages. The incumbent in Phoenix still employed field deputies under the antiquated fee system, while his colleague in New Mexico dispensed with them. The number of discordant elements along the international boundary perplexed the Arizona lawmen, while the New Mexico officers seldom fretted about this lonely area. Along with badmen, idealistic Mexican revolutionaries, and Chinese smugglers, county lawmen often obstructed the marshals as they attempted to enforce the laws along the border with Sonora. This trouble resembled the strife between Deputy Marshal Wyatt Earp and Sheriff John H. Behan in 1882, although the factions of 1900 fortunately did not come to blows.

While the Arizona marshals maintained their routine duties among the diverse races and religious factions within the territory, the post of federal lawman remained highly contested among political parties. As the statehood movement gained momentum after the turn of the century, each party desired exclusive control of the marshalcy. This goal was a natural one, but the consequences of the rivalry for the marshalcy were most unfortunate. The marshals often deliberately restricted their official activities, in order to avoid unnecessary exposure in the press. The enforcement of the federal laws in any territory was never a simple matter, but the shortsighted political parties compounded the frustrations of the Arizona marshals.

12

Conclusion

When the popular television series *Gunsmoke* ended a twenty-five-year run in 1975, a sigh of regret, no doubt, occurred among the American and European audiences. More than any other agency or person, Matt Dillon, the fictitious hero of *Gunsmoke*, molded in the popular mind a peculiar image of the frontier United States marshal. Bill O'Hallaren, a writer for *TV Guide*, perceived this fact in his post mortem about this popular show. "It is only right," he observed, "for the heavy thinkers to begin pondering what all those [*Gunsmoke*] shows have meant to our perceptions of . . . U. S. marshals," not to mention morality, violence, and other commonly held notions about the lawless West.[1]

Among the personalities on *Gunsmoke*, the protagonist and hero, U. S. Marshal Matt Dillon (actor James Arness), possessed all the attributes regarded as typical of the "western marshal." He was tall, athletic (but not comfortable in the saddle), quiet spoken, slow to anger, sound of judgment, and a determined and relentless manhunter. He used persuasion first but, if that failed, he used his six-gun remorselessly. In order to emphasize this latter trait, the *Gunsmoke* series opened with a violent scene in which Dillon dueled in the street with a badman. (Critics humorously noted that the outlaw—a quickdraw artist—always outdrew Arness.)

From these many distorted notions about the frontier marshal, it is difficult to draw a profile of the typical United States marshal of Arizona and New Mexico territories. Perhaps this is best. If the many federal lawmen of that era could suddenly materialize, they would present a diverse gathering. Yet, some uniformity might persist among them. They were middle-class property owners, many of them ardent practitioners of the capitalist creed. They were married men with family responsibilities. They were men of public affairs—although with varying degrees of devotion to duty—and members of either major political party. They adherred to the standard religious faiths of the nineteenth century. As occupants of federal office, they generally espoused the cause of federalism over provincialism, although with varying degrees of fervency. And while they were conservatives in social philosophy—some might even say stuffy or reactionary—these lawmen performed their duties with some sense of conviction in an atmosphere not very conducive to duty. Just as the pioneer farmers, cattlemen, and miners struggled against a hostile physical environment, the pioneer lawmen dealt with a stubborn, often unsympathetic, and rebellious human environment.

As the cycle of *Gunsmoke* episodes moved relentlessly from year to year, it became evident that some types of persons were conspicuously absent from Dodge City, Kansas, the seat of Matt Dillon's marshalcy. The county sheriff, city marshal, and precinct constable, among others, failed to appear in the show. After asking, with tongue in cheek, "Where was the Dodge City sheriff?," writer Bill O'Hallaren went on to comment that among television viewers, "hardly anyone seems to have noticed" the omission of these frontier lawmen from the scripts. The audience regarded "U. S. Marshal Matt Dillon" as the lone, and only necessary, defender of all laws in that violent cowtown. In fact, the federal lawmen performed the narrowest range of duties in frontier communities, those associated with violations of federal laws.[2]

Even the close associates of Matt Dillon—the deputies— lacked official personalities. Whereas frontier deputy marshals were the deputed subordinates of the chief lawman, Dillon's underlings appeared in *Gunsmoke* for comic relief or to titillate the female viewers. The gimpy Chester, the smelly Festus, and the muscular blacksmith, Quint Asper, did little to capture the authentic personalities of federal law enforcers of a century ago.

The American public has often confused the deputy marshals with that singular frontier character, the fastdrawing gunfighter. While such callous gunmen did thrive in the heated atmosphere of frontier communities, the marshals of Arizona and New Mexico seldom employed mankillers. The deputies were, as a rule, parttime, fee-earning officers of the federal courts. They were usually established citizens, possibly related to their superiors by family

ties and almost certainly by political ties. The deputies held substantially less property than their superiors but, as younger men,
they were "on the make." When the marshals required the assistance of gunfighters, the lawmen hired them as temporary, special
deputies. When the chief lawmen made the error of commissioning
mankillers as permanent deputies, these fractious men inevitably
blemished the reputation of federal justice.

When the United States marshalcy appeared in New Mexico in
1846 (more permanently in 1851) and in Arizona in 1864, Congress
regarded the first task of the federal lawmen to be the routine
service of process of the federal courts. These mundane jobs remained the foundation of the territorial marshalcies. The semian-
nual routine of serving the spring and fall sessions became a ritual-
like duty that the public anticipated with the seasons. In this
instance the frontier lawmen differed little from their colleagues in
the settled eastern states. Only occasionally were these ministerial
duties complicated by additional court duties, such as special land
cases.

When Congress mandated these duties in 1789, the lawmakers
possessed certain ideals about the nature of law enforcement
—equal enforcement of the laws of the land (nation) by lawmen
with limited authority. This ideal arose in the era of the American
Revolution when the Founding Fathers desired a body of laws to
unite, rather than to divide, as the state laws did, the American
people. The marshals, therefore, possessed the power to enforce
these novel laws that underpinned the unity of the nation.

Congress did not think it necessary for the marshals to pursue
criminals or to confront large bodies of rebellious citizens, since the
American people were peaceable and law-abiding. In fact, the
national legislators believed that every citizen was a potential law
enforcement officer and, through the medium of informants and
grand juries, the citizens would ferret out all evildoers. The
marshals would merely serve the warrants of arrest. This ideal
about the marshalcy—limited law enforcement—fitted into the
democratic ideology of the early nineteenth century, in which the
goal of the nation was to permit as much individual liberty (with
obligations) as possible.

Such idealism about the nature of the American citizens was to
some extent true, but better fitted the settled states in the East.
Many unique circumstances beset the territories. The marshals of

Arizona and New Mexico territories encountered many extremes. A sprawling desert district, which confined and isolated human inhabitants to remote river valleys, confronted and intimidated the federal lawmen. Racial hostilities among Anglos, Hispanos, and Indians endured. Political factions vied for the loyalty of these interest groups. Provincial territorials resisted the encroachments of federalism, something the marshals grappled with throughout the territorial period. Economic antagonisms were rife, as labor and capital collided, and as great ranchers bullied the small homesteader. All these vested interests united against newer arrivals— Chinese aliens or Mormons. Some persons—outlaws—withdrew from all protection of southwestern society. In the East, these freebooters would have found it difficult to avoid civilized communities completely, but the wastelands of the territories sheltered them easily.

A complacent Congress, armed with the ideal of limited law enforcement, failed miserably to comprehend the unique problems of the federal officers in Arizona and New Mexico. The national lawmakers provided weak and inefficient courts. The marshals, whom Congress regarded as mere ministerial officers, grappled with criminal activities that only a strong detective with resources for pursuit could have overcome. The Department of Justice encumbered these lawmen with "utterly impractible" bureaucratic restrictions and then left them "to keep the peace as best they could." One scholar has rightly concluded that the territorial judiciary was one of the "weakest" parts of that jerry-rigged government.[3]

When the marshals encountered violent resistance in the southwestern territories, they sought any available form of assistance. From 1854 to 1878, they deputized units of the regular army. When the Posse Comitatus Act of that year removed this privilege, the lawmen continued to use the military in limited ways. Sometimes the governors provided militiamen and, at other times, the marshals reluctantly summoned the unreliable *posse comitatus*. In 1908, the federal officers obtained the support of a new agency, the Bureau of Investigation. Private detectives also rendered worthwhile support. Congress regarded crime in the territories to be the exception to the rule; but the marshals encountered six decades of turbulence.

While some innovations occurred within the marshalcies, these changes were generally bureaucratic in nature and did little to assist the lawmen against lawlessness. These changes occurred during three periods of national stress, and reflected a fear on the part of authorities in Washington that the marshalcies were failing: in 1861, when, on the eve of the Civil War, the attorney general assumed supervisory powers over the marshals and district attorneys; in 1870, during Reconstruction, when the Department of Justice incorporated the marshalcies and other judicial agencies; and in 1896, during a period of intense labor unrest, when the marshals were placed on salary and more closely tied to Washington. These reforms rationalized the administration of the marshalcies, emancipated them from the county sheriffs (who often held concurrent deputyships), and made them more responsive to Washington. This centralization also revealed that the Department of Justice participated in a nationwide movement that historian Robert Wiebe has called *The Search for Order*. As Americans industrialized and urbanized, they uprooted the traditional agrarian society of America and sought to establish new rules of order. Bureaucratic methods, in which rapid communications permitted a constant flow of directives from headquarters to subordinate agencies in remote locations, fulfilled the need for order. Whereas, in the 1850s, southwestern marshals reacted alone to problems, the new sophisticated bureaucratic methods permitted the Department of Justice in Washington, D. C., to keep apprised of trouble spots on the frontier. The marshals thus headed off (or kept a close watch on) potential problems.[4]

While the Arizona and New Mexico marshalcies shared many of these developments, each district possessed some distinctive features. In New Mexico, where a large Hispano population greeted the first Anglo settlers, the marshals soon aligned with the natives. First as deputies, then as occupants of the chief position, the Hispanos helped to guide federal law enforcement. The location of the population in the Rio Grande Valley also helped the marshalcy to administer the federal courts more efficiently. In Arizona the Hispano population was smaller, more widely scattered, and lacked a closely knit aristocratic class. For this reason, the natives of Arizona failed to break into the ranks of the marshalcy during the territorial period. As large numbers of settlers swarmed into Arizona after the Civil War, they located in remote villages. The New Mexico lawmen centralized their administration in Albuquerque; the Arizona officers directed their office with the greatest difficulty. The presence of heavily used roads to the southern border of Arizona from Mexico aggravated the problems of the marshals. The lawmen of New Mexico suffered much less distress along the border of Chihuahua.

In addition to chief federal law enforcer, the marshals played many important roles in their districts. As appointees of the presidents, the lawmen represented the ruling party. As clients of senators or representatives, the marshals provided these economic imperialists with easy access to natural resources. By neglecting to enforce certain laws—for example, the land laws—the federal lawmen permitted political friends to ravage the public domain. An inoffensive census could have political repercussions for the marshals' political parties. The lawman might balloon the enumeration to make the territory appear ripe for statehood and thus elevate the prestige of his party.

As the Department of Justice ensnared the marshalcies in a tighter bureaucratic apparatus, the personalities of the marshals lost some of their force. But that was not always the case. Among the early marshals, the personality of a Milton B. Duffield or a William Kidder Meade reflected seriously in the performance of the office. As a servant of reform-minded Grover Cleveland, Meade sought to reform not only his post, but the territory. In the 1880s, both parties—Republican and Democrat—desired to "uplift" the territories and to prepare them for statehood. The marshals became energetic reformers (often against their will) as they enforced congressional reform laws.

While few marshals of Arizona and New Mexico became famous, they did help to spur the growth of popular literature about the frontier. The Southwest provided the lawless setting for the creation of heroes. The efforts of the marshals to capture notable outlaws, such as Billy the Kid and Black Jack Ketchum, produced many exciting journalistic episodes for public consumption. While the deputy marshals, and not the chief lawmen, performed most of the deeds of daring that went into this literature, a few marshals, such as William Kidder Meade and Robert Paul, approximated the image of the frontier marshal so revered by the American public. Perhaps that confrontation between Marshal Milton B. Duffield and badman Kennedy on the streets of Tucson in 1865 possessed some meaning after all.

With all their many roles, it is difficult to assess the effectiveness of the marshals in the enforcement of the federal laws. Many vested interests impinged upon them. If one reads the most massive scholarly work about lawlessness and law enforcement of the frontier, Hubert Howe Bancroft's *Popular Tribunals,* the reader can only conclude that vigilante justice ruled the West. One historian, Frank Richard Prassel, declares flatly that the Western lawmen, including the marshals, "did not bring peace and order to the American West." However, these commentators fail to take into consideration the ideal behind federal justice—limited law enforcement. The citizen was supposed to be the chief lawman.[5]

Whatever the case, for more than six decades the marshals of Arizona and New Mexico territories guided the destiny of federal law enforcement through numerous crises. They had experienced section conflict and survived to free Indian slaves and Hispano peons. They endured Indian wars and lived to see the warriors participate in the federal judicial process. The marshals helped to suppress brutal vendettas and observed the feudists return peacefully to their homes. They pursued murderous highwaymen and delivered them to prison. They encountered violent racial and religious conflicts and watched as these very lawbreakers soon expressed support for federal law. These federal policemen suppressed radical labor and political agitators and upheld the rights of property. They ran the gauntlet of political partisanship, sometimes succumbing to selfish party influences, but at other times transcending political dogmas. All these activities, when viewed collectively, reveal considerable achievement on the part of the federal lawmen. In spite of a rather doctrinaire attitude on the part of their superiors in Washington, the marshals demonstrated some ability to adapt to the peculiar problems of the frontier. When a law could not be enforced fully, the lawmen pressed it only as far as public opinion would permit. By the first decade of this century, as the territorial era closed, a measure of law and order prevailed in Arizona and New Mexico. While on a visit to his hometown in Ohio, in the early 1900s, Marshal Creighton M. Foraker declared to an audience of well-wishers: "We are having a quiet time in New Mexico now. . . . The West is the finest country on earth and I am well satisfied with it."[6]

Notes

Chapter 1

1. Duffield to William H. Seward, Secretary of State, December 1, 1865, quoted in Benjamin Sacks, *Arizona's Angry Man: United States Marshal Milton B. Duffield* (Tempe: Arizona Historical Foundation, 1970), pp. 31-32.

2. *Encyclopaedia Britannica*, 11th ed., s. v. "marshal."

3. Ibid.; see also s. v. "lord steward" and "marshalsea."

4. Herbert L. Osgood, *The American Colonies in the Seventeenth Century*, 3 vols. (Gloucester, Mass.: Peter Smith, 1957), 1:16, 45, 69 n4, 104; Edwin Powers, *Crime and Punishment in Early Massachusetts, 1620–1692: A Documentary History* (Boston: Beacon Press, 1966), pp. 431–32, 622 n53; Homer Cummings and Carl McFarland, *Federal Justice: Chapters in the History of Justice and the Federal Executive* (New York: Da Capo Press, 1970), p. 17; *Encyclopaedia Britannica*, 11th ed., s. v. "marshal."

5. Carl Ubbelohde, *The Vice-Admiralty Courts and the American Revolution* (Chapel Hill: University of North Carolina, Institute of Early American History and Culture, 1960), pp. 10–12.

6. Louis M. Hacker, *Alexander Hamilton: In the American Tradition* (New York: McGraw-Hill, 1957), pp. 87–88.

7. Charles M. Andrews, *England's Commercial and Colonial Policy*, The Colonial Period of American History, vol. 4 (New Haven: Yale University Press, 1964), p. 228.

8. Leonard D. White, *The Federalists: A Study in Administrative History, 1789–1801* (New York: Free Press, 1965), pp. 387–94; U.S., Congress, House, *Annals of Congress*, 1st Cong., 1st sess., 1789, 1:782–834.

9. U.S., *Statutes at Large*, 1(1789):73; Charles Warren, "New Light on the History of the Federal Judiciary Act of 1789," *Harvard Law Review* 37(1923):49–132.

10. See Rita W. Cooley, "The Office of United States Marshal," *Western Political Quarterly* 12(1959):123–40, for a brief discussion of the marshals; White, *Federalists*, pp. 411–12; Albert G. Langeluttig, *Department of Justice of the United States* (Baltimore: The Johns Hopkins University Press, 1927), pp. 82–89.

11. White, *Federalists*, pp. 411–21; U.S., *Statutes at Large*, 1(1789):570, 2(1807):445, 4(1830):417.

12. Carl Russell Fish, *The Civil Service and the Patronage*, Harvard Historical Studies, vol. 11 (Cambridge: Harvard University Press, 1904), pp. 82–83.

13. White, *Federalists*, pp. 414–15.

14. John C. Fitzpatrick, ed., *The Writings of George Washington*, 39 vols. (Washington, D.C.: GPO, 1931–44), 30:424.

15. White, *Federalists*, pp. 298–300.

16. Ibid.

17. *Report of the Attorney General [Edmund Randolph] Read in the House of Representatives, December 31, 1790* (Philadelphia: Francis Childs and John Swaine, 1791), p. 31 n21; Hamilton to George Washington, January 14, 1795, in, Harold C. Syrett, ed., *The*

Papers of Alexander Hamilton, 21 vols. (New York: Columbia University Press, 1961-), 18:42–43; Washington to Benjamin Lincoln, August 14, 1791, in, Fitzpatrick, ed., *Writings of Washington*, 31:335–36.

18. U.S., Congress, House, *Annals of Congress*, 2d Cong., 3d sess., 1793, 3:877.

19. U.S., *Statutes at Large*, 1(1799):624; White, *Federalists*, p. 413.

20. U.S., *Statutes at Large*, 1(1789):73; *Report of the Attorney General for 1791*, p. 16; Langeluttig, *Department of Justice*, pp. 86–87.

21. The position of office deputy was not made official until 1896. Langeluttig, *Department of Justice*, p. 86 n37.

22. See John A. Mallory, comp., *United States Compiled Statutes, Annotated*, 12 vols. (St. Paul, Minn.: West Publishing Co., 1916), 2:2164–65, sec. 1304, for legal opinions about the deputy marshals; *Report of the Attorney General for 1790*, p. 30 n14.

23. Alan Harding, *A Social History of English Law* (Baltimore: Penguin Books, 1966), pp. 27–28.

24. U.S., *Statutes at Large*, 1(1792):264; Mallory, comp., *Compiled Statutes*, 2:2176, sec. 1312 n1.

25. White, *Federalists*, p. 413; U.S., *Statutes at Large*, 12(1863):768.

26. White, *Federalists*, pp. 409, 413, 454–55; Jefferson to William B. Giles, March 23, 1801, in, Paul Leicester Ford, ed., *The Writings of Thomas Jefferson*, 10 vols. (New York: G. P. Putnam's Sons, 1892–99), 8:25–26.

27. See, Index to Names of U.S. Marshals, 1789-1960, Department of Justice, Record Group 60, National Archives, Washington, D.C., Micro. T-577.

28. White, *Federalists*, pp. 199–209.

29. Ibid.

30. Ibid., pp. 454–55.

31. Ibid., pp. 199–209; Carl Russell Fish, *Removal of Officials by the Presidents of the United States*, Annual Report of the American Historical Association for the Year 1899, 2 vols. (Washington, D.C.: GPO, 1900), 1:67-86.

32. Cummings and McFarland, *Federal Justice*, pp. 142–60.

33. U.S., *Constitution*, Art. 2, sec. 3; Edward S. Corwin, *The President, Office and Powers: History and Analyses of Practice and Opinion*, rev. ed. (New York: New York University Press, 1948), p. 76.

34. White, *Federalists*, p. 338; idem, *The Jeffersonians: A Study in Administrative History, 1801–1829* (New York: Free Press, 1965), pp. 163–65, 179, 179 n57.

35. White, *Jeffersonians*, pp. 204–5, 406–11; idem, *The Jacksonians: A Study in Administrative History, 1829–1861* (New York: Free Press, 1965), pp. 384–88.

36. William L. Stone to Rensselaer, January 23, 1841, in, Catharina V. R. Bonney, comp., *A Legacy of Historical Gleanings*, 2d ed., 2 vols. (Albany: J. Munsell, 1875), 2:149; Daniel Webster to Fletcher Webster, April 12, 1849, in, J. W. McIntyre, ed., *The Writings and Speeches of Daniel Webster*, 18 vols. (Boston: Little, Brown & Co., 1903), 16:520.

37. U.S., *Statutes at Large*, 5(1842):475, 483; White, *Jacksonians*, pp. 389–90.

38. U.S., *Statutes at Large*, 10(1853):161–69; White, *Jacksonians*, pp. 391–93, discusses federal compensation practices.

39. U.S., *Statutes at Large* 1(1789):96; White, *Federalists*, pp. 402–4.

40. Cummings and McFarland, *Federal Justice*, pp. 366–83; White, *Federalists*, pp. 415–17.

41. Cummings and McFarland, *Federal Justice*, pp. 267–68, 544.

42. Ibid., pp. 368–69, 543–44.

43. Ibid., p. 8; William Blackstone, *Commentaries on the Laws of England: In Four Books, with an Analysis of the Work*. Notes by Christian, Chitty, Lee, Hovenden, and Ryland. 2 vols. (New York: J. B. Lippincott, 1857), 1:259, sec. 344, 2:85, sec. 122; Cummings and McFarland, *Federal Justice*, p. 544; Harding, *English Law*, pp. 60, 270.

44. Mallory, *Compiled Statutes*, 2:2176, sec. 1311 *n*11.

45. U.S., *Statutes at Large*, 1(1792):264, 2(1807):506; White, *Federalists*, pp. 417–23; Cummings and McFarland, *Federal Justice*, pp. 545–49; Corwin, *The President*, pp. 166–67.

46. Corwin, *The President*, pp. 168–69, 169–70; by an Act of July 29, 1861, Congress removed the requirement for the proclamation.

47. James G. Randall, *Constitutional Problems under Lincoln*, rev. ed. (Urbana: University of Illinois Press, 1964), p. 160, 160 *n*41.

48. Ibid.

49. Ibid.

50. U.S., *Statutes at Large*, 1(1789):73; Max Farrand, *The Legislation of Congress for the Government of the Organized Territories of the United States, 1789-1895* (Newark, N.J.: William A. Baker, 1896), pp. 8–12.

51. Arthur St. Clair to George Washington, August [n.d.] 1789, in, Clarence E. Carter, ed., *Territorial Papers of the United States: Northwest Territorial Papers, 1787-1803*, 28 vols. (Washington, D.C.: GPO, 1934-75), 2:204–12; Max Farrand, "The Judiciary Act of 1801," *American Historical Review* 5(1899–1900):682–86; idem, *Legislation for the Territories*, pp. 25, 58.

52. U.S., *Statutes at Large*, 2(1807):445–46; Petition of Robert Robinson [1810?], in, Carter, ed. *Territorial Papers of the United States: Illinois Territorial Papers, 1809-1814*, 28 vols. (Washington, D.C.: GPO, 1934-75), 16:93–94; Lawrence M. Friedman, *A History of American Law* (New York: Simon and Schuster, 1974), p. 142.

53. U.S., *Statutes at Large*, 2(1897):445; Roy M. Robbins, *Our Landed Heritage: The Public Domain 1776–1936*, (Lincoln: University of Nebraska Press, 1962), pp. 25–26; for a discussion of Michigan's problems, see Carter, ed., *Territorial Papers of the United States: Michigan Territorial Papers, 1805-1820*, 28 vols. (Washington, D.C.: GPO, 1934-75), 10:787–90; William Baskerville Hamilton, *Anglo-American Law on the Frontier: Thomas Rodney & His Territorial Cases* (Durham: Duke University Press, 1953), pp. 79-82, 94-95.

54. U.S., Congress, House, *Annals of Congress*, 12th Cong., 2d sess., 1812–13, 1:200, 929; Poindexter recommended a bill to constrain territorial judges to remain in their districts during their terms, *Annals of Congress*, 1:1015, 1017, 1074; U.S., *Statutes at Large*, 2(1813):806.

55. Farrand, *Legislation for the Territories*, pp. 20–25; William Claiborne, Governor, to Thomas Jefferson, October 22, 1804, in, Carter, ed., *Territorial Papers of the United States: Orleans Territorial Papers, 1804-1812*, 28 vols. (Washington, D.C.: GPO, 1934-75), 9:311; Index to Names of U.S. Marshals, Micro. T-577.

56. U.S., *Statutes at Large*, 9(1834):128–29; Glenn Shirley, *Law West of Fort Smith: Frontier Justice in the Indian Territory, 1834–1896* (New York: Collier, 1961), pp. 21–23.

57. St. Clair to George Turner, Territorial Judge, June 19, 1791, in, Carter, ed., *Northwest Territorial Papers*, 3:343–47.

58. Farrand, *Legislation for the Territories*, p. 24.

59. Frank Richard Prassel, *The Western Peace Officer: A Legacy of Law and Order* (Norman: University of Oklahoma Press, 1972), p. 221.

Chapter 2

1. Thomas James, *Three Years Among the Indians and Mexicans* (Philadelphia: J. B. Lippincott, 1962), p. 82; Josiah Gregg, *The Commerce of the Prairies* (Lincoln: University of Nebraska Press, 1967), p. 101; Harvey Fergusson, *Rio Grande* (New York: Alfred A. Knopf, Inc., 1931), p. 285.

2. Fergusson, *Rio Grande*, p. 252.

3. J. Ross Browne, *Adventures in the Apache Country: A Tour Through Arizona and Sonora, 1864* (Tucson: University of Arizona Press, 1974), p. 131.

4. Homer Wilkes, "Territorial Head Count," *Frontier Times* 44 (1970):64-65; see also, Hubert Howe Bancroft, *History of Arizona and New Mexico, 1530-1888,* vol. 17 of *The Works of Hubert Howe Bancroft,* 39 vols. (New York: Arno Press. n. d.), pp. 529, 543.

5. Bancroft, *Arizona and New Mexico,* p. 342, 342 n56; see comments of a Baptist missionary in the *New York Times,* September 21, 1852, and of an attorney, one "S. A. H.," in the November 19, 1853, issue; see, Fergusson, *Rio Grande,* pp. 76-105, for a sparkling account of "The Right People."

6. Bancroft, *Arizona and New Mexico,* pp. 462 n28, 658, 671–73; Fergusson, *Rio Grande,* p. 55.

7. See *Santa Fe Weekly Gazette,* March 5, 1864, for these remarks by Judge Joseph G. Knapp (hereafter cited as *WG*).

8. Howard R. Lamar, *The Far Southwest, 1846–1912: A Territorial History* (New York: W. W. Norton, 1970), pp. 36–49.

9. Arie W. Poldervaart, *Black-Robed Justice: A History of the Administration of Justice in New Mexico from the American Occupation in 1846 until Statehood in 1912* (Santa Fe: New Mexico Historical Society, 1948), Chap. 2, pp. 13–20.

10. Lamar, *Far Southwest,* p. 64; L. Bradford Prince, *Historical Sketches of New Mexico, from the Earliest Records to the American Occupation,* 2d ed. (New York: Leggat Brothers, 1883), p. 308; see also, the *Santa Fe Republican,* June 8, 9, 1848, for advertisements by Dallam's commercial house.

11. Poldervaart, *Black-Robed Justice,* pp. 1, 22.

12. Lamar, *Far Southwest,* pp. 65–69; Bancroft, *Arizona and New Mexico,* pp. 432-36; Prince, *Historical Sketches,* p. 329.

13. Howard Lewis Conard, *Uncle Dick Wootton: The Pioneer Frontiersman of the Rocky Mountain Region,* ed. Milo M. Quaife (Chicago: R. R. Donnelley & Sons, 1957), pp. 153–70.

14. Francis T. Cheetham, "The First Term of the American Court in Taos, New Mexico," *New Mexico Historical Review* 1(1926):23–41; Poldervaart, *Black-Robed Justice,* pp. 22–24; Bancroft, *Arizona and New Mexico,* p. 436.

15. Bancroft, *Arizona and New Mexico,* pp. 441–42; Ralph E. Twitchell, *The History of the Military Occupation of the Territory of New Mexico, from 1846 to 1851 by the Government of the United States* (Chicago: Rio Grande Press, 1963), p. 152; U.S., Congress, Senate, *Report of the Secretary of War in Relation to Civil Officers Employed in the Territory of New Mexico while under Military Government, May 3, 1852,* 32d. Cong., 1st sess., vol. 9 (Serial 620), Exec. Doc. 71, pt. 1, 8 pp., pt. 2, 1 p.; for a copy of the military order, No. 10, dated February 12, 1848, see *Santa Fe Republican,* February 12, 1848.

16. Twitchell, *Military Occupation,* pp. 154–55; Lamar, *Far Southwest,* pp. 71–82.

17. Index to Names of U.S. Marshals, Micro. T-577; for John G. Jones, see Annie H. Abel, ed., *The Official Correspondence of James S. Calhoun* (Washington: GPO, 1915), pp. 20–25, 48–58, 248–49, 313–16; see also, "Register of Proceedings," Executive Record of the Governor of New Mexico, 1851–1867, State Records Center and Archives of New Mexico, Santa Fe, pp. 4, 17.

18. Ralph E. Twitchell, *Leading Facts of New Mexican History,* 5 vols. (Cedar Rapids, Iowa: Torch Press, 1917), 5:318; *Daily Missouri Democrat* (St. Louis), April 30, 1853.

19. Lansing B. Bloom, ed., "Historical Society Minutes, 1859–1863," *New Mexico Historical Review* 18(1943):394–428; *WG,* July 10, 1858; George Rutledge Gibson, *Journal of a Soldier under Kearny and Doniphan, 1846–1847,* ed. Ralph P. Bieber, vol. 3 of The Southwest Historical Series (Glendale, Calif.: Arthur H. Clark, 1953), p. 41 n81.

20. Twitchell, *Leading Facts*, 2:411 n337; *WG*, February 14, 1857, July 24, 1858; Index to Names of U.S. Marshals, Micro. T-577.

21. Earl S. Pomeroy, *Territories and the United States, 1861–1890: Studies in Colonial Administration* (Philadelphia: Univerity of Pennsylvania Press, 1947), Chap. 5, pp. 51–61; see, John S. Goff, "Isham Reavis, Pioneer Lawyer and Judge," *Nebraska History* 54(1973):1-46, and "John Titus: Chief Justice of Arizona, 1870-1874," *Arizona and the West* 14(1972):25–44, for some common features of the territorial judiciaries.

22. Pomeroy, *Territories*, p. 61; Bancroft, *Arizona and New Mexico*, p. 637, n10; Lamar, *Far Southwest*, pp. 84–85.

23. U.S., *Statutes at Large*, 1(1789):73; Pomeroy, *Territories and the United States*, p. 58; for data about the territorial judiciary in the 1850s, see, Twitchell, *Leading Facts*, 2:393–98.

24. William Watts Hart Davis, *El Gringo: Or New Mexico and Her People* (Santa Fe: Rydal Press, 1938), pp. 204–5; *New York Times*, November 8, 1862, lists Smith as a court interpreter in Albuquerque; *WG*, May 29, 1858.

25. Frank Hall, *History of the State of Colorado*, 4 vols. (Chicago: Blakely Printing Co., 1889–95), 4:92–94.

26. Davis, *El Gringo*, pp. 154–200; *WG*, April 5, 1856, March 14, 1857, September 4, October 9, 1858.

27. U.S., *Statutes at Large*, 11(1856):49–51, 11(1858):366; Davis, *El Gringo*, p. 300; *WG*, July 10, 1858.

28. Abraham Rencher to James L. Collins, Superintendent of Indian Affairs, March 16, 1860, Governor's Papers, New Mexico State Records Center and Archives, Santa Fe.

29. Caleb Sherman, Court Clerk, Santa Fe, to Grafton Baker, Territorial Justice, August 30, 1858, enclosed in, Baker to Millard Fillmore, December 24, 1851, in Abel, ed., *James S. Calhoun*, pp. 406–11; Davis, *El Gringo*, p. 174.

30. Davis, *El Gringo*, pp. 160–61; see, Report to the Governor by Sheriff and Others and Conditional Pardon by Governor, March 31, 1852, Governor's Papers, New Mexico State Records Center and Archives, Santa Fe.

31. Rencher to Territorial Legislature, December 7, 1859, State Department, Territorial Papers, New Mexico, National Archives, Microcopy T-17 (hereafter cited as State Dept. Ter. Papers, Micro. T-17); see, *Santa Fe New Mexican* (weekly), February 20, 1864 (hereafter cited as *NM*), for recollections about this prison.

32. Ralph E. Twitchell, ed., *Historical Sketch of Governor William Carr Lane: Together with [a] Diary of His Journey from St. Louis, Mo., to Santa Fe, N. M., July 31st, to September 9, 1852* (Santa Fe: The Historical Society, 1917), pp. 5–21; Leland R. White, "Relations of the United States and Mexico, 1847–1853," (Master's thesis, University of Missouri, 1950), pp. 224-26.

33. U.S., *Statutes at Large*, 10(1854):335; *WG*, October 11, December 13, 1856.

34. *WG*, December 13, 1856, July 4, 1857; see, *Rio Grande Republican* (Las Cruces), September 1, 1893, for the recollection of Samuel Bean; J. Morgan Broaddus, Jr., *The Legal Heritage of El Paso* (El Paso: Texas Western Press, 1963), pp. 58–59.

35. In James H. Tevis, *Arizona in the '50s* (Albuquerque: University of New Mexico Press, 1954), see p. 39 for a description of rare visit by Bean to Arizona in 1858; W. Claude Jones to David Meriwether, July 11, 1856, Governor's Papers, New Mexico State Records Center and Archives, Santa Fe; Recollections of Charles D. Poston, in, Frederick A. Tritle Scrapbooks, Arizona Historical Society, Tucson.

36. Joe A. Stout, "Henry A. Crabb—Filibuster or Colonizer? The Story of an Ill-Starred Gringo Estrada," *American West* 8(1971):4–9; *New York Times*, April 15, 1857; James B. O'Neil, *They Die But Once: The Story of a Tejano* (New York: Knight Publications, 1935), p. 30, declares that Bill Ake and other filibusters surrendered at Mesilla and were cleared, presumably by the federal court.

37. Adlai Feather, "The Territories of Arizona," *New Mexico Historical Review* 39(1964):16–31; *New York Times*, December 1, 1856.

38. Rencher to Lewis Cass, Secretary of Interior, April 10, 1858, State Dept. Ter. Papers, Micro. T-17; see also Rencher to William H. Seward, Secretary of State, February 27, March 16, 1863, in State Dept. Ter. Papers, Micro. T-17; *New York Times*, January 19, 1859.

39. Robert G. Athearn, *William Tecumseh Sherman and the Settlement of the West* (Norman; University of Oklahoma Press, 1956), p. 346; Hubert Howe Bancroft, *Popular Tribunals*, vols. 31–32 of *The Works of Hubert Howe Bancroft*, 39 vols. (San Francisco: The History Company, 1887), 31:719–20; Prassel, *Western Peace Officer*, pp. 194–95.

40. *WG*, March 6, May 1, June 26, July 10, 25, 1858.

41. Aurora Hunt, *Major General James Henry Carleton, 1814–1873: Western Frontier Dragoon* (Glendale, Calif.: Arthur H. Clark Co., 1958), pp. 117–18; James S. Calhoun to John G. Jones, Marshal, May 1, 1852, in Abel, ed., *James S. Calhoun*, pp. 544–46.

42. Sumner to Charles M. Conrad, Secretary of War, May 27, 1852, reprinted in *New York Times*, January 11, 1853; the previous year Sumner established a military police force to support civil authorities (Sumner to John G. Jones, Marshal, April 22, 1852, in Abel, ed., *James S. Calhoun*, pp. 525–26).

43. Twitchell, *Leading Facts*, 3:13–16; see *WG*, August 1, 1857, for official notices in Spanish, and see also *WG*, April 18, 1857.

44. *WG*, October 31, 1857, October 9, 1858.

45. *WG*, February 14, 1857.

46. *Missouri Democrat* (St. Louis), April 30, 1853; *WG*, February 27, 1858; Lamar, *Far Southwest*, pp. 100-108.

47. Thomas H. Hopkins to Jacob Thompson, Secretary of the Interior, June 27, 1858, and A. M. Jackson to Thompson, March 21, 1859, Attorney General's Papers, Letters Received, New Mexico, Record Group 60, National Archives, Washington, D.C. (hereafter cited as AG Papers, Letters Received, RG 60, NA).

48. *New York Times*, July 10, 1861.

Chapter 3

1. Feather, "Territories of Arizona," pp. 16–31.

2. Aurora Hunt, *Kirby Benedict* (Glendale, Calif.: Arthur H. Clark, 1961), p. 155.

3. Levi Keithly to Bates, June 9, 1861, AG Papers, Letters Received, RG 60, NA; *New York Times*, July 10, 1861.

4. Hunt, *Kirby Benedict*, p. 155; Archibald to Bates, January 20, 1862, Clever to Bates, December 7, 1861, AG Papers, Letters Received, RG 60, NA; Morris F. Taylor, *Trinidad, Colorado Territory* (Trinidad: Trinidad State Junior College, 1966), pp. 12–25.

5. Roy P. Basler, ed., *Collected Works of Abraham Lincoln*, 9 vols. (New Brunswick, N.J.: Rutgers University Press, 1953–55), 8:488; Abraham Cutler to Bates, August 16, 1862, AG Papers, Letters Received, RG 60, NA; Benedict to Bates, August 17, 1862, quoted in Hunt, *Kirby Benedict*, pp. 162–63; *Leavenworth Daily Times* (Kansas), May 14, 1862.

6. Sacks, *Arizona's Angry Man*, pp. 1–16.

7. U.S., *Statutes at Large*, 12(1861):319, 589, two acts; Randall, *Constitutional Problems*, pp. 275–77; Cummings and McFarland, *Federal Justice*, pp. 197–200.

8. Randall, *Constitutional Problems*, p. 281; Circular to District Attorneys and Marshals, January 8, 1863, Attorney General's Letter Book B5, pp. 340–43, Record Group 60, National Archives, Washington, D.C.

9. Lawrence R. Murphy, "William F. M. Arny, Secretary of New Mexico Territory, 1862-1867," *Arizona and the West* 8(1966):323–38.

10. Constance Wynn Altshuler, "The Case of Sylvester Mowry: the Mowry Mine,"

Arizona and the West 15(1973):149–74; idem, "The Case of Sylvester Mowry: The Charge of Treason,"*Arizona and the West* 15(1973):63-82.

11. Murphy, "William F. M. Arny," pp. 323–38; the literature concerning the confiscations in New Mexico Territory is voluminous; see, Edward D. Tittman, "The Exploitation of Treason," *New Mexico Historical Review* 4(1929):128–45; Clarence Wharton, "Spruce McCoy Baird," *New Mexico Historical Review* 27(1952):300–314; Hunt, *James Henry Carleton*, pp. 265–72; *NM*, June 9, 1865; C. L. Sonnichsen, *The Story of Roy Bean, Law West of the Pecos* (Greenwich, Conn.: Fawcett Publishing Co., 1972), pp. 44–45, says that Mrs. Samuel Bean refused to be ejected from her home, and the Unionists admitted defeat.

12. *NM*, December 15, 1865; Poldervaart, *Black-Robed Justice*, pp. 31–32.

13. Broaddus, *El Paso*, pp. 80–81. *NM*, December 8, 22, 29, 1865, January 5, 12, 1866; Frank Harder, Lieutenant, to Edward Bates, Attorney General, December 16, 1865, AG Papers, Letters Received, RG 60, NA.

14. Watts to Carleton, October 8, 1864, reprinted in, *NM*, December 15, 1865; Hunt, *James Henry Carleton*, p. 271; W. W. Mills, *Forty Years at El Paso, 1858–1898: Recollections of War, Politics, Adventure, Events, Narratives, Sketches, Etc.* (Chicago: W. B. Conkey Co., 1901), pp. 126–30.

15. Poldervaart, *Black-Robed Justice*, pp. 31–32; Tittman, "Exploitation," pp. 128–45.

16. Poldervaart, *Black-Robed Justice*, pp. 32–33.

17. Tittman, "Exploitation," pp. 128–45; William Waldrip, "New Mexico during the Civil War," *New Mexico Historical Review* 28(1953):251–90; Broaddus, *El Paso*, pp. 80–81.

18. Sylvester Mowry, *Arizona and Sonora* (New York: Harper & Bros., 1864), p. 207; *NM*, March 12, 1864.

19. Tittman, "Exploitation," pp. 128–45.

20. Ibid.; see, *NM*, April 20, 1867, for attachment notice against Cutler.

21. Hunt, *James Henry Carleton*, p. 271; Lamar, *Far Southwest*, p. 430; Cornelius C. Smith, Jr., *William Sanders Oury: History Maker of the Southwest* (Tucson: University of Arizona Press, 1968), pp. 150–51; Ebenezer R. Hoar, Attorney General, to the District Attorneys of Arizona and New Mexico, March 2, 1869, Attorney General's Instruction Book A2, pp. 184-85, Record Group 60, National Archives, Washington, D.C. (hereafter cited as Instruction Book ...., NA, pp. .....).

22. For Banta's recollections, see, *Albuquerque Morning Journal*, June 16, 1908 (hereafter cited as *Albuquerque Journal*); Randall, *Constitutional Problems*, pp. 147–49, notes that "the line of demarcation between the military and civil authority was often blurred," and that the provost-marshals often encroached upon the duties of the marshals.

23. *NM*, March 17, November 10, 1865; Knapp to Carleton, October 31, 1864, reprinted in, *NM*, January 13, 1865.

24. Carleton to W. F. M. Arny, Acting Governor, January 27, 1863, *War of the Rebellion Records*, Series 1, vol. 15, pp. 665–66; Cutler to Carleton, October 3, 1862, B[enjamin] Sacks Collection, Arizona Historical Foundation, Hayden Library, Arizona State University, Tempe, Arizona (hereafter cited as Sacks Collection); *New York Times*, August 24, 1861.

25. Broaddus, *El Paso*, p. 72.

26. Proclamation of Acting Governor William F. M. Arny, March 28, 1863, Sacks Collection; see also, James M. Taylor, Probate Judge, Dona Ana County, to Arny, December 1, 1863, Governor's Papers, New Mexico State Records Center and Archives, Santa Fe, for remarks about Arny's request for "harmonious" relations with the army.

27. Altshuler, "Sylvester Mowry," pp. 63–82.

28. Jay J. Wagoner, *Arizona Territory, 1863–1912: A Political History* (Tucson: University of Arizona Press, 1970), pp. 26–33.

29. Ibid., p. 36.

30. Carleton to Edward B. Willis, November 25, 1863, Sacks Collection; Sacks, *Arizona's Angry Man*, pp. 16–21.

31. Sacks, *Arizona's Angry Man*, pp. 17–25, 34 n 4; U.S., Congress, House, *Report of the Committee on Claims in the Case of Milton B. Duffield*, April 4, 1878, 45th Cong., 2d sess., 1878 (Serial 1823), Vol. 2, rpt. 459; *Arizona Miner* (Prescott), March 9, April 6, August 24, 1864 (hereafter cited as *AM.*).

32. *AM*, June 22, September 7, 1864; *Rio Abajo Weekly Press* (Albuquerque), June 7, 1864, in, State Dept. Ter. Papers, Micro. T-17; Sacks, *Arizona's Angry Man*, pp. 31–32; Howard R. Lamar, "Carpetbaggers Full of Dreams, A Functional View of the Arizona Pioneer Politician," *Arizona and the West* 7(1965):187–206; Wagoner, *Arizona Territory*, p. 36.

33. Duffield to William H. Seward, Secretary of State, December 1, 1865, quoted in, Sacks, *Arizona's Angry Man*, pp. 31–32.

34. Ibid., pp. 33–34.

35. *AM*, May 25, October 5, 1864, February 22, 1868.

36. *AM*, June 15, 1867; House Committee on Claims, *Duffield Report* (Serial 1823), Rpt. 459; Message of Governor Richard C. McCormick to the Fourth Legislature of Arizona, September 9, 1867, in State Dept. Ter. Papers, Micro. M-342.

37. *New York Tribune*, August 27, 1867, reprinted in, *AM*, October 19, 1867.

38. *AM*, May 23, October 13, 1866; Poston to Lincoln, January 10, 1865, in, Basler, ed., *Works of Abraham Lincoln*, 8:214 n.

39. Lamar, *Far Southwest*, p. 132.

Chapter 4

1. Lamar, *Far Southwest*, p. 130; in 1867 Judge John P. Slough ruled that the federal government possessed no jurisdiction over the Indians of the Territory of New Mexico and alleged that Congress failed to declare the New Mexican tribes a part of the "Indian Country." The Indian Appropriation Act of February 27, 1851 (U.S., *Statutes at Large*, 9 [1851]:587), extended this jurisdiction very clearly. See, Henry Stanberry, Attorney General, to Stephen B. Elkins, District Attorney, November 23, 1867, in, Thomas B. Catron Papers, Special Collections Department, Zimmerman Library, University of New Mexico, Albuquerque (hereafter cited as Catron Papers).

2. Bancroft, *Arizona and New Mexico*, pp. 795-96.

3. Victor Westphall, *Thomas Benton Catron and His Era* (Tucson: University of Arizona Press, 1973), p. 99.

4. Lamar, *Far Southwest*, pp. 136–39.

5. Pratt to James Speed, Attorney General, April 23, August 3, 1866, Department of Justice Source-Chronological Files, New Mexico, Record Group 60, National Archives, Washington, D.C. (hereafter cited as Source-Chronological Files); Samuel J. Crawford, *Kansas in the Sixties* (Chicago: A. C. McClurg, 1911), p. 390.

6. Lamar, *Far Southwest*, p. 128.

7. For incidental information about some deputies, see, U.S., Congress, House, *Papers in the Case of J. Francisco Chavez vs. Charles P. Clever, Delegate from the Territory of New Mexico*, Santa Fe, October 1, 1867, 40th Cong., 2d sess., 1868 (Serial 1350), Misc. Doc. 154, pp. 56–46; Pratt to Elkins, July 9, 1867, Catron Papers.

8. *NM*, November 3, 10, 1866.

9. Pratt to Elkins, July 10, 1867, Stevens to Elkins, September 4, 1867, Catron Papers.

10. Edward Jordan, Solicitor of the Treasury, to Elkins, July 10, September 19, 1867, Catron Papers.

11. John S. Watts, Territorial Justice, to Amos T. Akerman, Attorney General, March 21, June 25, October 24, 1871, Source-Chronological Files.

12. Farrand, *Legislation for the Territories*, pp. 44, 77, 79.

13. U.S., *Statutes at Large*, 14(1867):546; Lawrence R. Murphy, "Reconstruction in New

Mexico," *New Mexico Historical Review* 43(1968):99–115; Twitchell, *Leading Facts*, 2:324–25.

14. Pratt to Elkins, September 26, 1868, Senate Territorial Papers, New Mexico, Record Group 46, National Archives, Microcopy M-200 (hereafter cited as Senate Ter. Papers, Micro.....).

15. U.S., *Statutes at Large*, 14(1868):264.

16. Pratt to Elkins, September 26, 1868, Elkins to George Getty, General, September 28, 1868, Senate Ter. Papers, Micro. M-200.

17. Murphy, "Reconstruction in New Mexico," pp. 99–115.

18. *NM*, September 14, October 5, 1867; William J. Parish, "The German Jew and the Commerical Revolution in Territorial New Mexico, 1850-1900," *New Mexico Historical Review* 35(1960):1-29.

19. *NM*, February 4, 1868; *Papers in the Case of J. Francisco Chavez*, 40th Cong., 2d sess., 1868 (Serial 1350), Misc Doc. 154, pp. 92–95, 107–11.

20. *Papers in the Case of J. Francisco Chaves*, 40th Cong , 2d sess., 1868 (Serial 1350), Misc. Doc. 154, pp. 129-31, 147–48, 157-61.

21. *Daily New Mexican*, July 18, September 1, 1870 (Issues after January 1, 1870, refer to the daily, hereafter cited as *Daily NM*); Carl Coke Rister, "Harmful Practices of Indian Traders of the Southwest, 1867-1876," *New Mexico Historical Review* 6(1931):231-48; Charles L. Kenner, *A History of New Mexican-Plains Indians Relations* (Norman: University of Oklahoma Press, 1969), pp. 96-97.

22. *NM*, August 10, 1867.

23. Kenner, *New Mexican-Plains Indians Relations*, p. 176.

24. *Daily NM*, July 25, 1871.

25. Kenner, *New Mexican-Plains Indians Relations*, pp. 177–78.

26. *Daily NM*, October 26, 30, November 11, 13, 1871.

27. *Daily NM*, November 2, 1871; *Weekly Arizonian* (Tucson), February 25, 1871.

28. The Second Annual Message of Acting Governor William F. M. Arny, December [?], 1866, pp. 36–39, Governor's Papers, New Mexico State Records Center and Archives, Santa Fe.

29. See memorials to Congress, January 1, 1859, January 31, 1866, January 25, 1867, Senate Ter. Papers, Micro. M-200. U.S., *Statutes at Large*, 13(1864):74–75; Pratt to George A. Williams, Attorney General, March 14, 1873, Source-Chronological Files Box 543; see also, Pratt to Williams, March 25, 1874; George Thompson, "The History of Penal Institutions in the Rocky Mountain West, 1846-1900" (Ph. D. diss., University of Colorado, 1965), pp. 51–59; Cummings and McFarland, *Federal Justice*, pp. 352–65.

30. Newhall to Williams, April 17, 1873, Source-Chronological Files Box 543; *Daily NM*, February 5, 1872, November 13, 1873.

31. U.S., *Statutes at Large*, 16(1870):162-65; Cummings and McFarland, *Federal Justice*, pp. 218–25.

32. Cummings and McFarland, *Federal Justice*, pp. 225–29.

33. *Report of the Attorney General for the Fiscal Year Ending June 30, 1873*, 43d. Cong., 1st sess., Exec. Doc. no. 6 (Serial 1606), pp. 6, 17-18.

34. Williams to Pratt, November 30, 1874, Instruction Book E, NA, p. 168; Pratt to Williams, August 20, December 10, 1874, Source-Chronological Files Box 544; *Report of the Attorney General for 1870* (Serial 1454), pp. 1-20; Circular to Marshals, August 1, 1876, Instruction Book F, NA, pp. 571–72, 574, Instruction Book G, NA, pp. 599, 607, 608.

35. See, Cummings and McFarland, *Federal Justice*, pp. 366–72, for a general discussion of detective powers.

36. U.S., *Statutes at Large*, 18(1874):72–75; *Report of the Attorney General for the Fiscal Year Ending June 30, 1874* (Serial 1638), pp. 20–21.

37. *Report of the Attorney General for the Fiscal Year Ending June 30, 1874*, pp. 20-21.

38. Twitchell, *Leading Facts*, 2:411–12; Bancroft, *Arizona and New Mexico*, p. 773, 773 n9.

39. *Daily NM*, June 30, 1870.

40. *NM*, April 27, 1866; George B. Anderson, *History of New Mexico*, 2 vols. (Los Angeles: Pacific States, 1907), 2:529–30.

41. Anderson, *History of New Mexico*, 2:529–30; Frank McNitt, *Indian Traders* (Norman: University of Oklahoma Press, 1962), p. 110, 110 n; Robert G. Athearn, *Rebel of the Rockies: A History of the Denver & Rio Grande Western Railroad* (New Haven: Yale University Press, 1962), p. 10; Jim Berry Pearson, *Maxwell Land Grant* (Norman: University of Oklahoma Press, 1961), pp. 49–50; *Daily NM*, March 21, 1870, October 12, 1871, August 22, 1876; Paul A. F. Walter, "New Mexico's Pioneer Bank and Bankers," *New Mexico Historical Review* 21(1946):209–25.

42. Pearson, *Maxwell Land Grant*, pp. 49–50; see also, William A. Keleher, *Maxwell Land Grant: A New Mexico Item* (New York: Argosy-Antiquarian, 1942) passim; Lamar, *Far Southwest*, pp. 151–54.

43. Lamar, *Far Southwest*, pp. 151–54; Chris Emmett, *Fort Union, and the Winning of the Southwest* (Norman: University of Oklahoma Press, 1965), pp. 369–70; see, Farrand, *Legislation for the Territories*, p. 45, for bankruptcy legislation; Pratt was the messenger in a bankruptcy case in 1868 (*NM*, June 2, 1868).

44. Pearson, *Maxwell Land Grant*, pp. 70–71; Philip J. Rasch, "The People of the Territory of New Mexico vs. the Santa Fe Ring," *New Mexico Historical Review* 47(1972):185–202; F[ather] Stanley (Stanley Crocchiola), *Clay Allison* (Denver: World Press, 1956), pp. 119–52.

45. Westphall, *Thomas Benton Catron*, pp. 116–17; Norman Cleaveland, with George Fitzpatrick, *The Morleys: Young Upstarts on the Southwest Frontier* (Albuquerque: Calvin Horn, 1971), pp. 93–94.

46. Cleaveland, *The Morleys*, pp. 115–16; Westphall, *Thomas Benton Catron*, pp. 117–21.

47. Westphall, *Thomas Benton Catron*, pp. 117–21.

48. See Westphall, *Thomas Benton Catron*, pp. 161–63; *NM*, June 22, 1869; William A. Pile to Ulysses S. Grant, President, June 15, 1869, Governor's Papers, New Mexico State Records Center and Archives, Santa Fe.

49. *NM*, August 31, 1869; see the letter of Chavez to Kirby Benedict, May 1, 1871, published in *Daily NM*, May 5, 1871.

50. *Daily NM*, December 9, 1870, December 6, 1871, July 3, 1873, March 30, December 23, 1875, July 7, 1876.

51. Lansing Bloom, ed., "Bourke on the Southwest," *New Mexico Historical Review* 9(1934):33–77, with some paraphrasing by the present writer.

52. Elkins to Jones, October 27, 1881, quoted in, Pomeroy, *Territories*, pp. 85–86.

53. *Daily NM*, October 24, 1876.

Chapter 5

1. *AM* (Prescott), March 28, April 11, October 13, 1866. (Citations to *AM*, prior to August 10, 1867, refer to the semimonthly issues, through 1877 to the weekly, and from January 1, 1878, to the daily.)

2. *AM*, November 6, 1869, April 23, July 9, 1870.

3. *AM*, December 25, 1869; Rowell to Amos T. Akerman, Attorney General, August 5, 1870, AG Papers, Letters Received, RG 60, NA, Box 5.

4. M. F. Pleasants, Chief Clerk, to Rowell, and Edward Phelps, September 9, 1870, two letters, Instruction Book A2, NA, pp. 591–92; see also, Pleasant to Phelps, and Rowell, September 9, 1870, two letters, in Instruction Book B1, NA, p. 113.

5. Phelps to Akerman, October 9, 1870, AG Papers, Letters Received, RG 60, NA, Box 5.

6. *AM*, June 13, November 30, 1866; Gilbert C. Smith, Assistant Quartermaster, Camp Lowell, to E[dward] Phelps, July 4, 1868, photostatic copy in, Smith, *William Sanders Oury*, p. 290.

7. *AM*, October 13, 1866, June 15, 1867, July 18, 1868; *Weekly Arizonian* (Tucson), August 21, 1869.

8. *Weekly Arizonian*, n. d., quoted in *AM*, December 3, 1870; *AM*, October 1, 1870.

9. *Weekly Arizonian*, January 28, February 25, 1871.

10. *AM*, February 24, April 6, 1871; *Weekly Arizonian*, February 25, March 18, 1871.

11. Akerman to Rowell, March 17, 1871, Instruction Book B1, NA, p. 357.

12. *AM*, May 23, February 22, 1866, March 21, September 19, 1868, June 26, August 14, 1869, July 16, September 3, 1870, September 9, 1871; Dan L. Thrapp, *Al Sieber, Chief of Scouts* (Norman. University of Oklahoma Press, 1964), pp. 66–67; Asbury Harpending, *The Great Diamond Hoax and Other Stirring Incidents in the Life of Asbury Harpending*, ed. James H. Wilkins (Norman: University of Oklahoma Press, 1958), pp. 145–91.

13. James R. Hastings, "The Tragedy of Camp Grant in 1871," *Arizona and the West* 1(1959):146–60; Smith, *William Sanders Oury*, pp. 186–203.

14. See Smith, *William Sanders Oury*, pp. 87, 186–203; *AM*, September 11, 1874.

15. Akerman to Rowell, July 13, August 22, Akerman to Dickason, September 5, 1871, three letters, Instruction Book B1, NA, pp. 592–93, 607–8; Dickason to Akerman, August 14, 1871, Source-Chronological Files, Box 138.

16. Rowell to Akerman, September 9, 1871, Source-Chronological Files, Box 138; clippings from *AM*, September 2, 1872, enclosed in, Source-Chronological Files, Box 138; *AM*, September 2, 9, 1871.

17. Bristow to Dickason, and Bristol to Rowell, September 27, 1871, two letters, Instruction Book B1, NA, pp. 646–48.

18. Dickason to Akerman, October 18, December 19, 1871, Source-Chronological Files, Box 138.

19. *AM*, November 11, 18, December 2, 30, 1871; Rowell to Akerman, December 29, 1871, Source-Chronological Files, Box 138.

20. Don Schellie, *Vast Domain of Blood: The Story of the Camp Grant Massacre* (Los Angeles: Westernlore Press, 1968), pp. 42, 53, 230–42.

21. Edward H. Spicer, *Cycles of Conquest: The Impact of Spain, Mexico, and the United States on the Indians of the Southwest, 1533–1960* (Tucson: University of Arizona Press, 1962), p. 409.

22. *Arizona Citizen*, January 20, February 3, 24, 1872.

23. *AM*, April 26, 1873; *Yuma Sentinel*, September 13, 1873, quoted in *AM*, September 27, 1873; *NM*, n. d., in *AM*, April 17, 1873.

24. McCaffry to George A. Williams, Attorney General, August 31, September 13, 1871, two letters, Source-Chronological Files, Box 138.

25. *AM*, July 27, 1878, November 19, 1879, June 7, 1880; Orlando Allen, Postmaster, to Williams, October 18, 1873, Source-Chronological Files Box 138; *Weekly Arizonian*, February 25, 1871.

26. *AM*, July 27, September 14, 1872, April 12, July 12, 1873, October 9, November 20, 1874; Laurence P. James, "George Tyng's Last Enterprise, A Prominent Texan and a Rich Mine in Utah," *Journal of the West* 8(1969):429–37.

27. *AM*, October 9, 1874.

28. Tyng to Williams, August 21, September 2, November 15, 1874, three letters, Source-Chronological Files, Box 138; Williams to Tyng, September 18, 1874, Instruction Book E, NA, p. 36.

29. *AM*, April 26, 1873, November 13, December 24, 1874; *Daily Citizen* (Tucson),

January n. d., 1890; *Weekly Arizonian*, October 29, 1870; Duffield to George A. Williams, Attorney General, March 20, 1872, Department of Justice Appointment Papers, Arizona, 1863-77, RG 20, NA, Box 33 (hereafter cited as Dept. of Justice Appointment Papers).

30. Goodwin to Williams, February 13, 1875, Source-Chronological Files Box 138; E. B. Pomeroy, District Attorney, to Wiley W. Standefer, Deputy U.S. Marshal, July 16, 1876, enclosed in Standefer to Alphonso TAFT, Attorney General, July 22, 1876, Source-Chronological Files, Box 138.

31. Pomeroy to Taft, December 13, 1876, Source-Chronological Files Box 138.

32. Diary of Phocian Way, quoted in, W. Clement Eaton, "Frontier Life in Southern Arizona," *Southwestern Historical Quarterly* 36(1933):173–92; *New York Times*, June 15, 1858.

33. *Arizona Citizen* (Tucson), November 4, 1871.

34. *AM*, December 31, 1875; January 5, 1876; *Arizona Citizen*, December 30, 1871, enclosed in Anson P-K. Safford, Governor, to Hamilton Fish, Secretary of State, December 29, 1871, State Dept. Ter. Papers, Micro. M-342; Goodwin to Edwards Pierrepont, Attorney General, December 9, 1875, Source-Chronological Files Box 138.

35. Ignacio Pesqueira, Governor of Sonora, to John N. Goodwin, January 5, 1865, enclosed in, C. Trumbull Hayden, Probate Judge, First Judicial District, to Goodwin, January 28, 1865; Shaffenburg to Richard McCormick, Governor, August 11, 1868, in Governor's Papers, Arizona State Library and Archives, Phoenix.

36. Safford to Fish, February 14, 1871, State Dept. Ter. Papers, Micro. M-342, Wagoner, *Arizona Territory*, pp. 105, 113–17.

37. Wagoner, *Arizona Territory*, pp. 105, 113–17.

38. Ibid., pp. 113, 121; *AM*, January 11, 1873.

39. Biennial Message of Governor Anson P-K. Safford, January 6, 1875, reprinted in, *AM*, January 7, 1875; Fred Harrison, *The West's Territorial Prisons, 1861-1912* (New York: Ballantine Books, 1973), pp. 110–15.

40. See the photostatic copies of the Return of Fees and Emoluments of Edward Phelps, I. Q. Dickason, George Tyng, and Francis H. Goodwin, in the Sacks Collection.

41. *AM*, February 22, March 7, May 23, 1868, January 9, September 4, 1869, July 30, November 12, 1870.

42. *AM*, September 9, 1871, August 9, 1873; William F. Hogan, "John Miller: Pioneer Lawman," *Arizoniana: (Journal of Arizona History)* 4(1963):41–45; George Tyng, Deputy U.S. Marshal, to George A. Williams, June 17, 1872 and James E. McCaffry, District Attorney, to Williams, September 30, 1873, two letters, Source-Chronological Files Boxes 138 and 141, resp.

43. *AM*, February 5, April 2, August 27, 1875, April 14, 1876.

44. See *n* 40 supra.

45. For some very enlightening comments about the territorial bench of Arizona see, John S. Goff, "William T. Howell and the Howell Code of Arizona," *American Journal of Legal History* 11(1967):221–33; idem, "Michigan Justice in Arizona: Henry T. Backus," *Michigan History* 52(1968):109–22; idem "Isham Reavis," pp. 1–46.

46. *AM*, September 25, 1874; Circular to Marshals of Arizona and New Mexico, September 1, 1874, Instruction Book E, NA, pp. 12–13; Farrand, *Legislation for the Territories*, pp. 74–75.

47. Goodwin to Edwards Pierrepont, January 20, 1876, in Sacks Collection.

48. Bancroft, *Arizona and New Mexico*, pp. 604–5 *n* 18.

49. John G. Bourke, *On the Border with Crook* (Lincoln: University of Nebraska Press, 1971), p. 72.

Chapter 6

1. William A. Keleher, *Violence in Lincoln County, 1869–1881* (Albuquerque: University of New Mexico Press, 1957), p. 185; *Daily NM*, January 18, 1879.

2. *Daily NM*, July 20, 21, 1876.

3. See, *Daily NM*, December 31, 1875, March 25, May 22, 29, and June 24, 1876, for reports on these and other murders.

4. See, *Daily NM*, November 29, 1875, January 17, 21, 1876, for stagecoach robberies.

5. *Daily NM*, February 18, 19, July 17, 1876; Keleher, *Violence in Lincoln County*, pp. 16–17.

6. Poldervaart, *Black-Robed Justice*, pp. 97–98; for Arny's remarks about the sheriffs, see, the Second Annual Message of Acting Governor William F. M. Arny, December [?], 1866, pp. 36-39, Governor's Papers, New Mexico State Records Center and Archives, Santa Fe.

7. Quoted in *Daily NM*, July 12, 24, 1876.

8. *Daily NM*, January 7, 1876; Lamar, *Far Southwest*, p. 146.

9. Lamar, *Far Southwest*, pp. 136–48.

10. *Daily NM*, November 21, 23, 27, December 11, 16, 18, 1876, January, 6, 8, 1877.

11. Brief of Petition by Oscar P. McMains, [n. d., but received in Department of Justice, March 16, 1877], Source-Chronological Files, Box 544; see also McMains to Charles Devens, Attorney General, April 2, 1877, in Source-Chronological Files, Box 544; *Colorado Chieftain* (Pueblo), n. d., quoted in *Daily NM*, April 2, 1877.

12. Breeden to Devens, March 29, April 8, 1877, two letters, Axtell to Devens, April 3, 1877, two telegrams, Source-Chronological Files, Box 544; Devens to Sherman, March 31, 1877, Instruction Book G, NA, p. 206; see the *Daily NM*, April 2, 20, 28, May 12, 14, 1877, for information about the McMains case; Poldervaart, *Black-Robed Justice*, p. 98.

13. Bancroft, *Arizona and New Mexico*, pp. 795–96, 796 n 10.

14. Keleher, *Violence in Lincoln County*, pp. 13–15; Philip J. Rasch, "The Horrell War," *New Mexico Historical Review* 31(1956):223–31.

15. *Daily NM*, September 3, 17, October 8, December 18, 1877.

16. For the finest narrative account of the Lincoln County War, see Robert N. Mullin, ed., *Maurice Garland Fulton's History of the Lincoln County War* (Tucson. University of Arizona Press, 1968).

17. Affidavit of Alexander A. McSween to Frank W. Angel, Special Agent, Dept. of Justice, June 1, 1878, in Keleher, *Violence in Lincoln County*, pp. 266–80, 88–90; this volume is especially valuable for the reprint of many valuable documents.

18. Report of John E. Sherman to Lew Wallace, Governor, October 5, 1878, reprinted in, Keleher, *Violence in Lincoln County*, pp. 184–85; see also, pp. 106–7; Bruce T. Ellis, "Lincoln County Postscript: Notes on Robert A. Widenmann, by His Daughter, Elsie Widenman," *New Mexico Historical Review* 50(1975):213–30. (Miss Widenman changed the spelling of the family name.)

19. Affidavit by Robert A. Widenmann, June 6, 1878, taken before Juan B. Patron, Deputy Probate Clerk, Lincoln County, reprinted in, Keleher, *Violence in Lincoln County*, pp. 260–66; Mullin, ed., *Fulton's Lincoln County War*, pp. 130–33; Devens to Sherman, March 26, 1878, Instruction Book G, NA, p. 792; Sherman to Devens, November 30, 1877, Source-Chronological Files, Box 545.

20. Mullin, ed., *Fulton's Lincoln County War*, pp. 130–34.

21. Ibid., pp. 150–57; Widenmann to R. Guy McClellan, February 26, 1878, appeared in *NM*, March 23, 1878, in English, and in the March 30 edition in Spanish. References to *NM* from January 1, 1878, to August 16, 1880, refer again to the *Weekly New Mexican*.

22. See Affidavit by D. P. Shields, attorney and brother-in-law of Alexander McSween, June 11, 1878, reprinted in Keleher, *Violence in Lincoln County*, pp. 93–95, for the confrontation between Widenmann and Axtell; see the proclamation of Axtell, dated March 9, 1878, in ibid., pp. 92–93.

23. *NM*, March 30, 1878.

24. *News and Press* (Cimarron), April 11 (?), 1878, reprinted in Mullin, ed., *Fulton's Lincoln County War*, pp. 150–57.

25. *NM*, April 6, 1878, reported that Marshal Sherman "did not know Widermann's [*sic*] base conduct when he reappointed" the deputy and that the marshal intended to investigate the matter.

26. *News and Press* (Cimarron), April 4, 1878, quoted in Mullin, ed., *Fulton's Lincoln County War*, pp. 150–57; *NM*, March 30, 1878.

27. *News and Press* (Cimarron), April 4, 1878, quoted in Mullins, ed., *Fulton's Lincoln County War*, pp. 150–57; see also, *News and Press* (Cimarron), April 11, 1878, and *NM*, April 6, 1878.

28. Mullin, ed., *Fulton's Lincoln County War*, p. 162.

29. Ibid., pp. 195, 201, 222–23; *NM*, April 6, 1878.

30. *NM*, May 25, 1878; Devens to Sherman, June 1, 1878, telegram, Instruction Book H, NA, p. 122; Sherman to Devens, June 1, 1878, Source-Chronological Files, Box 545.

31. *NM*, April 20, 27, June 15, 1878; *Grant County Herald* (Silver City), June 29, 1878.

32. "S" to *Grant County Herald*, May 31, 1878, reprinted in, *NM*, June 22, 1878.

33. Ibid.

34. One complainant, Dr. Montague R. Leverson, of Douglas County, Colorado (a former resident of New Mexico) wrote to Secretary of Interior Carl Schurz, April 1, 1878, and charged that all the United States officers in the territory, except for Marshal Sherman and his deputies, were at the head of a "gang of veritable thieves" (Mullins, ed., *Fulton's Lincoln County War*, pp. 169–71); Devens to Sherman, April 16, 1878, Instruction Book H, NA, p. 44; for a discussion of the "Angel Report," see Westphall, *Thomas Benton Catron*, Chap. 7, pp. 122-34.

35. Lee Scott Thiesen, ed., "Frank Warner Angel's Notes on New Mexico Territory, 1878," *Arizona and the West* 18(1976):333-70; for a sketch of Fiske's life, see, Twitchell, *Leading Facts*, 2:507 *n*423; in the absence of the marshal, Fiske "attended" his duties (*Daily NM*, February 23, 1877); the two men rented office space jointly (*Daily NM*, May 14, 1877.

36. Thiesen, ed., "Frank Warner Angel's Notes of New Mexico Territory, 1878," pp. 333-70; Keleher, *Violence in Lincoln County*, pp. 106, 106 *n*6, 260; Mullin, ed., *Fulton's Lincoln County War*, p. 237.

37. Angel to Rutherford B. Hayes, May 16, 1878, Department of Interior Appointment Papers, New Mexico, Record Group 48, National Archives, Microcopy M-750 (hereafter cited as Dept. of Int. Appointment Papers).

38. Affidavit by George W. Peppin, reprinted in Keleher, *Violence in Lincoln County*, p. 131.

39. Mullin, ed., *Fulton's Lincoln County War*, pp. 229, 232–33.

40. U.S., *Statutes at Large*, 20(1878):145-52, 21(1880):110-14; Mullin, ed., *Fulton's Lincoln County War*, p. 235; Larry D. Ball, "Our Useful Army: The Impact of the Posse Comitatus Act on Law Enforcement in the Southwest," Paper read at the Western History Association Conference, October 3, 1974, at Rapid City, South Dakota.

41. *New York Times*, July 11, 1878, two articles re the Posse Comitatus Act; *Colorado Chieftain* (Pueblo), August 15, 1878.

42. Catron to Axtell, May 30, 1878, quoted in Westphall, *Thomas Benton Catron*, pp. 89–90; Postal Agent Adams's report, n. d., is quoted in, *NM*, August 3, 1878.

43. Mullin, ed., *Fulton's Lincoln County War*, pp. 253–61.

44. Keleher, *Violence in Lincoln County*, pp. 142–44.

45. *NM*, April 16, July 27, 1878.

46. Ellis, "Lincoln County Postscript," pp. 213–30; Keleher, *Violence in Lincoln County*, p. 106 n6.

47. Philip J. Rasch, "Exit Axtell: Enter Wallace," *New Mexico Historical Review*, 32(1957):231–45; for a subsequent report, dated October 3, 1878, see Dept. of Int. Appointment Papers.

48. Charles Devens, Attorney General, to Catron, October 19, November 11, 1878, Instruction Book H, NA, pp. 337, 370, resp.; Westphall, *Thomas Benton Catron*, pp. 122–34.

49. Report of Sherman to Wallace, October 5, 1878, quoted in, Keleher, *Violence in Lincoln County*, pp. 183–85.

50. Ibid.

51. U.S., *Statutes at Large*, 20(1878):806–7; the test of the amnesty is conveniently reprinted in, Keleher, *Violence in Lincoln County*, pp. 194–95.

52. Mullin, ed., *Fulton's Lincoln County War*, pp. 304–5; Philip J. Rasch, "The Murder of Houston I. Chapman," *Los Angeles Westerners' Brand Book* 8(1959):69–82.

53. Sherman to Devens, February 25, 1879, Source-Chronological Files, Box 545.

54. Mullin, ed., *Fulton's Lincoln County War*, pp. 333, 339–40; Keleher, *Violence in Lincoln County*, pp. 213, 216, 218, 219; for Wallace's recollections about these events, see Lewis Wallace, *Lew Wallace: An Autobiography*, 2 vols. (New York: Harper & Brothers, 1906), 2:913–15; Irving McKee, *"Ben-Hur" Wallace: The Life of General Lew Wallace* (Berkeley: University of California Press, 1947), pp. 141–61.

55. *NM*, August 23, 1879; F. Stanley, *Dave Rudabaugh: Border Ruffian* (Denver: World Press, 1961), pp. 83–117; Keleher, *Violence in Lincoln County*, pp. 281–82.

56. Ed Bartholomew, *Wyatt Earp, 1879 to 1882: the Man & the Myth* (Toyahvale, Texas: Frontier Book Company, 1964), pp. 15–17 (Earp was a member of the "sporting men" in Las Vegas); *NM*, August 23, September 6, October 18, 1879.

57. James Dunagan to Lew Wallace, August 10, 1879, Samuel Ellison Papers, 1863-1889, in Catron Papers.

58. For accusations against David Mather see, *Las Vegas Gazette*, November 4, 1879, reprinted in, Nyle H. Miller and Joseph W. Snoll, eds,, *Great Gunfighters of the Kansas Cowtowns, 1867-1886* (Lincoln: University of Nebraska Press, 1963), pp. 320–21.

59. Bartholomew, *Wyatt Earp*, p. 34; *NM*, August 30, September 6, 20, 27, October 18, November 1, 1879.

60. Commissioner Ellison sometimes held hearings in Marshal Sherman's office. *NM*, April 6, 1878.

61. Charles Devens, Attorney General, to Rutherford B. Hayes, February 20, 1880, U.S., Congress, House, *Compensation of United States Marshals . . .* , 46th Cong., 2d sess., (Serial 1922), Exec. Doc. 44, 2 pp.; *Report of the Attorney General for 1879* (Serial 1913), p. 15; when Devens advised his marshals to use their own "discretion" in this financial predicament, one editor observed that "the marshals know as much about what Congress will do as he [Devens] does. . . ."; *NM*, July 19, 1879.

62. *Daily NM*, November 11, 1880, February 13, 15, 1881.

63. Devens to Sidney M. Barnes, District Attorney, June 3, 1880, Instruction Book K, NA, p. 108; Barnes to Devens, June 9, 28, 1880, Source-Chronological Files, Box 545; in 1880, the acting agent for the Navajos, Captain F. T. Bennett, complained that it was "almost impossible to get the U.S. Marshal [Sherman] to take hold of such [whiskey] cases and very difficult to convict them upon the strongest evidence." Henry E. Fritz, *The Movement for Indian Assimilation, 1860–1890* (Philadelphia: University of Pennsylvania Press, 1963), pp. 146–51.

64. Barnes to Devens, May 6, 1881, Barnes to Wayne MacVeagh, Attorney General,

June 1, 1881, Source-Chronological Files, Box 545; *Daily NM*, May 19, 1881.

65. For works about this subject see, Leon Claire Metz, *John Selman: Texas Gunfighter* (New York: Hastings House, 1966), Chap. 11, pp. 96-111; idem, *Pat Garrett: The Story of a Western Lawman* (Norman: University of Oklahoma Press, 1973), Chaps. 3 & 4, pp. 42-66.

66. See Keleher, *Violence in Lincoln County*, pp. 216-17, for Leonard's note, Wallace's observations, and for the failure of the Mounted Rifles.

67. Wallace to Schurz, April 1, 1879, quoted in, Keleher, *Violence in Lincoln County*, p. 217; Lily Klasner, *My Childhood among Outlaws*, ed. Eve Ball (Tucson: University of Arizona Press, 1972), p. 186.

68. Metz, *Pat Garrett*, pp. 52, 55, 61; Keleher, *Violence in Lincoln County*, pp. 205-6, 346 n2; Klasner, *Childhood among Outlaws*, p. 186; *News and Press* (Cimarron), March 11, 1880.

69. Wild to Brooks [?], October 2, 1880, quoted in Metz, *Pat Garrett*, p. 59.

70. Metz, *Pat Garrett*, pp. 54-57; Pat. F. Garrett, *The Authentic Life of Billy, the Kid: The Noted Desperado of the Southwest* (Norman: University of Oklahoma Press, 1954), Chap. 16, pp. 98-102; for the pointed remark about Wild's courage, see *Daily NM*, January 9, 1881.

71. Keleher, *Violence in Lincoln County*, p. 303 n3; Garrett, *Authentic Life of Billy, the Kid*, p. 102; Metz, *Pat Garrett*, p. 59.

72. Garrett, *Authentic Life of Billy, the Kid*, pp. 116-21.

73. Barnes to Sherman, December 23, 1880, enclosed in Barnes to Devens, December 23, 1880, Source-Chronological Files, Box 545; *Daily NM*, December 29, 1880.

74. William H. Bonney to Wallace, March 4, 1881, reprinted in Keleher, *Violence in Lincoln County*, pp. 301-2; *Daily NM*, February 10, March 1, 1881.

75. *Daily NM*, April 3, 6, 1881.

76. Sidney M. Barnes to Wayne MacVeagh, May 30, 1881, Source-Chronological Files, Box 545; *Las Vegas Daily Optic*, May 3, 1881, reprinted in *Billy the Kid: Las Vegas Newspaper Accounts of His Career, 1880-1881* (Waco, Texas: W. M. Morrison-Books, 1958), pp. 18-19.

77. *Daily Optic*, July 18, 1881; *Daily NM*, May 5, 1881.

78. F. Stanley, *The Private War of Ike Stockton* (Denver: World Press, 1959), Chap. 4, pp. 81-104; S. F. Phillips, Acting Attorney General, to Sherman, April 1, 1881, Instruction Book K, NA, p. 495; Wallace to Samuel J. Kirkwood, Secretary of the Interior, March 25, April 8, 1881, Interior Department Territorial Papers, New Mexico, Record Group 48, National Archives, Washington, D.C., M-364 (hereafter cited as Interior Dept. Ter. Papers, Micro.....).

79. Wallace to Frost, Adjutant General, March 27, 1881, Wallace to Kirkwood, May 12, 1881, in, Interior Dept. Ter. Papers, Micro. M-364, in which he apprises the Secretary of Interior that the disturbance was coming under control; for additional details see Wallace's correspondence with William B. Haines, Captain, San Juan Guards, May 21, November 2, 1881, Governor's Papers, New Mexico State Records Center and Archives, Santa Fe.

80. Sherman to Wayne MacVeagh, August 25, 1881, Source-Chronological Files, Box 545.

81. MacVeagh to Sherman, August 27, 1881, Instruction Book L, NA, p. 101; Sherman to MacVeagh, August 30, 1881, Source-Chronological Files, Box 545.

82. Leonard D. White, *The Republican Era: A Study in Administrative History, 1869-1901* (New York: Free Press, 1965), pp. 378-79; U.S., Congress, House, *Testimony Taken by the Committee on Expenditures in the Department of Justice* (1884), 48th Cong., 1st sess., Misc. Doc. 38 (Serial 2233), vol. 1, pt. 1; (Serial 2234), vol. 1, pt. 1, con'd. (hereafter cited as *Testimony*).

83. Testimony of Examiner Joel W. Bowman, in *Testimony* (Serial 2233), pt. 1, p. 271.

84. *Grant County Herald*, July 4, 1879, quoted in, Keleher, *Violence in Lincoln County*,

pp. 186–87; *Evening Review* (Albuquerque), March 2, 1882; *Daily NM*, November 27, 1877.

85. *Evening Review*, March 2, 3, 1882.

86. *Evening Review*, March 2, 3, 4, 1882; see also *Evening Review*, March 6, 1882, quoted in, Prassel, *Western Peace Officer*, p. 221; White, *The Republican Era*, pp. 375–76; Index to Names of U. S. Marshals, Micro T-577; *NM*, August 31, 1878.

87. Report of Sherman to Lew Wallace, Governor, October 5, 1878, quoted in, Keleher, *Violence in Lincoln County*, pp. 183–85.

Chapter 7

1. A scholarly survey of banditry in Arizona does not exist. However, Richard P. Dillon, *Wells, Fargo Detective: The Biography of James B. Hume* (New York: Coward-McCann, 1969), serves as an introduction.

2. *AM*, August 20, 1878; *Arizona Citizen* (Florence and Tucson), August 30, 1878.

3. *AM*, May 18, 1877; Silent to Charles Devens, Attorney General, September 6, 1878, Source-Chronological Files, Box 138; Dake to Devens, July 14, 1879, Source-Chronological Files, Box 139; *Arizona Citizen*, August 23, 1878.

4. Index to Names of U. S. Marshals, Micro T-577; *AM*, August 6, 1875, April 28, December 22, 1876, March 16, July 13, 1877.

5. G. L. Seligman, Jr., "Vignettes of Arizona Pioneers: Crawley P. Dake, U. S. Marshal," *Arizoniana* 2(1961):13–14; *AM*, June 29, 1878, November 18, 1879; *Arizona Citizen*, June 21, August 9, 1878; T. W. Terry, Senator from Michigan, to Benjamin Brewster, Attorney General, June 20, 1882, Dept. of Justice Appointment Papers, Box 36.

6. *AM*, February 23, April 13, May 18, 25, June 1, September 28, 1877.

7. *AM*, March 15, 22, 1878.

8. *AM*, April 20, May 20, 27, June 17, 1878.

9. *AM*, June 17, 1878.

10. *AM*, June 19, 22, 24, July 11, 29, August 5, 6, 14, 20, 1878; for Swilling's statement, see, *AM*, September 9, 1878; for additional details, see *Arizona Sentinel* (Yuma) June 22, July 20, August 3, 24, October 5, 1878.

11. *AM*, August 3, 17, 24, 28, September 17, 1878; additional appointments included Josephus Phy of Phoenix, George L. Turner of McMillanville, and John C. Loss of Florence, *AM*, September 12, 1878.

12. *AM*, September 10, 1878.

13. Phillips to Dake, June 25, 1878, August 20, 1878, Instruction Book H, NA, pp. 159–60, 468, resp.; Dake to Charles Devens, Attorney General, August 19, 1878, Source-Chronological Files, Box 138; *Arizona Sentinel* (Yuma), August 24, 1878.

14. Evans to Torres, October 12, 1881, enclosed in M. Romero, Mexican Legation, WEAEAC., to Frederick Frelinghuysen, Secretary of State, April 6, 1882, Interior Dept. Ter. Papers, Micro. M-429.

15. Dake to Devens, September 5, Silent to Devens, September 6, Hoyt to Devens, September 9, 1878, Source-Chronological Files, Box 138.

16. *AM*, September 26, October 7, 1878; *Arizona Citizen*, September 6, 1878; *Colorado Chieftain* (Pueblo), September 26, 1878.

17. *Arizona Citizen*, August 23, 1878.

18. Ibid.; *AM*, October 1, 2, 1878; *Cheyenne Daily Leader* (Wyoming), September 12, 13, 14, 21, 28, October 15, 1878.

19. Dake to Devens, March 7, July 14, 1879, Source-Chronological Files, Boxes 138, 139, resp.; Devens to Dake, March 8, 1879, Instruction Book I, NA, p. 16.

20. Dake to Devens, July 14, 1879, Source-Chronological Files, Box 139.

21. Devens to Dake, July 15, 1879, reprinted in, *AM*, July 16, 1879; *Arizona Citizen*, July 5, 13, 25, 1879.

22. Dake to Devens, July 15, 1880, Source-Chronological Files Box 139; Samuel Mulliken, General Agent, Department of Justice, July 17, 1880, Instruction Book K, NA, p. 162; Dake to Devens, August 25, 1880, Source-Chronological Files Box 139; *New York Times*, June 23, August 6, 18, 25, 26, 27, 1880.

23. *AM*, August 25, 1880, March 22, 1881; Luis Torres, Governor of Sonora, to U.S. Officers in Tucson, August 27, 28, 1879, two letters, enclosed in, Robert Walker, Chief Deputy Marshal, to Devens, September 6, 1880, Source-Chronological Files Box 139; Dake to Devens, September 7, 11, 1880, two telegrams, in Source-Chronological Files Box 139; *Arizona Citizen*, August 28, 1880; for Dake's first two years as marshal see, Larry D. Ball, "Pioneer Lawman: Crawley P. Dake and Law Enforcement on the Southwestern Frontier," *Journal of Arizona History* 14(1973):243–56.

24. M. de Zamacona, Mexican Ambassador to the United States, to William H. Evarts, Secretary of State, December 6, 1878, Interior Dept. Ter. Papers, Micro. M-429; Carl Schurz, Secretary of Interior, to John C. Fremont, December 16, 1878, letter lost but mentioned in, Fremont to Schurz, January 6, 1879; see also, Fremont to Schurz, February 16, 1879, January 16, 1881, Interior Dept. Ter. Papers, Micro. M-429; *Arizona Citizen*, June 13, 1879.

25. Frank Waters, *The Earp Brothers of Tombstone: The Story of Mrs. Virgil Earp*, (New York: Clarkson N. Potter, 1960), pp. 120–23; Clifford P. Westermeier, *Trailing the Cowboy* (Caldwell, Idaho: Caxton Printers, 1955), pp. 140–43; Fremont to Schurz, January 26, 1879, Interior Dept. Ter. Papers, Micro. M-429.

26. *AM*, February 18, December 23, 1871; January 4, 1873, October 5, 1874, August 20, 1875, March 10, August 4, November 10, 1876. John H. Behan lost the race for sheriff of Mohave County in 1878 (*AM*, May 8, 1878); *AM*, November 29, 1879, March 13, 1881.

27. An adequate biography of Wyatt Earp has not yet appeared. Stuart N. Lake, *Wyatt Earp: Frontier Marshal* (Boston: Houghton Mifflin, 1931), is laudatory; Ed Bartholomew's *Wyatt Earp: The Untold Story, 1848-1880* (Toyahvale, Texas: Frontier Book Company, 1963), and, *Wyatt Earp: The Man & the Myth 1879-1882* (1964), are malignantly biased against the Earps, but contain many new facts.

28. *AM*, October 19, 1877, September 3, December 3, 1878.

29. *AM*, February 26, March 16, September 13, October 10, 1881, January 13, 1882; Virgil Earp to Fremont, April 7, 1881, Governor's Papers, Arizona State Library and Archives, Phoenix.

30. *AM*, March 16, 22, 1881, January 13, 1882; Carolyn Lake, ed., *Under Cover for Wells, Fargo: the Unvarnished Recollections of Fred Dodge* (Boston: Houghton Mifflin, 1969), pp. 7–81, recounts much of the highway robbery.

31. *Arizona Daily Star* (Tucson), February 24, 1881; see also, Waters, *Earp Brothers*, pp. 143–44; *AM*, August 4, 1881.

32. John C. Fremont to Carl Schurz, January 16, 1881, Joseph Boyer, Galeyville, Arizona, to John J. Gosper, Acting Governor, September 17, 1881, enclosed in, Gosper to Blaine, September 30, 1881, Interior Dept. Ter. Papers, Micro. M-429; Pat Jahns, *The Frontier World of Doc Holliday* (New York: Hastings House, 1957), pp. 176–77.

33. *Daily Arizona Journal* (Tucson), March 31, 1881, enclosed in, M. de Zamacona, Mexican Ambassador, to Blaine, April 13, 1881, Interior Dept. Ter. Papers, Micro. M-429; *Tombstone Epitaph*, August 13, 1881, quoted in, Douglas D. Martin, ed., *Tombstone's Epitaph* (Albuquerque: University of New Mexico Press, 1957), pp. 149–50; *AM*, March 17, 1881.

34. Gosper to Kirkwood, May 5, 1881, Interior Dept. Ter. Papers, Micro. M-429; MacVeagh to Dake, June 15, August 10, 1881, two letters, Instruction Book L, NA, pp. 16, 85, resp; Dake to MacVeagh, August 25, 1881, Source-Chronological Files, Box 139.

35. French to MacVeagh, September 2, 1881, Source-Chronological Files, Box 139; MacVeagh to Dake, August 27, Samuel J. Phillips, Acting Attorney General, to Dake, December 2, 1881, Instruction Book L, NA, pp. 101, 225, resp.

36. Report of the Acting Governor of Arizona to the Secretary of Interior for the Year 1881, October 6, 1881, Interior Dept. Ter. Papers, Micro. M-429.

37. Gosper to Blaine, September 30, 1881, Interior Dept. Ter. Papers, Micro. M-429.

38. Waters, *Earp Brothers*, pp. 110–11, 223–24; *AM*, March 13, June 2, July 9, 1881; William M. Breakenridge, *Helldorado: Bringing the Law to the Mesquite* (Boston: Houghton Mifflin, 1928), pp. 121–25, 139–40.

39. Testimony of Wyatt Earp, November 16, 1881, in the hearing over the deceased men at the "Gunfight at the OK Corral," reprinted in, Jahns, *Doc Holliday*, pp. 202–12.

40. The transcript of the hearing points to a deliberate premeditation on the part of the Earps; see ibid., pp. 185-215; but Josephine Earp, wife of Wyatt, alleges that Morgan Earp and Doc Holliday, intoxicated at the fight, drew their guns precipitously (Glenn G. Boyer, ed., *I Married Wyatt Earp: The Recollections of Josephine Sarah Marcus Earp* [Tucson: University of Arizona, 1976], pp. 88-90).

41. *AM*, November 10, 24, 1881, February 10, 1882; the *Tombstone Epitaph*, March 13, 1882, took offense at *Harper's Weekly*, which portrayed the lawmen of Arizona as incompetent and recommended the army as the only solution. "That our affairs are now in a better condition is . . . due," said the editor, "to our own people, backed by Judge [William H.] Stillwell and United States Marshal Dake."

42. Samuel F. Phillips, Acting Attorney General, to Dake, November 17, 28, 1881, two letters, Instruction Book L, NA, pp. 206–7, 217, resp.

43. Dake to Gosper, November 28, 1881, Governor's Papers, Arizona State Library and Archives; Gosper to Dake, November 28, 1881, Interior Dept. Ter. Papers, Micro. M-429; Gosper may have initiated a secret investigation after the gunfight at the OK Corral, since, on October 22, 1881, he appointed Frank Marsh as a "private detective for the purpose of discovering facts in a secret manner, connected with crime in the territory." Governor's Papers, Arizona State Library and Archives, Phoenix.

44. Dake to Phillips, Gosper to Phillips, December 8, 1881, two telegrams, Reference Service Report on Marshal Crawley P. Dake, dated December 9, 1966, National Archives, Diplomatic, Legal, and Fiscal Records Division.

45. Virgil Earp's telegram to General Willcox is mentioned in, Miller and Snell, eds., *Great Gunfighters*, pp. 91–92; Gosper to Kirkwood, April 29, 1882, Interior Dept. Ter. Papers, Micro. M-429; for the hearing of Virgil Earp and his party, see Gary Roberts, "Gunfight at O. K. Corral: The Wells Spicer Decision," *Montana, the Magazine of Western History* 20(1970):62–74.

46. Wyatt Earp to Dake, December 29, 1881, telegram, reprinted in *AM*, December 30, 1881; *AM*, January 27, 1882.

47. *AM*, January 27, 1882; Works Projects Administration, *The Private Journal of George Whitwell Parsons* (Phoenix: Arizona Statewide Archival and Records Project, 1939), entries for January 25, 26, 1882; Jahns, *Doc Holliday*, pp. 223–24; Bartholomew, *Wyatt Earp*, pp. 293-95; Breakenridge, *Helldorado*, pp. 141–42, 154–55; Lake, *Wyatt Earp*, pp. 315-16.

48. Two articles, *AM*, February 17, 1882; Works Projects Administration, *George Whitewell Parson*, entry for February 15, 1882.

49. Works Projects Administration, *George Whitewell Parson*, entries for March 19, 20, 21, 1882; Jahns, *Doc Holliday*, pp. 228–31, reprints testimony at the inquest over Stilwell.

50. Works Projects Administration, *George Whitwell Parson*, entries for March 22, 23, 1882; Boyer, ed., *I Married Wyatt Earp*, pp. 107-8.

51. Jahns, *Doc Holliday*, pp. 232–36; Waters, *Earp Brothers*, p. 208; *Colorado Chieftain* (Pueblo), May 18, 1882.

52. Tritle to Arthur, March 31, William T. Sherman to Benjamin Brewster, Attorney

General, April 11, 1882, U.S. Congress, House, *Lawlessness in Arizona*, April 26, 1882, 47th Cong., 1st sess., Exec. Doc. 188 (Serial 2030).

53. U.S., *Statutes at Large*, 22(1882):1035; Henry P. Walker, "Retire Peaceably to Your Homes: Arizona Faces Martial Law, 1882," *Journal of Arizona History* 10(1969):1–18.

54. *Arizona Star*, May 22, 27, 1882, quoted in Scrapbook No. 4, Frederick A. Tritle Collection, Arizona Historical Society, Tucson.

55. *Virginia City Enterprise*, May 21, 1882, quoted in, *Arizona Democrat*, June 5, 1882, in ibid.

56. *AM*, November 16, 23, December 7, 1877; *Daily NM*, December 6, 22, 1877; see *AM*, May 30, June 27, 1879, for the election of Cooley.

57. Ball, "Pioneer Lawman," pp. 243–56; see Bartholomew, *Wyatt Earp*, pp. 115–16 and *AM*, March 15, 1881, for deputies Evans and Paul.

58. See the Return of Fees and Emoluments of Crawley P. Dake for August 1, 1878, to December 31, 1880, in the Sacks Collection.

59. Ibid.

60. Dake to Brewster, September 14, 1881, Reference Service Report on Marshal Crawley P. Dake, dated December 9, 1966, National Archives, Diplomatic, Legal and Fiscal Records Division; Samuel Mulliken, Chief Clerk, Department of Justice, to Dake, April 12, 1882, Benjamin Brewster, Attorney General, to Dake, May 4, 1882, Instruction Book L, NA, pp. 460, 511, resp.

61. Unidentified newspaper clipping, enclosed in Silent to Devens, June 28, 1880, Source-Chronological Files, Box 139.

62. Dake to Devens, October 31, 1878, reprinted in, Harrison, *Territorial Prisons*, pp. 115–16.

63. *AM*, December 5, 1878.

64. S. R. Martin, Special Agent, to Brewster, April 19, 1882, Dept. of Justice Appointment Papers, Box 36; U.S., Congress, House, *Testimony Taken by the Committee on Expenditures in the Department of Justice* (1884), 48th Cong., 1st sess., Misc. Doc. 38 (Serial 2233), vol. 1, pt. 1; (Serial 2234), vol. 1, pt. 1, cont'd.

65. Dake to Brewster, May 7, 1883, Sacks Collection; Dake to Brewster, June 21, 1882, Dept. of Justice Appointment Papers, Box 36.

66. Van Arman to Brewster, July 10, 1882, Terry to Brewster, June 20, 1882, Dept. of Justice Appointment Papers, Box 36.

67. Brewster to Dake, August 5, 1882, Instruction Book M, NA, pp. 138–39; Zan L. Tidball, United States Marshal of Arizona, January 11, 1883, Reference Service Report on Marshal Crawley P. Dake, December 9, 1966, National Archives, Diplomatic, Legal and Fiscal Records Division.

68. Chalmers to Brewster, August 13, September 3, 1885, Reference Service Report on Marshal Crawley P. Dake, December 9, 1966, National Archives, Diplomatic, Legal and Fiscal Records Division.

69. Zabriskie to Brewster, January 22, 1885, ibid.; *Arizona Journal-Miner* (Prescott), February 11, May 25, 1886.

70. Bert M. Fireman, "Fremont's Arizona Adventure," *American West* 1(1964):8–19; Lamar, *Far Southwest*, pp. 468–72; for some of Dake's investments see, *AM*, May 12, 1881.

Chapter 8

1. Lamar, *Far Southwest*, pp. 171–76; Bancroft, *Arizona and New Mexico*, pp. 723–24, 727.

2. Lamar, *Far Southwest*, pp. 162–66; interview with Thornton, in *Rio Grande Republican* (Las Cruces), April 21, 1893.

3. Anderson, *History of New Mexico*, 2:643.

4. Lamar, *Far Southwest,* pp. 170, 180.

5. For Romulo Martinez see, *Silver City Enterprise,* January 30, February 27, March 6, 30, April 3, December 25, 1885; *Daily NM,* June 10, 1885; Frank D. Reeve, "The Government and the Navajo, 1878-1883," *New Mexico Historical Review* 16(1941):275–312; Howard R. Lamar, "Edmund G. Ross as Governor of New Mexico Territory: A Re-Appraisal," *New Mexico Historical Review* 36(1961):177–209; Ross to Ingalls, June 3, 1886, Governor's Papers, New Mexico State Records Center and Archives, Santa Fe (hereafter cited as Governor's Papers); author's interview with Romulo Martinez, Santa Fe, June 26, 1975, grandnephew and namesake of United States Marshal Romulo Martinez, and Laura Mullins, niece of the marshal, Santa Fe, June 26, 1975; for Don Romulo's badge see, *Daily NM,* May 27, 1886.

6. Twitchell, *Leading Facts,* 2:406, n331; author's interview with Hilario Romero, great-grandnephew of Marshal Trinidad Romero, Santa Fe, July 10, 1973.

7. *Daily NM,* February 25, 1890.

8. *Daily NM,* May 16–31, 1893, March 24, 1894, September 12, 1895; H. B. Hening, ed., *George Curry, 1861-1947: An Autobiography* (Albuquerque: University of New Mexico Press, 1958), pp. 75–77.

9. See *Silver City Enterprise,* November 6, 13, December 18, 1885, January 29, 1886, April 22, 1887, for Edward Hall's activities in Grant County; and *Daily NM,* May 23, 1893, for family data.

10. *Albuquerque Evening Review,* March 2, 1882, three articles, and March 3, 1882, one article.

11. Morrison to Brewster, May 18, 1882, Source-Chronological Files, Box 546; see, Samuel Phillips, Acting Attorney General, to Morrison, March 11, 1884, Instruction Book P, NA, p. 194, for Morrison's problems with the account—$475. 25—for transportation of Dye to prison in Missouri.

12. *Albuquerque Evening Review,* March 1, two articles, and 2, 3, 1882.

13. Cummings and McFarland, *Federal Justice,* pp. 260–71.

14. Victor Westphall, "The Public Domain in New Mexico, 1854–1891," *New Mexico Historical Review* 33(1958):24–52, 128–43.

15. Morrison to Brewster, August 9, 1883, Source-Chronological Files, Box 546; Westphall, "Public Domain in New Mexico," pp. 128–43.

16. *Silver City Enterprise,* February 8, 15, 1884.

17. Ibid., February 8, 1884; Miguel A. Otero, *My Life On the Frontier, 1864-1897,* 2 vols. (Albuquerque: University of New Mexico Press, 1939), 2:215–17.

18. *Daily NM,* March 13, 1890.

19. *San Marcial Reporter,* March [?], 1890, quoted in *Daily NM,* March 17, 1890; *Daily NM,* January 25, 1890; Otero, *My Life,* 2:215-17.

20. *Rio Grande Republican,* April [?], 1886, quoted in *Daily NM,* April 9, 1886.

21. Westphall, "Public Domain in New Mexico," pp. 128–43.

22. Romero to William H. H. Miller, Attorney General, October 12, November 9, 1891, Department of Justice Year Files, New Mexico, Record Group 60, National Archives, Washington, D. C., File 10587-1889 (hereafter cited as Year File); for a general discussion of the land grants and land court, see, Twitchell, *Leading Facts,* 2:451-79.

23. E. H. Cookridge, *The Baron of Arizona* (New York: John Day, 1967); *Daily NM,* May 1, June 10, 15, 25, 26, 1895.

24. Cookridge, *Baron of Arizona,* pp. 242–43.

25. *Silver City Enterprise,* August 1, 1890; *Springer Stockman,* quoted in, *Daily NM,* May 16, 1894; Felix Martinez is quoted in, *Daily NM,* May 31, 1893.

26. *Silver City Enterprise,* May 10, 1889, April 11, July 27, October 10, 1890.

27. Lee Myers, "An Experiment in Prohibition," *New Mexico Historical Review* 40(1965):293–306; Dee Harkey, *Mean as Hell* (New York: Signet Press, 1951), pp. 50–57.

28. *Rio Grande Republican*, April 26, May 10, 1895; David H. Stratton, *The Memoirs of Albert B. Fall*, Southwestern Studies, Monograph No. 15 (El Paso: University of Texas, 1966), pp. 42–44, 60 n39. Fall championed the poor Hispanos and charged that the federal lawmen pressed these cases to avoid appearing sympathetic "in the matter of vice."

29. *Daily NM*, June 18, 1896.

30. Judson Harmon, Attorney General, to Hall, February 10, 1869, Instruction Book 62, NA, p. 288, Harmon to Hall, March 6, 1896, Instruction Book 63, NA, p. 377, Harmon to Hall, May 16, 1896, Instruction Book 66, NA, p. 281; Harmon to Daniel S. Lamont, Secretary of War, February 3, 1896, Year File 14289-1895; Petition of Citizens of Raton to Thornton, February 1, 1896, Governor's Papers.

31. Hall to Harmon, February 11, 1896, Year File . .89-1895; Hall to Harmon, February 12, 20, 1896, in Year File 14289-1895; Dick King, "The Fight That Almost Kayoed Boxing," *Frontier Times* 33(1959):26–27, 56–t *Daily NM*, February 21, 1896.

32. *New York Times*, February 12–17, 19–22, 1896; Hening, ed., *George Curry*, pp. 90–92.

33. Richard Olney, Attorney General, to Hall, June 27; to J. H. H. Hemmingway, District Attorney, July 2; Hall to Olney, June 27, 1894, all in U.S., Congress, House, *Appendix to the Annual Report of the Attorney-General . . .for the Year 1896*, January 23, 1897, 54th Cong., 2d sess. (Serial 3499), Doc. 9, pt. 2, pp. 154–56; *Daily NM*, June 30, 1895.

34. Hall to Olney, July 16, 1894, *Appendix to the Annual Report of the Attorney-General*, pp. 160–62; Edwards P. Seeds to Olney, July 2, 1894, *Appendix to the Annual Report of the Attorney-General*, p. 157; *Daily NM*, June 28, 30, 1894.

35. Hall to Olney, July 3, July 16, 1894, *Appendix to the Annual Report of the Attorney-General*, pp. 158, 160–62, resp.

36. Hall to Olney, July 4, 5, 1894, ibid., pp. 158, 159, resp.; *Daily NM*, July 6, 7, 9, 13, 1894.

37. *Daily NM*, July 7, 10, 1894; *Raton Range*, July 5, quoted in, *Daily NM*, July 10, 1894; Hall to Olney, July 16, 1894, *Appendix to the Annual Report of the Attorney-General*, pp. 160–62.

38. Philip J. Rasch, "The Rustler War," *New Mexico Historical Review* 39(1964):257–73.

39. Ibid.; Arrell M. Gibson, *The Life and Death of Colonel Albert Jennings Fountain* (Norman: University of Oklahoma Press, 1965), pp. 108–25; Philip J. Rasch, "John Kinney: King of the Rustlers," *English Westerners' Brand Book* 4 (1961):10-12; *Daily NM*, January 19, 1883, quoted in, A. Gibson, *Albert Jennings Fountain*, p. 112.

40. *Report of Edward L. Bartlett, Adjutant General of the Territory of New Mexico, from March 1, 1882 to January 1, 1884*, p. 136, Governor's Papers; *Albuquerque Daily Democrat*, May 16, 1883, quoted in, F. Stanley, *Longhair Jim Courtright: Two Gun Marshal of Fort Worth* (Denver: World Press, 1957), pp. 102–4; *Silver City Enterprise*, April 13, 1883.

41. *Albuquerque Daily Democrat*, May 17, 23, 31, 1883, quoted in Stanley, *Longhair Jim Courtright*, pp. 104–13; *Daily NM*, May 26, 1883; Jim McIntire, *Early Days in Texas: A Trip to Hell and Heaven* (Kansas City, Missouri: McIntire Pub. Co., 1902), pp. 148–61; Philip J. Rasch, "Murder in the American Valley," *English Westerners' Brand Book* 7 (1965):2-7.

42. *Daily NM*, October 10, 1883, quoted in Stanley, *Longhair Jim Courtright*, pp. 123-36; some uncertainty exists about the presence of Logan. He arrived in Albuquerque on May 5, according to the *Weekly Review*, May 12, 1883. Stanley believes that Logan wanted the ranch of the murdered men, *Longhair Jim Courtright*, p. 138; the *New York Times* followed Logan's activities in New Mexico; see May 7, 29, 30, 1883, July 6, October 20, 21, 22, November 8, 1884.

43. *Albuquerque Daily Democrat*, May 29, 31, 1883, quoted in Stanley, *Longhair Jim Courtright*, pp. 112–20; *Silver City Enterprise*, April 2, 1886; McIntire merely states that

before leaving with Senator Logan he was given a badge to serve "some papers" in Kingston (McIntire, *Early Days in Texas*, pp. 150-52).

44. Lamar, *Far Southwest*, p. 193; the Republicans criticized Marshal Martinez for assigning "eight armed, bulldozing ruffians . . . at each poll in New Mexico" in the 1888 elections, in order to help Antonio Joseph win the delegateship. See, *Daily NM*, July 10, August 13, September 5, 17, 1890.

45. "Our Platform" [White Caps], August 8, 1890; clippings from the *Las Vegas Daily Optic*, July 31, August 6, 1890; O. D. Barrett, Employee of Benjamin Butler, to Butler, July 21, 1890, enclosed in, Butler to John W. Noble, July 29, 1890, Interior Dept. Ter. Papers, Micro. M-364; Benjamin Butler owned a portion of the disputed Mora Grant near Las Vegas, *Daily NM*, October 15, 1890; for a general discussion of the radical politics of New Mexico Territory, in which the White Caps flourished, see, Robert W. Larson, *New Mexico Populism: A Study of Radical Protest in a Western Territory* (Boulder: Colorado Associated University Press, 1974).

46. William H. H. Miller to Romero, August 19, Miller to Eugene A. Fiske, District Attorney, September 2, 1890, Instruction Books 4 and 5, NA, pp. 426 and 127, resp.; Romero to Miller, August 29, September 29, October 29, 1890, Year File 3062-1890; L. C. Booth to Prince, August 21, 1890, Governor's Papers.

47. Siringo to Prince, April 4, 1891, Governor's Papers; Robert Johnson Rosenbaum, "*Mexicano versus Anglo-Americano.* A Study of Hispanic-American Resistance to Anglo-American Control" (Ph.D. diss., University of Texas, 1972), pp. 247–48; Otero, *My Life on the Frontier*, 2:248–52.

48. For the latest statement about this dark episode see, Westphall, *Thomas Benton Catron*, Chap. 12, pp. 208-29; *Daily NM*, March 13, 20, 28, 29, 31, April 19, June 3, July 17, 25, 26, August 26, 27, 1890.

49. *Albuquerque Democrat*, August 29, quoted in, *Daily NM*, August 29, 1890; see also, *Daily NM*, September 4, 1890.

50. *Daily NM*, August 26, 27, 1890; Catron appealed the case to the Territorial Supreme Court, *Daily NM*, July 25, 1892; Westphall, *Thomas Benton Catron*, p. 216.

51. *Daily NM*, January 3, February 22, March 28, August 15, 21, 1890; Westphall, *Thomas Benton Catron*, pp. 216-20.

52. Westphall, *Thomas Benton Catron*, pp. 219–20; Lawman Dee R. Harkey considered Tucker very unsavory, *Mean as Hell*, pp. 124–28; *Daily NM*, April 12, 1894.

53. *Daily NM*, January 10, 11, 12, 15, 1894.

54. *Daily NM*, January 12, March 15, 1894.

55. *Daily NM*, March 16, 17, 1894.

56. *Daily NM*, April 21 1894.

57. *Daily NM*, May 1, 3, 1894, March 18, 1895.

58. *Daily NM*, May 28, 1894, December 2, 13, 26, 1895.

59. *Daily NM*, January 9, 10, 12, 1894; Lamar, *Far Southwest*, p. 195.

60. Morrison to Brewster, August 30, 1883, Source-Chronological Files, Box 546; *Silver City Enterprise*, January 20, 1888; *NM*, July 26, 1879.

61. Record Book of Edward L. Hall, New Mexico State Records Center and Archives, Santa Fe.

62. J. Monroe Heiskell, Examiner, to Judson Harmon, Attorney General, April 20, 1896, in, Reference Service Report on Edward L. Hall, July 8, 1965, National Archives, Diplomatic, Legal, and Fiscal Records Division; Hall announced the appointment of Neustatter in, *Daily NM*, May 3, 1894.

63. For the examiner's visit to Morrison, see Brewster to Morrison, February 12, 1883, Instruction Book N, NA, pp. 440–45; to Romero, see *Rio Grande Republican*, May 20, 1892; to Hall, see Leigh Chalmers, Examiner, to Richard Olney, Attorney General, September 4, 1893, in, Reference Service Report on Edward L. Hall, July 8, 1965, National Archives, Diplomatic, Legal and Fiscal Records Division.

64. For Morrison's appointments see, *Daily NM*, January 27, 1883; for Romero's see, *Albuquerque Morning Democrat*, November 19, 1889; for Hall's see, *Daily NM*, May 31, 1893; Romulo Martinez chose a reliable Hispano, Miguel A. Romero of Las Vegas, as chief deputy and accountant, Otero, *My Life on the Frontier*, 2:215–17.

65. Farrand, *Legislation for the Territories*, pp. 88, 91; J. H. Campbell, Examiner, to Judson Harmon, March 9, 1897, Reference Service Report on Edward L. Hall, July 8, 1965, National Archives, Diplomatic, Legal and Fiscal Records Division; *Daily NM*, August 30, 1895.

66. U.S., Congress, House, *Report of the Attorney General for 1883*, pp. 22-23; C. P. Berry to Harmon, February 11, 1896, Reference Service Report on Edward L. Hall, July 8, 1965, National Archives, Diplomatic, Legal and Fiscal Records Division; on railroad passes see, U.S. Congress, House, *Annual Report of the Attorney General for 1887*, pp. xx, 272–73.

67. *Daily NM*, January 10, February 3, 1890.

68. *Las Vegas Daily Optic*, quoted in *Daily NM*, May 18, 1896; R. J. Danials [his spelling], to Ross, March 22, 1886, Governor's Papers.

69. *Daily NM*, July 3, 1894, May 18, 1896; *Rio Grande Republican*, May 22, 1896; Governor William Thornton removed two sheriffs, George Sena of Lincoln County and Guadalupe Ascarate of Dona Ana in March 1896 for failure to enforce the law, *Daily NM*, March 19, 21, 1896; Bursum to Loomis, October 2, 1896, quoted in, Donald R. Moorman, "Holm O. Bursum, Sheriff, 1894," *New Mexico Historical Review* 39(1964):333–44.

70. Farrand, *Legislation for the Territories*, pp. 89, 91; Morrison to Brewster, August 4, 1882, Source-Chronological Files, Box 546.

71. For background on Albert Fall see, A. Gibson, *Albert Jennings Fountain*, pp. 192–98; Metz, *Pat Garrett*, pp. 161–70; Stratton, ed., *Memoirs of Albert B. Fall*, reveals the extraordinary ease with which Fall could forget his past.

72. Richard Olney to Hall, September 13, 1893, Instruction Book 33, NA, pp. 61–62, mentions Hall's inquiry of September 8 about the procedure for applying for funds for Fall's bodyguard; an 1890 decision of the Supreme Court upheld the procedure; Prassel, *Western Peace Officer*, p. 226.

73. For Ben Williams see, William A. Keleher, *The Fabulous Frontier: Twelve New Mexico Items* (Santa Fe: Rydal Press, 1945), pp. 187–88, 220–21, 226, 236; *Rio Grande Republican*, September 9, 23, 29, October 20, 1894; telegram, Hall to Williams, October 29, 1894, in *Rio Grande Republican*, November 3, 1894.

74. *Daily NM*, November 12, 1894; for Williams's version of this rivalry see, Williams to Editor, August 15, 1895, *Rio Grande Republican*, also August 16, 1895; A. Gibson, *Albert Jennings Fountain*, p. 204.

75. *Rio Grande Republican*, December 8, 1894; *Daily NM*, March 19, 28, 30, 1895.

76. *Daily NM*, August 23, 1895; *Rio Grande Republican*, August 23, September 16, 17, 20, 21, 30, 1895; Keleher, *Fabulous Frontier*, pp. 187–88.

77. Gibson, *Albert Jennings Fountain*, pp. 235–42; *Daily NM*, February 22, 1896; Hening, ed., *George Curry*, pp. 91–92.

78. Gibson, *Albert Jennings Fountain*, pp. 243–44.

79. *Daily NM*, February 22, 1896; the Republican Territorial Committee commended Governor Thornton and Marshal Hall for upholding the law, *Daily NM*, February 24, 1896.

80. Metz, *Pat Garrett*, p. 233.

Chapter 9

1. Lamar, *Far Southwest*, pp. 475, 484.

2. Bancroft, *Arizona and New Mexico*, pp. 529–31, 543.

3. Wagoner, *Arizona Territory*, pp. 56–57 *maps*, 36, 181, 504.

4. Edward Platt to Chester A. Arthur, June 12, 1882, note of endorsement on wrapper of, Tidball to William E. Chandler, May 31, 1882, Dept. of Justice Appointment Papers, Box 37; *AM*, July 14, 1882.

5. Wagoner, *Arizona Territory*, p. 224.

6. See *Arizona Daily Citizen* (Tucson), January 1, 1890, for biography of Meade; *AM*, March 27, July 3, August 7, 1885.

7. Wagoner, *Arizona Territory*, pp. 224–26.

8. James M. Barney, "Bob Paul—Early Arizona Sheriff," *The Sheriff Magazine* 8(1949):3, 8–10; idem, "Who Was Elected Sheriff?," *The Sheriff Magazine* 8(1949):11; *Silver City Enterprise*, March 23, 1888.

9. Both items quoted in, *Arizona Daily Citizen*, January 9, 18, 1890.

10. Hughes to Scott White, Tombstone, June 14, and to C. B. Kelton, Customs Officer, June 14, 1893, Letter Book of Louis C. Hughes, University of Arizona Special Collections, Tucson; clipping, *Arizona Republican*, November 27, 1894, Louis C. Hughes Scrapbook, vol. 3, p. 3, University of Arizona Special Collections, Tucson.

11. Benjamin Brewster, Attorney General, to Tidball, October 27, 1882, Instruction Book M, NA, pp. 282–83; Cummings and McFarland, *Federal Justice*, pp. 253–60.

12. Tidball to Brewster, November 16, 1882, Department of Justice, Letters Received, Arizona, Record Group 60, National Archives, Box 139 (hereafter cited as Letters Received, NA).

13. Cummings and McFarland, *Federal Justice*, p. 260; *New York Times*, March 17, 1883; clipping, "Choice Mortals," Frederick A. Tritle Scrapbook No. 2, p. 15, Arizona Historical Society, Tucson.

14. James A. Zabriskie, District Attorney, to Brewster, October 22, 1882, Source-Chronological Files, Box 139; a telegram from Brewster to Tidball, October 26, 1882, instructed the marshal to "bring certified copy of indictment [of Tiffany] immediately" to New York City (Instruction Book M, NA, p. 301); see also Tidball's comments to Brewster in letter, October 3, 1882, Source-Chronological Files, Box 139; John Bret Harte, "The Strange Case of Joseph C. Tiffany, Indian Agent in Disgrace," *Journal of Arizona History* 16(1975):383–404; Ralph Hedrick Ogle, *Federal Control of the Western Apaches, 1848-1886* (Albuquerque: University of New Mexico Press, 1970), pp. 191–212 n171, says that Tidball seized a letter from Tiffany which linked him to the freighting firm of Lord & Williams.

15. Harte, "Strange Case of Joseph C. Tiffany," pp. 383–404.

16. Ibid., Tidball to Brewster, March 10, Tidball to Springer, February 10, 1884, Source-Chronological Files, Box 141; Brewster to Tidball, February 20, 1884, Instruction Book P, NA, p. 133; U.S., Congress, House, *Testimony Taken by the Committee on Expenditures in the Department of Justice* (1884), 48th Cong., 1st sess. (Serial 2233), vol. 1, Misc. Doc. 38, pt. 1.

17. JoAnn W. Bair and Richard L. Jensen, "Prosecution of the Mormons in Arizona Territory in the 1880s," *Arizona and the West* 19(1977):25-46; Lamar, *Far Southwest*, p. 472.

18. *Arizona Weekly Journal* (Prescott), August 12, 1885, *Apache Chief* (St. Johns), May 30, 1884, both quoted in, David King Udall, *Arizona Pioneer Mormon: David King Udall, His Story and His Family*, Pearl Udall Nelson, collab. (Tucson: Arizona Silhouettes, 1959), pp. 122–23.

19. Wagoner, *Arizona Territory*, pp. 205–6, 242–43; *New York Times*, December 7, 1884; Lamar, *Far Southwest*, p. 472;

20. Wagoner, *Arizona Territory*, pp. 275–76; *New York Times*, January 27, October 31, November 1, 1887; Udall, *Arizona Pioneer Mormon*, pp. 130–31; Bair and Jensen, "Prosecution of the Mormons in Arizona Territory in the 1880s," pp. 25-46.

21. David Udall to Ida Udall, December 20, 1886, quoted in, Udall, *Arizona Pioneer Mormon*, p. 111; Meade to Augustus Garland, January 13, 1886, Letter Book of William Kidder Meade, July 28, 1885–June 20, 1887, United States Marshals' Records. 1882-1927, Arizona Historical Society, Tucson, p. 102 (hereafter cited as Meade Letter Book, 1885–1887); Richard E. Sloan, *Memories of an Arizona Judge* (Stanford, California: Stanford University Press, 1932), pp. 116–20.

22. *Silver City Enterprise*, December 7, 1882, August 17, September 7, 1883, October 9, 1885; *Arizona Journal-Miner*, April 5, 1886.

23. U.S., *Statutes at Large*, 22 (1885):58-61, 25:479; Larry D. Ball, " 'Of Different Clay': The United States Marshals and the Chinese Deportations, 1890-1912," paper delivered to Southwest Conference on Asian Studies, October 12, 1973.

24. Telegram, Robert H. Paul to William H. H. Miller, July 2, 1890, Year Files 980-1884; *Daily Star* (Tucson), June 10, July 6, 8, 10, 1890.

25. *Daily Star*, July 11, 22, 26, 1890.

26. Christ to John V. Paul, September 10, 1890, enclosed in, Robert H. Paul to Miller, October 3, 1890, Year File 980-1884; the *Daily Star*, May 1, 2, 4, 1890, noted Marshal Robert Paul escorting six Chinese to Sonora.

27. Robert H. Paul to Miller, October 3, 1890, Year File 980-1884.

28. Ibid.

29. Ibid.

30. See Dillon, *Wells, Fargo Detective*, esp. pp. 7-108, Eugene B. Block, *Great Train Robberies of the West* (New York: Coward-McCann, 1959), esp. pp. 13-167.

31. Hume quoted in, Dillon, *Wells, Fargo Detective*, pp. 228–29.

32. Lake, ed., *Under Cover for Wells, Fargo*, pp. 87-91.

33. *Arizona Journal-Miner*, May 6, 19, 21, November 8, 1887; *Silver City Enterprise*, May 13, 1887; Larry D. Ball, " 'This High-Handed Outrage,' Marshal William Kidder Meade in a Mexican Jail," *Journal of Arizona History* 17(1976):219–32; Block, *Great Train Robberies*, pp. 53–65.

34. Dispatch to the *New York Times*, March 13, 1888; a copy of Tucker's letter was enclosed in, Tucker to Hamilton [?], March 18, 1888, Files of Mrs. Burton Devere, Rose Tree Inn Book Shop, Tombstone.

35. Zulick to Bayard, April 18, 1888, Arizona State Library and Archives, Phoenix.

36. Meade to Bayard, March 20/21, 1888, Meade Letter Book, 1887–1889.

37. *Silver City Enterprise*, May 18, 1888.

38. Otto Miller Marshall, *The Wham Paymaster Robbery: Boldest in Arizona History, May 11, 1889* (Pima, Arizona: Pima Chamber of Commerce, April, 1967), pp. 1-5.

39. Breakenridge, *Helldorado*, pp. 218–21; *Silver City Enterprise*, May 31, 1889.

40. Unidentified clipping in Marshall, *Wham Paymaster Robbery*, pp. 19–20; Richard E. Sloan, *Memories of an Arizona Judge*, (Stanford: Stanford University Press, 1932), pp. 88–90.

41. Quoted in, Marshall, *Wham Paymaster Robbery*, p. 37; Louis C. Hughes, United States Commissioner, to William H. H. Miller, Attorney General, June 22, William Herring, Special Attorney, to Miller, November 12, 1889, Year File 4265-1889.

42. Harry R. Jeffords, United States District Attorney, to Miller, November 22, 1889, Year File 4265-1889; *Arizona Daily Citizen*, October 12, 13, 14, 15, 1889; for some details of the investigation see, "Extraordinary Expense in Wham Case, 1890," United States Marshals' Records, 1882-1927, Arizona Historical Society, Tucson.

43. Miller, *Wham Paymaster Robbery*, pp. 54–74; Breakenridge, *Helldorado*, p. 221.

44. Tichenor to Samuel Klotz, January [7?], 1890, Bryan W. Tichenor Correspondence, Folder 3, University of Arizona Special Collections, Tucson.

45. Quoted in *Arizona Daily Citizen*, February 18, 1890; for the efforts of Paul to apprehend the Wham robbers see, Harry Jeffords to Miller, n. d. [received December 23,

1889], Year Files 4265-1889; Miller to Thomas F. Wilson, United States District Attorney, December 23, 1891, Instruction Book 18, NA, p. 162; Miller to Wilson, August 1, 1892 Instruction Book 23, NA, p. 385.

46. *Arizona Daily Star*, May 10, 18, 20, 1890.

47. Judson Harmon, Attorney General, to Meade, June 4, 1895, Instruction Book 52, NA, p. 393; Meade to John Wanamaker, Postmaster General, January 26, 1894, Year File 1770-1894.

48. William H. Barnes to Richard Olney, Attorney General, December 12, 1894, Year File 1770-1894; Meade to Olney, December 10, 1894, Barnes to Olney, December 12, Year File, 1770-1894.

49. Report of General John Pope, Commander, Department of the Missouri, to Robert T. Lincoln, September 22, 1881, U.S., Congress, House, *Annual Report of the Secretary of War for 1881*, November 10, 1881, 44th Cong., 1st sess., Exec. Doc. 1, pt. 2 (Serial 2010), p. 118; Report of General William T. Sherman to Robert T. Lincoln, October 27, 1883, *Annual Report of the Secretary of War for 1883*, November 15, 1883, 48th Cong., 1st sess., Exec. Doc. 1, pt. 2 (Serial 2182), p. 45.

50. Paul I. Wellman, *The Indian Wars of the West* (Garden City, N.Y.: Doubleday & Co., 1947), pp. 411–15.

51. Crawley P. Dake to Wayne MacVeagh, October 3, 1881, AG Papers. Letters Received, NA, Box 139; George H. Turner, Sr., to Dake, September 26, 1881, reprinted in, *AM*, October 3, 1881; Turner filed charges against Indian Agent Tiffany for the death of his son, George Jr.; Benjamin Brewster to Dake, February 25, 1882, Instruction Book L, NA, p. 344.

52. E. B. Pomeroy, District Attorney, to Brewster, March 2, 1882, AG Papers, Letters Received, NA, Box 139; Brewster to Pomeroy, February 28, March 13, 1882, two letters, Instruction Book L, NA, pp. 344, 377, resp.; Dake to MacVeagh, October 8, 1881, AG Papers, Letters Received, NA, Box 139; MacVeagh to Dake, October 8, 1881, Instruction Book L, NA, p. 144.

53. Alexander B. Adams, *Geronimo: A Biography* (New York: G. P. Putnam's Sons, 1971), pp. 257–61; in a strange (and possibly tongue-in-cheek) statement in his report of September 27, 1883, Brigadier General George Crook extended his thanks to the "Hon. Z. L. Tidball, United States Marshal for Arizona . . . for the valuable assistance rendered me, and without which my work [among the Apaches] would have been more difficult" (*Annual Report of the Secretary of War for 1883*, pp. 159–82).

54. *Arizona Journal-Miner*, March 25, April 3, 14, 1886.

55. Breakenridge, *Helldorado*, pp. 204–5.

56. U.S., *Statutes at Large*, 23 (1885):362–85; for the extension of U.S. jurisdiction over the Indians see, Felix S. Cohen, *Felix Cohen's Handbook of Federal Indian Law* (Albuquerque: University of New Mexico Press, 1971), Chap. 18; Fritz, *Indian Assimilation*, pp. 142, 215–17.

57. Ex Parte Wilson (1891), 11 Sup. Ct. 870, cited in, Mallory, comp., *Compiled Statutes*, sec. 4149, 5:4943–51 n 13.

58. Meade to Sieber, October 2, 1888, Meade Letter Book, 1887-1889, p. 296, to Bullis, November 13, 1888, p. 334.

59. Breakenridge, *Helldorado*, pp. 206–8; Meade to E. A. Howard, Indian Agent, Pima Reservation, October 10, 1886, Meade Letter Book, 1885–1887, p. 272.

60. Meade to Augustus Garland, Attorney General, April 20, to A. J. Falls, Lawyer, April 20, 1887, Meade Letter Book, 1885–1887, pp. 387, 388–89, resp.

61. Prassel, *Western Peace Officer*, p. 223; Meade to Frank Porter, San Carlos Indian Agency, May 15, 1887, Meade Letter Book, 1885–1887, p. 418; Meade directed his Chief Deputy, C. T. Dunavan, at the outset of his first term, to take *"triplicate* paper in *every* [his italics] instance . . . [and to] be very particular in keeping these records." July 28, 1885, Meade Letter Book, 1885–1887, pp. 2–3.

62. *Arizona Daily Citizen*, November 23, 1889; *Arizona Daily Star*, August 2, 1891; William H. H. Miller, Attorney General, August 20, 1891, Instruction Book 15, NA, p. 13; Miller to Paul, June 14, 1892, Instruction Book 22, NA, p. 363; O'Neill to Paul, July 1, 1892, General Correspondence of the United States Marshals of Arizona, United States Marshals' Records, 1882-1927, Arizona Historical Society, Tucon; Paul to Miller, September 12, 1891, Year File 3116-1890.

63. Meade to Harrison, September 21, 1886, Meade Letter Book, 1885-1887, pp. 256-57.

64. Hughes to M. [Mike] J. Hickey, June 1, 1893, Louis C. Hughes Letterbook, University of Arizona Special Collections, Tucson, p. 121; Hereford to Bartleson, June 7, 1893, Hereford Collection, Arizona Historical Society, Tucson, Envelope no. 121.

65. *Tombstone* (Tombstone, Arizona), quoted in *Arizona Journal-Miner*, March 19, 1886.

66. Cummings and McFarland, *Federal Justice*, p. 366; these United States grand juries were also critical of the thirteenth session of the assembly (1885), the "thieving thirteenth," which exceeded the budget permitted by Congress (Wagoner, *Arizona Territory*, pp. 219–20); *Arizona Journal-Miner*, February 9, 16, April 10, 1886.

67. *Journal-Miner*, February 8, 11, 1886, *Tucson Citizen*, quoted in *Journal-Miner*, February 16, 1886.

68. Kercheval to Miller, March 7, April 9, 11, 1892, Year File 3116-1890; the examiner who had visited Paul in 1890 found the office in good order (Frank Crosthwaite to Miller, June 30, 1890, Year File 3116-1890).

69. Campbell to Joseph McKenna, Attorney General, April 10, 1897, Year File 2417-1886.

Chapter 10

1. Prince to John W. Noble, Secretary of Interior, April 23, 1892, quoted in, Lamar, *Far Southwest*, p. 196.

2. Westphall, *Thomas Benton Catron*, pp. 269-77; Catron to Price, December 11, 1896, Catron Papers.

3. Otero to Catron, December 7, 1896, January 8, 1897, two letters, Serapio Romero to Catron, December 9, 1896, Catron to Otero, December 14, 1896, Catron Papers.

4. Miguel A. Otero, *My Nine Years as Governor of New Mexico, 1897-1906* (Albuquerque: University of New Mexico Press, 1940), pp. 5–6.

5. *Daily Optic*, n. d., quoted in, *Rio Grande Republican*, March 19, July 23, 1897; Otero, *Nine Years as Governor*, pp. 1–3; Westphall, *Thomas Benton Catron*, pp. 274-75.

6. Westphall, *Thomas Benton Catron*, pp. 278–82.

7. Anderson, *History of New Mexico* 1:351; *Silver City Enterprise*, October 30, 1885, February 12, April 9, 1886, June 17, August 5, October 21, 1887; Creighton Foraker's brother, Joseph B. Foraker, in *Notes of a Busy Life*, 2 vols. (Cincinnati: Stewart & Kidd, 1916), 1:5–6, maintained that the new marshal earned his position without help from the family. Interview with Miss Mary Foraker, August 12, 1976, Albuquerque, New Mexico. Miss Foraker is the only surviving child of Creighton M. Foraker; Foraker Family Album, in the possession of Jane Foraker-Thompson, niece of Creighton M. Foraker, Santa Fe, Ne2 Mexico.

8. Undated clipping, *New Mexican*, Foraker Family Album.

9. U.S., *Statutes at Large*, 29(1896):181-83; U.S., Congress, House, *Report of the Attorney General for the Year 1883*, 48th Cong., 1st sess. (Serial 2193), Exec. Doc. 8, pp. 22–23; see also the *Annual Reports* for 1884 (Serial 2296), p. 17, for 1885 (Serial 2387), p. 12, and for 1895 (Serial 3390), pp. 5-6.

10. The instructions to marshals became elaborately regulated, see, *Instructions to United States Marshals, Attorneys, Clerks, and Commissioners, January 1, 1899*

(Washington: GPO, 1898), for 107 pages of guidelines; see, *Instructions to United States Marshals, Attorneys, Clerks, and Commissioners, April 1, 1904* (Washington: GPO, 1904), for 154 pages devoted to marshals; see also, *Duties and Compensation of United States Marshals: Adverse Report* [by the Committee on the Judiciary], 51st Cong., 1st. sess. (Serial 2809), vol. 3, rpt. no. 814.

11. U.S., Congress, House, *Report of the Attorney General for the Year 1896*, 54th Cong., 2d sess. (Serial 3499), Doc. 9, pt. 1, pp. vii–xi.

12. Foraker to Joseph McKenna, Letter Book of C. M. Foraker, August 9, 1897-August 25, 1898, Marshal's Papers, Special Collections Department, Zimmerman Library, University of New Mexico, Albuquerque. This volume is part of a vast collection of official documents of the New Mexico marshalcy spanning 1897–1950, donated to the Special Collections Department by United States Marshal Dorotero N. Baca in 1973 (all letter books hereafter cited as Letter Book of C. M. Foraker, inclusive dates, and page number if available).

13. Ibid.

14. J. J. Sheridan, Chief Office Deputy (for Foraker), to Griffith, October 13, 1898, Official Correspondence of C. M. Foraker with the Auditor of the Treasury, State [Department], and other Depts., June 30, 1897-May 1, 1899, Marshal's Papers, Special Collections Department, Zimmerman Library, University of New Mexico, Albuquerque (hereafter cited as Official Corr. of C. M. Foraker with the Auditor of the Treasury).

15. Ibid.

16. Ibid.

17. Foraker to William H. Ramsey, August 10, 1897, Letter Book of C. M. Foraker, 1897–1898, p. 32; Foraker to Charles J. Bonaparte, Attorney General, July 13, Aug. 31, 1906, Letter Book of C. M. Foraker, January 15, 1906-November 19, 1906, pp. 170, 303, resp.; when the courts of West Virginia entertained a case in which deputy marshals were considered for the Civil Service, Foraker inquired. See, Foraker to Bonaparte, August 10, 1907, Letter Book of C. M. Foraker, July 28, 1907-February 24, 1908, p. 33.

18. Foraker to Billy [William] Smith, July 23, 1906, Letter Book of C. M. Foraker, 1906, p. 200; Foraker to Bonaparte, July 28, 1906, p. 209.

19. Foraker to "Al" [?], April 13, 1898, Letter Book of C. M. Foraker, 1897-1898, p. 373; Foraker to Hall, June 21, 1901, Letter Book of C. M. Foraker, April 1, 1901-October 14, 1901, p. 239; Foraker to H. F. Curren, August 9, 1897, Letter Book of C. M. Foraker, 1897-1898, p. 10.

20. Foraker to W. G. Cullen, Postmaster, December 12, 1897, Letter Book of C. M. Foraker, 1897–1898, p. 235; *Albuquerque Journal*, February 23, 1907, January 10, 1910.

21. Foraker to W. K. Irwin, Martinez, New Mexico, January 1, 1898, Letter Book of C. M. Foraker, 1897-1898, p. 258; Foraker to A. F. Miller, Farmington, New Mexico, February 15, 1905, Letter Book of C. M. Foraker, January 1, 1905-January 15, 1906, p. 51.

22. Foraker to Philander C. Knox, February 4, 16, 1903, two letters, Letter Book of C. M. Foraker, September 30, 1902-October 26, 1903, pp. 136, 164, resp.; Foraker to T. H. Goodman, Railroad Agent, San Francisco, California, July 3, 1900, Letter Book of C. M. Foraker, January 2, 1900-March 29, 1901, p. 358; *Albuquerque Journal*, September 7, 1908; telephone interview with J. Benson Newell, December 31, 1976, Las Cruces, New Mexico. Newell is a prominent attorney and, at the age of ninety years, still practices law.

23. Foraker to Knox, July 2, 1904, Letter Book of C. M. Foraker, October 27, 1903-December 31, 1904, p. 262; *Albuquerque Journal*, June 1, 1907, July 5, December 1, 1908, February 20, 1910.

24. Foraker to Knox, January 3, 1902, Letter Book of C. M. Foraker, October 18, 1901-September 27, 1902, p. 126; Foraker to Knox, May 14, 1901, Letter Book of C. M. Foraker, 1901, p. 116; *Albuquerque Journal*, August 14, 1907; author interview with Miss Mary Foraker, August 12, 1976, Albuquerque, New Mexico.

25. *Albuquerque Journal*, May 27, 1910.

26. *Albuquerque Journal*, October 29, 1907, April 29, 1910; on the night of May 11, 1910, two young Oklahomans robbed a passenger train one mile from Phoenix (*Albuquerque Journal*, May 12, 13, 14, 1910).

27. Wiley to Foraker, October 8, 1904, February 19, March 21, 1905, Letters Received, Marshal's Papers, Special Collections Department, Zimmerman Library, University of New Mexico, Albuquerque (hereafter cited as Letters Received, C. M. Foraker); Twitchell, *Leading Facts*, 2:575, n484.

28. Foraker to Childers, March 19, 1904, Letter Books of C. M. Foraker, 1903–1904, p. 110; see also Foraker to Philander C. Knox, Attorney General, June 8, 1904, p. 202.

29. *Albuquerque Journal*, August 16, September 1, October 4, 1907.

30. Biographical File, Secundino Romero, Special Collections Department, Zimmerman Library, University of New Mexico, Albuquerque; clipping, *Albuquerque Evening Herald* [?], Foraker Family Album.

31. McFarland and Cummings, *Federal Justice*, pp. 534–35.

32. The Secundino Romero Papers, nine linear feet of material, is one of the most revealing collections concerning the administration of law enforcement in New Mexico Territory. The letters reveal the routine, inner workings of the court clerk's office (Special Collections Department, Zimmerman Library, University of New Mexico, Albuquerque [hereafter cited as Romero Papers]); see, Foraker to Romero, January 13, 1898, April 20, 1899, June 1, 1899, January 21, 1907; Harry Cooper to Romero, January 29, 1907; Romero to Foraker, January 18, 1907, Letter Book of Secundino Romero, 1906-1907, p. 113, Romero Papers.

33. Hall to "Friend Charley" [Charles C. Shirk], March 16, 1900, Romero Papers.

34. Pickard to Shirk, June 8, 11, 1900, Romero Papers; for the opening game of Marshal Edward L. Hall's challenge baseball exhibition see, *NM*, June 12, 14, 1895.

35. Hall to Shirk, December 19, 1900, Romero Papers.

36. Foraker to Moody, June [?], 1906 Letter Book of C. M. Foraker, 1906, p. 120; Foraker to Cleofes Romero, October 7, 1901, Letter Book of C. M. Foraker, 1901, n. p.

37. Foraker to Philander C. Knox, Attorney General, June 17, 1901, Letter Book of C. M. Foraker, 1901, pp. 219–21.

38. For the investigation of federal prisoners see, W. B. Childers to Philander C. Knox, May 27, 1901, and enclosure, Letters Received, C. M. Foraker; see also, Frank Strong, General Agent, Department of Justice, to J. H. Campbell, Deputy Marshal, June 6, 23, 1901, two letters, Letters Received, C. M. Foraker; Foraker to Knox, June 17, 1901, Letter Book of C. M. Foraker, 1901, pp. 219–21.

39. Charles J. Bonaparte, Attorney General, to Foraker, June 1, 1907, Letters Received, C. M. Foraker; *Albuquerque Journal*, January 15, 24, 1907.

40. Campbell to Frank Strong, General Agent, June 17, 1901, Letter Book of C. M. Foraker, 1901, p. 222; Foraker to Charles Emory Smith, Postmaster General, July 18, 1901, Letter Book of C. M. Foraker, 1901, p. 292.

41. U.S., *Statutes at Large*, 32 (1902):729; the most accessible record of train robberies is the *New York Times Index*.

42. For some account of the many Black Jacks see, Jeff Burton, *Black Jack Christian: Outlaw*, Western Americana Series, No. 14 (Santa Fe: Press of the Territorian, 1967); idem, *Dynamite and Six-Shooter* (Santa Fe: Palomino Press, imprint of the Press of the Territorian, 1970); Larry D. Ball, "Outlaws of the Southwest, 1895–1905," *Denver Westerners' Brand Book* 20 (1964): 281–99; idem, "Black Jack Ketchum: The Birth of a Folk Hero," *Mid-South Folklore* 1 (1973):19–25.

43. Hall to Joseph McKenna, Attorney General, March 25, 1897, Year File 13065-1896; Foraker to McKenna, October 26, 1897, Correspondence of C. M. Foraker with the U.S. Attorney General, August 3, 1897-May 26, 1900, Marshal's Papers, Special Collections

Department, Zimmerman Library, University of New Mexico, Albuquerque (hereafter cited as Correspondence with Attorney General); Foraker to Guy Beckam, Butte, Montana, November 29, 1897, Letter Book of C. M. Foraker, 1897–1898, p. 223.

44. Hall to McKenna, October 13, 1896, Foraker to McKenna, June 9, 1898, Year File 13065-1896; Foraker to McKenna, October 26, 1897, Correspondence of C. M. Foraker with the Attorney General; James McCauley, *A Stove-Up Cowboy's Story* (Dallas: Southern Methodist University Press, 1943), pp. 33–34.

45. McKenna to Foraker, November 2, 1897, Instruction Book 88, NA, p. 258; Foraker to McKenna, November 6, 12, 1897, two letters, Year File 13065-1896; *Rocky Mountain News* (Denver), April 30, 1897.

46. Foraker to McKenna, April 9, June 9, August 13, September 14, 1898, four letters, Year File 13065-1896; Foraker to J. E. Hurley, July 1, 1898, Letter Book of C. M. Foraker, 1897-1898, p. 463; Foraker sent Deputy Memphis Elliot on a stillhunt for the remnants of the Black Jack Ketchum band (see, John W. Griggs, Attorney General, to Foraker, September 12, 1899, Instruction Book 116, NA, p. 112).

47. William French, *Some Recollections of a Western Ranchman: New Mexico 1883-1899* (London: Methuen, 1927), pp. 203–9.

48. Walter Hovey, "Black Jack Ketchum Tried to Give Me a Break!" *True West* 19 (1972):6–18, 48–52; Miss Mary Foraker recalled that when Cipriano Baca visited her father the children were all "agog" at the noted Hispano lawman. Author interview with Miss Mary Foraker, August 12, 1976.

49. Ibid.; Foraker to Fred Dodge, December 30, 1897, Letter Book of C. M. Foraker, 1897–1898, p. 256.

50. Burton, *Dynamite and Six-Shooter*, pp. 53-60; for the version favorable to Marshal Foraker, see J. Evetts Haley, *Jeff Milton: A Good Man with a Gun* (Norman: University of Oklahoma Press, 1948), pp. 280–90.

51. Burton, *Dynamite and Six-Shooter*, pp. 73–90.

52. Foraker to George H. Green, United States Marshal, Dallas, Texas, February 26, Foraker to J. A. Franklin, Deputy Sheriff, Dalhart, Texas, February 26, 1907, Letter Book of C. M. Foraker, 1906–1907, pp. 203, 205, resp.; for the trial of George Musgrave see, *Albuquerque Journal*, July 25, 1907, September 21, 1908, January 5, 7, 9, 13, 25, 26, March 9, May 28, June 1, 2, 3, 4, 1910.

53. Foraker to McKenna, October 26, 1897, Correspondence with Attorney General.

54. Joseph Miller, ed., *The Arizona Rangers* (New York: Hastings House, 1972), pp. 1-15; Twitchell, *Leading Facts*, 2:574, n484, for mention of Mounted Police Act; Cornelius C. Smith, Jr., *Emilio Kosterlitzky: Eagle of Sonora and the Southwest Border* (Glendale, California: Arthur H. Clark Co., 1970) details his life.

55. Foraker to Philander C. Knox, Attorney General, March 21, 1902, Letter Book of C. M. Foraker, 1901–1902, pp. 281–82; *Albuquerque Journal*, September 30, 1908.

56. U.S., Congress, House, *Report of the Attorney General for the Year 1907*, 60th Cong., 1st sess. (Serial 5356), 2 vols., Doc. 10, 1:9–10, 44–45; *Report of the Attorney General for 1908*, 60th Cong., 2d sess. (Serial 5445), Doc. 1043, p. 50.

57. Cummings and McFarland, *Federal Justice*, pp. 375–83.

58. John W. Griggs, Attorney General, to Childers, November 14, December 4, 1900, Instruction Books Nos. 134, 135, NA, pp. 402–3, 276, resp.; Childers to Griggs, November 28, 1900, Year File 11717-1900.

59. Fornoff to Foraker, January 17, 1901, enclosed in Childers to Griggs, April 20, 1901, Year File 11717-1900.

60. Childer's report is mentioned in, Griggs to Childers, October 8, 1901, General Correspondence of the United States Marshals of Arizona, Arizona Historical Society, Tucson; Foraker to Frank Maggio, December 7, 1901, to Rosario Maggio, March 10, 1902, Letter Book of C. M. Foraker, 1901–1902, pp. 82, 262, resp.

61. Foraker to Philander C. Knox, Attorney General, February 23, June 3, 1904, Year Files 28731-1904, 16-12, resp.; Knox to Foraker, February 21, June 15, 1904, Instruction Books Nos. 193, 199, pp. 92, 136, resp.; William H. H. Llewellyn, District Attorney, September 6, 1904, Year File 16-12.

62. Ethan A. Hitchcock, Secretary of Interior, to Philander C. Knox, September 20, 1902, Year File 15838-1902; Foraker to Knox, October 9, 27, 1902, Year File 15838-1902; Knox to Foraker, July 1, 1903, Instruction Book No. 180, NA, p. 332.

63. Anderson, *History of New Mexico*, 1:351; *Arizona Republican* (Phoenix), December 12, 1903; author interview with Miss Mary Foraker, August 12, 1976, Albuquerque.

64. Stephen Easton, Bernalillo, New Mexico, to Foraker, March 13, 1905, James Black, Leavenworth Prison, to Foraker, October 9, 1910, Letters Received, C. M. Foraker; Foraker to J. R. Massagee, May 12, 1902, Letter Book of C. M. Foraker, 1901–1902, p. 333; Foraker to John A. Ball, National Soldiers' Home, Tennessee, November 27, 1906, Letter Book of C. M. Foraker, 1906, p. 2.

65. Hening, ed., *George Curry*, pp. 264–65; Twitchell, *Leading Facts*, 5:123.

Chapter 11

1. Lynn I. Perrigo, *The American Southwest: Its Peoples and Cultures* (New York: Holt, Rinehart and Winston, 1971), pp. 302, 322–23; Wagoner, *Arizona Territory*, p. 504.

2. John Alexander Carroll, ed., *Pioneering in Arizona: The Reminiscences of Emerson Oliver Stratton & Edith Stratton Kitt* (Tucson: Arizona Pioneers Historical Society, 1964), p. 102; *AM*, December 30, 1878; *Daily Citizen* (Tucson), December 5, 1889, February 23, 1890; *Arizona Republican* (Phoenix), June 24, 1901.

3. Effie R. Keen, "Arizona's Governors," *Arizona Historical Review* 3(1930):7-20; Charles H. Herner, "Arizona's Cowboy Cavalry," *Arizoniana* 5(1964):10-26; *Weekly Republican* (Phoenix), July 2, 1903; *Arizona Republican*, June 9, 1901.

4. Nyle H. Miller and Joseph W. Snell, eds., *Why the West Was Wild: A Contemporary Look at the Antics of Some Highly Publicized Kansas Cowtown Personalities* (Topeka: Kansas State Historical Society, 1963), pp. 126–29; Theodore Roosevelt, *The Rough Riders*, vol. 11, *The Works of Theodore Roosevelt*, Executive Edition (New York: P. F. Collier & Sons, 1899), p. 174; Henry F. Pringle, *Theodore Roosevelt: A Biography* (New York: Harcourt, Brace, Harvest Books, 1956), pp. 139-40, *Weekly Republican*, January 14, 1904; *Rocky Mountain News* (Denver), October 21, 1901, January 9, 1902.

5. *Weekly Republican*, February 6, 27, March 6, 1902; *Rocky Mountain News*, October 22, 1901, January 11, February 9, 11, 14, 1902; Elting E. Morison, ed., *The Letters of Theodore Roosevelt*, 8 vols. (Cambridge, Mass.: Harvard University Press, 1951-54), 3:234–35.

6. Roosevelt to Daniels, February 22, 1902, Roosevelt to Brodie, June 6, 1902, in Morison, ed., *Letters of Theodore Roosevelt*, 3:234–35, 270, 270n3, resp.

7. Frederick J. Dodge to Roosevelt, December 18, H. P. Myton to Roosevelt, December 14, 1901, enclosed in, Roosevelt to Clarence D. Clark, December 8, 1905, Morison, ed. *Letters of Theodore Roosevelt*, 5:104–5.

8. Roosevelt to Clark, December 8, 1905, Roosevelt to Trevelyan, October 11, 1911, Morison, ed., *Letters of Theodore Roosevelt*, 5:104–5, 7:348–49, resp.

9. *Weekly Republican*, May 10, 1906; *Kansas City Journal*, quoted in *Weekly Republican*, April 5, 1906; Mossman is quoted in, Glenn Shirley, "Cap Mossman—and the Apache Devil," *True West* 5(1957):4-6, 32-34; for the official correspondence about Daniels see, Reference Service Report on Benjamin Daniels, March 20, 1964, National Archives, Diplomatic, Legal, and Fiscal Records Division.

10. Biographical Files, Arizona Historical Society, Tucson.

11. Judson Harmon, Attorney General, to Meade, June 29, 1896, Instruction Book 68, NA, pp. 20–21.

12. Meade to Harmon, July 6, 1896, Meade Letter Book, 1896-1897, pp. 24–25; Harmon to Meade, November 11, 1896, Instruction Book 74, NA, p. 1.

13. Meade to Richard R. McMahon, July 6, 1896, Meade Letter Book, 1896-1897, p. 22.

14. Meade to McMahon, September 19, 1896, Meade Letter Book, 1896-1897, p. 233; Meade to J. M. Pratt, October 12, 1896, p. 299; under the private contract between marshals and field deputies, the subordinate officer received only three-fourths of his mileage fees (Harmon to Meade, January 5, 1897, Instruction Book 76, NA, p. 182); in 1906 the attorney general again abolished double fees (W. T. Gregory, Deputy Marshal, to Benjamin F. Daniels, Marshal, January 3, 1906, Letter Book of Benjamin F. Daniels, August 19, 1905-September 24, 1909, United States Marshals' Records, 1863-1912, Arizona Historical Society, Tucson, only 49 pages extant).

15. McCord to Philander C. Knox, September 7, 1901, Letter Book of Myron McCord, June 6, 1901-December 24, 1902, Archives Branch, Bell, California, National Archives and Record Service, p. 79 (hereafter cited as Letter Book of Myron McCord); *Arizona Republican*, June 9, 13, 17, 20, 1901.

16. McCord to Knox, July 11, 1901, two letters, Letter Book of Myron McCord, pp. 18–20.

17. McCord to Knox, July 13, 1901, Letter Book of Myron McCord, 1901-1902, pp. 30–32.

18. McCord to Knox, March 4, 1904, Letter Book of Myron McCord, December 25, 1902-September 27, 1904, p. 260.

19. *Arizona Republican*, September 22, 1904; McCord to George R. Davis, Associate Justice, September 22, 1904, Letter Book of Myron McCord, 1902–1904, p. 481.

20. Frank Hereford to Adeline Rockwell, Milwaukee, Wisconsin, July 14/15, 1900, Frank Hereford Collection, Arizona Historical Society, Tucson.

21. *Arizona Republican*, June 21, 1900.

22. *Arizona Republican*, April 18, 21, June 12, 18, 19, 1900; Wagoner, *Arizona Territory*, pp. 379–81.

23. *Arizona Republican*, July 2, August 13, 1900.

24. Martin, ed., *Tombstone's Epitaph*, pp. 250–67.

25. *Weekly Republican*, January 24, 1901, September 11, 1902.

26. *Arizona Republican*, July 16, 30, 1903.

27. Frederick C. Nave, District Attorney, to Philander C. Knox, Attorney General, November 25, 1902, McCord to Knox, July 6, 11, 1903, Year File 19413-1902; Knox to McCord, July 7, 11, 1903, Instruction Books 180 and 181, NA, pp. 449, 118, resp.; *Weekly Republican*, July 16, 1903.

28. McCord to Knox, December 5, 1903, Year File 10552-1901; Knox to McCord, December 7, 1903, Instruction Book 188, NA, p. 358; *Weekly Republican*, December 17, 1903.

29. Mexican Embassy to Alvey Adee, Secretary of State, September 13, 1905, enclosed in L. B. Loomis, Acting Secretary of State, to William H. Moody, Attorney General, September 15, 1905; Daniels to Moody, November 30, 1905, Millay to Daniels, October 15, 1905, enclosed in, J. D. Harris, Examiner, to Moody, April 30, 1906, Tener to Moody, December 6, 1905, all in Year File 64459-1905.

30. Milton to Harris, enclosed in, Harris to Moody, April 30, 1906, Year File 64459-1905.

31. Welles to McCord, July 12, 1903, Letter Book of Myron McCord, 1902-1904, p. 170.

32. *Albuquerque Journal*, January 28, February 11, 1907, January 2, August 15, December 21, 1908.

33. George H. Kelly, comp., *Legislative History: Arizona, 1864-1912* (Phoenix: Manufacturing Stationers, 1926), pp. 212, 224–26; Miller, ed., *Arizona Rangers*, pp. 17-53.

34. McCord to Philander C. Knox, May 6, 1902, Year File 9332-1901; Knox to McCord, August 26, 1902, Instruction Book 165, NA, p. 221; Knox to Creighton M. Foraker, April 4, 1902, Instruction Book 158, NA, p. 158; *Weekly Republican*, July 10, 1902.

35. See, John W. Griggs, Attorney General, February 24, April 5, 1899, Instruction Books 108 and 110, NA, pp. 505, 427, resp., for commission and rescindment of Selman's badge; *Arizona Republican*, January 22, 1899.

36. Larry D. Ball, ed., " 'No Cure, No Pay': A Tom Horn Letter," *Journal of Arizona History* 8(1967):200–202; A. Kinney Griffith, *Mickey Free: Manhunter* (Caldwell, Idaho: Caxton, 1969), pp. 184, 191.

37. John Kenneth Turner, *Barbarous Mexico*, intro. by Sinclair Snow (Austin: University of Texas Press, 1969), pp. 237–38. This book was originally published in 1910–11, at the outbreak of the Mexican Revolution; *Weekly Republican*, September 20, 1906.

38. Hopkins to Daniels, September 5, 1906, General Correspondence of the United States Marshals of Arizona, United States Marshals' Records, 1882–1927, Arizona Historical Society, Tucson (hereafter cited as General Correspondence, AHS); Daniels to Moody, September 10, 1906, Year File 43718-1906.

39. *Weekly Republican*, December 28, 1906.

40. Ibid.

41. McCord to Moody, October 19, 1904, Daniels to Moody, July 28, 1906, Year File 43718-1904; Kosterlitsky to Daniels, April 30, 1907, General Correspondence, AHS.

42. Turner, *Barbarous Mexico*, pp. 234–35.

43. Ibid., pp. 238–40; *Albuquerque Journal*, July 2, 6, 13, 1907; Mother [Ann] Jones *Autobiography of Mother Jones*, ed. Mary Field Parton (Chicago: Charles H. Kerr, 1925), pp. 136–40.

44. *Albuquerque Journal*, July 13, 1907; Turner, *Barbarous Mexico*, pp. 238–40; Charles J. Bonaparte to Daniels, July 6, 1907, General Correspondence, AHS.

45. *Albuquerque Journal*, August 26, September 17, November 28, December 22, 1907, April 30, June 28, July 26, November 10, December 23, 1908; *Weekly Republican*, March 4, 1909.

46. Daniels to Bonaparte, May 27, 1909, Year File 60444-8-1905; H. D. Guery, Deputy Marshal, to Daniels, May 16, 19, 1909, General Correspondence, AHS; *Weekly Republican*, May 13, 14, 15, 17, 1909.

47. Alexander to Torres, October 3, 1906, Alexander to Overlock, June 12, 14, 1912, two letters, J. L. B. Alexander Papers, Special Collections, Hayden Room, Arizona State University, Box 7.

48. Marshall Eberstein to Overlock, February 11, 1910, General Correspondence, AHS.

49. Anderson to Overlock, March 8, 1910, General Correspondence, AHS; *Albuquerque Journal*, November 23, 1908; for Overlock's efforts to police the Mexican refugees, see, Anne Pace, "Mexican Refugees in Arizona, 1910-1911," *Arizona and the West* 16(1974):5–18.

50. Gregory to Alexander, October 7, Gregory to Daniels, October 12, 1905, Letter Book of Benjamin F. Daniels, 1905–1909, Arizona Historical Society, pp. 15, 17, resp.; *Arizona Republican*, May 20, 1909.

51. McCord to Philander C. Knox, Attorney General, April 30, 1903, Letter Book of Myron McCord, 1902-1904, pp. 104–8; Knox to McCord, April 23, May 7, 1903, Instruction Book 177, NA, pp. 62, 409–10, resp.; *Weekly Republican*, April 30, 1903; *Albuquerque Journal*, July 2, 4, 8, 1907; for the "suppression" of a Papago "scare," see, *Albuquerque Journal*, September 17, 18, 23, 25, 1907.

52. Porterie to Griffith, July 1, 6, 1898, April 25, 1899, General Correspondence, AHS; McCord to Philander C. Knox, April [26 ?], 1904, Letter Book of Myron McCord, p. 396.

53. *Arizona Republican*, August 24, November 9, December 10, 1905; Gregory to Daniels, August 22, 1905, Letter Book of Ben Daniels, 1905-1909, General

Correspondence, AHS, p. 4, Bair and Jensen, "Prosecution of the Mormons in Arizona Territory in the 1880s," pp. 25-46.

54. Ball, "Of Different Clay"; McCord to Commissioner General of Immigration, September 22, 1904, Letter Book of Myron McCord, pp. 494-95.

55. *Tucson Citizen*, August 14(?), 1907, in *Albuquerque Journal*, August 15, 1907.

56. Wagoner, *Arizona Territory*, p. 453.

57. Hoval Smith to Cameron, May 4, 1909, Ralph Henry Cameron Papers, Special Collections, University of Arizona Library, Tucson (hereafter cited as Cameron Papers); *Arizona Republican*, September 22, 1900.

58. Overlock to Cameron, May 12, 1909, Cameron Papers.

59. Overlock to Cameron, August 23, 1909, Smith to Hitchcock, August 12, 1909, Cameron Papers.

60. John S. Goff, "The Organization of the Federal District Court in Arizona, 1912-1913," *American Journal of Legal History* 8(1964):172–79.

Chapter 12

1. Bill O'Hallaren, "When Chester Forgot to Limp," *TV Guide* 23(August 23, 1975):10–13.

2. O'Hallaren, "When Chester Forgot to Limp," pp. 10–13.

3. Cummings and McFarland, *Federal Justice*, pp. 250–51; Pomeroy, *Territories*, p. 61.

4. Robert H. Wiebe, *The Search for Order, 1877–1920* (New York: Hill and Wang, 1967), p. 145.

5. Hubert Howe Bancroft, *Popular Tribunals*, vols. 31 & 32 of *The Works of Hubert Howe Bancroft*, 39 vols. (San Francisco: History Publishing Co., 1887); Prassel, *Western Peace Officer*, p. 253.

6. Undated clipping, Foraker Family Album.

Bibliography

PUBLISHED DOCUMENTS

House of Representatives. *Annals of Congress.* 1st Cong., 1st sess., 1789, vol. 1; 2d Cong., 3d sess., 1793, vol. 3; 12th Cong., 2d sess., 1812-13, vol. 1.
——. *Papers in the Case of J. Francisco Chaves vs. Charles P. Clever, Delegate from the Territory of New Mexico, Santa Fe, October 1, 1867.* 40th Cong., 2d sess., 1868, Misc. Doc. no. 154.
——. *Report on the Case of Milton B. Duffield, April 4, 1878.* 45th Cong., 2d sess., 1878, vol. 2, rpt. 459.
——. *Compensation of United States Marshals, Message from the United States President, Transmitting a Letter from the Attorney General, February 24, 1880.* 46th Cong., 2d sess., 1880, vol. 21, Exec. Doc. 44.
——. *Lawlessness in Parts of Arizona, Message from the President . . . , February 2, 1882.* 47th Cong., 1st sess., 1881–82, vol. 19, Exec. Doc. 58; *April 26, 1882,* vol. 22, Exec. Doc. 188.
——. *Testimony Taken by the Committee on Expenditures in the Department of Justice.* 48th Cong., 1st sess., 1884, vol. 1, pt. 1, vol. 2, pt. 1.
——. Committee on the Judiciary. *Duties and Compensation of United States Marshals; Adverse Report.* 51st Cong., 1st. sess., 1889–90, vol. 3, rpt. 814.
——. *Biographical Directory of the American Congress, 1774–1927.* 69th Cong., 2d sess., Doc. 783.

Justice Department. *Annual Reports of the Attorneys General for 1870–1912.* 43 vols.
——. *Report of the Attorney-General [Edmund Randolph] Read in the House of Representatives, December 31, 1790* (Philadelphia: Francis Childs and John Swaine, 1791, facsimile ed.).
——. *Appendix to the Annual Report of the Attorney General of the United States for the Year 1896, . . . Relating . . . to the Interruption by Force of Interstate Commerce, the Carriage of the Mails, Etc., in the Year 1894. January 23, 1897.* 54th Cong., 2d sess., 1897, Doc. no. 9, pt. 2.
——. *Instructions to United States Marshals, Attorneys, Clerks, and Commissioners, January 1, 1899* (Washington: GPO, 1899); *April 1, 1904* (Washington: GPO, 1904).

War Department. *Report of Secretary of War in Answer to Resolution of the Senate, Calling for Information in Relation to Civil Officers Employed in the Territory of New Mexico While Under Military Government, May 3, 1852.* 32d Cong., 1st sess., 1852, vol. 9, 2 pts., Exec. Doc. 71.
——. *Annual Report of the Secretary of War for 1881, November 10, 1881.* 44th Cong., 1st sess., Exec. Doc. 1, pt. 2, *for 1883, November 15, 1883.* 48th Cong., 1st sess., Exec. Doc. 1, pt. 2.

United States Constitution, Art. 2, sec. 3.
United States, *Statutes at Large*, vols. 1–32.

Unpublished Documents and Manuscripts

Washington, D. C., National Archives.
Record Group 48. Interior Department:
    Territorial Papers of Arizona, 1868–1913. Microcopy M-429. 8 rolls.
    Territorial Papers of New Mexico, 1851–1914. Microcopy M-364. 15 rolls.
    Appointment Papers of New Mexico, 1850–1907. Microcopy M-750. 18 rolls.
Record Group 60. Justice Department:
    Appointment Papers of Arizona, 1863–1889. Boxes 33-37.
    Attorney General's Papers. Letters Received. 1 box.
    Arizona Territory, 1863–1870.
    Attorney General's Papers. Letters Received. New Mexico Territory, 1853–1870.
        4 boxes.
    Source-Chronological Files, Arizona, 1871–1884. 4 boxes.
    Source-Chronological Files, New Mexico, 1871–1884. 4 boxes.
    Year Files, Arizona and New Mexico. 980–1884; 2417–1886; 4265, 10587–1889;
        3116–1890; 1770–1894; 14289–1895; 13065–1896; 11717–1900; 9332, 10552–1901;
        15838, 19413–1902; 16–12, 28731, 43718–1904; 60444–8, 64459–1905.
    Index to Names of U. S. Marshals, 1789–1960. Microcopy T-577. 1 roll.
    Letter Books of the Attorney General, 1862–1869. 6 vols.
    Instruction Books of the Attorney General, 1867–1904. 227 vols.
    Diplomatic, Legal, and Fiscal Records Division. Reference Service Reports: Benjamin
        F. Daniels, March 20, 1964; Edward L. Hall, July 8, 1965; Crawley P. Dake,
        December 9, 1966.
Record Group 46. Senate:
    Territorial Papers of New Mexico, 1851–1873. Microcopy M-200. Rolls 14 and 20.
Record Group 59. State Department:
    Territorial Papers of Arizona, 1864–1872. Microcopy M-342. 1 roll.
    Territorial Papers of New Mexico, 1851–1872. Microcopy T-17. 2 rolls.
Bell, California. National Archives Branch:
    Letter Books of Myron McCord, 1901–1904. 2 vols.
Albuquerque, New Mexico. University of New Mexico. Zimmerman Library. Special
    Collections Department:
    United States Marshal's Papers, 1897-1950.
    Secundino Romero Papers, 1898-1908.
    Biographical File—Secundino Romero.
    Thomas B. Catron Papers.
Santa Fe, New Mexico. State Records Center and Archives:
    Governor's Papers, 1852-1894.
    Record Book of Edward L. Hall for the Fiscal Year 1896.
    ————. Foraker Family Album. Property of Jane Foraker-Thompson.
        Phoenix, Arizona. State Library and Archives.
    Governor's Papers, 1865–1893.
Tempe, Arizona. Arizona State University. Hayden Library:
    J. L. B. Alexander Papers. Box 7.
    ————. Arizona Historical Foundation. Hayden Library.
    Benjamin Sacks Collection.

Tombstone, Arizona. Mrs. Burton Devere:
  William Kidder Meade File.
Tucson, Arizona. Arizona Historical Society:
  United States Marshals' Records, 1882–1927.
  Biographical Files—Charles A. Overlock.
  Frederick A. Tritle Scrapbooks. 6 books.
  Frank H. Hereford Collection.
———. University of Arizona Library. Special Collections:
  Ralph Henry Cameron Papers.
  Louis C. Hughes Collection.
  Bryan W. Tichenor Correspondence, 1887–1896. 1 box.

PRIMARY PUBLISHED SOURCES

Abel, Annie Heloise, ed. *The Official Correspondence of James S. Calhoun, While Indian Agent at Santa Fe and Superintendent of Indian Affairs in New Mexico, 1849-1852.* Washington: GPO, 1915.

Basler, Roy P., ed. *The Collected Works of Abraham Lincoln.* 9 vols. New Brunswick: Rutgers University Press, 1953–55.

Bonney, Catharina V. R., comp. *A Legacy of Historical Gleanings.* 2d ed., 2 vols. Albany: J. Munsell, 1875.

Bourke, John G. *On the Border with Crook.* 1891. Reprint. Lincoln: University of Nebraska Press, 1971.

Boyer, Glenn G., ed. *I Married Wyatt Earp: The Recollections of Josephine Sarah Marcus Earp.* Tucson: University of Arizona Press, 1976.

Breakenridge, William M. *Helldorado: Bringing the Law to the Mesquite.* New York: Houghton Mifflin Co., 1928.

Browne, J. Ross. *Adventures in the Apache Country: A Tour Through Arizona and Sonora, 1864.* 1869. Reprint. Tucson: Unisity of Arizona Press, 1974.

Caroll, John Alexander, ed. *Pioneering in Arizona: The Reminiscences of Emerson Oliver Stratton & Edith Stratton Kitt.* Tucson: Arizona Pioneers Historical Society, 1964.

Carter, Clarence E., and John Porter Bloom (after 1961), eds. *The Territorial Papers of the United States.* 28 vols. Washington: GPO, 1934-.

Davis, W. W. H. *El Gringo: Or New Mexico and Her People.* 1856. Reprint. Santa Fe: Rydal Press, 1938.

Fitzpatrick, John C., ed. *The Writings of George Washington.* 39 vols. Washington: GPO, 1931–44.

Foraker, Joseph Benson. *Notes of a Busy Life.* 2 vols. Cincinnati: Stewart & Kidd Co., 1916.

Ford, Paul Leicester, ed. *The Writings of Thomas Jefferson.* 10 vols. New York: G. P. Putnam's Sons, 1892–99.

French, William. *Some Recollections of a Western Ranchman: New Mexico, 1883-1899.* London: Methuen, 1927.

Garrett, Pat. F. *The Authentic Life of Billy, the Kid: The Noted Desperado of the Southwest.* Norman: University of Oklahoma Press, 1954; orig. pub. 1882.

Gibson, George Rutledge. *Journal of a Soldier Under Kearny and Doniphan, 1846-1847.* Vol. 3. The Southwest Historical Series. Edited by Ralph P. Bieber. Glendale, Calif.: Arthur H. Clark Co., 1935.

Gregg, Josiah. *The Commerce of the Prairies.* Abridged ed. Lincoln: University of Nebraska, 1967; orig. pub. 1844.

Harkey, Dee. *Mean as Hell.* New York: Signet Press, 1951.

Hening, H. B., ed., *George Curry, 1861–1947: An Autobiography.* Albuquerque: University of New Mexico Press, 1948.

James, Thomas. *Three Years Among the Indians and Mexicans.* Philadelphia: J. B. Lippincott, 1962; orig. pub. 1846.

Jones, Mother [Ann]. *Autobiography of Mother Jones.* Edited by Mary Field Parton. Chicago: Charles H. Kerr, 1925.

Klasner, Lily. *My Childhood among Outlaws.* Edited by Eve Ball. Tucson: University of Arizona, 1972.

Lake, Carolyn, ed. *Under Cover for Wells, Fargo: The Unvarnished Recollections of Fred Dodge.* Boston: Houghton Mifflin, 1969.

McCauley, James Emmit. *A Stove-Up Cowboy's Story.* Dallas: Southern Methodist University Press, 1943.

McIntire, Jim. *Early Days in Texas: A Trip to Hell and Heaven.* Kansas City, Mo.: McIntire Publishing Co., 1902.

McIntyre, J. W., ed. *The Writings and Speeches of Daniel Webster.* 18 vols. Boston: Little, Brown & Co., 1903.

Mallory, John A., comp. *United States Compiled Statutes: Annotated.* 12 vols. St. Paul: West Publishing Co., 1916.

Martin, Douglas D., ed. *Tombstone's Epitaph.* Albuquerque: University of New Mexico Press, 1958.

Miller, Joseph. ed. *The Arizona Rangers.* New York: Hastings House, 1972.

Miller, Nyle H., and Joseph W. Snell, eds., *Why The West Was Wild: A Contemporary Look at the Antics of Some Highly Publicized Kansas Cowtown Personalities.* Topeka: Kansas State Historical Society, 1963. Abridged as, *Great Gunfighters of the Kansas Cowtowns, 1867–1886.* Lincoln: University of Nebraska Press, 1963.

Mills, W. W. *Forty Years at El Paso, 1858–1898: Recollections of War, Politics, Adventure, Events, Narratives, Sketches, Etc.* Chicago: W. B. Conkey Co., 1901.

Morison, Elting E., ed. *The Letters of Theodore Roosevelt.* 8 vols. Cambridge, Mass.: Harvard University Press, 1951–54.

Mowry, Sylvester. *Arizona and Sonora: The Geography, History, and Resources of the Silver Region of North America.* 3d ed., rev. & enl. New York: Harper & Brothers, 1864.

Otero, Miguel A. *My Life on the Frontier, 1864–1897.* 2 vols. Albuquerque: University of New Mexico Press, 1939.

———. *My Nine Years as Governor of the Territory of New Mexico, 1897-1906.* Albuquerque: University of New Mexico Press, 1940.

Roosevelt, Theodore. *The Rough Riders.* Vol. 11, Executive Edition of the *Works of Theodore Roosevelt.* New York: P. F. Collier & Son, 1899.

Sloan, Richard E. *Memories of an Arizona Judge.* Stanford: Stanford University Press, 1932.

Stratton, David H., ed. *The Memoirs of Albert B. Fall.* Monograph No. 15, Southwestern Studies. El Paso: University of Texas, 1966.

Syrett, Harold C., ed. *The Papers of Alexander Hamilton.* 21 vols. New York: Columbia University Press, 1961-.

Tevis, James. *Arizona in the 50's.* Albuquerque: University of New Mexico Press, 1954.

Twitchell, Ralph E., ed. *Historical Sketch of Governor William Carr Lane: Together with [a] Diary of His Journey from St. Louis, Mo., to Santa Fe, N.M., July 31st, to September 9, 1852.* Santa Fe: N.M. Historical Society, 1917.

Udall, David King, and Pearl Udall Nelson. *Arizona Pioneer Mormon; David King Udall: His Story and His Family, 1851-1938.* Tucson: Arizona Silhouettes, 1959.

Wallace, Lewis. *Lew Wallace: An Autobiography.* 2 vols. New York: Harper & Brothers, 1906.

War of the Rebellion Records. 130 vols. Washington: GPO, 1880–1901.

Works Projects Administration. *The Private Journal of George Whitwell Parsons.* Phoenix: Arizona Statewide Archival and Records Project, 1939.

NEWSPAPERS

Arizona.

Tucson *Daily Star*, April 17, 1890–August 31, 1891.

Phoenix *Arizona Republican* (daily and weekly), 1898–1906, January-August 1909.

Prescott *Arizona Journal-Miner* (weekly and daily), 1864–83, 1886–89.

Tubac and Tucson *Weekly Arizonian*, 1859–71.

Florence and Tucson *Arizona Daily Citizen*, May 29, 1878–August 28, 1879, October 1, 1889–March 15, 1890.

Yuma *Arizona Sentinel*, June 22–October 12, 1878.

Colorado.

Denver *Rocky Mountain News*, 1896–1903.

Pueblo *Colorado Chieftain*, June 27-October 10, 1878, January 5-June 29, 1882, February 22-June 7, 1883.

Kansas.

Leavenworth *Daily Times*, April 10-August 31, 1862, December 30, 1865-February 28, 1866.

Missouri.

St. Louis *Missouri Democrat*, April 5-December 31, 1853.

New Mexico.

Albuquerque *Evening Review*, February 20–March 4, 1882.

Albuquerque *Daily Democrat*, November 15–19, 1889.

Albuquerque Morning Journal, January 1, 1907–June 7, 1910.

Albuquerque *Weekly Review*, April 28–May 26, 1883.

Albuquerque *Rio Abajo Weekly Press*, June 7, 1864.

Cimarron News and Press, November 29, 1879–January 7, 1882.

Las Cruces *Rio Grande Republican*, January 8, 1892–December 31, 1897.

Las Vegas *Daily Optic*, 1879–81.

Santa Fe Weekly Gazette, 1853, 1856–59, 1860–67.

Santa Fe *New Mexican* (weekly and daily), 1849, 1863–69, 1870–77, 1880–81, 1882–86, January 1-December 31, 1890, July 1-November 30, 1892, May 16-September 30, 1893, January 1, 1894-June 30, 1896.

Santa Fe Republican, January 1, 1847-September 23, 1848.

Silver City Enterprise, November 16, 1882-June 26, 1891.

Silver City *Grant County Herald*, June 15-September 28, 1878.

New York

New York Times, 1851–1906. By index.

Wyoming.

Cheyenne Daily Leader, June 7-September 13, 1878.

SECONDARY PUBLISHED SOURCES

Adams, Alexander B. *Geronimo: A Biography*. New York: G. P. Putnam's Sons, 1971.

Anderson, George B. *History of New Mexico: Its Resources and People*. 2 vols. Los Angeles: Pacific States Publishing Co., 1907.

Andrews, Charles M. *The Colonial Period of American History*. 4 vols. New Haven: Yale University Press, 1964.

Athearn, Robert G. *Rebel of the Rockies: A History of the Denver and Rio Grande*. New Haven: Yale University Press, 1962.

———. *William Tecumseh Sherman and the Settlement of the West*. Norman: University of Oklahoma Press, 1956.

Bancroft, Hubert Howe. *The Works of Hubert Howe Bancroft*. 39 vols. New York: Arno Press, n. d.

Bartholomew, Ed. *Wyatt Earp*. 2 vols. Toyahvale, Texas: Frontier Book Co., 1963-64.

Billy the Kid: Las Vegas [New Mexico] Newspaper Accounts of His Career, 1880-1881. Waco, Texas: W. M. Morrison-Books, 1958.

Blackstone, William. *Commentaries on the Laws of England: In Four Books, with an Analysis of the Work.* Notes by Christian, Chitty, Lee, Hovenden, and Ryland. 2 vols. New York: J. B. Lippincott, 1857.

Block, Eugene B. *Great Train Robberies of the West.* New York: Coward-McCann, 1959.

Broaddus, J. Morgan, Jr. *The Legal Heritage of El Paso.* El Paso: Texas Western Press, 1963.

Burton, Jeff. *Black Jack Christian: Outlaw.* Western Americana Series, no. 14. Santa Fe: Press of the Territorian, 1967.

———. *Dynamite and Six-Shooter.* Santa Fe: Palomino Press, Imprint of the Territorian, 1970.

Cleaveland, Norman, with George Fitzpatrick. *The Morleys: Young Upstarts on the Southwest Frontier.* Albuquerque: Calvin Horn, 1971.

Cohen, Felix, ed. *Felix Cohen's Handbook of Federal Indian Law.* 1942. Reprint. Albuquerque: University of New Mexico Press, 1971.

Conard, Howard Lewis. *Uncle Dick Wootton: The Pioneer Frontiersman of the Rocky Mountains.* Edited by Milo Quaife. Chicago: R. R. Donnelley & Sons, 1957.

Cookridge, E. H. *The Baron of Arizona.* New York: The John Day Company, 1967.

Corwin, Edward S. *The President, Office and Powers: History and Analyses of Practice and Opinion.* 2d ed. rev. New York: New York University Press, 1948.

Crawford, Samuel J. *Kansas in the Sixties.* Chicago: A. C. McClurg, 1911.

Cummings, Homer, and McFarland, Carl. *Federal Justice: Chapters in the History of Justice and the Federal Executive.* New York: Macmillan Co., 1937.

Dillon, Richard. *Wells, Fargo Detective: The Biography of James B. Hume.* New York: Coward-McCann, 1969.

Emmet, Chris. *Fort Union and the Winning of the Southwest.* Norman: University of Oklahoma Press, 1965.

Encyclopaedia Britannica. 11th ed. s. v., "lord steward," "marshal," "marshalsea."

Farrand, Max. *The Legislation of Congress for the Government of the Organized Territories of the United States, 1879-1895.* Newark, N.J.: Wm. A. Baker, 1896.

Fergusson, Harvey. *Rio Grande.* New York: Alfred A. Knopf, 1931.

Fish, Carl Russell. *The Civil Service and the Patronage.* Vol. 11. Harvard Historical Studies. Cambridge, Mass.: Harvard University Press, 1904.

Friedman, Lawrence M. *A History of American Law.* New York: Simon and Schuster, 1974.

Fritz, Henry E. *The Movement for Indian Assimilation, 1860-1890.* Philadelphia: The Pennsylvania State University Press, 1963.

Gibson, Arrell M. *The Life and Death of Colonel Albert Jennings Fountain.* Norman: University of Oklahoma Press, 1965.

Griffith, A. Kinney. *Mickey Free: Manhunter.* Caldwell, Idaho: Caxton Press, 1969.

Hacker, Louis. *Alexander Hamilton, in the American Tradition.* New York: McGraw-Hill, 1957.

Haley, J. Evetts. *Jeff Milton: A Good Man with a Gun.* Norman: University of Oklahoma Press, 1948.

Hall, Frank. *History of the State of Colorado: Embracing Accounts of the Pre-Historic Races and Their Remains; the Earliest Spanish, French and American Explorations . . . from 1858 to 1890.* 4 vols. Chicago: The Blakely Printing Co., 1889–95.

Hamilton, William Baskerville. *Anglo-American Law on the Frontier: Thomas Rodney & His Territorial Cases.* Durham, N.C.: Duke University Press, 1953.

Harding, Alan. *A Social History of English Law.* Baltimore: Penguin Books, 1966.

Harpending, Asbury. *The Great Diamond Hoax and Other Stirring Incidents in the Life of Asbury Harpending*. Edited by James H. Wilkins. No. 10, The Western Library. Norman: University of Oklahoma Press, 1958.

Harrison, Fred. *The West's Territorial Prisons, 1861–1912*. New York: Ballantine Books, 1973.

Hunt, Aurora. *Kirby Benedict: Frontier Federal Judge*. Glendale, Calif.: Arthur H. Clark Co., 1961.

———. *Major General James Henry Carleton, 1814-1873: Western Frontier Dragoon*. Glendale, Calif.: Arthur H. Clark Co., 1958.

Jahns, Pat. *The Frontier World of Doc Holliday*. New York: Hastings House, 1957.

Keleher, William A. *The Fabulous Frontier: Twelve New Mexico Items*. Santa Fe: Rydal Press, 1945.

———. *Maxwell Land Grant: A New Mexico Item*. New York: Argosy-Antiquarian, 1942.

———. *Violence in Lincoln County, 1869-1881: A New Mexico Item*. Albuquerque: University of New Mexico Press, 1957.

Kelly, George H., comp., *Legislative History: Arizona, 1864-1912*. Phoenix: Manufacturing Stationers, 1926.

Kenner, Charles L. *A History of New Mexican-Plains Indian Relations*. Norman: University of Oklahoma Press, 1969.

Lamar, Howard Roberts. *The Far Southwest, 1846-1912: A Territorial History*. New York: W. W. Norton, 1970.

Langeluttig, Albert G. *Department of Justice of the United States*. Baltimore: The Johns Hopkins University Press, 1927.

Larson, Robert W. *New Mexico Populism: A Study of Radical Protest in a Western Territory*. Boulder: Colorado Associated University Press, 1974.

McKee, Irving. *"Ben-Hur" Wallace: The Life of General Lew Wallace*. Berkeley: University of California Press, 1947.

McNitt, Frank. *The Indian Traders*. Norman: University of Oklahoma Press, 1962.

Metz, Leon C. *John Selman: Texas Gunfighter*. New York: Hastings House, 1966.

———. *Pat Garrett: The Story of a Western Lawman*. Norman: University of Oklahoma Press, 1973.

Marshall, Otto Miller. *The Wham Paymaster Robbery: Boldest in Arizona History, May 11, 1889*. Pima, Ariz. Pima Chamber of Commerce, 1967.

Mullin, Robert N., ed., *Maurice Garland Fulton's History of the Lincoln County War*. Tucson: University of Arizona Press, 1968.

Ogle, Ralph Hedrick. *Federal Control of the Western Apaches, 1848-1886*. Albuquerque: University of New Mexico Press, 1970.

O'Neil, James B. *They Die But Once: The Story of a Tejano*. New York: Knight Publications, 1935.

Osgood, Herbert L. *The American Colonies in the Seventeenth Century*. 3 vols. Gloucester, Mass.: Peter Smith, 1957.

Pearson, Jim Berry. *The Maxwell Land Grant*. Norman: University of Oklahoma Press, 1961.

Perrigo, Lynn I. *Our Spanish Southwest: Its Peoples and Cultures*. New York: Holt, Rinehart and Winston, 1971.

Poldervaart, Arie W. *Black-Robed Justice: A History of the Administration of Justice in New Mexico from the American Occupation in 1846 until Statehood in 1912*. Vol. 13, Historical Society of New Mexico Publications in History. Santa Fe: The Society, 1948.

Pomeroy, Earl S. *The Territories and the United States, 1861–1890: Studies in Colonial Administration*. Philadelphia: The Pennsylvania State University Press, 1947.

Powers, Edwin. *Crime and Punishment in Early Massachusetts, 1620-1692: A Documentary History*. Boston: Beacon Press, 1966.

Prassel, Frank Richard. *The Western Peace Officer: A Legacy of Law and Order.* Norman: University of Oklahoma Press, 1972.

Prince, L. Bradford. *Historical Sketches of New Mexico: From the Earliest Records to the American Occupation.* 2d ed. New York: Leggat Brothers, 1883.

Pringle, Henry F. *Theodore Roosevelt: A Biography.* New York: Harcourt, Brace, Harvest Books, 1956.

Randall, James G. *Constitutional Problems Under Lincoln.* Rev. ed. Urbana: University of Illinois Press, 1964.

Robbins, Roy M. *Our Landed Heritage: The Public Domain, 1776-1936.* Lincoln: University of Nebraska Press, 1962.

Sacks, B[enjamin]. *Arizona's Angry Man: United States Marshal Milton B. Duffield.* No. 1, Arizona Monographs. Tempe: Arizona Historical Foundation, 1970.

Schellie, Don. *Vast Domain of Blood: The Story of the Camp Grant Massacre.* Los Angeles: Westernlore Press, 1968.

Shirley, Glenn. *Law West of Fort Smith: Frontier Justice in the Indian Territory, 1834-1896.* New York: Collier Books, 1961.

Smith, Cornelius C., Jr. *Emilio Kosterlitzky: Eagle of Sonora and the Southwest Border.* Glendale, Calif.: Arthur H. Clark Co., 1970.

———. *William Sanders Oury: History Maker of the Southwest.* Tucson: University of Arizona Press, 1968.

Sonnichsen, C. L. *The Story of Roy Bean: Law West of the Pecos.* Greenwich, Conn.: Fawcett Publishing Co., 1972.

Spicer, Edward H. *Cycles of Conquest: The Impact of Spain, Mexico, and the United States on the Indians of the Southwest, 1533-1960.* Tucson: University of Arizona Press, 1962.

Stanley, F. [Stanley Crocchiola]. *Clay Allison.* Denver: World Press, 1956.

———. *Dave Rudabaugh: Border Ruffian.* Denver: World Press, 1961.

———. *Longhair Jim Courtright: Two Gun Marshal of Fort Worth.* Denver: World Press, 1957.

———. *The Private War of Ike Stockton.* Denver: World Press, 1959.

Taylor, Morris F. *Trinidad, Colorado Territory.* Trinidad: Trinidad State Junior College, 1966.

Thrapp, Dan L. *Al Sieber, Chief of Scouts.* Norman: University of Oklahoma Press, 1964.

Turner, John Kenneth. *Barbarous Mexico.* Intro. by Sinclair Snow. Reprint. Austin: University of Texas Press, 1969.

Twitchell, Ralph E. *The History of the Military Occupation of the Territory of New Mexico From 1846 to 1851 by the Government of the United States.* 1909. Reprint. Chicago: Rio Grande Press, 1963.

———. *The Leading Facts of New Mexican History.* 5 vols. Cedar Rapids, Iowa: Torch Press, 1911–17.

Ubbelohde, Carl. *The Vice-Admiralty Courts and the American Revolution.* Chapel Hill: University of North Carolina Press, 1960.

Wagoner, Jay J. *Arizona Territory, 1863–1912: A Political History.* Tucson: University of Arizona Press, 1970.

Waters, Frank. *The Earp Brothers of Tombstone: The Story of Mrs. Virgil Earp.* New York: Clarkson N. Potter, 1960.

Wellman, Paul I. *The Indian Wars of the West.* Garden City, N.J.: Doubleday and Co., 1947.

Westermeier, Clifford P., comp. & ed., *Trailing the Cowboy: His Life and Lore as Told by Frontier Journalists.* Caldwell, Idaho: Caxton Printers, 1955.

Westphall, Victor. *Thomas Benton Catron and His Era.* Tucson: University of Arizona Press, 1973.

White, Leonard D. *The Federalists: A Study in Administrative History, 1789–1801*. New York: Free Press, 1965.
——. *The Jeffersonians: A Study in Administrative History, 1801–1829*. New York: Free Press, 1965.
——. *The Jacksonians: A Study in Administrative History, 1829–1861*. New York: Free Press, 1965.
——. *The Republican Era: A Study in Administrative History, 1869–1910*. New York: Free Press, 1965.
Wiebe, Robert H. *The Search for Order, 1877–1920*. New York: Hill and Wang, 1967.

JOURNAL AND PERIODICAL ARTICLES

Altshuler, Constance Wynn. "The Case of Sylvester Mowry: The Charge of Treason." *Arizona and the West* 15.63 82.
——. "The Case of Sylvester Mowry: The Mowry Mine." *Arizona and the West* 15:149–74.
Bair, JoAnn, and Jensen, Richard L. "Prosecution of the Mormons in Arizona Territory in the 1880s." *Arizona and the West* 19:25–46.
Ball, Larry D. "Black Jack Ketchum: The Birth of a Folk Hero." *Mid-South Folklore* 1:19–25.
——. "Pioneer Lawman: Crawley P. Dake and Law Enforcement on the Southwestern Frontier." *Journal of Arizona History* 14:243–56.
——. " 'No Cure, No Pay': A Tom Horn Letter." *Journal of Arizona History* 8:200–202.
——. Outlaws of the Southwest, 1895–1905. *Denver Westerners' Brand Book* 20:281–99.
——. " 'This High-Handed Outrage,' Marshal William Kidder Meade in a Mexican Jail." *Journal of Arizona History* 17:219–32.
Barney, James M. "Bob Paul—Early Arizona Sheriff." *The Sheriff Magazine* 8:3, 8–10.
——. "Who Was Elected Sheriff?" *The Sheriff Magazine* 8:11.
Bloom, Lansing, ed. "Bourke on the Southwest." *New Mexico Historical Review* 8:1–30; 0:33–77, 159–83, 273–89, 375–435; 10:1–35, 271–322; 11:77–122, 188–207, 217–82; 12:41–77, 337–79; 13:192–238.
——. "Historical Society Minutes, 1859–1863." *New Mexico Historical Review* 18:247-311, 394-428.
Cheetham, Francis T. "The First Term of the American Court in Taos, New Mexico." *New Mexico Historical Reivew* 1:23–41.
Cooley, Rita W. "The Office of United States Marshal." *Western Political Quarterly* 12:123–40.
Eaton, W. Clement. "Frontier Life in Southern Arizona, 1858-1861." *The Southwestern Historical Quarterly* 36:173–92.
Ellis, Bruce T., ed. "Lincoln County Postscript: Notes on Robert A. Widenmann, by His Daughter, Elsie Widenman." *New Mexico Historical Review* 50:213–30.
Farrand, Max. "The Judiciary Act of 1801." *American Historical Review* 5:682–86.
Feather, Adlai. "The Territories of Arizona." *New Mexico Historical Review* 39:16–31.
Fireman, Bert M. "Fremont's Arizona Adventure." *American West* 1:8–19.
Fish, Carl Russell. "Removal of Officials by the Presidents of the United States." *Annual Report of the American Historical Association for the Year 1899*. 2 vols. 1:67–86.
Goff, John S. "Isham Reavis, Pioneer Lawyer and Judge." *Nebraska History* 54:1–46.
——. "John Titus, Chief Justice of Arizona, 1870–1874." *Arizona and the West* 14:25–44.
——. "Michigan Justice in Arizona: Henry T. Backus." *Michigan History* 52:109–22.
——. "The Organization of the Federal District Court in Arizona, 1912–1913." *American Journal of Legal History* 8:172–79.

——. "William T. Howell and the Howell Code of Arizona." *American Journal of Legal History* 11:221–33.

Harte, John Bret. "The Strange Case of Joseph Tiffany, Indian Agent in Disgrace." *Journal of Arizona History* 16:383–404.

Hastings, James R. "The Tragedy at Camp Grant in 1871." *Arizona and the West* 1:146–60.

Herner, Charles H. "Arizona's Cowboy Cavalry." *Arizoniana (Journal of Arizona History)* 5:10–26.

Hogan, William F. "John Miller: Pioneer Lawman." *Arizoniana (Journal of Arizona History)* 4:41–45.

Hovey, Walter C. "Black Jack Ketchum Tried to Give Me a Break!" Edited by Doris Sturges. *True West* 19:6–11, 48–52.

James, Laurence P. "George Tyng's Last Enterprise: A Prominent Texan and a Rich Mine in Utah." *Journal of the West* 8:429–37.

Keen, Effie R. "Arizona's Governors." *Arizona Historical Review* 3:7–20.

King, Dick. "The Fight That Almost Kayoed Boxing." *Frontier Times.* New Series 33:26–27, 56–57.

Lamar, Howard Roberts. "Carpetbaggers Full of Dreams: A Functional View of the Arizona Pioneer Politician." *Arizona and the West* 7:187–206.

——. "Edmund G. Ross as Governor of New Mexico: A Reappraisal." *New Mexico Historical Review* 36:177–209.

Moorman, Donald R. "Holm O. Bursum, Sheriff, 1894." *New Mexico Historical Review* 39:333–44.

Murphy, Lawrence R. "Reconstruction in New Mexico." *New Mexico Historical Review* 43:99–115.

——. "William F. M. Arny, Secretary of New Mexico Territory, 1862-1867." *Arizona and the West* 8:323–38.

Myers, Lee. "An Experiment in Prohibition." *New Mexico Historical Review* 40:293–306.

O'Hallaren, Bill. "When Chester Forgot to Limp." *TV Guide* 23:10–13.

Pace, Anne. "Mexican Refugees in Arizona, 1910-1911." *Arizona and the West* 16:5–18.

Parish, William J. "The German Jew and the Commercial Revolution in Territorial New Mexico, 1850-1900." *New Mexico Historical Review* 35:1–29.

Rasch, Philip J. "Exit Axtell: Enter Wallace." *New Mexico Historical Review* 32:231–45.

——. "The Horrell War." *New Mexico Historical Review* 31:223–31.

——. "John Kinney: King of the Rustlers." *English Westerners' Brand Book* 4:10–12.

——. "Murder in American Valley." *English Westerners' Brand Book* 7:2–7.

——. "The Murder of Houston I. Chapman." *Los Angeles Westerners' Brand Book* 8:69–82.

——. "The People of the Territory of New Mexico vs. the Santa Fe Ring." *New Mexico Historical Review* 47:185–202.

——. "The Rustler War." *New Mexico Historical Review* 39:257–73.

Reeve, Frank D. "The Government and the Navajo, 1878-1883." *New Mexico Historical Review* 16:275–312.

Rister, Carl Coke. "Harmful Practices of Indian Traders of the Southwest, 1867–1876." *New Mexico Historical Review* 6:231–48.

Roberts, Gary. "Gunfight at O. K. Corral: The Wells Spicer Decision." *Montana, the Magazine of Western History* 20:62–74.

Seligman, G. L., Jr. "Vignettes of Arizona Pioneers: Crawley P. Dake, U. S. Marshal." *Arizoniana (Journal of Arizona History)* 2:13–14.

Shirley, Glenn. "Cap Mossman—And the Apache Devil." *True West* 5:4–6, 32–34.

Stout, Joe A. "Henry A. Crabb—Filibuster or Colonizer? The Story of an Ill-Starred Gringo Entrada." *American West* 8:4–9.

Thiesen, Lee Scott, ed. "Frank Warner Angel's Notes on New Mexico Territory, 1878." *Arizona and the West* 18:333–70.

Tittman, Edward. "The Exploitation of Treason." *New Mexico Historical Review* 4:128–45.

Waldrip, William F. "New Mexico During the Civil War." *New Mexico Historical Review* 28:163–82, 251–90.

Walker, Henry P. "Retire Peaceably to Your Homes: Arizona Faces Martial Law, 1882." *Journal of Arizona History* 10:1–18.

Walter, Paul A. F. "New Mexico's Pioneer Bank and Bankers." *New Mexico Historical Review* 21:209–25.

Warren, Charles. "New Light on the History of the Federal Judiciary Act of 1789." *Harvard Law Review* 37:49–132.

Westphall, Victor. "The Public Domain in New Mexico, 1854-1891." *New Mexico Historical Review* 33:24–52, 128–43.

Wharton, Clarence. "Spruce McCoy Baird." *New Mexico Historical Review* 27:300–314.

Wilkes, Homer. "Territorial Head Count [of Arizona County, 1860]." *Frontier Times*. New Series. 44:64–65.

THESES AND DISSERTATIONS

Rosenbaum, Robert Johnson. "*Mexicano versus Anglo-Americano:* A Study of Hispanic-American Resistance to Anglo-American Control." Ph.D. dissertation, University of Texas, 1972.

Thompson, George. "The History of Penal Institutions in the Rocky Mountain West, 1846-1900." Ph.D. dissertation, University of Colorado, 1965.

White, Leland R. "Relations of the United States and Mexico, 1847–1853." Master's thesis, University of Missouri, 1950.

AUTHOR INTERVIEWS

Hilario Romero, Santa Fe, N. M. July 10, 1973.

Laura Mullins, Santa Fe, N. M. June 26, 1975.

Romulo Martinez, Santa Fe, N. M. June 26, 1975.

Mary Foraker, Albuquerque, N. M. August 12, 1976.

J. Benson Newell, Las Cruces, N. M. December 31, 1976. Telephone.

SCHOLARLY PAPERS

Ball, Larry D. " 'Of Different Clay': The United States Marshals and the Chinese Deportations, 1890-1912." Paper read at Southwest Conference on Asian Studies, October 12, 1973, at North Texas State University, Denton.

———. "Our Useful Army: The Impact of the Posse Comitatus Act on Law Enforcement in the Southwest." Paper read at Western History Association Conference, October 3, 1974, at Rapid City, South Dakota.

Index